Flowering Natives For Home Gardens

Flowering Natives For Home Gardens

DENISE GREIG

Angus&Robertson
An imprint of HarperCollins*Publishers*

To my mother, Gladys Greig,
with love and thanks, also to my children,
Katie and Alex Fallows

Angus&Robertson
An imprint of HarperCollins*Publishers,* Australia

First published in Australia by Angus & Robertson Publishers in 1987
as *The Australian Gardener's Wildflower Catalogue*
This edition published in 1996
Reprinted in 1998, 1999, 2000, 2001, 2002, 2003
by HarperCollins*Publishers* Pty Limited
ABN 36 009 913 517
A member of the HarperCollins*Publishers* (Australia) Pty Limited Group
www.harpercollins.com.au

HarperCollins*Publishers*
25 Ryde Road, Pymble, Sydney, NSW 2073, Australia
31 View Road, Glenfield, Auckland 10, New Zealand
77-85 Fulham Palace Road, London W6 8JB, United Kingdom
Hazelton Lanes, 55 Avenue Road, Suite 2900, Toronto, Ontario M5R 3L2
and 1995 Markham Road, Scarborough, Ontario M1B 5M8, Canada
10 East 53rd Street, New York NY 10022, USA

National Library of Australia Cataloguing-in-Publication data:

Greig, Denise, 1945– .
Flowering natives for home gardens: the Australian gardener's wildflower catalogue.
Rev. ed.
Bibliography.
Includes index.
ISBN 0 207 18413 5.
1. Wild flowers – Australia. 2. Wild flower gardening – Australia.
I. Greig, Denise, 1945– . Australian gardener's wildflower catalogue.
II. Title. III. Title: Australian gardener's wildflower catalogue.
635.96760994

Printed in Singapore by Kyodo Printing Co. on 115gsm Matt Art

12 11 10 9 8 7 03 04 05 06

Contents

ACKNOWLEDGEMENTS

I would like to sincerely thank the many people who have given encouragement and generous assistance with the preparation of this book.

I am extremely grateful to the Australian plant growers for their patience, knowledge and willingness in supplying information — without their support there would be no book. In particular, Sharon and Russell Costin, John Rose and his staff, Brian and Nola Parry, and Tony Clark, who provided valuable information on drought-tolerant plants and their cultivation.

Appreciation is expressed to the many people who have kindly allowed me to photograph their lovely private gardens. I have also photographed in many public gardens and would like to thank the staff for their assistance in the identification and tracking down of elusive species. Special thanks to Jack Moon and Robert Miller who work at the Bankstown Council Wildflower Garden.

I would also like to thank the staff of the National Herbarium of New South Wales and the National Botanic Gardens in Canberra for their assistance. Grateful acknowledgement is also made of the references used, a list of which is included at the back of the book for further reading.

Thanks to Tessa Riordan for her meticulous typing of the original manuscript and Patricia Anderson for typing the revision. Many thanks to my mother who was a willing assistant at all times and to my children Katie and Alex who were patient and understanding during the preparation of this book.

Photograph on page ii: Telopea *'Wirrimbira White';*
this page: Eucalyptus leucoxylon

Rhodanthe chlorocephala ssp. *rosea*

INTRODUCTION

When I began photographing Australian plants many years ago I had the beginner's fantasy of photographing all our flora in its natural habitat. After working for years in the bush I began to discover that many of these plants also grow very well in public and private gardens. I still experience great delight in finding in someone's garden a healthy specimen of a plant that I last saw years ago in the bush on the other side of the country. It's like meeting an old acquaintance again.

We have a magnificent wealth in our flora and for me it is the most beautiful in the world. I love the fields of dainty flowers in the desert, the rainforest showoffs, the summer alpines and the outback battlers. Then there is the incredible range of foliage types and the very smell of the bush to add to my pleasure in native flora. All are part of our environment and can beautifully become part of our gardens and lives.

I have intended this book to be a practical as well as visual guide to the most popular available Australian plants that have found their way into our gardens. Some plants will be only seasonally available and some will only be found at nurseries specialising in native flora. Only a handful of irresistible or rare beauties may not always be available. Popular and successful cultivars have also been included.

In preparing this book I have worked very closely with Australian plant specialists across the country. Most are enthusiastic and helpful and an enormous source of information about what thrives in their area. Many different species are brought into cultivation each year and a chat with your nearby nurseryman will help you find out which plants have proved reliable in your district.

An Australian plant, like any other plant in the world, will only respond to cultivation if it has been selected with care to suit the situation in which it is planted and my aim is to guide you through the enormous range available. Every species mentioned is illustrated, described and presented with cultivation notes. Landscaping suggestions are also discussed for each. This book is written for all those gardeners who wish to do their own selection, planning and design to create the Australian landscape of their choice.

Melaleuca fulgens (salmon-coloured form)

How to Use this Book

A great number of Australian plants, regardless of their origin, are quite adaptable and can be grown under a variety of garden conditions, while others do best in conditions similar to their natural habitat. In this book I have included the most attractive, popular and most reliable native plants for Australian gardens. It is a catalogue, intended as a helpful reference guide to be consulted not only by the landscape architect and the native plant enthusiast, but also by the average gardener who may prefer to grow a combination of native and exotic plants, or by those who wish to have a native section in the garden. The coverage is by no means exhaustive as many new species, forms and hybrids are brought into cultivation each year. Others, for various reasons, are available only in small numbers or seasonally.

PLANT NAMES

Universally accepted botanic names are given to plants so that they can be readily identified irrespective of the language of the country. Under this system, the major groups are known as families (e.g. Myrtaceae). Plants with similar characteristics are placed in the same genus (e.g. *Eucalyptus*) and individual plants within the genus are called species. The species name often describes an important feature of the plant, e.g. *Eucalyptus macrocarpa* means large-fruited eucalypt.

In this book, the genera (plural of genus) are arranged in alphabetical order and within each genus the species are also listed alphabetically. This is how many nursery catalogues are presented and also how most native plant specialists arrange their plants. (Some nurseries also have plants divided into sections according to habit and size, for example mat plants and ground covers; shrubs; trees; climbers and creepers.) The name of the family to which each genus belongs will be found following the name of the genus.

It is always advisable when preparing buying lists or consulting with a nursery to use botanical names, as common names may cause confusion because they vary from State to State, and because several plants may share the same common name. Some plants do not even have a common name, but where they do the name in common usage is included under the botanical name.

EXPLANATION OF TERMINOLOGY

Origin

'Origin' indicates the State or in some cases the States where the plant naturally occurs. It may be used as a guide to the selection of the plant and suitable companions to grow with it. It should be noted, however, that Australia has a wide diversity of environments, and a large number of different plant habitats occur in each State. While three eastern States might be listed for a plant, climate considerations would limit the range of the plant within those States.

Standard abbreviations are used for the names of States. The Australian Capital Territory is not included.

Climate

Australia is a vast continent and climatic conditions vary considerably. The two major elements in the make-up of climate are water and heat. Although a great number of Australian plants are extremely adaptable, the most suitable plants for any given climate are those occurring naturally in that climate or in a reasonably similar one. Certain plants are more accommodating than others, and some species will be found suitable for two or more climate zones.

For easy reference, Australia has been divided into seven major climatic zones. These zones are listed below and shown on Fig. 1. For each individual species covered in this book, the zones in which it will grow are listed, to enable the reader to select species suitable for any region. It should be noted, however, that this is simply a guide and numerous local factors such as soil conditions, prevailing winds and aspects and origin of the plants themselves should be taken into consideration.

In many cases, the magnificent flowering plants from Western Australia do not respond well to the summer rainfall and excessive humidity of the coastal Sydney region, but flourish in the western districts of New South Wales, parts of Victoria and around Adelaide; for this reason Melbourne and Adelaide have been given the same zoning as Perth. As well as local species, a wide selection of plants can be grown in this zone, including some from dry areas, mountains and rainforests.

In recent years, a great deal of research has gone into the cultivation of Australian plants in semiarid and arid areas. Many spectacular native plants are particularly well adapted to long periods without water and these are becoming more available in these areas. In many cases, these plants will survive in arid areas or in arid centres where there is adequate town water. The desert annuals of course look marvellous in these gardens.

In tropical areas where there is a dry winter and a very wet summer, plants need to be selected that will tolerate long periods of high humidity, heavy rainfall and even floods and then little moisture for long periods. Selection of local species is recommended and a wide range of native plants is now available to create a lush garden and attract the marvellous native birds and butterflies found in that region.

Highland climates vary greatly, as they may occur at any latitude, and the species listed under this category are for cool highland areas only. In the Atherton Tableland and other highland areas in Queensland, many of the plants suited to tropical and subtropical zones may be grown.

Shade

Plants have differing requirements for healthy growth. While many Australian plants need exposure to plenty of sun to flourish, others are scorched by direct sun and need varying amounts of shade. Almost all gardens have shady beds and this provides the opportunity for growing shade-loving plants. Shade may be provided by trees and tall shrubs, buildings, or other structures such as pergolas through which filtered light can pass.

The table below explains the meaning of the phrases used to indicate shade tolerance for the individual species throughout the book.

None to light Plants which do not tolerate shade and prefer maximum sunshine for most of the day. Some rainforest species that grow naturally in filtered or heavy shade will become more compact and flower better in full sun.

Light to filtered Plants which prefer light shade or filtered sunlight, such as dappled shade provided by a foliage canopy or a position that is not exposed to hot summer sun.

Filtered to full shade Plants which require protection from the sun's rays and are suitable for heavy shade. These may be grown under densely canopied trees or between buildings or in entrance ways.

Fast-growing

A large number of species are fast growing and flower while young. Those plants listed as FAST-GROWING have a growth rate of 1 m or more in one growing season. As this particularly refers to rapid growth in the early part of the plant's life it could prove an especially useful characteristic to look for where a quick and effective screen is required. However, eventual height or spread of the plant must be taken into consideration as well, as a climber or tree that affords a very quick effect may eventually be too large for the site where it is planted.

Specimen Plant

Any species listed as a SPECIMEN PLANT has been selected for outstanding form, habit, foliage, colour or other attribute which would make it attractive when seen as an individual plant. Such a plant should be grown where it may display its best features.

Salt-tolerant

SALT-TOLERANT indicates that a plant can withstand exposed coastal conditions of blustery sea winds and salty spray. Only a minority of Australian plants occur naturally in front line coastal situations, but any species indicated as salt-tolerant will stand up under the most vigorous conditions. If planted thickly such plants will provide a protective

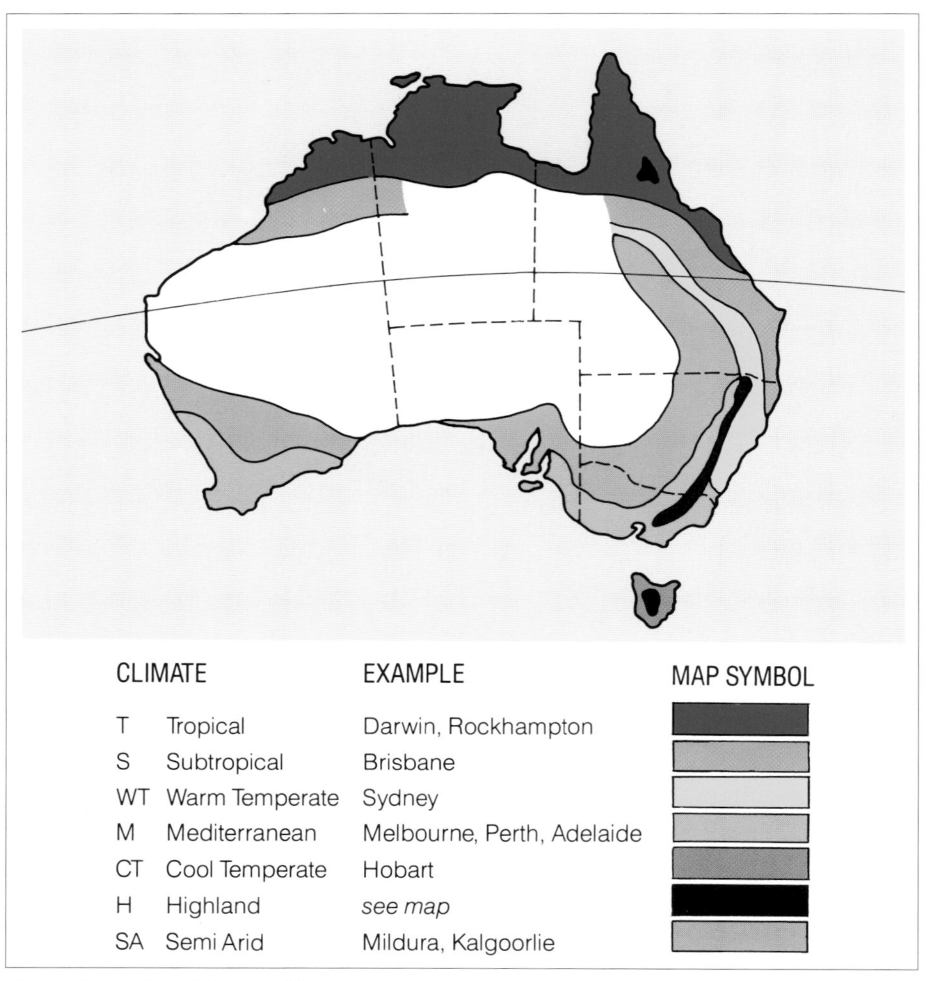

Fig 1. Australian Climatic Zones

environment for less salt and wind-tolerant species. In exposed gardens plant growth is often slowed down or stunted and it is recommended that plants be grown fairly close together so they will benefit from mutual protection against the effects of strong winds.

Drought-resistant

The annotation DROUGHT-RESISTANT identifies plants which, once established, should survive in gardens in areas which receive less than 375 mm annual rainfall. Most species native to dry regions do not grow without water, but are generally adapted to survive long dry periods with minimal growth. In the garden, most will perform better and flower longer with extra care and watering. In drier areas several factors must be especially considered such as the use of mulches to insulate and prevent evaporation, and continued care to reduce the degree of weed competition. Poor soil texture and permeability, the slope of the land, which may allow water to drain too rapidly, and drying winds also have an effect on the plant's ability to withstand drought, and work carried out in improving soil, making terraces or erecting windbreaks will reap benefits.

Ornamental Foliage

Plants annotated ORNAMENTAL FOLIAGE have unusual or beautiful foliage. Although most of us grow plants for their flowering beauty, the use of a variety of leaf types and colour can create interest and contrast throughout the year even when flowering is somewhat sparse.

Other Features

Species that are fragrant or have aromatic foliage, that attract birds and that are suitable for growing in containers have been highlighted throughout and separate indexes at the end of the book group species by these special features.

Cultivation and Maintenance

Hundreds of species of Australian plants are now available for planting into home gardens. Although a large proportion of native plants, irrespective of their State of origin, are very adaptable and can be easily cultivated under a wide variety of garden conditions, consideration should be given to species known to be indigenous to the area. Nothing will look as natural in your garden as the local plants. A knowledge of local environmental conditions is necessary and a visit to established successful gardens or observation of plants in the local bushland will help in your final selection. Many nurseries now have display gardens and are a useful source of information on what thrives in your area. Climate, soil conditions, aspect and the characteristics of the plant, including its estimated mature size and growing habits, should all be taken into account.

With good planning and an understanding of growing conditions the native garden will provide years of pleasure and aesthetic satisfaction. The maintenance required by such a garden will decrease as plants develop and adapt to their environment.

SOIL PREPARATION AND DRAINAGE

Generally, native plants require well-drained soil. Badly drained areas may need the installation of underground agricultural pipes or plastic pipes to remove excess water from the soil. Surface drains will also assist so that the water does not lie around the base of the plants. A retaining wall will need a good supply of large weep holes at the base and good drainage behind it.

For those with a flat garden site with heavy, badly drained soil it is sometimes better and more aesthetically pleasing to build up a raised section of the garden at least 1 m high. Raised beds can be retained by logs, sleepers, bricks or rock. If gardens are surrounded by stone or brick work, make provision for weep holes at the bottom of the surround. Avoid building up beds around valued existing trees and shrubs. An established tree or shrub will not survive a metre of new soil around its trunk.

Soil types vary greatly throughout Australia, making generalised statements about conditioning methods impossible. Most soils will require some improvement while sandy soil and, at the other extreme, clay soil will require special attention if a wide range of plants is desired in the garden.

Although clay is usually rich in nutrients and a large variety of plants will thrive on it, clay and heavy clay loams retain water and have poor aeration. If you wish to grow a wide range of native plants it is essential that the naturally poor drainage of the clay be improved. This can be achieved by the addition of gypsum at the rate of 1 to 1.5 kg a square metre, spread and incorporated evenly. This will break up the compacted clay particles so that nutrients become more readily available to the plants and aeration of the soil is improved. Organic matter, such as compost, manures and leaf litter, and coarse river sand added to the soil will also help to improve the structure of the clay.

Very sandy soil may rapidly dry out and it is best to incorporate a moisture retaining agent into it. Well-rotted cow or horse manure, peatmoss, leaf mould and garden compost are all good moisture-holding materials and will rot down further. They also supply plants with valuable nutrients. A light mulch will also assist in water retention and help prevent movement of the soil by strong winds.

ACID OR ALKALINE SOIL

Acidity or alkalinity of the soil affects plant growth to varying degrees. The degree of acidity or alkalinity is measured in terms of the pH scale, which ranges roughly from pH 0 to pH 14. A value of pH 7 is neutral, while all figures below 7 are acid and those over 7 are alkaline. Most native plants grow satisfactorily in slightly acid soils in the pH 5.5 to 7 range.

Parts of South Australia and areas around Perth have large areas of predominantly alkaline soils. These soils have a high lime content and if you live in such an area it is best to choose plants tolerant of alkaline conditions. Some very attractive Western Australian species, including some members of the family Proteaceae, have shown a preference for alkaline soil.

WEEDS

All weeds should be removed from a garden bed before it is planted, as later removal may disturb the plant. By spending time going over the site thoroughly you will benefit in low maintenance later on. To suppress large areas of weeds, place newspapers and opened out cardboard cartons over the weeds. Cover with wood chips, pruning materials and leaves to prevent the cardboard from blowing away. All these will eventually rot into materials which will improve the soil. Weeds grow best in bare, cultivated soil so that once an area is planted a mulch will be essential to keep them at bay.

SELECTION OF PLANTS

Care in selecting plants is just as important as soil preparation. It is best to buy plants from specialist nurseries, forestry departments or good garden centres. As a general rule, it is recommended to buy a small, healthy plant in a large container, as a plant too large for its pot is often rootbound and is unlikely to do well in the ground. Never buy spindly trees in a sale. These will rarely develop into the lovely specimens you envisaged. Quite often they have lost their labels and their eventual size and cultivation needs are a matter of guesswork.

Before finalising your selection of trees and shrubs, find out the ultimate size of the plant and consider the extent of root competition from existing trees and large shrubs. When planning plantings beneath overhead power lines ensure that species chosen are of an appropriate height so that they won't become entangled. Consider the position of the sun during winter and summer so that there is sufficient sun during the cooler months and shade is where it will be needed during the hottest months. A tree should be planted at least 3 m from a neighbouring fence so that it may gracefully display its beauty and spread without being hampered or becoming a nuisance.

Some Australian plants have different growing forms within a species. For example *Grevillea banskii* may be a tall bushy shrub to 3 m or more high with either bright red or cream flowers, or a completely prostrate shrub spreading 2 to 3 m across with either cream or red flowers. It is always wise to check to ensure you are buying the desired form.

The size of fully grown plants is given for each species and variety throughout this book but, as a native species can vary widely in size even in its habitat, let alone under different cultivation conditions, these measurements can only be approximate.

Many nurseries have a good range of seasonally flowering plants on display. This makes it easy to see what you are purchasing and gives you instant colour in the garden. However, many beautiful flowering shrubs and trees which do not display their full beauty as plants in pots have high potential for use in gardens. These may be overlooked at nurseries and it is a good idea to spend time reading some of the labels.

PLANTING

Following the purchase of plants, they should be planted out as soon as possible. If this is not possible, pots should be placed in a sheltered position and thoroughly watered at least once a day. Unless species are shade-loving, do not store plants in a very shady spot or bush house. Most nursery plants are used to full sun.

Saturate a plant thoroughly before removing it from its container. This can be done by submerging it in a bucket of water and allowing it to drain properly before planting out. The hole to take the plant should only be a little deeper than the depth of the soil in the container, but at least twice the width so that plenty of good soil can be worked in below and around it. If the soil is dry, fill the hole with water and allow it to drain away before planting. Place about a tablespoon of slow release fertiliser suitable for native plants or Agriform tablets in the bottom of the hole and mix thoroughly with the soil to prevent young roots coming in contact with fresh fertiliser. Carefully remove the plant from its container and when positioning it place a few centimetres of good soil in the bottom of the hole to settle the plant at the same level as or slightly below the surrounding soil. If the roots are coiled tightly or matted, carefully ease them out at the base and generally loosen the root ball, taking care not to break the main root zone. Use clean sharp secateurs to remove any old, matted roots. This will allow new roots to take a good hold of their new surroundings more quickly. Firm the soil around the plant and water in well to settle the soil around the roots. Add mulch, which will prevent water loss, maintain an even soil temperature and eliminate weed growth, but do not spread it right up to the trunk or stem of the plant.

STAKING

Staking is not generally necessary for young plants, as they usually grow stronger without support. The sway caused by the wind is a natural process which has the effect of strengthening stems. In extremely exposed windy areas, a strong stake can be driven in alongside the plant, but not through the root ball. To this the stem is secured, not too tightly, with a soft tie. A better, stronger root system will develop if the plant is allowed to move a little in an enclosure of

Scaevola aemula, Purple Fanfare

three stakes with the tie circling outside the stakes. The tie should be of soft material so that it will not rub the stem. Old stockings and pantyhose are ideal.

MULCHING

A mulch is a layer of material covering the soil above the roots of the plants. Not only does it look good, but mulching is recommended for its many beneficial effects. Many native plants form surface feeder roots and mulching acts as a barrier to excessive evaporation from the surface of the soil. It also helps control soil temperature and an even soil temperature is often most favourable for plant growth. Suppression of weeds is another important result of mulching, as native plants resent root disturbance from surface cultivation. Mulch softens the effect of heavy rain, preventing it from compacting the soil or washing it away on slopes. Depending on the material used as a mulch, it could also add nutrients to the soil and improve the soil structure by adding humus as it decays.

Mulches are many and varied and include compost, pine bark, hardwood chips, grass clippings, fallen leaves, casuarina needles and other plant litter. Some gardeners prefer inorganic mulches such as gravel, pebbles, crushed rock or coarse sand. Each has its advantages and disadvantages and when considering what kind of mulch to use, consult a nurseryman specialising in native plants to find out what is the best available material in your area.

Since organic mulches retain water, they can increase frost damage to plants in areas where temperatures drop to freezing in winter. A mulch using inorganic material such as coarse sand or gravel would be best in such areas. If organic mulches are used, they may cause a nitrogen deficiency in the soil, as the bacteria that decompose these materials absorb nitrogen and food from the soil. This can be counteracted by applying blood and bone before mulching. Organic mulches will need to be topped up when time and weather have reduced them to part of the soil. For native plants, it is preferable to add a new mulch over the old to avoid disturbing the soil.

Mulches should be kept well clear of trunks and stems of the plants or they may cause collar rot.

Another means of mulching is by growing carpeting or prostrate plants around shrubs. The Native Violet *Viola hederacea*, *Pratia pedunculata* and *Mazus pumilio* are all quite suitable for this kind of cover.

Once established, your native garden should provide you with all the natural garden mulch you need, in the form of fallen leaves, bark, spent flowers and small branches. Grass clippings should be allowed to dry out before use and are best mixed with manure or leaf mould to allow free access of air and moisture to the soil.

WATERING

In the first few weeks after planting and until the plant is established, watering must not be neglected. As plants mature, watering can be reduced, and in some seasons it may become unnecessary. Once a plant is established, the need to water it will vary with the season, the origin of the plant, soil type and the natural rainfall. If space permits, it is best to grow plants in separate sections of the garden according to their watering requirements. For example, some Western Australian species are from low summer rainfall areas and may prefer a period of summer dormancy, while moisture-loving plants would perish very quickly without water during hot dry summers.

Once plants are established, water only when soil below the surface becomes dry. As many species are naturally equipped to withstand dryness, overwatering should be avoided because it may cause the roots to rot.

When watering is carried out, it must be thorough and at well-spaced intervals. If the surface only is watered each time, the plant will not grow strong deep roots but will develop surface roots; this could cause the plant to die during hot dry weather or fall over during a high wind. Plants chosen for a low rainfall planting must be encouraged to put roots deep down into the soil in their search for subsoil moisture.

In sandy soils, watering may be necessary more often because the water simply dries out more quickly than in other soils and the dry soil may even become water-repellent. In this kind of soil, add plenty of organic material to give the soil better moisture holding capacity.

In the summer or other hot periods, water should always be given during a cool spell of weather or, if that is not possible, be given early in the morning; otherwise the sun and heat will evaporate much of it before it can properly soak into the ground. Watering at night is not recommended, as water left on the leaves and stems could encourage the spread of fungal disease.

FERTILISERS

With the regular use of adequate quantities of organic material such as mulch and compost and sparing use of slow release fertilisers, all native garden plants will give a more than satisfactory performance. Many Australian plants are adapted to infertile soils, and therefore should not be heavily fertilised. Agriform tablets used during planting will feed new plants for at least 15 months. For extra feeding after that or for feeding existing plants, use a light application of slow release fertiliser such as Green Label Osmocote, which lasts up to 9 months. It should be applied during the warmer months when the plants are in active growth.

Most native plants grow in soil low in phosphates, so fertilisers containing superphosphate should be totally avoided. Blood and bone is another safe and effective fertiliser. A light application should be mixed well into the soil or mulch, avoiding direct root contact, then watered in thoroughly. Very well rotted cow, horse or a well-pelleted form of poultry manure may also be used. Before fertilising, the garden should be watered well. The fertiliser should then be spread, lightly cultivated into the soil and watered in.

ORGANIC MATTER

Gardeners can greatly reduce their use of fertilisers by conserving organic kitchen and garden waste and returning them to the soil as compost. Not only does well-rotted organic material provide nutrients for the soil organisms and for plants, but it also improves the physical condition of the soil. In a native garden one does not usually have the opportunity of reworking the bed annually and it is best to blend organic material into the soil before planting.

A compost heap is an asset to all gardens and you can make your own easily. It can be made in a construction of bricks, timber or wire netting, or it can just be an open pile on the ground. The floor must be bare earth to allow the beneficial action of earthworms penetrating the heap. The compost heap should be sited in a warm, sunny position.

The basic principle behind composting is to gradually build up vegetable refuse, peelings, pulled up weeds, lawn clippings, leaf litter and animal manure into a heap which, with the aid of moisture and heat, will rot down. Each addition to the heap is covered with a layer of soil and it is important that the whole be kept moist, but not too wet, otherwise loss of valuable properties may occur through leaching or running off in the drainage. Compost is ready when it is earthy and dark brown and shows no traces of the original materials. It breaks down faster in warm seasons and climates, but in any case it should be ready for use after three to six months.

IRON DEFICIENCY

When a plant is not able to take up enough iron, blanching or yellowing of the leaves occurs, particularly in the young growth. The condition is often due to high pH, which makes it possible for other elements to interfere with the absorption of iron. It occurs often on soils that are high in lime, but it may also be caused by over-irrigation or poor drainage. Iron deficiency can be rectified by applying a dressing of iron chelates to the soil.

PRUNING

Pruning is an important but often overlooked aspect of the maintenance of Australian plants. It will keep them healthier and more compact and will encourage new growth and fresh flowering.

Tip pruning is carried out while plants are young and ensures a neater and bushier appearance throughout the plant's life. It is done by simply pinching out the fresh new growth with the finger and thumb at the beginning of warm weather, and continuing to do so throughout the growing season.

Many shrubs benefit if flowering stems are cut back after they finish flowering and before new growth begins. This promotes new growth and vigour and encourages more blooms the following season. Some plants may need shaping or may look rather straggly once they are a few years old, and these will respond well to **light pruning**. Cut the shrub back all over after flowering, taking care not to cut into the old wood. Where possible, all pruning cuts should be made just above an outward-facing bud.

On some occasions it is necessary to **heavily prune** or shape vigorous growing species. Many plants will stand this type of pruning provided that ample foliage is left on the plant. When heavy pruning is required always try to preserve the natural growing habit of the plant. This is best achieved by removing only small portions at a time until you are satisfied with the results. Any large pruning cuts should be painted over with a wound sealant to prevent entry of insects and plant diseases.

Native trees require little pruning and it is best to remove only unwanted, dangerous or dead limbs. Cut branches clearly and flush to the trunk.

Always use very sharp, disease-free pruning tools so that you make a clear, sharp cut without tearing plant tissue.

PROPAGATION

Having established a native garden, people often develop an interest in propagating their own plants. There are several books on native plants which deal with propagation at some length. Anyone who wants to grow native plants would be well advised to join their local branch of the Society for Growing Australian Plants (SGAP). It is at Society meetings that propagation is discussed and cuttings and seed are exchanged. The Society publishes the quarterly journal *Australian Plants* as well as regional newsletters. Both are available to all members. Membership enquiries may be directed to any of the state branches listed on page 325.

Propagation is usually carried out from seed or from cuttings and mention of this is included with every genus entry. I have often referred to hot water treatment for some seeds. This is because very hard seeds, such as those produced by acacias, the pea family and cassias need pretreatment before sowing. Such seed may be covered with near boiling water and left in the water until they swell. This may take a few hours or overnight.

Species which are difficult to grow from seed can often be propagated from cuttings. Native plants are usually best propagated from half-ripened new season's tip cuttings but some species will require hardwood cuttings. Good results may be obtained by striking cuttings in moist sand.

Half-ripened tip cuttings A small cutting, 6 to 8 cm long, is taken from early summer to early autumn, after the new season's growth is finished.

Hardwood cuttings A cutting up to 10 cm long may be taken in winter when last spring growth has hardened and become woody.

PEST AND DISEASE CONTROL

Pests

By growing Australian plants, you will soon attract many birds to the garden that will feed on the nectar, seeds and fruits and also on insects. Some birds are completely insectivorous, while most species include some insects in their diet. It is they who will all play a major role in controlling insect pests in the garden, making the use of toxic sprays unnecessary.

By attacking the insects with sprays, you kill not only the insects but also the birds and other small beneficial creatures that prey upon the pest species. This upsets the normal balance of your garden, which may necessitate continued spraying to control the problem.

Make sure the damage being caused to a garden is serious enough to warrant special control measures. Remember, a natural balance can often be attained if some damage is tolerated.

Garlic spray is a natural, safe spray which can be effectively used to control a range of insect pests including aphids and caterpillars. Crush 85 g of garlic cloves and pour over 10 mL of paraffin oil. Cover and soak for 48 hours. Then make a solution of 7 g of pure soap in 500 mL of hot water. Pour over the garlic mixture, mix thoroughly, strain and when cool store in a container. Use as needed in dilutions of 1 part to 100 parts of water, or less depending on the strength required.

Where there is a huge infestation of pests and you must use a commercial spray, choose a pesticide such as derris dust (Rotenone) or pyrethrum which will have the least effect on the nearby environment. Read the instructions carefully, and use sparingly and only when absolutely necessary. After spraying store all pesticides out of reach of children, wash out the utensils used and wash the hands thoroughly.

Healthy, vigorous plants will soon recover from insect attack. The following strategies can be applied to help control your pest situation.

Caterpillars overlooked by the birds can easily be picked off and squashed. Always look under the leaves as there are usually more congregated there than above. Take care, as some caterpillars have stinging hairs which can irritate the skin.

Webbing caterpillars tend to attack species of *Leptospermum* and *Melaleuca*, particularly those with narrow leaves. They are the larvae of various species of moths, and they feed together in a group and shelter in a protective mass of webbing. If the habitation is discovered early the mass of webbing may be removed by hand or pruned off and the grubs squashed. If the web cannot be removed manually and it is necessary to spray it may be difficult to penetrate the web and a wetting agent applied first may assist. This can be made up by mixing in about two teaspoons of washing up detergent per litre of water.

Sawflies are the larvae of some common wasp-like insects. They resemble caterpillars and are often black and covered with short white hairs. They congregate in a revolting mass during daylight hours and may seriously defoliate a small tree when they spread out and feed at night. The Steel-blue Sawfly *Perga dorsalis* feeds chiefly on *Eucalyptus* species, but species of *Callitris*, *Callistemon*, *Leptospermum* and *Angophora* are also hosts to various species of sawfly larvae. They can easily be controlled by removing a small branch with a group of larvae attached to it. The larvae may then be squashed (if you can bear it) or dropped into boiling water.

Sawfly larvae, *Perga dorsalis*

Aphids and thrips are small sapsucking insects usually found on the new growing tips of plants. They can be dislodged by a strong blast of water from the hose or they can be sprayed with garlic spray. Aphids have many natural enemies, and these are often sufficient to control the aphid infestation.

Scale infestations are caused by insects and may appear as a white or brown crusty covering on the stems and leaves. In early stages scale can be scrubbed off with a toothbrush and soapy water, or badly encrusted branches can be removed and burned. If the infestation is heavy it can be treated with white oil. On ferns and soft foliaged plants use about three quarters the recommended strength.

Lerps Commonly found on eucalypts, these small sucking insects cause unsightly discolouration and dry patches on leaves and, in severe cases, defoliation. Further, lerps secrete honeydew which attracts Sooty Mould. They are identified by the small, waxy, scale-like coverings they build and a silvering of leaves where there is a bad infestation. They are usually controlled by natural predators but for bad infestations consult your nurseryman.

Galls are unsightly swellings found on leaves, flowers and stems and are caused by a variety of insects, or in some cases by fungi. Secretions by the insects cause the plant tissue to grow in an abnormal manner, resulting in galls taking such forms as reddish bubble-like lumps on the surfaces of gum leaves or greenish brown balls on the flowers of various wattles. Leaves and stems infested by galls can be cut off and burned. Water and fertilise the plant to promote healthy regrowth.

Borers are an enemy of a wide range of plants, including species of *Acacia*, *Banksia* and *Eucalyptus*. The presence of borers is indicated by little piles of gummy sawdust around their holes on trunks, branches or around the base of a shrub or tree. Borers should be removed when they are first noticed and can be dug out with a flexible piece of wire. A few drops of methylated spirits or kerosene injected into the hole should cause the grub to emerge in a hurry and it can then be killed, or the hole can be sealed with wood putty immediately after treatment.

With a sharp knife, pare back damaged wood down to a healthy layer and paint with a wound sealant. Prune off any severely damaged limbs and fertilise the plant.

DISEASES

Native plants are attacked by a number of diseases, which may be caused by fungi, bacteria and viruses. Fungi cause most diseases in Australian plants and can attack the roots or above-ground parts of the plant in many ways. The basic fungal growth is a network of fine filaments which spreads throughout the plant parts from which nourishment is drawn. During this process the plant tissue is disrupted or destroyed, resulting in various symptoms of disease.

Fungi cause many different types of disease in native plants and the following are perhaps the most commonly seen.

Damping-off is the collapse at soil level and subsequent death of young seedlings owing to the attack of soil inhabiting fungi. It is often increased by overthick sowing of seeds and overly moist and humid conditions. Damping off is best prevented by sowing seeds in sterilised soil and paying careful attention to watering.

Ink Disease is a common complaint of kangaroo paws and appears as black spots on stems and leaves. These may become so numerous that they cover large areas. Species vary in their susceptibility, but the Red and Green Kangaroo Paw (*Anigozanthos manglesii*) seems to be the worst affected. The disease is most severe in damp and protected positions and the best means of prevention or control is to grow plants in an open situation and avoid watering them from above. Cutting back of the plant after flowering and removal of waste material will promote healthy new growth and may serve to check spread of ink disease. Badly infected plants should be removed and burned.

Powdery mildews are a group of fungi which produce a white powdery coating on the leaves, young shoots and sometimes fruits and flowers of their hosts. They can spread very rapidly, especially in humid conditions, and a commercially available fungicide such as Benlate may have to be applied.

Sooty Mould is a dark fungal growth which forms on the surfaces of leaves and stems where scale insects or aphids are feeding or on plants growing beneath lerp-infested trees. A mould grows on the honeydew secreted by the insects and if the insects are controlled the Sooty Mould will disappear.

Collar rot is caused by fungal disease found in the soil and first appears as a split near the soil line which may exude gum. Affected bark looks dark and water-soaked and if the ground is wet there may be a sour smell. Like most fungi this thrives in damp, humid conditions, so provision of good drainage and improved air circulation near the trunk are important in control. Damaged bark should be cut away and the wound painted with Bordeaux paste. Unless the disease is treated the plant may be ringbarked and die.

Cinnamon Fungus (*Phytophthora cinnamomi*) is a root rot fungus which causes death of plants, single specimens and large stands alike. The fungus starts by infecting the fine feeding roots and eventually weakens the whole root system of its host. In times of stress such as drought or during hot weather the plant may deteriorate rapidly and die. Cinnamon Fungus is common in gardens and is favoured by wet soil conditions. It is often found in ground with impeded drainage or following wet periods. Control of this fungus is very difficult so the best way to overcome the disease is to improve drainage and grow healthy plants with a vigorous root system. In areas known to be infected with Cinnamon Fungus or sites prone to drainage problems choose species known to be resistant to the disease or those that grow naturally in waterlogged soils.

Members of the family Proteaceae originating in Western Australia and grown in the eastern states with a high summer rainfall are particularly sensitive to this disease and their collapse could be an early warning of the presence of Cinnamon Fungus in your garden.

Landscaping Ideas

When planning a native garden you must first decide what type of garden you want. There are basically two types of native gardens, the informal or bush garden and the more formal garden with lawns and garden beds or selected groupings. This chapter looks at ideas that best suit a purely native garden; however, they are suggestions that could be incorporated into any garden.

If you are lucky enough to purchase a block of land with natural bush and existing trees, it is of course best to keep what healthy trees and shrubs you wish to feature in the garden and protect them from the builders. Try to organise that builders do not dump excavation rubble too near the trunks. It is probably best to rope off areas to guard the existing vegetation as much as possible while work is being carried out. This will give you time to identify what plants you have and learn their times of flowering. Time too to appreciate foliage features, growth patterns and natural arrangements that exist on your block. Even ground covers, perennials and some native grasses are worth saving to prevent erosion and give your garden an established look. Choose additional plants compatible with the bush in your area as they will be in their right habitat, fully adapted to soil and climate and perfectly happy.

If you do not have a bush garden to begin with, and most people do not, it is still possible to achieve a low maintenance garden though it does takea greater initial expenditure of time and money. If you have decided on an all-native garden and have an existing garden dominated by exotics, it may be best to take a deep breath and make a clean sweep from the start. Without the competition of roots, the native plants will grow faster, and will also be healthier and bushier. Also it is much easier to chop out old trees and shrubs if you do not have to worry about ruining valued plants.

With the unique foliage textures, subtle colours and fascinating flowers of Australian plants, it is easy to create a harmonious landscape and enjoy a close relationship with our native plants. The bird life attracted by native plants is an additional joy.

PLANTING FOR VARIETY OF HEIGHT

When planning a native garden, always begin with the overall concept in mind and gradually refine the plan by filling in detail. Visit your local bushland and observe the relationships of trees, shrubs, undershrubs, clumps, and ground covers. In the natural landscape trees form the framework and there is gradation in height down to shrubs and prostrate plants. Height must always be considered in the early stages of planning. Plant the backbone of trees first, as they are the most permanent things in the garden and take the longest time to reach maturity, then add dominant shrubs, smaller shrubs and ground covers to develop the areas in between.

Trees

Trees have many useful functions in the garden. They can be planted to screen traffic, to hide eyesores, to soften adjacent buildings, to give privacy and to provide shade. The ability of trees to absorb carbon dioxide from the atmosphere and purify the air we breathe, and their ability to cut out wind, reduce the temperature of air passing through them or reduce noise make them useful in any garden and worthy of consideration in landscape design. But apart from their usefulness, trees have an aesthetic appeal of their own. Taller trees can frame a beautiful vista, not merely block off an unpleasant view or provide privacy from neighbours or the street.

In nature trees usually grow in groups together with others of their kind. Thus, if space permits, consider planting a small community of trees of the one species. A grove of casuarinas enhances the natural look with a delicate mass of foliage that filters rather than blocks light. Some eucalypts highly prized for their beautiful white trunks look marvellous planted in groups. The Wallangarra White Gum *Eucalyptus scoparia* is one such. It has graceful, drooping foliage and bark which peels off to reveal a stunning pure white trunk. Other lovely eucalypts for group planting are the lemon-scented gum *E. citriodora* and the Sydney blue gum *E. saligna*, which has a trunk with a bluish hue. There is little to surpass the beauty of a mature red flowering ironbark *E. sideroxylon* — but when planted in a group this species looks even more magnificent.

Remember, large plants usually have large root systems and can cause damage to drains and foundations. However, in an area next to a driveway or path, a tree which develops a tall trunk will occupy less space at ground level than a large, bushy shrub.

Shrubs

Shrubs too have many uses in the garden. They can help unite house and garden, soften and beautify hard architectural angles, conceal fences and ugly sites and provide privacy. When planted between the trunks of trees or in rows, they form windbreaks. Shrubs may provide fill-in plants of varying heights or, when carefully sited, a shrub of particular beauty may become an outstanding specimen and feature of the garden. The aim should be to achieve unity in the garden complemented by close range surprises. It is in the latter particularly that the subtlety of some of our native plants can be used so cleverly.

Clumping Plants

Plants forming tussocks with grass or reed-like foliage offer an appealing contrast throughout the year, and as these perennials grow side by side with shrubs in the wild, no native garden looks complete without a clump or two.

Acacia spathulifolia, Chamelaucium ciliatum, Dryandra sessilis

Many are spectacular when in flower — for instance the kangaroo paws and *Conostylis* species — and some have long been favourite wildflowers — for instance Christmas bells and native irises. Tufting species combine very well with ground-covering plants, rocks and water and create a natural effect at path edges and under trees. *Lomandras* are beautiful clumping plants which may form large tussocks and make striking accent plants near a water garden or for softening paved and walled areas such as driveways and courtyards. *Poa australis* is a charming native grass which grows as a low, tufted clump, making it an ideal edging and rockery plant. For a truly Australian touch to the landscape the grass trees with their fine crown of long, narrow, tough leaves make excellent feature plants.

Ground Covers and Creepers

A ground cover is a prostrate, semiprostrate or mat-forming shrub or herbaceous plant that clings closely to the ground and is wider than its height. There is a wide range of native groundcovers that can be allowed to thread their way between shrubs and under trees, or be used to soften rocky slopes and bare banks, to tumble over walls or to edge paths. Apart from increasing the variety of species in the garden and making it more interesting at ground level, ground cover plants provide the most effective, natural and pleasing form of soil insulation. At the same time they reduce weed growth, eliminate soil erosion, conserve moisture and provide a vegetative mulch.

When selecting ground covers try to establish the plant's eventual spread. Larger areas may have to be covered by a vigorous-growing species but such a species, when grown in a small garden, might become entangled and swamp its neighbours. *Kennedia nigricans, K. rubicunda* and *Hibbertia scandens*, for example, should never be grown too close to other shrubs and trees. Some smaller species like the *Pratia pedunculata* and *Viola hederacea* might daintily get out of control whereas others such as *Scleranthus biflorus* might need to be planted fairly closely to ensure good coverage.

Many ground covers are more effectively displayed if allowed to cascade over retaining walls, rocky slopes or raised garden beds. Massed plantings of one or two species in bold sweeps will give a greater feeling of space and continuity either in the large garden or in the smaller landscape.

PLANTING FOR VARIETY OF FOLIAGE

In planning any garden, native or otherwise, the texture, shape and colour of the foliage of all plants should be carefully considered in order to place them to their best advantage. With such a diversity of foliage in Australian plants, this can be one of the most striking features of a native garden. It should be remembered that it is the foliage, not the flowers, that is the permanent feature, and by the introduction of a variety of leaf types interesting effects can be created all the year round, even when flowering is sparse.

Australian plants are mostly evergreen and they are highly adapted to sometimes hostile environments. There are basically two foliage types: the broad-leaved plants adapted to warm, moist conditions or rainforests; and the sclerophyll or hard-leaved species which include eucalypts, wattles, banksias, grevilleas and melaleucas — in fact, the majority of trees and shrubs of the Australian bush. The characteristic hard leaves of the latter group are a protection against evaporation, as is the often reduced size of the leaves.

Rainforest species may be grown as single specimens or planted in some close arrangement to create a rainforest environment. Many have impressive dark glossy foliage, and a cool green community can be achieved with the additional planting of palms, lacy tree ferns and ground ferns. Some rainforest species are excellent foliage plants for containers. The Umbrella Tree *Schefflera actinophylla*, the Black Bean *Castanospermum australe*, the Kangaroo Vine *Cissus antarctica* and *Ficus* species are all suited to containers. Plants in containers may be moved around in the garden to suit their seasonal requirements for shade or sun. Rainforest species are also useful as indoor plants, as most will tolerate fairly dark conditions.

Most species from the sclerophyll group relate very well when planted together. Although the flowers of the different genera of Proteaceae are very different in appearance, one outstanding feature is prominent, and that is the hard leathery texture of the mature foliage in many of the species. There is an extraordinary diversity of forms of foliage within the family and one of the most outstanding members is undoubtedly the genus *Grevillea*. Apart from their colourful flowers, grevilleas differ very much in foliage and form and could be used exclusively in a home garden without producing monotony. The leaves may be oak-like (*G. barklyana*); very divided (*G. pteridifolia* and *G. robusta*); holly-like (*G. aquifolium*); oval (*G. laurifolia*); hard and prickly (*G. juniperina*); or soft (*G. lanigera*).

Prickly Foliage

Many native plants have prickly or needle-like foliage and most of these can be used successfully as a barrier against unwanted traffic, as a dense hedge or as a secure nesting site for small birds. A safe garden position where people may not get caught up in them should be chosen for species with prickly foliage or spines.

As well as attracting beautiful native birds, a bush garden will emit delightful fragrances all year round.

Eremophila nivea is a decorative silver-foliaged plant that will withstand dry conditions.

Coloured Foliage

Australian plants offer a wide range of foliage colours, including different greens, greys, reds and plum colours. A species selected to provide a foliage contrast can become a dazzling feature point. Some plants light up with pink new growth and in some species of *Callistemon* the new foliage is so richly coloured that the display is just as attractive as the flowers. *Casuarina torulosa* is an outstanding foliage tree with very fine, drooping plum-coloured foliage. Many grevilleas have attractive pink or bronze new growth, for instance *Grevillea caleyi*, *G. venusta* and *G.* x *gaudichaudii*.

Be sure that colourful-foliaged species blend well into the garden. It is best to plan for one plant or a small group of the same species rather than a wide variety as too many different leaf colours in view can result in an uneasy landscape.

Silver Foliage

Australia has a wealth of silver-foliaged plants and interesting highlights or features may be formed by the introduction of these plants. *Acacia iteaphylla* has marvellous drooping silver-grey foliage that makes a feature of this plant all year. Other silvery-foliaged wattles include the beautiful Coastal Myall *A. binervia* and the popular Queensland Silver Wattle *A. podalyriifolia*, which has foliage like silvery velvet. *Acacia cultriformis* has slender grey branches and attractive triangular silvery blue leaves. And not all eucalypts are planted for their flowers and trunks. *Eucalyptus cinerea* and *E. gunnii* both have beautiful silver juvenile foliage that is often retained throughout life. *Eucalyptus tetragona* is a very decorative small bushy tree with silvery white stems, branches, foliage and fruit.

Some of the arid area shrubs have a silvery glaucous appearance and, if conditions suit, a garden consisting entirely of silvery foliage plants can be created. *Eucalyptus macrocarpa*, *Eremophila nivea*, *Cassia artemisioides*, *Hakea petiolaris* and *Einadia nutans* are all beautiful silvery-foliaged species which withstand dry conditions.

PLANTING FOR YEAR-ROUND COLOUR

By careful planning, thought and selection you can create a garden that will reward you with flowers and colour throughout the year. With a native plant garden it is normal to expect a flush of flowering in spring; however a study of the flowering times of species will help ensure that there is something in flower for as much of the year as possible. Some species which do not have showy flowers may have attractive foliage, new growth or fruits.

Australia has some outstanding flowering trees, enough to provide colour and interest through every season. Many of them come from northern rainforests, but are adaptable and will flourish in a protected garden as far south as Melbourne. Some make impressive specimen plants and when grown in open positions may become dense and bushy. In a good season, the Flame Tree *Brachychiton acerifolius* with its blaze of brilliant red waxy flowers is one of the most spectacular of native rainforest trees. It flowers from late spring to midsummer. Also in spring the familiar and adaptable Silky Oak *Grevillea robusta* will put on a wonderful display of golden orange flowers which attract a multitude of birds. The attractive Black Bean *Castanospermum australe* has handsome glossy foliage and produces masses of colourful red and yellow pea-shaped flowers clustered along the branches during late spring and early summer. The Firewheel Tree *Stenocarpus sinuatus* has an outstanding display of bright red flowers arranged in clusters like the spokes of a wheel from late summer almost throughout autumn. The amazingly adaptable White Cedar *Melia azedarach* var. *australasica* will grow in most climates, including that of dry inland towns. It is deciduous during winter and provides good shade in summer; and it has perfumed lilac flowers in late spring and bird-attracting yellow fruit in autumn and early winter.

Where soil is fairly moist many *Melaleuca* species and bottlebrushes (*Callistemon*) will give a striking display of native plant colour during late spring and early summer. All through winter and spring there is a wide variety of wattles that add a splash of yellow to the landscape. There are also a number of wattles that bloom at other times of the year. *Acacia iteaphylla* bears masses of small ball-shaped blossoms through autumn into winter. Other autumn-flowering acacias include *A. flexitolia* and *A. terminalis*, while the Cedar Wattle *A. elata* blooms throughout summer.

Fruit

While most native plants are grown for their flowers, some are also selected for their colourful fruit. These provide extra colour, often in the off-season for flowers, and some are also attractive to native birds. Examples of these are the pretty pinkish red fruits of *Acmena* and *Syzygium* species, the blue or purple berries of *Sollya* and *Dianella* species and the colourful winged fruits of the *dodonaeas*. *Pittosporum rhombifolium* is an excellent all-rounder in form, foliage, flowers and fruit. It grows to a neat 10 m and has dark green, glossy leaves, and large clusters of white flowers in early summer, followed by bunches of bright orange berries from autumn to late winter. The Blueberry Ash *Elaeocarpus reticulatus* is another decorative tree with a massed display of cream or pink fringed, bell-shaped summer flowers followed by bright blue berries from autumn through to spring.

A list of native plants that have particularly attractive fruits is included on page 344.

Apart from providing interesting colour to the garden in autumn, the bright orange berries of *Pittosporum rhombifolium* are great for indoor decoration.

PLANTING WITH A COLOUR SCHEME IN MIND

The choice of colour in the garden will ultimately bring your garden to life in an individual way. Just as some people feel happier wearing certain colours, some also prefer particular flowering colours for the garden and for indoor decoration. Some people prefer masses of different colours throughout the garden at the one time and this can work very well. Others enjoy choosing colours which create a pleasing harmony in the landscape. Some prefer a tranquil setting of a predominantly green garden of lush-foliaged shrubs and trees, ferns, ground covers and moss.

Like beauty, colour is in the eye of the beholder and if your favourite colour is blue, as mine is, you will find there are quite a number of beautiful blue flowering native plants available. As many are low-growing or procumbent they can be tucked in all round the garden, spilling over walls, steps, rocks, garden edges, containers or in bold sweeps as borders. The genus *Dampiera* has some beautiful species worthy of cultivation. It is named after William Dampier, the explorer and naturalist who is known to have remarked upon the prevalence of blue flowers in the new land, and this colour is certainly well represented by the dampieras. A favourite wildflower of many is the Western Australian *Lechenaultia biloba*, which comes in many lovely shades of blue and has a wonderful cultivar known as 'White Flash' which has a white centre surrounded by a vibrant deep blue.

You may decide to plant a patch of garden with a collection of pink flowering plants, for instance the robust *Grevillea* 'Misty Pink', the delicate pink-flowering weeping *Hypocalymma angustifolium*, the long-flowering *Bauera rubioides* and a pink boronia underplanted with the pink form of the creeping *Myoporum parvifolium* with its star-like flowers. If the garden opens out to a sunny enclosure where the sun penetrates more freely, this could be planted with a framework of smaller growing pink grevilleas and some sunloving paper daisies *Rhodanthe chlorocephala* ssp. *rosea* or clumps of pink kangaroo paws.

Some people might prefer to sprinkle their colourful gardens with touches of white or soft pastels. As in a good floral arrangement, the quiet beauty of white flowers will enhance and quite often perfume the garden. White flowers will also light up a garden at night against the background of dark green. Flannel flowers are a favourite wildflower and as well as their dancing white flowers, they have beautiful grey foliage. The Wedding Bush *Ricinocarpos pinifolius* bears profuse fragrant white flowers and so too does the taller *Kunzea ambigua*. Several good species of *Leptospermum* produce masses of white flowers, often on arching branches, and there are several outstanding white-flowering melaleucas, including the spectacular snow-in-summer *M. linariifolia*, which is covered in scented flowers in early summer. Two beautiful white-flowering climbers are *Clematis aristata*, which bears masses of starry blossoms in summer followed by decorative cotton-like fruits, and the Wonga Vine *Pandorea pandorana* 'Snow Bells' which has white, velvety bell flowers in late winter and spring. Some smaller white-flowering plants will create a mass of ground cover flowers on either side of a path. These include *Pratia pedunculata*, *Micromyrtus ciliata*, *Myoporum parvifolium*, the dwarf *Baeckea virgata*, and the white-flowering forms of *Brachycome multifida* and *Scaevola albida*.

PLANTING A FRAGRANT GARDEN

One of the joys of gardening is the pleasure of experiencing the scent of freshly dug soil. The fragrances of the garden, some subtle, others strong, contribute to our overall appreciation of this environment and can be of great benefit to our spiritual and physical wellbeing. Many Australian plants have aromatic foliage and exquisitely perfumed flowers and indeed, a scented garden consisting entirely of native plants could easily be created.

In planning your garden, fragrant plants should be strategically sited along

The colourful fruits of *Acmena smithii* were popular with early settlers for making jam and jelly.

paths and near outdoor living areas or frequently opened doors or windows where the perfume may be enjoyed. Many native plants with aromatic foliage release their perfume even with gentle brushing and can bring pleasure all the year round.

Most of us who have spent time in the bush will recall its imposing, but impossible to describe, aroma. Fragrance is one of the striking features of the bush and it is the species with highly odoriferous foliage that give off the predominant aroma on a hot or rainy day.

The Myrtaceae, the dominant oil-bearing family in many plant communities, includes a wealth of plants with foliage of the 'crush and smell' variety. These range from the many hundreds of eucalypts, melaleucas, tea-trees, bottlebrushes, darwinias and thryptomenes to little ground-hugging *Micromyrtus* species and astarteas. *Backhousia citriodora* has powerful lemon-scented leaves as does the widely cultivated Lemon-scented Tea-tree *Leptospermum petersonii.* Both are reminiscent of several other myrtaceous plants, especially *Eucalyptus citriodora*, which in early days was used to scent linen.

The foliage of many species of the mint bushes, *Prostanthera*, is rich in volatile oils, giving it a pleasant or pungent odour on warm days. Mint bushes belong to the family Lamiaceae, which contains many aromatic kitchen garden herbs including sage, basil and mint.

The fragrant family Rutaceae, which contains the important cultivated genus *Citrus*, includes many attractive Australian genera with aromatic foliage. Some of these are species of *Boronia*, *Crowea*, *Eriostemon* and *Zieria*.

There are many Australian plants with beautifully perfumed flowers. A large number of wattles have sweetly scented blossoms and it is possible to select from the large variety available to have one or two wattles flowering and perfuming the air in all seasons.

For mornings in late winter who would want to be without the wonderful perfume of the Brown Boronia *Boronia megastigma* or its varieties? For early spring, other sweetly scented boronia blossoms include *B. heterophylla*, *B. floribunda* and the native rose, *B. serrulata*.

Rhodanthe chlorocephala ssp. *rosea* is an excellent bedding plant and looks wonderful in cottage gardens.

The Native Frangipani *Hymenosporum flavum* is a lovely sight during spring and early summer. When it is flowering at its peak you can stand beneath the canopy and be totally overwhelmed by the delicious sweet perfume. Closely related is the genus *Pittosporum*, which also has species with sweetly perfumed flowers.

In warm areas, some epiphytic orchids can add to the fragrance in the late part of the day and evening.

In this catalogue special mention has been made of fragrance where it is a feature of a species and all plants having fragrant foliage or flowers have been grouped together for easy reference in a separate index on page 343.

LANDSCAPE FEATURES

There are a number of landscape features that can be constructed by the home owner or by the designer-landscaper, but even if you employ a professional it is best to have some understanding of what is involved and a knowledge of materials available. But do remember that all decks, pergolas, retaining walls, other garden structures, and in some cases fences, need council approval.

There are many different building materials available for use in the garden, but it is difficult to improve on employing natural materials such as timber, stone, brick and brush which merge easily with the native garden environment.

A garden is an extension of the home and will add considerable beauty to it. As more Australians enjoy entertaining outside, a living area complete with pergola and barbecue facilities might need to be part of the plan. Children need places to play and paths for bikes. Whether you are an active gardener or a passive garden user, you should derive pleasure from working in it, relaxing in it or looking at it.

Rocks

Rocks are an evocative element in any bush garden, as they give emphasis to and enhance the colour and texture of native plants. You may be fortunate enough to have rocky outcrops on your property which will already have balance and unity. The task for those introducing rocks to a garden is to try to reproduce that balance and weatherworn unity with the site. The placement of rocks is thus one of the most challenging aspects of landscaping.

If you do wish to introduce rocks into your landscape it is advisable to do so before anything else is planted. A few really big ones should be placed and settled while there is still room to move. Consider the natural character and symmetry of the rocks and set them into the ground so they look as though they have always been there. Any lichen and moss on the rocks should be shown to advantage.

Rocks provide a habitat for plants that like a cool root run and they allow levels to be changed in a garden in a most natural way. A rockery can be inspiring and, if sited correctly, will give the garden structural form and visual interest. It is best to make use of stones and rocks native to the locality as these blend more naturally with the landscape.

Paths

The basic aim of the native garden is to achieve an informal atmosphere and when planning paths in the landscape it is best to avoid straight lines wherever possible. Paths add character to a garden and irregular or winding paths of a natural appearance are more interesting because new focal points come into view as you meander along them.

A garden should be planned for wandering in and will seem larger because of a meandering path. As most people need to move freely around their gardens, main tracks or pathways should be wide enough to allow two people to walk comfortably side by side and to take a wheelbarrow easily.

Materials used in garden paths vary greatly. Care should be taken to select sympathetic materials which will blend into the garden and harmonise with the environment. Materials may include stepping stones, cobble stones, pine bark and sawn tree sections.

Secondhand bricks can make an attractive pathway and may be used to link the house with the garden. Their warm colouring and well-weathered appearance harmonise beautifully with the informal garden. Quite interesting designs can be formed and the bricks can be laid on edge, flat, or in a combination of both. Lay them on a levelled surface covered by a generous bed of damp sand, keeping the crevices between the bricks as uniform as possible. The margins may be edged with railway sleepers, pine log off-cuts and large stones. Fill the crevices and edges with soil and gently hose it in. The planting of small ground covers at the edges will eliminate the need for cement.

Random stepping stones are an alternative type of path. They can be flagstones of different sizes, rings of timber or natural flat bush stone interwoven with tiny ground covers, pebbles or woodchips. The stones should be placed reasonably close to each other for easy stepping, as walking along a path should be comfortable and not an obstacle course.

A quiet and charming path through a natural garden could be surfaced with pine bark, wood chips, gravel, crushed stone or fine river pebbles. All these materials give a soft surface that is pleasant to walk on and attractive in appearance. An edging of brick, logs or stone may be used to confine the margins of paths of this type. Wood chips soon weather to a pleasing colour and make an excellent path.

In an established bush garden the fallen litter will form a lovely natural carpet of dried leaves and twigs that are delightful to tread on and when crushed will add to the beautiful bush fragrance.

Ponds

A pond can be one of a garden's delights. It can evoke a feeling of tranquillity and cool relief on hot days as well as attracting many species of birds.

The size of a pond will depend on what the owner can afford and the size of the garden, but no area is too small for a compact water feature. Surprisingly little water is needed to create attractive effects and there are several models of pumps which will allow you to have moving and circulating water. By adding movement to the pond in the form of a waterfall or fountain, you can have the additional enjoyment of the soothing sound of dripping or splashing water.

The most important consideration when planning a garden pond is to capture a natural and realistic effect. It should be in a site where it does not intrude and can be a feature of a rockery or the climax of a walk flanked by tall shrubs or trees. Shrubs close to the pond afford safe roosting sites and protection for birds attracted to the water.

Any obviously visible concrete, fibreglass or artificial edgings may be concealed by well-placed rocks interplanted with ground covers and plants that thrive near the water's edge. Provision should be made for larger plants in the background. The overflow of water can be diverted down one side or into the ground beyond where beautiful bog plants can be grown. Many native plants thrive in moist or wet soil, but not actually under water. These include tufting plants, sedges, ferns, native violets and many shrubs, including a good range of melaleucas. Ferns complement a water feature and a lush ferny glade could be made up of tall tree ferns, big bird's nest ferns, moisture loving blechnums and small ground ferns. The Nardoo *Marsilea drummondii* with fronds like four-leaved clover leaves will cluster at the edge of the pond or float prettily on its surface. For larger ponds the water lilies *Nelumbo* and *Nymphaea* would be suitable and might be available through nurseries specialising in water plants. Neither have been included in this work as they are not widely available.

Steps

The important points to keep in mind when planning steps in the garden are that they should be safe to walk up and down, and in proportion to the location for which they are designed. They should be comfortable to use, and preference should be given to broad steps with a well-proportioned riser.

Steps can be made of natural cut stone, sandstone blocks, bricks, sleepers, logs or other materials. It is important here again to select materials which blend into the surroundings and are not slippery.

A very attractive flight of steps can be constructed with the combination of bricks forming broad steps retained by sleepers as the risers. Equally attractive is an informal flight of steps or change of level made with sleepers as risers and the tread consisting of packed earth and a mulch such as pine bark or wood chips.

Steps or stepping stones in a large rockery should be made of materials complementary to or the same as those used in the construction of the rockery.

Garden steps can be decorated and softened with low-growing plants such as prostrate grevilleas, scaevolas, dampieras, brachycomes and ferns.

Screening

While parts of a garden may be visible to neighbours and from the street, there are usually private areas, such as terraces, other sitting areas, a barbecue, little getaway areas or possibly a pool, that may have to be screened. As well as providing private recreational areas for members of the family, screens may also be needed to hide an unwanted view or to conceal the utility area from view. Good screenings may be effected by a manmade construction or a vegetative barrier.

Plants which grow to provide a screen or shelter may be planted together as hedges, groups of shrubs or belts of trees. Screen plants are often grown near the coast to protect the more tender plants from salt spray or drying winds. For a good dense screening effect it is best to use plants with varied growth habits so that they will mature to a range of heights which will ensure good density, particularly at the base of the screen. For example the taller trees or shrubs *Banksia integrifolia*, *Lagunaria patersonia* or *Melaleuca armillaris* could be underplanted with medium shrubs like *Acacia sophorae* or *Correa backhousia* and smaller shrubs like *Westringia fruticosa* and *Thomasia petalocalyx*. Among the more natural screening construction materials now commonly used are tea-tree, paperbark and brush. All have a natural, rough surface that merges with the colour of the garden.

Wire or mesh fencing is an effective screen which can be softened by surrounding it with shrubs and trees or encouraging the growth of leafy climbers. Some of the kennedias, the pandoreas and *Sollya heterophylla* will rapidly cover large areas.

A timber lattice trellis can be used as a screen if erected on a solid timber frame. Lattice is very decorative in itself, giving an airy, lacy charm wherever it is used in the garden. You can buy lath strips and make your own lattice; this will give you a complete choice of lattice patterns, degrees of screening and size of panels. The lattice may be stained with a timber finish to blend into the surrounding if you wish.

Pergolas

A well-planned outdoor living space in the garden will provide a positive, relaxed environment well suited to the informal Australian lifestyle and our wonderful climate. For convenience an outdoor eating area should be sited reasonably near the house. A vine-covered pergola along the rear of the house will give you practically another room. It will add coolness to the nearby rooms and create both a delightful spot for informal meals and protection for many plants.

A pergola is constructed from a simple timber post and beam system, with beams spanning across the structure, giving a feeling of semi-enclosure and a little shelter. In some cases a pergola may be completely or partially covered depending on the degree of shade protection and shelter required. Choice of covering materials should be guided by moderation as it is easy to overfill even a large space and some roofing materials such as fibreglass panels and canvas restrict ventilation to some degree. Pergola rafters combined with suitable climbing plants should cast sufficient shade to turn the whole of the outdoor living area into a big shade-house. Vigorous climbers such as *Kennedia macrophylla* and *K. nigricans*, *Cissus antarctica*, *Clematis aristata*, *Hardenbergia comptoniana* and *H. violacea*, *Hibbertia scandens* and the pandoreas are all suitable for training up posts and covering large areas.

With the use of a pergola an excellent outdoor living area may be created in the space between a house and its garage. Hanging baskets, potted plants and in-ground shrubs can all contribute to making a pleasant private retreat.

Most inner city terraces have little side areas leading from the kitchen or living room to the garden. Rather than leave them as bare corridors, have a pergola covered with creepers there: it will provide a charming entrance to the garden and give an appearance of a small courtyard from inside the house.

Furniture

Choose outdoor furniture to harmonise with the garden. Timber furniture blends beautifully with a native garden, as does traditional bush furniture, which is becoming a popular choice for outdoor settings and landscape design. Bush furniture is modelled on that of early bush settlers in the times when craftsmen made their own furniture using locally available materials. Generally ironbark and gum are used and because these woods come directly from the Australian bush, the furniture blends perfectly with a native garden. It is functional, long-lasting and surprisingly comfortable, and it has an air of permanence, giving you another good reason to use your garden for relaxing with friends or having quiet meals with the family.

Small Gardens and Containers

When selecting plants for a small garden, you need to incorporate and arrange the same group of elements used for a larger area. With careful planning, an illusion of space, balanced design and unity of theme can easily be created.

Consideration must first be given to permanent plantings that form the background framework of a garden. The textural interest that foliage provides is important in limited space. Australian native plants provide a wide range of foliage variation from the large-leaved or glossy rainforest species to the needles and feathery leaves of casuarinas and acacias. In a small space you have the option of choosing foliage that is similar in texture. Where in a large garden this would be visually boring, in a small area it conveys a sense of unity. A pleasing balance of light and shade is another desirable feature in any garden and it can best be achieved in small gardens by variation in the height of framework planting. Palms are ideal for adding height to small gardens because they do not have a tap root system, so however big they become you will not have to worry about roots getting into foundations or drains. If space permits, a few palms grouped fairly closely will give a natural grove effect and, perhaps because of their association with the tropics, a relaxed mood to a garden.

Where space is limited, density of foliage, rather than of planting, becomes another desirable ingredient in the garden's framework. Plants that retain their shrubby habit, such as bushy species of acacias, banksias, bottlebrushes, grevilleas and melaleucas, are ideal. Tall, lanky plants are not really suitable as they need constant trimming and renewal of underplanting.

When extra privacy needs to be gained, or unsightly boundaries or buildings need to be hidden, latticework is an indispensable feature to use against walls and fences. Then by adorning the latticework with cascading colour and climbing foliage, you can create a small vertical garden. *Hibbertia scandens*, *Kennedia macrophylla*, *Hardenbergia violacea*, *Pandorea jasminoides* and *P. pandorana* are all ideal for this.

Fill-in plants such as small species of *Brachycome*, *Pimelea*, *Dampiera*, *Hibbertia* and *Epacris* will create a more pleasing effect when planted en masse. If you like bright colour, a few plants of the Scrambling Flame Pea *Chorizema cordatum* will really light up the small garden in late winter and spring.

For low maintenance in a small garden, grow plenty of ground covers and carpeting plants such as *Dampiera diversifolia*, *Mazus pumilio* and *Pratia pedunculata*. The Native Violet *Viola hederacea* will daintily get out of hand and provide you with delicate chaos linking garden with paving or paths. Ground covers are ideal for small areas because the plants look after themselves and suppress weeds.

Once you have planned or planted a framework, a happy solution to the problem of limited space is a garden in pots. In any garden large or small potted plants can be positioned to give balance to areas, filling ground space, bench space and air space. Another advantage is that many native plants that have difficulty surviving in garden conditions are often happier in containers. The pot can also be filled with the type of soil the plant requires, making it possible to grow many eastern Australian plants in the west and to nurture some of the glorious Western Australian species like *Boronia megastigma* more reliably in eastern States. Moreover, containers can be moved with the seasons to ensure colour and greenery throughout the year.

There is a very wide range of plants that will provide year-round greenery, but possibly the most readily available and popular are palms and tree ferns. Both are ideal for potting, and situated together in a massed grouping they provide a graceful feature giving variety in foliage and height.

For an abundance of bright splashes of colour, *Lechenaultia formosa* in its many shades of red, orange and yellow in winter and spring is ideally suited to containers and hanging baskets. The spectacular blue *Lechenaultia biloba* which blooms in spring and early summer looks superb as a potted plant. Tip cuttings from both species will strike very easily so that bold groups of colour can be quickly achieved.

There are several *Hibbertia* species that are ideal for containers, with profuse bright yellow flowers in spring. *Pimelea ferruginea* has an almost perfect dome shape for a container and bears masses of deep pink flower heads in spring. For summer flowers, the Golden Everlasting *Bracteantha bracteata* 'Diamond Head' and 'Dargan Hill Monarch' and the White Everlasting *Chrysocephalum baxteri* bloom for a long period. Many of the correas are perfect for containers and will flower in autumn and winter.

PLANTS FOR SHADE OR INDOORS

Sections of small gardens are often shady because they are close to the house or boundaries and here shade largely governs the choice of plant material. Ferns in all their variety are ideal for shady nooks and team well with the graceful fronds of palms and the blue colour accents of the mint bushes (*Prostanthera* spp.) in spring. Most boronias prefer light shade and for such a position where a little height is needed, *Boronia muelleri*, *B. mollis* and the lightly perfumed greenish-flowering *B. clavata* are all suitable. *Eriostemon myoporoides* will tolerate considerable shade and its dense bushy habit, growing to a rounded 1.5 m, makes it a very attractive specimen for the small garden. For semishade, *Persoonia pinifolia* is a graceful weeping shrub with crowded pine-like leaves and beautiful spikes of yellow flowers at branch ends in summer, followed by clusters of green fruit. This is a lovely plant at all times of the year.

Many rainforest species, particularly the slow-growing ones, make excellent foliage plants in containers for shady parts of the garden, near entrances and for indoor decoration. While most will tolerate fairly dark indoor conditions, it is best to have spare plants in a protected outdoor situation to swap with those indoors. This will maintain a fresh look to the indoor display at all times. The Umbrella Tree and the Weeping Fig are well-known indoor plants. Not so widely used are the Firewheel Tree (*Stenocarpus sinuatus*), the Black Bean (*Castanospermum australe*) and *Cordyline* species, which all make decorative indoor foliage plants. With the exception of *Cordyline* species, do not be tempted to plant out a rainforest plant that has outgrown its container into the small garden. It will eventually grow far too big.

The uniquely Australian Grass Tree *Xanthorrhoea australis* is very well suited to container culture.

POTS AND POTTING

Containers for the small garden should be chosen with care and whether of ceramic, stone, terracotta or wood, should harmonise with house and other materials used for paths, paving and garden edging. Be it a slender urn or a generous half wooden cask, choose your pot so that it complements the planting. Colourful plastic pots do nothing for the plant or the garden. If plastic containers are used, black is preferable as it is more easily camouflaged by the vegetation. Plastic pots may be placed in cane baskets when being used as a feature. There are some marvellous baskets available, but those made with Lawyer Cane or Wait-a-while (*Calamus* species) will stand up very well to outdoor conditions, even harsh sun and rain.

Soil from the garden is seldom satisfactory for growing plants in containers. Soil mixtures should be well aerated but able to retain moisture sufficiently to maintain a healthy plant. The addition of peatmoss to a friable soil with good compost added would be suitable for many species. Soil mixture will vary according to the individual species and it is possible to buy good commercially prepared potting mixtures to suit the needs of most plants. A mulch can be placed on top of the potting mix to help retain moisture, or a pretty trailing plant such as the Native Violet *Viola hederacea* or *Pratia pedunculata* can be used as a ground cover in large planters.

It should be remembered that all plants grown in containers require careful watering. They should never be allowed to dry out completely, but will resent overwatering. Be guided by the condition of the soil below the surface. Most native plants will die if their roots are sodden, so watch that pots are not left standing in a saucer of water. Watering of hanging baskets has to be carefully administered as baskets dry out more quickly than pots.

Most plants in pots will benefit from a light feeding. A slow release fertiliser formulated for native plants applied during early spring is ideal.

Attracting Native Birds to the Garden

One of the great pleasures of growing native plants is that many species attract our marvellous birds to the garden. As well as being a source of endless entertainment with their movement, colour, chatter and song, these birds will efficiently control many insect pests.

Since the escalated interest in growing Australian plants in the past thirty years, the native bird population of settled areas has increased tremendously so that even in our cities and adjoining suburbs, we are now enjoying a varied bird life. In some newly developed outer housing areas, however, the birds are often few and far between because extensive clearing for housing, roads or early farming has destroyed their habitat. Sometimes existing trees have been protected, but the removal of understorey shrubs has prevented the important continuous supply of food throughout the year. By planting balanced native gardens in these areas birds can be re-introduced and with luck become regular visitors or residents once again. A balanced garden would contain trees, a framework of large shrubs and, filling the gaps, small plants such as species of *Anigozanthos*, *Correa*, *Epacris* and native grasses. Thus birds are provided with food, shelter and nesting sites. Native plants generally grow crowded together, so if you plan a garden like this the birds will soon seek refuge and nest in such vegetation. Birds need variety, so plan for tall trees such as *Eucalyptus* and *Angophora* with hollows for nesting and some dense, prickly shrubs as sanctuaries from predators. Some species of *Acacia*, *Grevillea* and *Hakea* have prickly foliage and make a good protective cover for small birds.

Water is an important requirement which you can provide by placing out water bowls or a bird bath, which should be kept clean and freshly supplied and should be out of reach of preying cats. A fresh water supply will be especially appreciated in warmer months.

Although many exotic plants are also good sources of food, you can be sure that native birds will instinctively feed more on native nectar, seed and fruits. By carefully selecting native plants that provide a succession of flowers, fruits and seeds you will provide a permanent source of food for both visiting birds and those who will become full-time boarders.

The most frequent visitors to any native garden are the nectar-feeding birds. They are attracted by the nectar of certain flowering plants, and indeed, some of these are among the most spectacular of all Australian plants. Long-flowering species of *Banksia*, *Grevillea* and *Hakea* and the outstanding *Lambertia formosa* are all excellent. Other plants loved by nectar-feeding birds include species of *Angophora*, *Anigozanthos*, *Callistemon*, *Correa*, *Eremophila*, *Eucalyptus*, *Kunzea* and *Melaleuca*. The soft, papery bark of some melaleucas also provides a favourite nesting material for many birds.

As well as providing shelter for smaller birds, a selection of *Acacia* species that flower at different times will ensure a continuous supply of seed for rosellas, parrots, cockatoos and other seed-eaters. Native pigeons and doves especially depend on *Acacia* seed as a major part of their diet.

Parrots and cockatoos may return to the same nesting site for many years and also enjoy the seed and fruit provided by species of *Callitris*, *Casuarina*, *Eucalyptus*, the White Cedar *Melia azedarach* var. *australasica* and *Pittosporum*.

Smaller seed-eaters such as finches and budgerigars feed almost entirely on the seeds of grasses and herbaceous plants. They do, however, need dense clumps of trees and shrubs to head to for cover and in which to build their nests.

The eucalypt is the most conspicuous element of the Australian vegetation, and what native garden would be without at least one? All bear flowers, some more flamboyantly than others, and these colourful blossoms provide rich nectar for the honeyeaters. Their flowers are followed by fruits which in turn attract the parrots and cockatoos. Insectivorous birds extract pests from the branches, foliage and trunks. Eucalypts are fast-growing and grow tall enough to attract birds in from some distance for a look around or to nest in the foliage. The fibrous, stringy barks of some species provide nesting materials for many birds.

Most native birds include insects in their diet and many, such as the pretty pardalotes, are completely insectivorous. Insects are an especially important food, particularly during the nesting period, for many of the attractive smaller garden birds such as silvereyes, robins, wrens and fantails.

Birds will ensure that the insect population is reduced to insignificant proportions, but you must avoid the use of toxic sprays and dusts whenever possible. Birds feeding on poisoned insects will gradually build up a concentration of the poison that will kill them. Initially you may have to tolerate a few insects until the plants are large enough to shelter the birds. Some pests can be controlled by removal by hand or by spraying them with a hose. White oil is useful for scale, Sooty Mould and leaf-webbing caterpillars.

Sulphur-crested cockatoo feeding on *Persoonia levis*

Diplolaena grandiflora

THE PLANTS

ACACIA

MIMOSACEAE

The common name 'wattle' by which these plants are known in Australia came into use when Acacia *species were used by early settlers to provide slender sticks for their dwellings built by a method known as 'wattle and daub'.*

Australia has a huge range of wattles — more than 700 different species ranging in size from prostrate ground covers to medium trees — and they are present in almost all plant communities. They are divided into two major groups, those with feathery bipinnate leaves and those with leaves modified to phyllodes. A phyllode is a flattened leaf stalk; it probably evolved as a means of conserving moisture in an arid climate. Phyllodes appear in a wide range of shapes and sizes including flat and broad, long and thin, triangular and needle-like, curved and pointed. Floral brilliance, superb foliage, diversity of form, landscaping adaptability, low maintenance and quick growth are some of the reasons why Acacia *species are such popular garden plants. Flowering times are most often in winter and early spring, but throughout the year there are always some in flower. Wattles attract native birds to the garden, providing them with protective cover. The seeds are an important source of food for parrots, rosellas and pigeons.*

Wattles are very hardy; most are frost-resistant, will grow in almost any well-drained soil and do not require excessive fertiliser. Regular trimming of flowering stems should be carried out during or immediately after flowering to improve bloom production and prolong life. Borers in shrubby species and galls are the main pests to watch out for in acacias.

Propagation is from seed in early spring. The seeds have a hard, shiny protective coat, but can be stimulated into germination by pouring boiling water over them to stand overnight. Sow those seeds which have swollen. Germination usually takes place within three weeks.

Acacia acinacea

GOLD DUST WATTLE

Origin NSW, Vic., SA
Climate S, WT, M, CT, SA
Shade Light to filtered

BIRD-ATTRACTING
CONTAINER PLANT

Description A much-branched, spreading small shrub to 2 m tall and 2 to 4 m across, with oblong to rounded phyllodes ending in a curved point. The bright yellow balls of flowers on long slender stalks bloom profusely from late winter to November.

A. acinacea var. *rotundifolia*, a form with more rounded phyllodes, was formerly known as *A. rotundifolia.*

Cultivation An adaptable and hardy species for most well-drained soils and most conditions. It will tolerate some shade, can survive dry periods and is frost-resistant. Prune lightly after flowering to encourage compact growth.

Landscape Use A most attractive species for small gardens. It will grow in a large container or can be used as a low hedge or windbreak.

Acacia adunca

(syn. *A. accola*)

WALLANGARRA WATTLE

Origin Qld, NSW
Climate S, WT, M, CT
Shade None to light

FAST-GROWING
FRAGRANT
BIRD-ATTRACTING

Description A small, shapely tree with a slightly weeping habit, to around 6 or 7 m high. It has narrow, dark green phyllodes and bears perfumed golden ball flowers in terminal clusters during winter and early spring.

Cultivation A hardy, adaptable species for a well-drained position. It is frost-resistant.

Landscape Use A shapely specimen tree for parks and gardens.

Acacia acinacea

Acacia adunca

Acacia amblygona

Origin Qld, NSW
Climate S, WT, M
Shade None to light
BIRD-ATTRACTING
CONTAINER PLANT
Description A variable spreading shrub up to 2 m high. It has sharply pointed triangular phyllodes and produces masses of yellow ball flowers from late winter to spring.

A prostrate form from southern Queensland has become very popular in cultivation. It has a spread of up to 3 m and is an excellent ground cover.

Cultivation A hardy wattle for subtropical areas that will also do well in cooler climates. It likes a sunny, open position with good drainage and is moderately frost-resistant.

Landscape Use Suitable for a large rockery and for controlling soil erosion. The prostrate form provides a good dense ground cover, especially for covering banks and tumbling over retaining walls or large tubs.

Acacia amblygona

Acacia aneura
MULGA; YARRAN

Origin Qld, NSW, SA, WA, NT
Climate M, SA
Shade None to light
BIRD-ATTRACTING
DROUGHT-RESISTANT
Description Mulga is one of the predominant plants of the dry inland. It is a variable small tree up to 7 m tall, often multibranched, with narrow grey-green phyllodes. Attractive yellow flowering spikes appear around August, especially after good rains. Mulga is well known for its beautiful grained timber, so widely favoured for souvenirs. It was used by Aborigines for spears and long narrow shields or 'mulgas'. A number of varieties exist. One attractive form has weeping grey foliage.

Acacia aneura

Cultivation This long-lived species is drought-resistant and moderately frost-resistant and is ideally suited to hot, dry inland gardens. It will tolerate a wide range of soils, including clay and limy, but good drainage is essential.

Landscape Use Plant singly or as a small group for shade.

Acacia baileyana
COOTAMUNDRA WATTLE

Origin NSW
Climate S, WT, M, CT, H
Shade None to filtered
FAST-GROWING
SPECIMEN PLANT
FRAGRANT
BIRD-ATTRACTING
ORNAMENTAL FOLIAGE
Description This spectacularly flowering small tree to 6 m high is probably the most popular wattle cultivated. It has silvery grey, feathery leaves, a handsome wide-spreading form and a graceful weeping habit. The massed clusters of rich golden yellow perfumed flowers bloom

Acacia baileyana

Acacia baileyana var. *purpurea*

during July and August. These early spring flowers attract insectivorous birds.

A. baileyana var. *purpurea* has the added feature of very attractive purplish new growth. Another form, *A. baileyana* var. *aurea*, has yellowish new growth.

Cultivation This very hardy plant is frost-resistant and moderately drought-resistant and will grow in almost any soil with reasonable drainage. It is also suited to protected coastal areas. Prune after flowering to prolong life and encourage lots of new growth, especially with the coloured foliage forms.

Landscape Use The Cootamundra wattle can be used in the larger landscape as a soft foliage background for other trees and shrubs, as a specimen or as a quick-growing plant for screens or windbreaks.

Acacia beckleri

BARRIER RANGE WATTLE

Origin NSW, SA
Climate WT, M, SA
Shade None to filtered

SPECIMEN PLANT
FRAGRANT
BIRD-ATTRACTING
DROUGHT-RESISTANT

Description An erect, open shrub up to 3 m. The leathery blue-green phyllodes are lanceolate and may be straight or curved ending in a dull point. New growth is often red and shining. The large flowers are bright yellow, globular-shaped balls and may appear singly or in terminal clusters. These are delicately fragrant and appear early in winter through to spring.

Cultivation Although this attractive plant naturally occurs in semiarid areas, it is adaptable to a wide range of conditions in

Acacia beckleri

an open, well-drained position. It is frost-hardy and drought-resistant, but requires watering during dry periods in the first year.

Landscape Use An attractive rounded shrub for the small or large garden or in rows as a low windbreak.

Acacia binervata

TWO-VEINED HICKORY

Origin Qld, NSW
Climate WT, M, H
Shade None to filtered

FAST-GROWING
BIRD-ATTRACTING

Description A medium-sized tree to 10 m, with broad phyllodes to 12 cm long with two or three prominent veins. The pale cream flower balls appear in long attractive clusters in spring.

Acacia binervata

Cultivation Grow in a sunny position in a well-composted soil with good drainage. It needs plenty of water and is frost-resistant.

Landscape Use This long-lived species is an excellent fast-growing screen or windbreak plant, or a dense specimen tree for the large garden or park.

Acacia binervia

(syn. *A. glaucescens*)

COASTAL MYALL

Origin NSW
Climate WT, M
Shade None to light

FAST-GROWING
SPECIMEN PLANT
FRAGRANT
BIRD-ATTRACTING
ORNAMENTAL FOLIAGE

Description This beautiful medium-sized tree may reach 18 m in height, but is usually smaller than this in cultivation. It has a compact crown of attractive silvery blue curved phyllodes and produces masses of lemon flower spikes during spring.

Cultivation This hardy species will do well in most well-drained soils. Although it likes plenty of moisture, it will withstand periods of dryness, and it may be grown in protected coastal gardens. It is moderately frost-resistant.

Landscape Use A very attractive wattle for form, foliage and flower. It makes an outstanding specimen tree for streets, parks and large gardens and is suitable for windbreaks on properties, as it is fairly long-lived. The foliage is, however, reported to be poisonous to stock.

Acacia binervia

Acacia boormanii

Acacia boormanii

(syn. *A. hunterana*)

SNOWY RIVER WATTLE

Origin NSW, Vic.
Climate WT, M, CT, H
Shade None to filtered

FAST-GROWING
SPECIMEN PLANT
FRAGRANT
BIRD-ATTRACTING

Description A graceful, slender-branched shrub to 5 m, with smooth silvery stems and a suckering habit. The grey-green phyllodes are linear and masses of bright yellow flower balls are borne in profusion in early spring. Small thickets provide nesting sites for smaller birds.

Cultivation Originating chiefly from the deep valley of the Snowy River, this lovely wattle will tolerate snow and frost. It is an adaptable plant for most well-drained soils and a wide range of climatic conditions, tolerating some dryness as well as extended wet periods.

Landscape Use This extremely attractive wattle makes an excellent specimen shrub. It may be grouped or planted as a screen or windbreak, where the suckers may be left to form an attractive informal hedge.

Acacia brachybotrya

(syn. *A. spillerana*)

GREY MULGA

Origin Qld, NSW, Vic., SA
Climate WT, M, CT, SA
Shade None to light

BIRD-ATTRACTING
DROUGHT-RESISTANT

Description A compact, rounded shrub to 3 m with leathery, grey-green oval

Acacia brachybotrya

phyllodes and dense, bright yellow flower balls which may be solitary or in groups. Flowers are numerous and appear from August to October. In north-western Victoria seeds provide food for the Mallee Fowl (*Leipoa ocellata*).

Cultivation This hardy, handsome shrub with an attractive silver-grey appearance is suited to dry conditions, but is adaptable to areas with higher rainfall. It requires well-drained soil.

Landscape Use An ornamental plant for brightening the dry-country garden. Suitable for group plantings as a low windbreak or hedge.

Acacia buxifolia

BOX-LEAF WATTLE

Origin Qld, NSW, Vic.
Climate S, WT, M
Shade None to filtered

BIRD-ATTRACTING

Description A variable erect shrub or small tree to about 4 m tall, with thick

Acacia buxifolia

pale green phyllodes, and a spectacular display of brilliant yellow ball flowers from spring to summer.

Cultivation This adaptable, widespread species is very hardy and will tolerate most climatic conditions, including frost and some dryness. Grow in well-drained soils in a sheltered position. Regular pruning will keep the plant to the desired size.

Landscape Use A handsome species which may be grown in the dappled shade of taller trees.

Acacia calamifolia

WALLOWA

Origin NSW, Vic., SA
Climate WT, M, CT, SA
Shade None to light

FAST-GROWING
BIRD-ATTRACTING
DROUGHT-RESISTANT

Description A graceful rounded shrub with slender, spreading branches up to 4 m high. The narrow grey-green phyllodes are hooked at the apex. From winter to November masses of perfumed, bright flower balls cover the bush. Mallee Fowl feed on the seed.

Acacia calamifolia

Cultivation Wallowa is a hardy, ornamental shrub adaptable to most conditions, including drought. It requires good drainage and may be grown in coastal gardens with adequate wind protection. It is frost-resistant.

Landscape Use This ornamental species will form an attractive low screen or hedge.

Acacia cardiophylla
WYALONG WATTLE

Origin NSW
Climate WT, M, CT, SA
Shade None to light

FAST-GROWING
SPECIMEN PLANT
FRAGRANT
BIRD-ATTRACTING
DROUGHT-RESISTANT
ORNAMENTAL FOLIAGE

Description A rounded shrub to 4 m. The finely divided, fern-like foliage is a soft green in colour and is attractive at all times. This is an outstanding foliage plant with long arching branches draped in spring with masses of bright yellow flower balls.

Cultivation This very hardy shrub is adaptable to a wide range of conditions including drought and frost. It likes good drainage and will grow in protected seaside gardens. Prune after flowering to keep shapely.

Acacia cardiophylla

Landscape Use This wattle makes a delightful year-round specimen shrub.

Acacia conferta
GOLDEN TOP

Origin Qld, NSW
Climate S, WT, M, CT, SA
Shade None to light

BIRD-ATTRACTING
DROUGHT-RESISTANT

Description A rounded shrub up to 4 m with pubescent branches and crowded linear grey-green phyllodes. Bright yellow ball flowers on slender hairy stalks at branch ends appear in spring.

Cultivation This attractive wattle will grow in a variety of soil types, but requires an open position and excellent drainage. It is adaptable to a wide range of climatic conditions, growing well from Brisbane to southern Australia. It is frost-resistant. Prune after flowering to shape.

Landscape Use Its dense growth makes this species suitable as a low screen plant. The conifer-like phyllodes provide an interesting foliage contrast.

Acacia cultriformis
KNIFE-LEAF WATTLE

Origin Qld, NSW
Climate S, WT, M, CT, H, SA
Shade None to light

SPECIMEN PLANT
FRAGRANT
BIRD-ATTRACTING
DROUGHT-RESISTANT
ORNAMENTAL FOLIAGE

Description This bushy shrub with attractive drooping branches will grow up to 4 m high. The grey-green, triangular phyllodes hug the slender grey branches, and very profuse, lightly perfumed yellow flower balls appear in spring.

Acacia conferta

Acacia cultriformis 'Austraflora Cascade'

A. cultriformis

Acacia dealbata

The prostrate form 'Austraflora Cascade' has a marvellous cascading habit and is ideal as a spill-over plant from rocks, banks or tall containers. This cultivar does not enjoy high humidity.

Cultivation This shrub will grow in a variety of soils and conditions, but needs good drainage. It is frost-resistant and drought-resistant and will grow on the coast with some protection.

Landscape Use This is a delightful feature plant. A habit that is dense at both upper and lower levels makes it an excellent screen or hedge plant. The attractive foliage is useful in floral arrangements.

Acacia dealbata
SILVER WATTLE

Origin NSW, Vic., Tas.
Climate WT, M, CT, H
Shade None to filtered

FAST-GROWING
FRAGRANT
BIRD-ATTRACTING

Description A variable small to medium-sized tree usually to about 8 m. This wattle sometimes occurs as a multistemmed shrub, but in Tasmania it may attain a height of up to 30 m. The stems and the divided feathery leaves have a mealy, silvery appearance. Masses of sweetly scented golden ball flowers cover the ends of the branches in spring. The seed pods are a food source for the Crimson Rosella.

Cultivation This adaptable species is suited to most soils and aspects, but is at its ornamental best when planted in moist, cool situations. It is frost-resistant.

Landscape Use A handsome, hardy species, suited to bank planting because of its suckering habit. A good specimen tree for the large garden or in parks. It can be used as a fast-growing shelter or shade tree.

Acacia deanei
DEANE'S WATTLE

Origin Qld, NSW, Vic.
Climate S, WT, M, SA
Shade None to filtered

FRAGRANT
BIRD-ATTRACTING

Description A shrub or small tree to about 7 m tall. The divided, ferny leaves are a yellow-green colour when young. The pale lemon flower balls are perfumed and appear sporadically throughout the year with a main flush in early winter. The attractive seed pods hang in clusters.

The subspecies *paucijuga* has more angular branches and longer leaflets. It has a more southerly distribution and flowers mainly in summer.

Cultivation This very hardy, adaptable species is suited to a wide range of soils and conditions. It will withstand dry periods and is frost-resistant.

Landscape Use A bushy shrub useful for windbreaks.

Acacia deanei

Acacia decurrens
EARLY BLACK WATTLE, GREEN WATTLE

Origin NSW
Climate S, WT, M, CT, H
Shade None to light

FAST-GROWING
SPECIMEN PLANT
FRAGRANT
BIRD-ATTRACTING

Description A small to medium-sized tree to 15 m high with a shapely crown of feathery dark green leaves. It is distinguished from its close relatives by its prominent angular or winged stems. The perfumed golden flower balls appear in dense clusters in late winter and early spring and provide a bold splash of colour when in full bloom. This tree provides shelter and food for insectivorous birds.

Cultivation A hardy tree, adaptable to a wide range of conditions, including hot, dry spells, frost and winter cold. Although

Acacia decurrens

very fast-growing, it is subject to attack by borer which may shorten its life.

Landscape Use This ornamental tree has been cultivated for many years as a specimen and shade tree. It is amongst the most popular trees on farms for quick shelter or windbreaks.

Acacia drummondii
DRUMMOND'S WATTLE

Origin WA
Climate WT, M, CT
Shade None to filtered

FAST-GROWING
BIRD-ATTRACTING
CONTAINER PLANT

Description This beautiful variable shrub has been divided into four subspecies which range considerably in height, from ssp. *candolleana* which may reach 3 m to the dwarf form ssp. *affinis* up to 1 m. The ferny foliage with green or slightly bluish leaflets is attractive in all forms. Showy canary yellow rods of flowers are produced at the ends of branches from July to October; ssp. *elegans* has very large flower heads up to 5 cm long.

Acacia drummondii

Cultivation This shrub is best planted with a little shade and shelter in a well-drained position. It is slightly frost-tender while young. A light pruning after flowering helps to maintain compactness.

Landscape Use A compact shrub useful where space is limited. It is suitable for low windbreaks or screens and is an ideal specimen plant for the large rockery. Subspecies *affinis* is a delightful plant for medium containers.

Acacia elata
CEDAR WATTLE

Origin NSW
Climate WT, M, SA
Shade None to filtered

FAST-GROWING
BIRD-ATTRACTING

Description A graceful spreading tree to around 12 m in cultivation. The dark green foliage is divided into large feathery leaflets. Young leaves are pinkish bronze. The large, fluffy pompom flowers are pale yellow and appear in summer.

Cultivation This adaptable tree from sheltered coastal gullies and nearby mountains will also tolerate dry situations and cold, but is slightly frost-tender while young. It may be grown in protected coastal gardens.

Acacia elata

A. drummondii ssp. *elegans*

Landscape Use A shapely ornamental tree for large gardens, street and parks. It is suited to windbreak planting.

Acacia fimbriata
FRINGED WATTLE

Origin Qld, NSW
Climate S, WT, M, CT
Shade None to filtered

FAST-GROWING
FRAGRANT
BIRD-ATTRACTING

Description A bushy shrub or small tree to 7 m with a graceful arching habit. The dark green phyllodes are narrow and fringed with fine hairs. New growth is bronze. Numerous sprays of sweetly perfumed flower balls cover the bush in spring. Flower colour varies in different regions from pale yellow to deep golden.

Cultivation A popular and hardy species in cultivation, and one which will grow in a variety of soils with good drainage. It is frost-resistant, but requires adequate

Acacia fimbriata

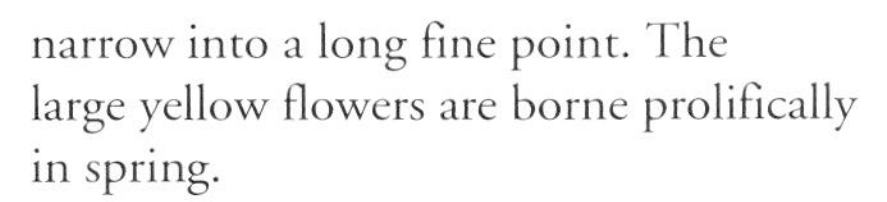

water. It is useful for protected coastal planting.

Landscape Use This acacia makes a lovely specimen plant. When planted in rows it will form a good dense screen or windbreak.

Acacia flexifolia
BENT-LEAF WATTLE

Origin Qld, NSW, Vic.
Climate WT, M, CT, SA
Shade None to filtered

FRAGRANT
BIRD-ATTRACTING
CONTAINER PLANT

Description An attractive rounded shrub to 2 m. The grey-green linear phyllodes are leathery and have a pronounced bend near the base. The profuse, dainty pale yellow flower balls are perfumed and appear in winter.

Cultivation A most adaptable wattle in many situations. However, a well-drained, dry, open position is most suitable. It is frost-tolerant. Pruning after flowering helps to maintain the shape and denseness of the bush.

Landscape Use A good ornamental for a moderately dry garden. It is suitable for a low windbreak or hedge.

Acacia floribunda
WHITE SALLOW WATTLE

Origin Qld, NSW, Vic.
Climate S, WT, M, CT
Shade None to filtered

FAST-GROWING
SPECIMEN PLANT
FRAGRANT
BIRD-ATTRACTING

Description A graceful, spreading small tree to 8 m. It has a weeping habit, particularly when laden with flowers. The light green phyllodes, up to 10 cm long, narrow into a long fine point. The large yellow flowers are borne prolifically in spring.

Acacia floribunda

Cultivation This very hardy wattle grows in a wide range of soils, including clay, and will tolerate frost and wet conditions. It is suitable for planting in a protected seaside position.

Landscape Use The willow-like habit makes this wattle an attractive specimen tree. When planted in rows it quickly forms an effective screen or wind break.

Acacia glaucoptera
CLAY WATTLE, FLAT WATTLE

Origin WA
Climate WT, M, CT, SA
Shade Light to filtered

BIRD-ATTRACTING
ORNAMENTAL FOLIAGE

Description A many-branched rounded shrub up to 1 m. The unusual flat grey-green phyllodes overlap continuously along the zig-zagging stem. New growth is often red or bronze. The large deep yellow flower balls emerge from the central stem in the spring months.

Cultivation This species does well in eastern Australia. However, it must have excellent drainage. Grows well beneath light cover of larger trees. Some pruning after flowering is recommended if bush becomes straggly and to encourage attractive red new growth.

Acacia flexifolia

Acacia glaucoptera

Landscape Use This curious foliage plant may be used as an interesting garden feature or in a partially shaded position in the rockery.

Acacia gracilifolia

Origin SA
Climate WT, M, CT, SA
Shade None to filtered

FAST-GROWING
BIRD-ATTRACTING
ORNAMENTAL FOLIAGE

Description A medium-sized open shrub to around 2 or 3 m high. It has very fine, long wispy phyllodes and bears golden ball flowers during spring. Flowers and foliage are good for light indoor arrangements.

Cultivation Hardy and adaptable for most well-drained soils. It will do well in dry country areas and is moderately frost-resistant.

Landscape Use A most ornamental shrub, useful as a feature or for a light foliage contrast amongst other shrubs.

Acacia gracilifolia

Acacia gunnii

(syn. *A. vomeriformis*)

PLOUGHSHARE WATTLE

Origin Qld, NSW, Vic., Tas., SA
Climate WT, M, CT
Shade None to filtered

BIRD-ATTRACTING

Description A small, spreading, prickly shrub rarely rising above 50 cm but spreading to 2 m across. More often the plant is decumbent. The rigid triangular phyllodes taper into a straight sharp point and the profuse pale yellow flower balls appear from late winter.

Acacia gunnii

Cultivation This species is tolerant of a wide range of conditions, but likes good drainage. It will tolerate dry periods and is frost-resistant.

Landscape Use A sprawling ground cover suited to a rockery or sloping bank.

Acacia howittii

STICKY WATTLE

Origin Vic.
Climate WT, M, CT
Shade None to filtered

FAST-GROWING
FRAGRANT
BIRD-ATTRACTING

Description A large shrub with a dense weeping habit up to 6 m. The sticky dark green phyllodes have a spicy aroma and masses of scented lemon flower balls appear in spring. The seeds provide food for native pigeons.

Cultivation An adaptable species for most well-drained soils. It likes plenty of moisture but will withstand dry spells. It is frost-resistant.

Landscape Use This graceful, weeping wattle makes a lovely specimen plant if given space in the suburban landscape. It also makes an excellent dense hedge or screening plant that will tolerate heavy pruning.

Acacia howittii

Acacia hubbardiana

(syn. *A. plagiophylla*)

Origin Qld
Climate T, ST, WT
Shade None to filtered

BIRD-ATTRACTING

Description A small, compact shrub which may reach 2 m but is usually smaller. It has bright green wedge-shaped phyllodes ending in a sharp point. The globular pale yellow flower heads on long slender stalks appear from late winter.

Cultivation This interesting small plant is hardy in tropical and subtropical gardens, where it will tolerate wet soil and protected coastal positions.

Landscape Use An attractive plant for the rockery or small garden.

Acacia hubbardiana

Acacia iteaphylla

FLINDERS RANGE WATTLE

Origin SA
Climate WT, M, SA
Shade None to light

FAST-GROWING
SPECIMEN PLANT
FRAGRANT
BIRD-ATTRACTING
DROUGHT-RESISTANT
ORNAMENTAL FOLIAGE

Description A beautiful, dense, weeping shrub to 5 m. It has long, narrow, drooping blue-green phyllodes with mauve young tips and has fragrant lemon ball flowers through autumn and winter. These are followed by decorative bunches of silvery pods. A less attractive upright form is also in cultivation.

Cultivation This hardy species will grow in most well-drained soils, including limy ones. It is drought-resistant and frost-resistant. Prune lightly after flowering to maintain compact shape.

Landscape Use A handsome decorative shrub to use as a feature or for foliage contrast. It is attractive even when not in flower and looks spectacular in rows, forming a good screen, informal hedge or windbreak.

Acacia iteaphylla

Acacia lanuginoisa

Origin WA
Climate WT, M, SA
Shade None to light

BIRD-ATTRACTING
DROUGHT-RESISTANT

Description A small to medium spreading shrub to around 2 m high with a spread to 3 m across. The small grey-green oblong phyllodes which broaden near the tip are covered in dense woolly hairs. Bright yellow ball flowers are produced on short stalks at the leaf axils in spring.

Cultivation This ornamental shrub with attractive felted foliage requires a well-drained soil. It is suited to dry conditions and will withstand heavy frost. Prune after flowering to shape.

Landscape Use A compact shrub suitable as a low hedge or screen.

Acacia lanuginoisa

Acacia longifolia

SYDNEY GOLDEN WATTLE; SALLOW WATTLE

Origin NSW, Vic., Tas., SA
Climate S, WT, M, CT
Shade None to light

FAST-GROWING
FRAGRANT
BIRD-ATTRACTING
SALT-TOLERANT

Description An upright, bushy small tree to 5 m. It has long bright green phyllodes and bears profuse golden rod-like flower spikes from late winter.

Cultivation This very adaptable species thrives in a wide variety of situations and soil conditions, but needs good drainage. It is one of the hardiest wattles for seaside gardens, tolerating salt-laden winds. It is frost-resistant.

Landscape Use This fast-growing wattle is particularly useful where a quick hedge or windbreak is needed. Its bold display when in full bloom makes it an attractive ornamental species.

Acacia longifolia

Acacia melanoxylon

BLACKWOOD WATTLE

Origin Qld, NSW, Vic., Tas., SA
Climate WT, M, CT, H
Shade None to filtered

SPECIMEN PLANT
BIRD-ATTRACTING

Description This handsome, widespread tree is a valuable timber tree prized for its close-grained and beautifully marked wood. It grows as a graceful upright tree to 30 m with a dense crown of drooping

Acacia melanoxylon

grey-green phyllodes. The masses of creamy flower balls in small clusters are carried in winter and spring.

Cultivation One of the more long-lived wattles, this species grows best in the rich soil of cool moist areas. It tolerates frost and snow.

Landscape Use The dense foliage makes this an ideal shade or shelter tree for the country property or very large garden. It is also useful for erosion control.

Acacia myrtifolia

MYRTLE WATTLE

Origin All states
Climate WT, M, CT, H
Shade None to filtered
FAST-GROWING
FRAGRANT
BIRD-ATTRACTING
DROUGHT-RESISTANT

Description This shrubby species, often with attractive red stems, varies in height from almost prostrate to 2.5 m tall. The dark green phyllodes are lanceolate with a prominently thickened margin. Large, pretty, sweetly scented lemon ball flowers appear in spring over an extended period.

Acacia myrtifolia

Cultivation A very adaptable species suited to a wide range of soils and conditions. It is frost-resistant. Prune after flowering to maintain shape and encourage attractive rosy-tinted new growth.

Landscape Use An ornamental shrub suitable for rockery planting. It is a useful wattle for the semishaded position and may be grown in groups as a low screen or windbreak.

Acacia paradoxa

(syn. *A. armata*)

KANGAROO THORN

Origin Qld, NSW, Vic., Tas., SA, WA
Climate WT, M, CT, SA
Shade None to light
BIRD-ATTRACTING

Description A many-branched, spreading shrub to 3 m high and up to 3 m across. It has wavy-edged phyllodes, and stems armed with stiff sharp spines. The profuse bright yellow flower balls are borne in spring.

Cultivation This very adaptable wattle is widely cultivated. It will withstand dry conditions but also tolerates wet periods and is suitable for coastal planting with some protection. It is frost-resistant.

Landscape Use Well known as a hedge plant, this prickly wattle also provides an ideal nesting site for small native birds.

Acacia paradoxa

Acacia pendula

WEEPING MYALL; BOREE

Origin Qld, NSW, Vic.
Climate M, SA
Shade None to light
BIRD-ATTRACTING
DROUGHT-RESISTANT

Description A beautiful weeping small tree which grows to about 12 m. The narrow silvery phyllodes and pendulous branches, often drooping almost to the ground, make a delightful sight against the clear blue skies of the inland. The small pale lemon yellow flower balls are inconspicuous and appear irregularly.

Acacia pendula

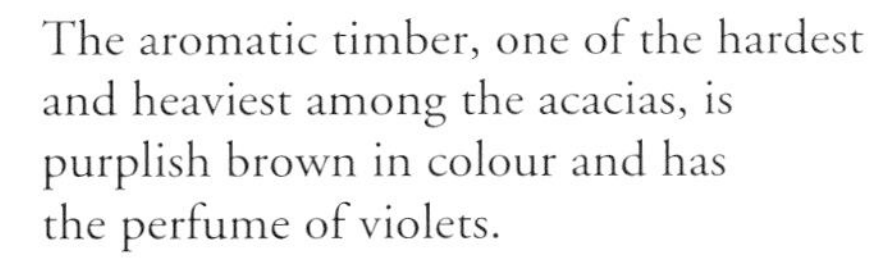

The aromatic timber, one of the hardest and heaviest among the acacias, is purplish brown in colour and has the perfume of violets.

Cultivation This handsome tree is found on fertile soils in semiarid regions and is ideal for planting in dry areas with medium to heavy soils and some ground moisture.

Landscape Use This is a handsome specimen tree and is useful as a shade and fodder tree or as a windbreak on farms.

Acacia perangusta

(syn. *A. fimbriata* var. *perangusta*)

BRISBANE WATTLE

Origin Qld, NSW
Climate S, WT
Shade None to filtered

FAST-GROWING
BIRD-ATTRACTING

Description A spreading, graceful small tree to 6 m and up to 5 m wide. It has narrow dark green phyllodes, and flowers profusely with yellow ball flowers in late winter.

Acacia perangusta

Cultivation This is a free-flowering, dense wattle suited to the subtropical garden. It is tolerant of all soil types and is frost-resistant.

Landscape Use A quick-growing species which will soon form a dense screen or hedge. Pruning encourages shrubby growth.

Acacia podalyriifolia

Acacia podalyriifolia
QUEENSLAND SILVER WATTLE

Origin Qld
Climate T, S, WT, M, CT
Shade None to light
FAST-GROWING
FRAGRANT
BIRD-ATTRACTING
ORNAMENTAL FOLIAGE

Description A most attractive dense tall shrub to 5 m. It has beautiful rounded silvery grey phyllodes and produces fragrant golden ball flowers forming dense clusters in midwinter.

Cultivation This species enjoys a sunny position and does not seem fussy as to soils provided the drainage is excellent. It can be grown near the coast if some protection is provided. May be sensitive to frost while young.

Landscape Use A popular specimen plant cultivated for its ornamental foliage and early winter flowers.

Acacia pravissima
OVENS WATTLE

Origin NSW, Vic.
Climate WT, M, CT, H, SA
Shade None to light
FAST-GROWING
SPECIMEN PLANT
FRAGRANT
BIRD-ATTRACTING
ORNAMENTAL FOLIAGE

Description This graceful large shrub or small tree grows up to 7 m. It has slightly pendulous branches and small olive green triangular phyllodes enfolding the stems. The perfumed bright yellow globular flower heads occur in profuse clusters in spring.

Acacia pravissima

Acacia prominens

A. pravissima 'Golden Carpet' is a beautiful low-growing prostrate form with a spread of up to 5 m.

Cultivation Widely grown in New South Wales, Victoria and Tasmania, this lovely species will grow in most soil types in full sun to partial shade. It will tolerate frost, snow and slight coastal exposure.

Landscape Use This hardy wattle is a beautiful showy garden subject. It is also well suited for hedges, windbreaks and screens. The prostrate form is a cascading shrub ideal for the large rockery or sloping bank.

Acacia prominens
GOLDEN RAIN WATTLE; GOSFORD WATTLE

Origin NSW
Climate WT, M, CT
Shade None to filtered
FAST-GROWING
SPECIMEN PLANT
FRAGRANT
BIRD-ATTRACTING

Description A tall shrub or small tree to 9 m; frequently taller in higher rainfall areas. The thinly textured lanceolate phyllodes are a grey-green colour and the tips of the young foliage are often silvery green tinged with pink. The long slender branches are massed with fragrant lemon flower balls in early spring.

Cultivation This delightful, hardy plant will grow in a wide variety of soils, but prefers moist well-drained positions. It will grow in full sun but also enjoys quite shady situations.

Landscape Use This acacia makes a spectacular specimen tree. It is long-lived and fast-growing and is ideal as a screen or windbreak.

Acacia pubescens
DOWNY WATTLE

Origin NSW
Climate S, WT, M
Shade None to filtered
SPECIMEN PLANT
FRAGRANT
BIRD-ATTRACTING
ORNAMENTAL FOLIAGE

Description A bushy tall shrub, 3 to 5 m high with arching branches covered in dense hair especially when young. The bright green bipinnate leaves consisting of 10 pairs of pinnae are subdivided into 20 pairs of leaflets. The sweetly scented bright yellow ball flowers are carried on dense drooping sprays in late winter and spring.

Cultivation This ornamental species has a very restricted distribution and is endangered in its natural habitat due to extensive land clearing. It has been in cultivation in Europe since 1790 and is very popular in the USA and should be more widely grown locally. It requires good drainage and watering during dry periods. It will grow in protected coastal gardens and is unaffected by frost. Suckers may develop around mature plants.

Landscape Use This is a lovely screening or specimen plant. Cut flowers last well indoors.

Acacia pubescens

Acacia pycnantha
GOLDEN WATTLE

Origin NSW, Vic., SA
Climate WT, M, CT, SA
Shade None to filtered

FAST-GROWING
FRAGRANT
BIRD-ATTRACTING
DROUGHT-RESISTANT

Description This beautiful pendulous shrub or small tree to 10 m is Australia's floral emblem. It has attractive bright green sickle-shaped phyllodes, and in spring has a spectacular showing of large golden flower balls in long loose clusters, filling the air with a delightful fragrance. It provides a nectar that is attractive to honeyeaters and small insectivorous birds. A pale-flowered variety which blooms in autumn is also available.

Cultivation This very adaptable plant tolerates dry conditions and is frost-resistant when mature. It may be used in coastal gardens with some protection from salt-laden winds. In wet conditions it needs excellent drainage.

Landscape Use A very attractive species and highly recommended for shade, shelter or ornamental planting. It is suitable for windbreaks and is useful in erosion control.

Acacia pycnantha

Acacia saligna
(syn. *A. cyanophylla*)
GOLDEN WREATH WATTLE

Origin WA
Climate S, WT, M, CT, SA
Shade None to light

FAST-GROWING
SPECIMEN PLANT
BIRD-ATTRACTING

Description A large shrub or small bushy tree reaching up to 10 m. It will form a dense crown of long, drooping green phyllodes and bears very large, fluffy golden flower balls in spring.

Cultivation This hardy species is suited to most soils and conditions. It may be grown in protected coastal gardens and is suitable for soil stabilisation. It will tolerate periods of dryness and is frost-resistant.

Landscape Use A very showy small shade tree for use as a feature or as a street or park specimen. It is useful for a quick screen or windbreak.

Acacia saligna

Acacia sophorae
(syn. *A. longifolia* var. *sophorae*)
COASTAL WATTLE

Origin Qld, NSW, Vic., Tas., SA
Climate S, WT, M, CT, SA
Shade None to light

FAST-GROWING
BIRD-ATTRACTING
SALT-TOLERANT

Description A large, bushy shrub to about 4 m high, but often less in exposed situations where it may have a spread up

Acacia sophorae

to 10 m wide. It has broad, elliptic phyllodes and has golden, rod-like flowers in spring.

Cultivation This very hardy plant is adaptable to a wide variety of situations, but is noted for its ability to withstand salt-laden winds and its use as a sand binder. It has been used extensively in dune regeneration work.

Landscape Use This is an excellent screen plant for seaside gardens. Low-growing forms will spread rapidly and may be used as a dense ground cover.

Acacia spectabilis
MUDGEE WATTLE

Origin Qld, NSW
Climate S, WT, M, SA
Shade None to light

FAST-GROWING
SPECIMEN PLANT
BIRD-ATTRACTING
DROUGHT-RESISTANT
ORNAMENTAL FOLIAGE

Description A beautiful, upright shrub or small tree to 5 m, slender and often weeping. The bark and branches often have a silvery bloom and the divided, ferny leaves are a lovely soft blue-green colour. The large yellow flower balls are carried on long sprays in late winter and spring.

Cultivation This very adaptable, frost- and drought-resistant wattle is widely grown throughout Australia. In coastal gardens it needs some protection. A light pruning after flowering will help form a more bushy shrub if this is desired.

Landscape Use This is a delightful ornamental species. In group plantings it forms a pretty, open screen.

Acacia spectabilis

Acacia suaveolens
SWEET-SCENTED WATTLE

Origin Qld, NSW, Vic., Tas., SA
Climate S, WT, M, CT, H
Shade None to filtered

FAST-GROWING
FRAGRANT
BIRD-ATTRACTING

Description Common along the coast and tablelands of eastern Australia, this variable shrub may be a dense, compact bush of 1 m to an upright slender shrub of 3 m. The blue-green phyllodes are usually quite narrow and the pale yellow flower balls, which bloom over a long period through winter and spring, have a sweet perfume. Attractive flattened bluish pods are produced after flowering. These provide seed for parrots such as rosellas. There is also a form with variegated phyllodes and deep yellow flowers.

Cultivation This is a hardy shrub in any well-drained soil. It is particularly suited to coastal and near-coastal gardens and is frost-resistant. Prune after flowering to encourage compact shape.

Landscape Use This attractive winter-flowering ornamental may also be used as a low screen plant.

Acacia suaveolens

Acacia terminalis
(syn. *A. botrycephala*, *A. discolor*)
SUNSHINE WATTLE

Origin NSW, Vic., Tas.
Climate WT, M, CT, SA
Shade None to filtered

FAST-GROWING
BIRD-ATTRACTING

Description This wattle is usually a small shrub to 2 m, but may occur as a small tree to 6 m. It has shiny, dark green divided foliage which may be bronze when young. The large sprays of pale cream to deep yellow flower balls appear from autumn to spring.

Cultivation This pretty wattle is adaptable to a variety of situations, including very dry and protected coastal. It will grow in sandy well-drained soil and does respond to some summer moisture. It is frost-resistant.

Landscape Use Grow this wattle for its welcome blossoms in the off-season.

Acacia terminalis

Acacia triptera
SPUR-WING WATTLE

Origin Qld, NSW, Vic.
Climate M, SA, CT
Shade None to light

BIRD-ATTRACTING
ORNAMENTAL FOLIAGE

Description This dry-country shrub may be spreading almost at ground level to 5 m across or open and upright to 4 m high. The unusual phyllodes are stiff, curved and pointed, spreading evenly around the stem. The numerous golden, rod-like flower spikes may occur from August to October.

Cultivation This beautiful shrub is best suited to lower rainfall areas. It must have good drainage. It is frost-resistant.

Landscape Use The prickly nature and branching habit of this shrub make it an excellent protective hedge plant. Grow also as a lovely feature plant for its profuse flowering and interesting foliage.

Acacia triptera

Acacia uncinata
(syn. *A. undulifolia*)
WEEPING WATTLE

Origin Qld, NSW
Climate WT, M, SA
Shade None to light

BIRD-ATTRACTING
DROUGHT-RESISTANT

Description A rather open medium shrub to 3 m tall with long pendulous branches. The almost rounded stem-clasping phyllodes have a pronounced hooked point. The bright yellow ball flowers are borne singly on slender stalks held well out from the phyllodes. Flowering is mainly in spring and summer, but it may produce odd flowers throughout the year.

Cultivation A very hardy and adaptable species suited to a wide range of conditions and soil types. For best results an open position and good drainage is required. It is frost-tolerant and will withstand very dry conditions. A little light pruning will keep the plant shapely.

Acacia uncinata

Landscape Use The long flowering period and hardiness make this a good species for a low maintenance bush garden. It will form a light screen.

Acacia verniciflua
VARNISH WATTLE

Origin Qld, NSW, Vic., Tas., SA
Climate S, WT, M, CT, SA
Shade None to filtered

FAST-GROWING
SPECIMEN PLANT
BIRD-ATTRACTING

Description A tall spreading shrub up to 4 m high. It has attractive pendulous foliage with glistening young growth and bears masses of bright, yellow flower balls during spring.

Cultivation This species is suited to most well-drained soils. It is a good wattle for lightly shaded positions and is frost-resistant.

Landscape Use An ornamental shrub for planting beneath tall trees. It can be used as a fence screen or low windbreak.

Acacia verniciflua

Acacia vestita
HAIRY WATTLE

Origin NSW
Climate WT, M, CT
Shade None to light

FAST-GROWING
SPECIMEN PLANT
BIRD-ATTRACTING
ORNAMENTAL FOLIAGE

Description This is one of the most beautiful wattles. It grows to 4 m tall and has a marvellous weeping habit and most attractive soft, hairy grey-green phyllodes. The masses of bright yellow ball flowers in heavy clusters appear in spring.

Cultivation This hardy species is widely cultivated. It will grow in most soils and will tolerate frost and some dryness. Prune gently after flowering to maintain shape.

Landscape Use This is an outstanding specimen plant. It also makes an excellent screen, informal hedge or low windbreak.

Acacia vestita

ACMENA
MYRTACEAE

This is a small genus of ornamental trees of the rainforest. Acmena *was formerly included in* Eugenia *and species are sometimes still sold under this name. These are handsome trees with glossy green foliage. New growth is particularly attractive, often being crimson, pink, copper or bronze. The fluffy flowers in summer are massed in small terminal sprays and are followed by attractive succulent fruits. These edible fruits are a showy feature of these trees and attract a variety of birds. Many species grow to great heights in their rainforest habitats, but in cultivation their size is reduced dramatically. They are very adaptable and will grow in sun or shade, but prefer good humus-enriched soil with ample moisture.*

Not usually pest prone, acmenas may occasionally suffer from scale and the bright-pink pimple gall. Propagation is from fresh seed taken from April to June.

Acmena smithii
(syn. *Eugenia smithii*)

Origin Qld, NSW, Vic., NT
Climate T, S, WT, M
Shade None to filtered

BIRD-ATTRACTING
SPECIMEN PLANT
RAINFOREST PLANT

Description A bushy dark green foliage tree which may reach a height of up to 20 m in tropical areas. It has glossy, lanceolate to ovate leaves and attractive bronzy pink new growth. Masses of small, fluffy cream blossoms in terminal sprays in summer are followed by attractive mauve, pink or purple rounded berries.

Acmena smithii var. *minor* is a more compact form with smaller leaves and rarely exceeding 7 m.

Cultivation A reliable and popular ornamental tree which adapts to a wide variety of soil types, provided ample moisture is available in dry periods. If grown in sandy soil, it benefits from the addition of organic matter. It is resistant to most frosts.

Landscape Use This long-lived, handsome tree is a perfect specimen and shade tree for parks and large gardens. It may be trimmed to form an attractive, bushy hedge.

Acmena smithii

ACTINODIUM
MYRTACEAE

There are only two species in this small Western Australian genus. One is currently unnamed and the other is the very similar and well-known Swamp Daisy, Actinodium cunninghamii.

Although these species have daisy-like flowers, they are in fact members of the myrtle family (Myrtaceae). *Both are ideal for container planting or for growing in a rockery pocket. The cut flowers are long-lasting and may be dried. Propagation is from cuttings taken in summer.*

Actinodium cunninghamii
SWAMP DAISY; ALBANY DAISY

Origin WA
Climate WT, M
Shade Light to filtered

CONTAINER PLANT

Description This twiggy little semishrub around 75 cm has tiny aromatic stem-clasping leaves. The daisy-like flowers, which are white with pale pink centres, appear in spring.

Actinodium cunninghamii

Cultivation The swamp daisy, as the name implies, likes moist conditions, but must have excellent drainage. It prefers a warm climate and does best in a partially shaded situation. It will tolerate light frosts.

Landscape Use This plant is especially suitable for growing in a container or as a decorative addition to the rockery.

ACTINOTUS
APIACEAE

This genus of some 17 species of small annual or perennial herbaceous plants occurs in all States in a wide range of conditions. They are commonly known as flannel flowers, as the daisy-like flower heads and the foliage have a whitish, felt-like appearance and texture. The lovely greyish foliage gives a marvellous colour contrast to a garden bed or rockery. Flowers appear in spring and summer and provide long-lasting cut flowers. Propagation is from semiripe cuttings or seed freshly collected in summer.

Actinotus helianthi
FLANNEL FLOWER

Origin Qld, NSW
Climate WT, M
Shade Light to filtered

ORNAMENTAL FOLIAGE
CONTAINER PLANT

Description This well-known and favoured wildflower is an erect-growing annual or perennial to 1.5 m. It has soft silver-grey deeply lobed leaves and showy, star-like flannel flowers of white or cream, often tipped green, from late winter to summer.

Cultivation It grows best in lightly filtered sunlight in a well-drained, preferably sandy, soil with a good mulch. It is generally short-lived, but if conditions are right it will self-seed in the garden.

Landscape Use Flannel flowers make excellent container plants and look attractive with terracotta colours. They are particularly suited to the rockery, which will provide the cool root run and the excellent drainage they demand.

Actinotus helianthi

ADENANTHOS

PROTEACEAE

A genus of some 30 species, confined to south-western Western Australia except for two species that extend to South Australia and Victoria. They range in size from prostrate to large shrubs and have most attractive foliage. The flowers are tubular, with long styles, varying in colour from yellow to pink and red. Many species attract honey-eating birds to the garden. Not many species of these ornamental shrubs are commonly seen in cultivation. However, some reliable species are available from specialist nurseries. Propagation is from half-ripened tip cuttings.

Adenanthos detmoldii

Origin WA
Climate WT, M
Shade Light to filtered
BIRD-ATTRACTING
Description An erect medium shrub to 4 m high or less. Young branches and leaves are densely covered with long white hairs. The linear leaves to about 8 cm long are spirally arranged along the stems. Attractive spidery yellow flowers with an orange throat and protruding hairy styles are produced mainly in late winter and spring, but odd flowers can be seen at other times.

Cultivation This endangered species naturally occurs in the extreme south-west of Western Australia in sandy swampy sites. Adequate moisture is required for best results in cultivation; good drainage is also necessary. It is frost-tolerant.

Landscape Use An attractive plant for growing amongst other shrubs. Partially opened flowers are suitable for picking.

Adenanthos detmoldii

Adenanthos obovata

BASKET FLOWER

Origin WA
Climate WT, M
Shade None to filtered
BIRD-ATTRACTING
Description This slender, many-stemmed shrub grows to 1 m and has narrow dark green leaves ending in a small point. The scarlet vase-shaped flowers appear in leafy sprays throughout the winter months. This plant is regularly visited by honeyeaters.

Cultivation This species prefers a sunny to lightly shaded position in a coarse, sandy soil. Although it is found in swampy areas, it does best in a well-drained situation. It is frost-resistant.

Landscape Use This small ornamental species is well suited to the rockery.

Adenanthos obovata

Adenanthos sericea

WOOLLYBUSH

Origin WA
Climate WT, M, SA
Shade None to light
FAST-GROWING
ORNAMENTAL FOLIAGE
Description This tall, rounded shrub grows to a height of 7 m. The small red flowers are partially hidden by the foliage,

which is silky grey and is the most decorative feature of this plant.

Cultivation This species does particularly well in sandy soil. It is frost-resistant and is moderately salt-tolerant if planted in a protected coastal garden. It requires excellent drainage.

Landscape Use This is a beautiful silver-foliaged plant which provides a lovely contrast in the garden. It will form an excellent dense windbreak.

Adenanthos sericea

Adiantum aethiopicum

ADIANTUM

ADIANTACEAE

Worldwide there are over 200 species of Adiantum, *including some nine species native to Australia, mostly from tropical areas. These delicate, small to medium ferns are commonly known as maidenhairs. They have a creeping rhizome, fan-shaped leaflets and polished stems. As a group they are among the most popular of cultivated ferns, providing year-round greenery and giving a lush tropical look to any setting.*

Maidenhair ferns grow well outside on protected patios, under pergolas, in ferneries or in the garden, but are best protected from the wind. In areas with frost, protection should also be provided. Suitable for containers, they like a potting mix with a high peat content. When used indoors as pot plants, maidenhairs prefer a situation that stays roughly the same in warmth and humidity. If growing them in a heated room, place each plant on a saucer filled with pebbles and water; this provides humidity as the water evaporates around the fern. Propagation is by division of the rhizomes or from spores.

Adiantum aethiopicum

COMMON MAIDENHAIR

Origin All States
Climate T, S, WT, M, CT
Shade Light to filtered

ORNAMENTAL FOLIAGE
CONTAINER PLANT

Description This is one of the best known cultivated native ferns. It has a wiry, creeping rhizome which suckers profusely and quickly spreads into a dense clump. The numerous lacy fronds up to 35 cm long have shiny stems and rounded to wedge-shaped leaflets with lobed margins.

Cultivation Although delicate in appearance, this fern is not difficult to grow providing it has adequate sun and abundant moisture in a sheltered position. It resents total shade and does best in positions where it gets some early morning sun or some filtered sun. When grown indoors, it needs warmth and light, but not direct sun.

Landscape Use Apart from its uses as an attractive indoor plant, this maidenhair will naturalise beautifully in sheltered garden spots in the rockery. It is also excellent for use in hanging baskets or containers.

Adiantum formosum

GIANT MAIDENHAIR; BLACK STEM MAIDENHAIR

Origin Qld, NSW, Vic.
Climate T, S, WT, M
Shade Light to filtered

ORNAMENTAL FOLIAGE
CONTAINER PLANT
RAINFOREST PLANT

Description A vigorous fern with a long creeping rhizome and erect dark green fronds up to 120 cm on shiny black stems. The leaflets are rhomboid in shape with deeply lobed margins.

Cultivation This easily grown, hardy species enjoys a warm, protected position in humus-enriched soil. It will tolerate some frost.

Landscape Use This is a handsome fern for a large tub or for growing in the ground in a protected ferny glen.

Adiantum formosum

Adiantum hispidulum

ROUGH MAIDENHAIR

Origin Qld, NSW, Vic., NT
Climate T, S, WT, M
Shade Light to filtered

ORNAMENTAL FOLIAGE
CONTAINER PLANT
RAINFOREST PLANT

Description This variable species has a short, wiry rhizome and erect fronds up to 35 cm long. The dark green leaflets are covered in minute white hairs and are serrated at the edges. New fronds have a pinkish tinge.

Cultivation This hardy species grows well in a warm, protected position. It will withstand some drying out and is frost-hardy.

Landscape Use The slight drooping habit and pretty pink new fronds makes this species a good basket or container plant.

Adiantum hispidulum

AGATHIS

ARAUCARIACEAE

A genus of about 20 species of conifers, three of which are found in Australia. These large trees with dark brown bark and massive trunks provide valuable softwood timber. They differ from other conifers in their large, flat leathery leaves. The male cones are elongated and the female ones are somewhat globular. When ripe, the whole cone falls from the tree and the seeds are released later. Propagation is from seed, which should be sown when fresh in summer.

Agathis robusta

(syn. *A. palmerstonii*)

QUEENSLAND KAURI PINE

Origin Qld
Climate T, S, WT, M
Shade None to light

FAST-GROWING
CONTAINER PLANT
RAINFOREST PLANT

Description In nature this is a tall, stately tree to 50 m, but it can be expected to grow up to 30 m in cultivation if conditions are good. It has attractive brown scaly bark and dark glossy green leaves up to 15 cm long.

Cultivation This is a fast-growing tree if cultivated in warm coastal areas. It will grow in a variety of soil types, but does best in a deep, well-mulched soil. It is widely cultivated in Brisbane parks and

Agathis robusta

gardens, but will also do well in southern gardens.

Landscape Use When young, this symmetrical tree makes an ideal pot plant, either indoors or outdoors, for a number of years. As an ornamental tree it is suited only to large gardens and parks.

AGONIS

MYRTACEAE

This genus of some 12 species is found only in Western Australia. They are shrubs to small trees with alternate simple leaves. When crushed the leaves and young stems emit a delicious, spicy perfume. The white to pale pink flowers are massed along the branches and resemble those of Leptospermum, *to which the genus is closely related.*

They are rapid growers and are adaptable to a wide range of soil and climatic conditions. Some species are tender to frost in their juvenile stage, but they are noted for their resistance to dry conditions. Most species are cultivated and have excellent landscape qualities. Pruning, if necessary, is best done after flowering. Propagation is from ripened seed or from half-ripened tip cuttings.

Agonis flexuosa

WILLOW MYRTLE; WILLOW PEPPERMINT

Origin WA
Climate S, WT, M, CT, SA
Shade None to light

SPECIMEN PLANT
AROMATIC FOLIAGE
BIRD-ATTRACTING
CONTAINER PLANT

Description A weeping dense small tree to 7 m with a spread of about 8 m. The broad dark green leaves narrow with age and have a marvellous bush fragrance when crushed. The small white flowers are clustered along the stems in spring and summer.

A. flexuosa 'Belbra Gold' is a small tree to 3 m with graceful yellow foliage.

A. flexuosa 'Fairy Foliage' is a slow-growing tree to 4 m with very narrow foliage.

A. flexuosa 'Nana' is an attractive dwarf shrub with coppery red new foliage.

A. flexuosa 'Variegata' has a shrubby growth habit with a height to 3 m and attractive cream and pink marked foliage. It is slow-growing and makes an attractive container plant for some time.

Agonis flexuosa

A. flexuosa 'Variegata'

A. flexuosa (flower)

Cultivation This is a hardy plant for most soils, including very sandy ones and those with a very high lime content. Once established, it will tolerate dry conditions and it can be planted in coastal gardens with some protection from the strongest salt-laden winds. It will withstand heavy frosts.

Landscape Use With fine willowy foliage, drooping almost to the ground, this species makes an ideal specimen tree. It can also be used as a screen plant or windbreak. *A. flexuosa* 'Nana' is suitable for pot culture and for rockeries.

Agonis juniperina

JUNIPER MYRTLE

Origin WA
Climate WT, M, CT
Shade Light to filtered

FAST-GROWING
AROMATIC FOLIAGE
BIRD-ATTRACTING

Description A handsome, upright small tree which quickly reaches a height of about 7 m in the garden. It has fine, small narrow leaves which are aromatic when crushed. Masses of white flowers appear mostly towards the tips of branches throughout the year, with the main flush in autumn. These flowers are long-lasting in water, and can be dried and used in decoration.

Agonis juniperina

Cultivation This is a very hardy and popular species that will grow in a wide range of soils and conditions, but is at its best in light shade. A light trimming will keep the bush in good shape.

Landscape Use The upright habit makes this plant especially useful for growing in narrow garden beds. It is also a good screen plant.

Agonis linearifolia

Origin WA
Climate S, WT, M
Shade None to filtered
BIRD-ATTRACTING

Description This is an upright, bushy shrub to 3 m with crowded linear foliage and small white flowers clustered along the stem. Flowers appear over extended periods and dainty sprays provide lovely cut flowers, remaining fresh for a long time.

Cultivation This plant inhabits swamps of the south-west and does very well in moist conditions. It will tolerate semishade and some frost.

Landscape Use This bushy shrub is suitable as a screen or windbreak.

Agonis linearifolia

AJUGA

LAMIACEAE

This genus of quick-growing carpeting plants comes mostly from Europe, but two species are endemic to Australia, of which one, Ajuga australis, *is well known to cultivation. Propagation is by root division, from cuttings or from seed which germinates easily.*

Ajuga australis

Ajuga australis

AUSTRAL BUGLE

Origin Qld, NSW, Vic., Tas., SA
Climate S, WT, M, CT, SA
Shade Light to filtered
CONTAINER PLANT

Description A suckering herb with a rosette of hairy purplish-green leaves and purple, blue or pink flowers borne on upright stems to 30 cm. Flowers occur in spring and summer.

Cultivation Although this hardy plant does best in filtered shade, it will tolerate full sun. It is not fussy about soil and will tolerate frost.

Landscape Use This is an excellent rockery plant and is a decorative ground cover, useful in preventing soil erosion on sloping sites.

ALOCASIA

ARACEAE

Alocasias are foliage plants mostly from Asia, with one species. A. macrorrhiza, *extending to Queensland and New South Wales. Although* Alocasia *is grown mostly for the attractive spade-shaped foliage, the arum-like 'flowers' are beautifully perfumed, and both foliage and flowers make striking floral arrangements. Propagation is by division of the rhizome during winter or from fresh seed.*

Alocasia macrorrhiza

(syn. *A. brisbanensis*)

CUNJEVOI; SPOON LILY

Origin Qld, NSW
Climate T, ST, WT, M
Shade Light to filtered
FRAGRANT
ORNAMENTAL FOLIAGE
CONTAINER PLANT
RAINFOREST PLANT

Description A rainforest plant to 1.5 m with very large heart-shaped leaves on long fleshy stems. Greenish cream inflorescences similar to those of the arum lily appear in summer and they have a beautiful perfume. All parts of this plant are highly poisonous. Aborigines are known to have eaten the toxic stems, but only after special preparation and cooking to clear the poisons.

Cultivation This plant is fairly hardy given a protected well-mulched, moist position. It is frost-tender.

Alocasia macrorrhiza

Landscape Use Grow near a water feature with tree ferns to create a lush rainforest environment. It looks superb planted in a damp, rocky pocket. Cunjevoi makes an excellent container plant inside the house or on a sheltered terrace.

ALPHITONIA

RHAMNACEAE

Of the 20-odd species in this tropical genus, there are about six in Australia, mostly native to the coastal rainforests of New South Wales and Queensland. These fast-growing erect trees are popular in tropical gardens, but will grow well as far south as Victoria. The fragrant, small white to cream flowers are followed by black, bird-attracting berries. Propagation is from fresh seed or cuttings.

Alphitonia petriei

PINK ALMOND; WHITE ASH

Origin Qld, NSW, NT
Climate T, S, WT, M
Shade None to filtered

FAST-GROWING
FRAGRANT
BIRD-ATTRACTING
RAINFOREST PLANT

Description This medium-sized to tall tree reaches 40 m in its rainforest habitat, but when grown in open situations the tree is much shorter, with a dense spreading canopy to around 12 m. The long ovate leaves with a whitish underside have an attractive silvered new growth. Clusters of tiny white fragrant flowers appear in spring and are followed by black berries.

Alphitonia petriei

Cultivation Attractive and hardy, this fast-growing tree will grow in a variety of soils and positions and is moderately frost-resistant.

Landscape Use This is a graceful, fast-growing shelter and shade tree.

ALYOGYNE

MALVACEAE

This genus of hibiscus-like shrubs has four species, all native to Australia. They are upright shrubs with usually soft, lobed leaves and hibiscus-like single flowers. Flowers can be white, yellow, pink or purple, and differ from those of the true hibiscus in having an undivided style. Propagation is from seed, which germinates readily, or from cuttings.

Alyogyne huegelii

(syn. *Hibiscus huegelii*)

LILAC HIBISCUS

Origin WA, SA
Climate WT, M, CT, SA
Shade None to filtered

FAST-GROWING
BIRD-ATTRACTING

Description This rounded shrub will reach a height of 3 m. It has soft, deeply lobed, dull green foliage, and attractive single lilac flowers, sometimes with darker throats, throughout spring and summer. Although each flower lasts for only a day, the shrub is capable of producing many blooms for a long time.

There are several different colour forms, including one with white flowers and brighter green leaves.

Alyogyne huegelii

A. huegelii (flower)

Cultivation This rapid-growing shrub is adaptable to a wide range of soil types in full or partial sun. It is frost-tolerant in most areas. Prune back hard after flowering to keep a compact shape.

Landscape Use This pretty, showy plant can be used as a long-flowering colour feature in the garden.

ALYXIA

APOCYNACEAE

A genus of some 80 species, of which nine are native to Australia. They are bushy shrubs or climbers with smooth, leathery leaves in whorls of 3–5, smallish fragrant flowers and decorative fleshy fruits, usually orange or red. Propagation is from fresh seed.

Alysia ruscifolia

CHAIN FRUIT; NATIVE HOLLY

Origin Qld, NSW, NT
Climate T, S, WT, M
Shade Light to full

FRAGRANT
CONTAINER PLANT
RAINFOREST PLANT

Description An upright shrub to 3 m. Leaves, usually in whorls of four, are glossy dark green with a sharp point. The small white flowers are delightfully perfumed and are followed by brightly coloured orange berries which are considered poisonous. The plant may produce flowers and fruits throughout the year, but the main season is winter and early spring.

Cultivation This species prefers warm conditions with plenty of water during summer. It will tolerate quite heavy shade and enjoys well-composted soil. It is frost-resistant.

Landscape Use This is a very useful and decorative plant for growing under trees where ample light is available. It is also an excellent container plant.

Alysia ruscifolia

ANGIOPTERIS

MARATTIACEAE

This genus of very large primitive ferns contains over 100 species, with one widespread species, Angiopteris evecta, *being found in tropical Queensland. All members of the genus are of considerable size, with large fleshy trunks and thick, coarse fronds. They are easily grown and make good specimen plants. Propagation is from the fleshy scales at the base of the frond.*

Angiopteris evecta

KING FERN; GIANT FERN

Origin Qld, NSW
Climate T, S, WT, M
Shade Filtered to full

SPECIMEN PLANT
ORNAMENTAL FOLIAGE
CONTAINER PLANT
RAINFOREST PLANT

Description A handsome large fern with massive weeping fronds up to 5 m long. With age this fern develops a black trunk that can be up to 1 m in diameter. This species is reputed to have the largest fronds of any fern.

Cultivation This easily grown species needs a moist, well-mulched situation. Will grow in southern areas, but needs protection from severe frost.

Landscape Use A magnificent specimen plant that needs plenty of room to show off its fronds. It makes a fine container plant when young.

Angiopteris evecta

ANGOPHORA

MYRTACEAE

Seven species of trees and shrubs belong to this genus, all being endemic to Australia and widely distributed throughout the eastern States. Angophora *is closely related to* Eucalyptus, *but differs in that* Angophora *usually has opposite leaves and lacks the operculum or cap covering the undeveloped flowers that is found in all eucalypts.*

Angophoras are highly ornamental with attractive foliage, particularly the new growth, interesting trunks and masses of creamy white, gum-like blossoms in spring and summer, the nectar of which attracts a variety of honeyeaters and nectar-feeding parrots. Insectivorous birds feed on the many insects that are attracted to the flowers and the genus is generally free of pests and diseases. The flowers are followed by ornamental, ribbed seed capsules. When ripe the capsule opens suddenly to release three or more flat seeds. Propagation is carried out from ripe seed, which is shed 4 to 6 months after flowering and will germinate readily.

Angophora costata

(syn. *A. lanceolata*)

SMOOTH-BARKED APPLE; SYDNEY RED GUM

Origin Qld, NSW
Climate S, WT, M
Shade None to filtered

FAST-GROWING
SPECIMEN PLANT
BIRD-ATTRACTING

Description This handsome, spreading tree growing to a height of up to 20 m is noted for its contorted branches and beautiful smooth bark which takes on many hues from red, salmon and pink to pale grey. The leaves are dark green and lanceolate, with lovely copper-red new growth during spring and summer. The very showy white flowers are produced in large clusters during summer and the ribbed fruit capsules are bell-shaped.

Cultivation This tree is adaptable and hardy, doing best in well-drained soils. It will grow in coastal gardens, but needs protection from strong winds as the timber is somewhat brittle and branches may break. When young it needs some protection from frost.

Landscape Use This is a beautiful specimen tree for its interesting form, but only for the large garden or park.

Angophora costata

Angophora hispida
(syn. *A. cordifolia*)
DWARF APPLE

Origin NSW
Climate S, WT, M, CT
Shade None to light

FAST-GROWING
SPECIMEN PLANT
BIRD-ATTRACTING

Description This interesting spreading shrub or small tree will reach a height of up to 6 m, but rarely exceeds 4 m. It has a marvellous twisted growth habit, gnarled branches and rough bark. The stem-clasping leaves are leathery and heart-shaped with wavy edges. Large, fluffy creamy white flowers appear in January and are followed by beautiful, ribbed seed capsules. Young branches and flower buds are covered in velvety rusty red hairs. All parts of this plant are extremely attractive in floral decoration. Birds and coloured beetles are drawn to this highly ornamental plant.

Cultivation This hardy shrub will grow in most well-drained soils. It is resistant to disease and pests and will grow in coastal gardens with some protection. It is frost-tender in some areas, especially when young.

Landscape Use This is a truly lovely plant for the informal bush garden. It can also be used as a low windbreak.

Angophora floribunda
(syn. *A. intermedia*)
ROUGH-BARKED APPLE

Origin Qld, NSW, Vic.
Climate WT, M
Shade None to filtered

FAST-GROWING
SPECIMEN PLANT
BIRD-ATTRACTING

Description This handsome, rugged tree has a spreading, gnarled growth habit and reaches a height of 20 m. It has a noticeably rough, fibrous bark, attractive red and green foliage, abundant white-cream flowers in summer and oval, ridged fruit capsules.

Cultivation This species will grow well in a wide range of soils, provided they are well drained. In cooler climates it needs protection from the worst frosts. It will tolerate fairly dry conditions.

Landscape Use This tall-growing tree is best suited to the large garden, park or public place. In the rural garden it is a lovely shade or shelter tree.

Angophora floribunda

Angophora hispida

ANIGOZANTHOS

HAEMODORACEAE

Kangaroo paws have been admired and grown the world over, and a considerable trade has developed in the cut flowers. There are 11 species, all from Western Australia. All are in cultivation and most are available from specialist native plant nurseries. They are clumping plants with strap-like leaves, and produce striking velvety tubular flowers on upright stems with an outstanding colour range. The flowers attract honeyeaters and spinebills to the garden and are excellent for picking as they remain fresh for weeks.

Colour and form may very according to growing conditions, but all varieties perform best in a sunny, open, well-drained position. Kangaroo paws are prone to a fungal attack, known as ink disease, which reduces their attractiveness and suitability for gardens. Natural hybrids have occurred and horticulturists have artificially hybridised and selected forms for disease resistance, long life, vigour and long life, vigour and long flowering period. With the modern technique of tissue culture being used to grow large numbers of the new hybrids, these hardy and extremely free-flowering varieties are becoming more widely available.

Kangaroo paws are excellent rockery subjects and container plants where good drainage can be guaranteed. Clumped plants benefit from division of root systems. They are best divided in autumn and replanted in pots until they are re-established. Propagation can also be carried out using fresh seed collected from spent flowers, but some types are more difficult than others.

Anigozanthos *'Bush Gem'* hybrids

Origin Bush Gems Nursery, Victoria
Climate WT, M, CT
Shade None to light

BIRD-ATTRACTING
CONTAINER PLANT

Description After an extensive breeding and selection programme, an outstanding range of colourful varieties of kangaroo paws which feature disease resistance and general vigour has become available from many nurseries and garden centres. They are compact, ornamental plants with prolific flowering over a long period, and provide excellent cut flowers. Flowering time is mainly through spring and summer.

Anigozanthos 'Bush Baby'

Cultivation Adaptable to a wide range of conditions, but prefer a sunny, well-drained position. Keep moist during dry periods. Remove old flower stems and dead leaves in late summer and autumn. They are frost-resistant.

Landscape Use These lovely kangaroo paws are ideal for group plantings, in the rockery or as container plants.

Anigozanthos flavidus

TALL KANGAROO PAW

Origin WA
Climate S, WT, M, CT, SA
Shade None to light

SPECIMEN PLANT
BIRD-ATTRACTING
CONTAINER PLANT

Description A long-lived species which forms large bushy clumps of reed-like foliage to 1 m. Long flowering stems up to 2 m have furry tubular flowers, usually yellow-green, but sometimes orange to rusty red. This is the most common and hardiest species in cultivation, and the one most often used as one of the parents of the more vigorous colourful hybrids. All of these are attractive to honey-eating birds and produce spectacular spikes of paw flowers for long periods.

Anigozanthos 'Dwarf Delight' (*A. flavidus* x *A. onycis*). This superb cultivar grows as a small compact clump with multibranched flower stems to 1 m, bearing apricot to red flowers in profusion throughout the warmer months.

Anigozanthos 'Harmony' (*A. flavidus* x *A. pulcherrimus*). This showy plant will grow into a rounded clump, with attractive green fleshy leaves and bright yellow flowers on brilliant red stems about 1 m long for a long period through spring and summer.

Anigozanthos 'Regal Claw' (*A. flavidus* x *A. preissii*). A cultivar with long, thin olive green leaves and flower spikes up to 1.5 m tall, with orange multiple flowers for long periods in spring and summer. The stems and flowers are covered with dense red hair.

Anigozanthos 'Pink Joey' (*A. flavidus* selected form). A compact clumping plant to about 50 cm with attractive smoky pink flowers.

Anigozanthos 'Red Cross' (*A. flavidus* x *A. rufus*). A vigorous cultivar with typical strap leaves and flower spikes to 1.5 m tall. The spikes are multi-branched and produce a spectacular showing of rich burgundy flowers. The flowers and stems are also covered in burgundy hairs.

Cultivation These showy plants will grow in any soils, provided the drainage is good, with adequate sun. If they are too shaded or are watered too much, this greatly increases the possibility of ink disease. They will tolerate humidity, extreme heat, dryness and quite a degree of frost.

Landscape Use There is a place in every garden for these outstanding display plants — in a prominent position, in narrow or elevated beds, in rockeries, near a water feature or in public landscaping. They make excellent flowering pot and tub specimens.

Anigozanthos flavidus

Anigozanthos 'Dwarf Delight'

Anigozanthos 'Harmony'

A. flavidus (red form)

Anigozanthos 'Regal Claw'

A. flavidus 'Pink Joey'

A. flavidus 'Red Cross'

Anigozanthos humilis

CAT'S PAW

Origin WA
Climate WT, M
Shade None to light
BIRD-ATTRACTING
CONTAINER PLANT

Description This species grows in a small clump with short, sickle-shaped leaves and flower stems up to 50 cm tall. The woolly yellow flowers in quite large heads are suffused with shades of orange or red and appear from late winter and spring.

Cultivation Grow in a very well drained, light-textured soil in full sun. During its dormant period, the plant may shed its foliage and watering should be reduced. It is tender to frost.

Landscape Use A lovely small subject for the rockery or container.

Anigozanthos humilis

Anigozanthos manglesii

RED AND GREEN KANGAROO PAW

Origin WA
Climate WT, M
Shade None to light
SPECIMEN PLANT
BIRD-ATTRACTING
CONTAINER PLANT

Description This well-known species is the floral emblem of Western Australia. It forms a reed-like clump of grey-green leaves and bears stunning bright red and green paw flowers on red woolly stems up to 1 m tall.

Cultivation This species needs a well-drained sandy soil in full sun. It is subject to ink disease and is unsuited to humid

Anigozanthos manglesii

conditions. It must be protected from frost and it is relatively short-lived in cultivation. To prolong life and vigour, it is recommended that plants be divided every two years.

Landscape Use This is a striking plant for the rockery, where it will get the sharp drainage it demands. As this species is particularly susceptible to leaf-eating pests, container culture may be preferable where slugs and snails can be easily controlled.

Anigozanthos pulcherrimus
GOLDEN KANGAROO PAW

Origin WA
Climate WT, M, CT
Shade None to light

SPECIMEN PLANT
BIRD-ATTRACTING
CONTAINER PLANT

Description This kangaroo paw will form a clump up to 1 m, with lovely greyish green leaves. The brilliant golden flowers are borne on red woolly stems 1–2 m high from November to February.

Anigozanthos pulcherrimus

Cultivation This species prefers a drier climate and demands excellent drainage in a sunny position. It is relatively frost-hardy.

Landscape Use An excellent rockery or container plant.

Anigozanthos rufus
RED KANGAROO PAW

Origin WA
Climate WT, M
Shade None to light

SPECIMEN PLANT
BIRD-ATTRACTING
CONTAINER PLANT

Description An ornamental species with spreading leaves to 50 cm forming a clump up to 1 m across. The striking red flowers on stems up to 1.5 m high are clothed with dense woolly hairs and are at their best from September to February.

Cultivation The Red Kangaroo Paw likes good drainage and lots of sun. It requires some protection from severe frosts, but

Anigozanthos rufus

given the right conditions will survive for many years.

Landscape Use Ideally suited to the rockery or elevated garden bed. Good container plant.

Anigozanthos viridis

Anigozanthos viridis
GREEN KANGAROO PAW

Origin WA
Climate WT, M
Shade None to filtered

SPECIMEN PLANT
BIRD-ATTRACTING
CONTAINER PLANT

Description This is one of the smaller species, with fine deep green leaves up to 30 cm long. Striking emerald green paw flowers appear on green woolly stems up to 50 cm tall from August to December.

Cultivation This plant is an inhabitant of winter-damp soils of south-western Western Australia and is, therefore, less particular about good drainage than most paws. It will grow in partial shade and tolerates light frosts.

Landscape Use The Green Kangaroo Paw makes an outstanding pot plant. It is a marvellous addition to the rockery.

Anigozanthos 'Bush Emerald'

AOTUS
FABACEAE

A small genus of pea-flowering hairy shrubs of which there are 15 species, all endemic and some occurring in all States. The plants produce a profusion of yellow flowers and are a lovely addition to the wildflower garden. Generally pest free, Aotus *may be subject to the occasional attack from scale insects but these can be easily treated with white oil. Propagation is from seed, which is produced in pods after flowering. Seed germinates readily, particularly with treatment. This is best done by pouring boiling water over the seed and leaving it to soak for 24 hours before sowing.*

Aotus lanigera
POINTED AOTUS

Origin Qld, NSW
Climate S, WT, M
Shade None to filtered

FAST-GROWING

Description A dense-growing shrub to 2 m with pointed leaves, shiny above and hairy below. The large yellow and brown flowers make a superb display when in full bloom in spring.

Cultivation Plant in a sunny, well-drained position. This species will tolerate protected coastal conditions and light frosts.

Landscape Use This shrub is very attractive in flower and is ideal for the native or seaside garden.

Aotus lanigera

ARAUCARIA
ARAUCARIACEAE

Of the 15 or so species of these magnificent conifers of the southern hemisphere, only two are endemic to Australia. Although the pyramidal Norfolk Island pine, A. heterophylla, *is widely planted on the eastern coast of Australia, it is endemic to Norfolk Island. Araucarias are tall trees with a single main trunk that is always densely clothed with side branches and have spirally arranged, sharp, pointed leaves. They are beautiful ornamental shade trees, but are suitable only for the large garden and parks. They also make excellent indoor or container plants for a number of years when young. Propagation is from seed, which is best sown when fresh.*

Araucaria bidwillii
BUNYA PINE

Origin Qld
Climate T, S, WT, M
Shade None to light

SPECIMEN PLANT
CONTAINER PLANT
RAINFOREST PLANT

Description A beautiful, dome-shaped tree to 30 m or more, with many horizontal branches radiating from the stout trunk. The glossy, dark green leaves are prickly and are crowded into great tufts towards the ends of the branches. The pineapple-like female cones, which produce woody edible nuts, are very large — up to 30 cm long. These were a highly prized food of the Aborigines, who ate them either raw or roasted, or ground and used as flour.

Cultivation This hardy ornamental tree may be slow-growing when young, but once it is established growth and frost resistance are good. It withstands moderate coastal exposure, but needs protection in the early stages.

Landscape Use A magnificent tree for public gardens, parks, roadsides, windbreaks and farms. It is an exceptionally good indoor or container plant. In the Brisbane City Botanic Gardens there is a Bunya Promenade — a lovely walk along the Brisbane River featuring historical bunya pines planted in 1858 in honour of colonist botanist James Bidwill.

Araucaria cunninghamii
HOOP PINE

Origin Qld, NSW
Climate T, S, WT, M
Shade None to filtered

FAST-GROWING
SPECIMEN PLANT
CONTAINER PLANT
RAINFOREST PLANT

Description Hoop pine is a straight, tall tree which attains a height of 30 m or

Araucaria bidwillii

more. It has small prickly leaves in bunched growth towards the ends of upward-pointing branches. The bark has a hoop-like formation, from which the tree gets its common name. It is one of Australia's best softwoods and has been used extensively in forestry.

Cultivation This species comes from high summer rainfall areas, but is adaptable to cooler climates provided there is adequate moisture. It will withstand moderate coastal exposure and is relatively frost tolerant.

Landscape Use This is a highly ornamental tree for the large garden or park. It is an excellent container plant when young.

Araucaria cunninghamii

ARCHONTOPHOENIX

ARECACEAE

A genus of two or three tall slender palms native to eastern Australia. The large graceful fronds are pinnately divided and form a crown. Produced below the base of the leaves are small flowers borne on many pendulous panicles which are first enclosed by a large, deciduous spathe. Flowering, which is often irregular, is followed by the production of bright red-skinned fruits.

These palms are most attractive for specimen planting, or as potted plants for shaded patios or light positions indoors. Fronds can be badly chewed by the translucent caterpillar of the palm dart butterfly. Look for larvae sheltered in leaflets webbed together. Propagation is from fresh seed. Germination may be slow.

Archontophoenix alexandrae

ALEXANDRA PALM

Origin Qld
Climate T, S, WT
Shade Light to filtered
SPECIMEN PLANT
BIRD-ATTRACTING
CONTAINER PLANT
RAINFOREST PLANT

Description A tall, single-stemmed tropical palm to 15 m or more. The straight trunk is distinctly ringed and the base is enlarged. The long, bright green

Archontophoenix alexandrae

fronds are curved and have a whitish undersurface. Flowers are creamy pink and fruits red.

Cultivation When grown in the garden, this palm needs warm conditions protected from frost. It does best in a well-composted soil with ample water. If used as an indoor plant, it needs a well-lit airy room where it receives some morning sun each day. Container plants respond to annual feeding with a slow release fertiliser.

Landscape Use This graceful specimen for the warm garden looks best planted in small groves. It is a good tub plant for sheltered pool surrounds, courtyards, patios or verandas.

Archontophoenix cunninghamiana
BANGALOW PALM; PICCABEEN PALM

Origin Qld, NSW
Climate T, S, WT, M
Shade Light to filtered
SPECIMEN PLANT
BIRD-ATTRACTING
CONTAINER PLANT
RAINFOREST PLANT

Description A tall, graceful palm to 20 m or more with a straight, smooth, grey trunk ringed by the scars of fallen fronds. The small mauve flowers in large panicles and the red fruits that follow are most attractive to a variety of birds and animals. The spathes which house the unopened flowers were used by Aborigines as water containers.

Cultivation When planted in the garden, this lovely palm needs a well-composted situation in deep soil with ample moisture. A plant of 5 m or more will tolerate full exposure to the sun but when young may be frost-sensitive.

Landscape Use This decorative palm is ideal for giving the tropical touch to outdoor living areas or for planting around pools, giving shade with a minimum of leaf problems. In nature, it often grows in large stands, and it looks particularly appealing when several are grouped fairly closely to give a palm grove effect. In its early years, it may be grown as a container plant, but it is not suitable for indoors.

ASPLENIUM
ASPLENIACEAE

This genus of epiphytic or terrestrial ferns is widely distributed throughout the world, with some 26 species extending to Australia. They are collectively known as spleenworts. A number of attractive species have become popular in cultivation and they may be grown in pots and baskets, or on rocks and trees. Propagation is from spores, by division of the rhizome or from the small bulbils that form in the upper part of the fronds in some species.

Asplenium australasicum
BIRD'S NEST FERN

Origin Qld, NSW
Climate T, S, WT, M
Shade Light to filtered
ORNAMENTAL PLANT
CONTAINER PLANT
RAINFOREST PLANT

Description The beautiful bird's nest fern has large, undivided leathery fronds up to 1 m or more long and to 20 cm broad, each with a dark brown midrib. They are a rich green colour and radiate from a central region that collects debris as a source of nutrients.

Cultivation This species grows naturally as an epiphyte on rocks and in the branches of rainforest trees. It will grow outdoors in filtered sunlight in humus-enriched soil with excellent drainage. It needs protection from frost. Because of the relatively small root system, it is highly recommended for growing in a large shallow container. It needs a potting mix with plenty of leaf mould.

Landscape Use This is a striking feature plant for use by a shady pool or under trees. An excellent container plant for the courtyard or patio or for indoors in a well-lit room.

Archontophoenix cunninghamiana

Asplenium australasicum

Asplenium bulbiferum
MOTHER SPLEENWORT

Origin Qld, NSW, Vic., Tas., SA
Climate T, S, WT, M, CT
Shade Light to filtered
ORNAMENTAL FOLIAGE
CONTAINER PLANT
RAINFOREST PLANT

Description An erect species with finely divided, semi-weeping fronds to 120 cm. Its interesting feature is that tiny reproductive plantlets form on the outer parts of the mature fronds. These eventually take root and may be transplanted when they are a reasonable size.

Cultivation This is a hardy fern for a sheltered position in the ground. It requires protection from frost.

Landscape Use A lush and attractive plant for the rocky parts of the garden, or near steps where the pendent fronds nay be seen to advantage. It combines well with taller tree ferns. It is an excellent hanging basket fern for growing under pergolas or beneath the cover of small trees.

Asplenium bulbiferum

Asplenium flabellifolium
NECKLACE FERN

Origin All States
Climate T, S, WT, M, CT
Shade Light to filtered
CONTAINER PLANT

Description This is a very dainty trailing species which forms miniature spreading colonies. It has slender light green fronds with small fan-shaped leaflets. These

Asplenium flabellifolium

prostrate fronds extend into a slender tail which may take root at the tip and form a new plantlet.

Cultivation This species will grow in a protected position in the ground or as an epiphyte, where it will probably be happier away from the snails and slugs that can completely denude it overnight.

Landscape Use A pretty, lacy fern for a small rockery pocket or for use as a tiny ground cover. It can be grown as a basket or pot plant.

ASTARTEA
MYRTACEAE

An endemic genus of attractive flowering shrubs of which there are five species in Western Australia and one in the Northern Territory. Two species are popular in cultivation. They are hardy and easily maintained and have abundant flowers almost all year round, providing attractive sprays of cut flowers. Dense growth can be encouraged by regular pruning. Propagation is from half-ripened tip cuttings taken from spring to autumn or from seed which is best sown when fresh.

Astartea fascicularis

Origin WA
Climate S, WT, M, CT, SA
Shade None to filtered
AROMATIC FOLIAGE

Description An upright, open shrub to 1 m with aromatic, narrow foliage. Sprays of whitish pink flowers are massed along the drooping stems over a long period, providing a good supply of cut blooms.

Cultivation This very hardy shrub likes most soils and conditions. It is frost-

Astartea fascicularis (flower)

A. fascicularis

resistant and will tolerate dryness and wind, although a sheltered position with good watering produces a denser, better flowering shrub. Dense growth can also be encouraged by regular pruning.

Landscape Use This is a particularly attractive shrub when grown in a raised garden bed where the arching branches and profuse flowers may be seen to advantage. It can also be grown as a small informal hedge or low windbreak if well trimmed. For this purpose, plants should be spaced at least 1 m apart.

Astartea heteranthera

Origin WA
Climate S, WT, M, CT, SA
Shade None to filtered
AROMATIC FOLIAGE
CONTAINER PLANT

Description A low-growing shrub with red stems and a compact growth habit up to 80 cm. The small, short, needle-like leaves

Astartea heteranthera

are aromatic, and dainty sprays of white flowers are studded on slender drooping branches in spring and summer.

Cultivation This adaptable small shrub will grow in most well-drained soils in full sun or partial shade. It will withstand considerable frost, but young plants need protection until established. Prune after flowering.

Landscape Use This is a good cascading plant suited to a well-drained rockery or for use as a ground cover. It can also be grown in containers.

ASTROLOMA

EPACRIDACEAE

A genus of some 20 Australian species belonging to the heath family. These interesting small shrubs have crowded foliage and brightly coloured tubular flowers which attract honeyeaters to the garden. Flowers are followed by small, fleshy berries, some of which have a sweet pulp when ripe, and were used as a food source by Aborigines and early settlers. In nature, these plants are usually understorey shrubs with the protection of other plants. A raised garden bed or rockery will provide the good drainage that this genus demands as some species occasionally suffer from fungus attacks. White oil will control the infestations of sap-sucking pests or scale that astrolomas are sometimes prone to. Propagation may be carried out from half-ripened tip cuttings, which in some species may be slow to strike.

Astroloma conostephioides
(syn. *Styphelia behril*)

FLAME HEATH

Origin NSW, Vic., SA
Climate WT, M
Shade None to filtered
BIRD-ATTRACTING
CONTAINER PLANT

Description A small, erect dwarf shrub to 1 m which features a bright display of red tubular flowers with red calyces in winter and spring. Honeyeaters flock to this plant when it is in bloom. The blue-green leaves are narrow and sharply pointed.

Cultivation This species demands excellent drainage in a position with full sun or partial shade. It is frost-resistant and will grow in coastal gardens with some protection.

Landscape Use A most attractive small plant when sited near the base of eucalypt

Astartea conostephioides

species. It is a charming shrub for the small garden and will fit snugly into any large rockery. It may also be grown in a large container.

Astroloma pinifolium

PINE HEATH

Origin NSW, Vic., Tas.
Climate WT, M, CT
Shade Light to filtered
BIRD-ATTRACTING
CONTAINER PLANT

Description A small, spreading shrub to 1 m or less, with dense pine-like foliage and pink or yellowish green flowers

Astartea pinifolium

crowded at the ends of branches and often partially hidden by the foliage.

Cultivation This species enjoys sandy soils with good drainage. A lightly shaded position is preferred. It will stand quite dry conditions and is frost-resistant.

Landscape Use A good place for this attractive plant is a partially shaded rockery where there is room to display its compact beauty. A good tub plant.

ATRIPLEX

CHENOPODIACEAE

There are some 60 species of this saltbush genus endemic to Australia. They are shrubs with attractive leathery, silvery-green leaves and showy fruits and are usually found in drier saline habitats. Their ornamental foliage, their soil-binding ability, their resistance to salt-spray, drought, frost and fire and their usefulness as fodder plants are all good reasons for growing these decorative plants. Propagation is from seed or by half-ripened tip cuttings.

Atriplex nummularia

OLD MAN SALTBUSH

Origin Inland Australia
Climate WT, M, SA
Shade None to light

SALT-TOLERANT
DROUGHT-RESISTANT
ORNAMENTAL FOLIAGE

Description The Old Man Saltbush is one of the better known and one of the largest species, growing to a height of 3 m. It has large, rounded silvery grey leaves covered with a scaly white layer. The separate clusters of male and female flowers are inconspicuous.

Cultivation This very adaptable species can withstand severe drought, periodic flooding, full coastal exposure and frost. It will tolerate most soils, but does best in a sunny, well-drained position.

Landscape Use Old Man Saltbush has been cultivated for a variety of purposes including hedges, windbreaks and firebreaks. It is an attractive silver accent plant against a background of dark green trees and shrubs.

Atriplex nummularia

AUSTROMYRTUS

MYRTACEAE

A genus of some 14 endemic species confined to moist coastal areas of eastern Australia. They are small to large shrubs with small glossy leaves, white flowers with numerous fluffy stamens and small berry-like fruits. A few ornamental species are in cultivation and they do best in partially shaded conditions. Propagation is carried out from cuttings or from fresh seed.

Austromyrtus tenuifolia

Origin Qld, NSW
Climate S, WT, M
Shade Light to filtered

CONTAINER PLANT

Description A small-growing shrub to 2 m. It has linear foliage and bears small pretty white flowers with many stamens in summer to autumn. These are followed by small edible berries.

Cultivation Grow in soil enriched with compost in a damp sheltered position. It is frost-resistant.

Landscape Use This is a good flowering plant for growing under taller trees and tree ferns in the 'rainforest' section of the garden. It also makes a decorative plant.

Austromyrtus tenuifolia

BACKHOUSIA

MYRTACEAE

This genus was named in honour of James Backhouse, a mid-nineteenth century nurseryman. It is a small genus comprising seven endemic rainforest species of tall shrubs to small trees which have strongly aromatic foliage. The small cup-shaped flowers with long stamens are grouped together into large showy clusters. Backhousias make excellent garden specimens and shade trees and do best in rich soil conditions with plenty of moisture. They are sometimes frost-tender. Propagation is from cuttings or from the small, fine seeds contained in the nut-like capsule.

Backhousia citriodora

LEMON-SCENTED MYRTLE; LEMON IRONWOOD

Origin Qld
Climate T, S, WT, M
Shade None to filtered

SPECIMEN PLANT
AROMATIC FOLIAGE
RAINFOREST PLANT

Description This attractive small tree, generally only 6 to 8 m in height, has

Backhousia citriodora

B. citriodora (flower)

dark green ovate leaves which, when crushed, give off a beautiful strong citrus fragrance. The leaves contain a high percentage of citral oil and yield a valuable commercial oil. The bouquets of small white flowers literally cover the tree through the summer months.

Cultivation Although from Queensland, this lovely plant can be grown as far south as Victoria. It likes a soil rich in humus with plenty of moisture during dry periods. It needs protection from winds and frosts when young. Prune lightly if you want to improve the shape or appearance. This provides an opportunity to collect the leaves, dry them, and use them in potpourri, or for making refreshing lemon-scented sachets.

Landscape Use This beautiful specimen may be used as a feature, as a shade tree or as a screening plant. It makes an excellent host for epiphytic orchids.

BAECKEA

MYRTACEAE

Named in honour of Abraham Baeck, a Swedish physician and friend of Linnaeus. There are over 70 indigenous species, found in all States and in a diversity of situations. They range in height from tall shrubs to almost prostrate species, all with a profusion of small tea-tree-like flowers from spring to summer, often in the summer months when little else is in bloom. Many species have adapted to cultivation and are readily available from specialist nurseries as well as general outlets. Propagation is from half-ripened tip cuttings prior to flowering.

Baeckea astarteoides

Origin WA
Climate WT, M, CT, SA
Shade None to filtered

CONTAINER PLANT

Description This dainty small shrub will grow up to 1 m. It has tiny leaves clustered along the stems and bears small pink flowers on arching branches for a long period in summer.

Baeckea astarteoides

Cultivation A hardy species suitable for both dry and moist conditions in filtered shade or full sun. It is frost-hardy. Prune lightly after flowering.

Landscape Use This is a pretty plant for the rockery or sloping bank where the pendulous branches may tumble over in a natural way. It may be used as a tub plant.

Baeckea camphorata

CAMPHOR BUSH

Origin Qld, NSW
Climate S, WT, M
Shade None to filtered

FAST-GROWING
AROMATIC FOLIAGE
CONTAINER PLANT

Description A small open shrub to 2 m with small oblong leaves which give off a spicy aroma when crushed. Dainty white flowers appear all year; may be used as a cut flower.

Cultivation This is a reliable plant in most soils, but it prefers a well-drained position with adequate moisture. It is frost-tolerant and will withstand limited coastal exposure. It responds well to tip pruning to encourage branching.

Landscape Use An attractive branching shrub for the garden or larger rockery.

Baeckea crenatifolia

FERN-LEAF BAECKEA

Origin Vic.
Climate WT, M, CT, H
Shade Light to filtered

CONTAINER PLANT

Description This very attractive shrub to 3 m has small rounded leaves, rather fern-like, on slender stems with pendulous tips. Masses of tiny white flowers appear in summer.

Cultivation This species, from the Victorian Alps, does best in a cool, partially shaded location with a moist but well-drained soil. It will tolerate frost and snow.

Landscape Use This is a charming garden shrub which blooms when little else is in

Baeckea camphorata

Baeckea densifolia

Origin NSW
Climate S, WT, M, CT
Shade None to filtered
CONTAINER PLANT
Description A small upright shrub to 1 m with crowded narrow leaves and masses of tiny white flowers in summer which are excellent for picking.

Cultivation This is a hardy plant for most soils and conditions. It will grow in a protected coastal garden and will withstand frost. Prune lightly after flowering.

Landscape Use This is a profuse-flowering shrub for the lightly shaded garden or rockery. It may also be trimmed into a low hedge.

Baeckea linifolia
WEEPING BAECKEA

Origin Qld, NSW, Vic.
Climate S, WT, M, CT
Shade None to filtered
SPECIMEN PLANT
AROMATIC FOLIAGE
CONTAINER PLANT
Description A fine species, with a delicate weeping habit, which grows up to 3 m. The fine, glossy leaves, which have a spicy perfume when bruised, often turn an attractive bronzy colour in flower. It may be trimmed to form a low hedge or screen plant and can be grown in a large tub.

Baeckea crenatifolia

Baeckea densifolia

winter. Delicate, tiny white flowers appear in great masses along the branches in late summer, autumn and winter. Sprays of cut flowers last well indoors.

Cultivation This popular, adaptable plant can be planted in most soils and situations. Although it will withstand dry periods, it does best in a moist, well-drained position, with a little shade in hot areas. It is usually frost-resistant. A light pruning after flowering helps to maintain a compact bush.

Landscape Use This is a beautiful shrub for planting near a path or gateway where the tiny white flowers may be appreciated and aromatic leaves may be picked and crushed by passers-by. It may also be used as a light screen plant.

Baeckea linifolia

Baeckea ramosissima

ROSY BAECKEA

Origin NSW, Vic., Tas., SA
Climate WT, M, CT, H
Shade None to light
CONTAINER PLANT

Description A low, spreading, sparsely leaved shrub with wiry branches up to 1 m high and 1.5 m across. Lovely white to rosy pink flowers appear in winter and spring. This is a variable species from a variety of habitats, and several different forms are at present in cultivation.

Cultivation A hardy little shrub for the sunny, well-drained position. It will tolerate most soils and is frost-resistant.

Baeckea ramosissma

Landscape Use A pretty, sprawling shrub for rockery and ground cover purposes. It makes a good cascading tub plant.

Baeckea virgata

TWIGGY BAECKEA; TALL BAECKEA

Origin Qld, NSW, Vic., NT
Climate T, S, WT, M, CT, SA
Shade None to light
FAST-GROWING
CONTAINER PLANT

Description An erect, dense shrub or small tree to 4 m with small lanceolate leaves on arching branches. From the upper leaf axils masses of loose clusters of small white flowers appear in summer, providing good cut flowers. This is an extremely variable shrub and several good prostrate and dwarf forms are available.

Cultivation An adaptable species, tolerating a wide range of soil types and climatic conditions. It does best in a sunny position with summer watering. It tolerates both frost and dry conditions. Prune lightly after flowering to retain bushiness.

Landscape Use This is an attractive, hardy shrub for background or screen planting. The dwarf forms are also hardy and make plants for rockeries and tubs.

Baeckea virgata

B. virgata (dwarf form)

BANKSIA

PROTEACEAE

The magnificent banksias are among the most attractive of all the plants of the bush. There are some 70 known species, found only in Australia with the exception of B. dentata, *a tropical species which extends from northern Australia to New Guinea. The genus* Banksia *commemorates the name of Sir Joseph Banks, the British botanist who travelled with Captain Cook.*

Banksias vary from prostrate shrubs to gnarled, twisted, low-branching trees. When in bloom they carry spectacular flower spikes consisting of hundreds of densely packed, spirally arranged individual flowers. Their liberal quantities of nectar hold a great attraction for nectar-feeding birds and small marsupials. As the flowers die, the spike develops into the familiar woody fruiting cone which attracts seed eaters such as parrots and cockatoos.

Banksias are grown for their handsome form, foliage and flowers. Left on the bush or cut for indoors, flowers last for many weeks. Dried flowers and cones are also popular for floral decoration.

Of all the native plants, banksias have the reputation for being the most difficult in cultivation, particularly those grown far from their natural habitats. They are sunlovers and most demand excellent drainage.

Many of the Western Australian species are susceptible to a fungal root rot caused by Phytophthora cinnamomi, *the cinnamon fungus. This occurs mainly in the eastern States when simultaneous heavy rains and hot weather are experienced. These plants demand excellent drainage, such as a bank or hill, preferably with sandy soil mixed with loose gravel, and if possible in a dry position in the garden. In nature a dense covering of plant litter ensures a cool root run and this can similarly be applied in cultivation. Mulch or ground covers may be used to control weeds, but always leave a clear area around the trunk. Pruning, although seldom necessary, may be lightly carried out to improve unshapely bushes. Taking lots of cut flowers encourages vigour and better flower production.*

Propagation is from seed. To extract seeds, soak the cone in water for two or three days, then quickly dry in a warm oven. The seed has a papery wing and should drop easily from the valves or, failing that, may be extracted with tweezers. Germination takes three to ten weeks. Care should be taken to avoid damping off of seedlings by careful garden hygiene and use of fungicide. Some banksias can also be grown from half-ripened cuttings.

Banksia aemula

Banksia aemula
(syn. *B. serratifolia*)
WALLUM BANKSIA

Origin Qld, NSW
Climate T, S, WT, M
Shade None to light

SPECIMEN PLANT
BIRD-ATTRACTING
SALT-TOLERANT

Description Found in sandy coastal heaths and dune ridges, this is a spreading shrub or small, gnarled and twisted tree to 5 m. It has bright green serrated leaves and silvery gold cylindrical flower spikes. It is closely related to *B. serrata*, but may be distinguished by the tiny club-shaped stigma, which is smaller than that of *B. serrata* and not as pointed. Aborigines were gatherers of honey from the flowers and gave the plant the name 'wallum', a name also applied to an area of coastal lowland in south-east Queensland in which this particular banksia thrives. Its red-grained timber is prettily marked and has been used in cabinet work.

Cultivation This is a hardy, adaptable plant suited to coastal and cooler locations. It likes a moist, well-drained soil but will also tolerate a poorly drained situation. It is frost-resistant.

Landscape Use This is a beautiful specimen shrub for the coastal garden.

Banksia ashbyi
ASHBY'S BANKSIA

Origin WA
Climate WT, M, SA
Shade None to light

SPECIMEN PLANT
BIRD-ATTRACTING

Description This beautiful leafy shrub of the warm sandheaths of Western Australia will reach a height of 3 m. The long narrow leaves, up to 25 cm long, are deeply lobed almost to the midrib and long-lasting, rich orange flower spikes appear from August to November. The cut flowers and handsome foliage are beautiful for indoor arrangements.

Cultivation This species requires warm conditions in an open, well-drained soil. It will tolerate some frost and dry conditions.

Landscape Use This is a spectacular specimen plant for a special spot.

Banksia ashbyi

Banksia baueri
POSSUM BANKSIA

Origin WA
Climate WT, M, CT, SA
Shade None to filtered

SPECIMEN PLANT
BIRD-ATTRACTING

Description This dense, rounded shrub which grows to a height of about 3 m has toothed oblong leaves. It is easily recognisable by the large, soft, hairy flower spikes ranging in colour from pale mauve to a bright tan colour. Often flowering close to the ground, this species hides its lovely flower spikes like small furry animals huddled in the leaves — a feature from which it derives its common name. This species produces some of the largest flowers among banksias. The flowering period is winter and spring.

Cultivation This is a relatively easy species to establish, and adapts well to full sun or partial shade. It prefers light soil in a well-drained site and will withstand dry periods. It is frost-resistant.

Banksia baueri

Landscape Use An interesting and ornamental banksia which may be used as a feature. It is also suitable for a screen or for low windbreak planting.

Banksia baxteri
BIRD'S NEST BANKSIA

Origin WA
Climate M, SA
Shade None to light

SPECIMEN PLANT
BIRD-ATTRACTING
ORNAMENTAL FOLIAGE

Description A large, erect shrub to 3 m high with ornamental triangular-lobed leaves with blunt ends. The very attractive silvery green globular flower spikes are set in a rosette of leaves during summer. Flower spikes are on long slender stalks and are ideal for picking.

Cultivation A very well drained sandy soil and minimum summer rainfall are necessary for this species. It will grow in a protected coastal garden and is frost-resistant.

Landscape Use A beautiful flowering species that can be used as a feature, for a low windbreak and for cut flowers.

Banksia blechnifolia

Origin WA
Climate WT, SA
Shade None to filtered

BIRD-ATTRACTING
ORNAMENTAL FOLIAGE

Description A prostrate creeping shrub with a spread of around 2 m. The deeply lobed erect leaves to about 50 cm long are covered in rusty hairs when young. The highly attractive flower heads are produced at branch ends in spring and early summer. They are oblong spikes to 20 cm long in glowing shades of bronze and rosy-red.

Cultivation Although best suited to areas with low summer rainfall, good specimens of this plant can be seen in gardens west of Sydney. It likes good drainage, will tolerate dry conditions and light frosts.

Landscape Use This is a beautiful ground cover species for sloping banks, raised garden beds, foreground planting and large rockeries.

Banksia baxteri

Banksia blechnifolia

Banksia coccinea
SCARLET BANKSIA; ALBANY BANKSIA

Origin WA
Climate M
Shade None to light
SPECIMEN PLANT
BIRD-ATTRACTING

Description This is a stiff upright shrub to 4 m or more. The undersurface of the rounded toothed leaves is white or greyish and the erect branches are thickly coated with soft matted fur. The spectacular globular flower spikes of scarlet and grey sit in a rosette of leathery leaves. This is one of the best known banksias and one that is widely cultivated and used extensively in the cut flower trade.

Cultivation This plant of the south coast of Western Australia needs conditions as near as possible to those of its natural habitat — a deep sandy soil in a warm area with a good winter rainfall and a dry summer. It will withstand frost. A light pruning will improve shape and increase flowering.

Landscape Use This ornamental banksia may be used as a feature and will grow under the shelter of tall trees.

Banksia coccinea

Banksia ericifolia
HEATH BANKSIA

Origin Qld, NSW
Climate S, WT, M, CT
Shade None to light
FAST-GROWING
SPECIMEN PLANT
BIRD-ATTRACTING
SALT-TOLERANT
CONTAINER PLANT

Description This is a tall, shapely shrub to 7 m with a spread of about 2 m, branching from near ground level, with crowded heath-like foliage backed with silver. The erect torch flowers scattered throughout the bush during winter and early spring are usually a golden orange shade, but some forms are deep orange-red to burgundy and others pale yellow. This is an excellent source of nectar for honeyeaters and is a good species for cut flowers.

The cultivar 'Giant Candles' is a supposed hybrid between *B. ericifolia* and *B. spinulosa*. It is noted for its huge burnt orange flower spikes up to 40 cm long.

An excellent dwarf compact form, 1 m high and 2 m across is now available from some nurseries in eastern Australia. It bears spectacular orange-red flowers from autumn right through to spring.

Cultivation This is a robust, healthy grower and one of the easiest banksias to grow. It grows in well-drained soils with some summer moisture. It will grow in seaside gardens if given some protection when young. It is wind- and frost-resistant.

Landscape Use This is a handsome garden specimen in all seasons. It is used extensively in municipal plantings and may be grown as an informal hedge, windbreak or screen. It is also successfully grown in large tubs.

B. ericifolia (tree)

Banksia ericifolia

Banksia hookerana
HOOKER'S BANKSIA

Origin WA
Climate M, CT
Shade None to light
SPECIMEN PLANT
BIRD-ATTRACTING

Description This lovely spreading shrub reaches a height of 3 m and has long, narrow, serrated leaves. It is often crowded with flowers at various stages of development, varying in colour from soft velvety white to deep orange. The flowering period is mainly winter to summer.

Cultivation This species requires an open sunny position, light well-drained soil, water in winter and a dry summer and autumn. It will tolerate frost and extended dry periods.

Landscape Use A beautiful ornamental species. Its dense compact shape makes it suitable for a low windbreak.

Banksia hookerana

Banksia integrifolia
COAST BANKSIA

Origin Qld, NSW, Vic., Tas.
Climate T, S, WT, M, CT
Shade None to light
FAST-GROWING
SPECIMEN PLANT
BIRD-ATTRACTING
SALT-TOLERANT

Description This fast-growing gnarled tree of the coast will reach a height of 15 m or more. The attractive, entire leaves are a rich glossy green with silvery, felted undersides. The plant bears masses of honey-laden, pale yellow flower spikes from early autumn through to spring.

A prostrate form with a spread of around 2 m across is in cultivation. Large yellow flowers are produced for most of the year. A good groundcover for coastal gardens.

Cultivation This hardy banksia adapts well to cultivation and will grow in almost any soil from sand to heavy clay. It is found along Australia's east coast and will withstand exposure to harsh sea winds and drifting sand. It will also grow inland and is frost-resistant.

Landscape Use Coast banksia may be used as a specimen tree, for privacy screens, for shelter or as a windbreak in seaside gardens. The prostrate form is suitable for foreground planting and large containers.

Banksia marginata
SILVER BANKSIA

Origin NSW, Vic., Tas., SA
Climate S, WT, M, CT, H, SA
Shade None to filtered
BIRD-ATTRACTING
SALT-TOLERANT
CONTAINER PLANT

Description This is a variable, fairly dense shrub or small tree which may grow to a height of about 10 m, but is usually much smaller. It sometimes occurs as a low shrub in coastal and rocky areas. The common name is derived from the narrow green leaves which are white on the underside, giving the tree a silvery appearance. It has a long flowering season, from winter to summer and sometimes in autumn. The flowers at bud stage are greenish, becoming pale to bright yellow. The flowers are most

Banksia integrifolia

attractive to honeyeaters, and cockatoos feed on the seed.

Cultivation This banksia has a wide distribution and will tolerate a variety of climatic conditions from coastal and mountainous to those of moderately dry inland areas. It prefers full sun but will grow in some shade and is frost-resistant.

Landscape Use Dense forms of this plant are used as a windbreak. It is an attractive plant for the seaside garden. The stunted forms make an attractive tub plant.

Banksia media
SOUTHERN PLAINS BANKSIA

Origin WA
Climate WT, M
Shade None to light
SPECIMEN PLANT
BIRD-ATTRACTING

Description A compact bushy shrub which grows to a height of 6 m. Branches are densely covered with tiny white hairs and the attractive small, shiny green leaves are irregularly toothed along the margins. The prominent flower spikes, which vary in colour from creamy yellow to golden bronze or almost orange, vary also in shape and size. It usually blooms from February to October.

Cultivation This species prefers a light, well-drained soil in full sun or partial

Banksia marginata

Banksia media

shade. It will tolerate frost, periods of dryness and some coastal exposure.

Landscape Use This is an outstanding specimen shrub.

Banksia menziesii

MENZIES' BANKSIA

Origin WA
Climate M, CT
Shade None to light
SPECIMEN PLANT
BIRD-ATTRACTING

Description A shrub or small twisted tree to 15 m but usually much smaller in cultivation. It has long, toothed leaves and striking silky pink to red flowers in autumn and winter. These are followed by attractive patterned seed cones with a few prominent furry capsules.

Cultivation This species prefers a dry summer and has been successfully cultivated in Western Australia and South Australia. It needs a medium, well-drained soil and is moderately frost-resistant. Take cut flowers or prune to keep shapely.

Landscape Use A showy banksia for use as a feature or windbreak.

Banksia menziesii

Banksia oblongifolia

(syn *B. asplenifolia*)

FERN-LEAVED BANKSIA

Origin Qld, NSW
Climate T, S, WT, M, CT
Shade None to filtered
BIRD-ATTRACTING
CONTAINER PLANT

Description This species varies from a low spreading, bushy shrub about 1.5 m wide to a tall open shrub which may reach 3 m high. The dark green leaves are leathery and mainly entire, with a silvery undersurface; the soft new growth has a contrasting rust colour. The pale yellow flower spikes are often tinged silvery blue when in bud, and occur mainly from autumn to winter; they make beautiful cut flowers.

Cultivation This is a hardy, adaptable species in cultivation, where soils are well drained and moisture is adequate. It will grow in coastal gardens, but needs some protection from heavy salt-laden winds. It will tolerate frost.

Landscape Use This is an attractive banksia for the bush garden, where it will grow in the filtered sunlight of taller trees and provide food and shelter for visiting native birds.

Banksia oblongifolia

Banksia occidentalis
RED SWAMP BANKSIA

Origin WA
Climate WT, M, CT
Shade None to light
SPECIMEN PLANT
BIRD-ATTRACTING

Description This erect shrub or small tree can reach 7 m but is usually smaller in cultivation. It has slender toothed or entire green leaves with a white undersurface, and ornamental ruby red flower spikes in great numbers from summer to autumn.

Cultivation This species is an inhabitant of swampy but sandy soils and adapts well to garden conditions, provided it is watered well during dry periods. It is frost-tolerant.

Landscape Use A neat ornamental specimen that is attractive even when not in flower. It responds to pruning and may be used as a privacy screen.

Banksia occidentalis

Banksia paludosa
MARSH BANKSIA

Origin NSW
Climate WT, M, CT
Shade None to filtered
BIRD-ATTRACTING
CONTAINER PLANT

Description A low, bushy, spreading shrub to 1.5 m across with entire or toothed foliage in a whorled arrangement. It bears numerous narrow golden flower spikes in late autumn and winter.

Cultivation This hardy species will grow in most well-drained soils It will withstand summer rainfall and may be used in protected coastal gardens. It is frost-resistant.

Landscape Use An attractive low-growing species for a rocky slope or garden foreground or in large tub.

Banksia paludosa

Banksia praemorsa
CUT-LEAF BANKSIA

Origin WA
Climate M, CT
Shade None to light
BIRD-ATTRACTING
SALT-TOLERANT

Description A shapely medium or large shrub to 4 m. It has short toothed leaves and beautiful large flower spikes in colours of wine shading to yellow near the base. These appear in late winter and spring and make lovely cut flowers.

Cultivation This species prefers a well-drained soil, but is moderately lime- and salt-tolerant. It comes from windswept coastal areas near Albany in Western Australia and may be used in seaside gardens. It is moderately frost-resistant.

Landscape Use An attractive erect shrub to grow among other plants or to use as a windbreak in coastal gardens.

Banksia praemorsa

Banksia prionotes
ORANGE BANKSIA; ACORN BANKSIA

Origin WA
Climate M, CT, SA
Shade None to light
SPECIMEN PLANT
BIRD-ATTRACTING
CONTAINER PLANT

Description A tall spreading shrub or erect tree to 10 m, but usually less in cultivation. It has long narrow scalloped leaves and large orange flower spikes with soft woolly white buds. These beautiful flowers appear mainly in autumn and are often sold by florists.

Cultivation This species has been successfully grown commercially for the cut flower trade. It prefers full sun and a very well drained soil and may be used in protected coastal gardens. It is frost-resistant.

Banksia prionotes

Landscape Use An outstanding feature plant that may also be used as a windbreak. It is suitable for large tubs.

Banksia repens
CREEPING BANKSIA

Origin WA
Climate M, CT, SA
Shade None to light

SPECIMEN PLANT
BIRD-ATTRACTING

Description This is a prostrate banksia with a spread of 50 cm and particularly handsome foliage. The long erect leaves are divided to the midrib and young growth and horizontal stems are covered with rusty red velvety hairs. The oblong flower spikes of dusky pink, red or pale brown appear at the ends of the branches at ground level in spring and summer.

Cultivation This species occurs in sandheaths in the south of Western Australia. Soils there are mainly acid sands with good drainage and this species will grow well in similar garden conditions in an open sunny position. It will tolerate frost and prefers dry conditions away from the areas of high humidity.

Landscape Use This interesting ornamental plant is ideal for rockeries and sloping banks.

Banksia robur
SWAMP BANKSIA

Origin Qld, NSW
Climate T, S, WT, M, CT
Shade None to light

SPECIMEN PLANT
BIRD-ATTRACTING

Description This is a handsome small shrub to 2 m with marvellous large rumpled leaves to 30 cm long with serrated margins and a woolly underside. The new foliage is velvety pink to deep red. The flower spikes are at first a metallic green, but turn yellowish green as the flowers open, darkening with age to bronze and then brown. The flowering period is usually winter and spring but flowers may appear at other times. Flowers are most attractive to honeyeaters and are excellent for dried arrangements.

Cultivation This species adapts well to cultivation in a variety of soils and conditions, including very wet places in the garden. It will tolerate a dry site, providing adequate water is available, but must be grown in full sun for good flowering. It is resistant to frost. Mulch well to assist in water retention.

Landscape Use An ornamental species that stands out well on its own. Its branching habit and huge leaves give a dramatic effect in pool surrounds and water features.

Banksia serrata
SAW BANKSIA

Origin Qld, NSW, Vic., Tas.
Climate S, WT, M, CT
Shade None to light

SPECIMEN PLANT
BIRD-ATTRACTING
SALT-TOLERANT

Description A strong-growing, gnarled tree from 10 to 15 m tall. The rigid, deep green leaves are coarsely serrated. The flowers are a beautiful silvery grey at first, opening to a yellowish colour as the flower matures. The flowers appear from spring through to autumn and are followed by large grey cones. This banksia is a valuable source of food for a variety of native birds including honeyeaters, Rainbow Lorikeets, rosellas and cockatoos.

An attractive, spreading prostrate form registered as 'Austraflora Pygmy Possum' is available from specialist nurseries. It has horizontal branches that spread to about 2 m across.

Cultivation An adaptable and frost-tolerant species suited to a variety of soils and climatic conditions from coastal to mountain locations. It prefers good drainage and a sunny position.

Landscape Use An excellent plant for the seaside garden, where it is especially useful

Banksia repens

Banksia robur

Banksia serrata (fruit)

B. serrata

as a windbreak to protect less salt-tolerant plants. The prostrate form may be used as a ground cover or in a large rockery.

Banksia speciosa
SHOWY BANKSIA

Origin WA
Climate M
Shade None to light

SPECIMEN PLANT
BIRD-ATTRACTING
SALT-TOLERANT
ORNAMENTAL FOLIAGE

Description This tall, spreading shrub could reach 6 m high by 6 m wide and has very long triangular-lobed leaves. They may be up to 40 cm long and spring out from woolly white branches. Large oblong yellow flower spikes with velvety white buds are set in a rosette of leaves. These are produced mainly in summer and autumn and make spectacular indoor arrangements.

Cultivation Grow in a very well drained, light-textured soil. It may be grown in coastal areas and is moderately frost-resistant.

Landscape Use This is a marvellous garden subject that can be used as a feature or as a dense hedge or screen.

Banksia speciosa

Banksia spinulosa
HAIRPIN BANKSIA

Origin Qld, NSW, Vic.
Climate T, S, WT, M, CT
Shade None to filtered

SPECIMEN PLANT
BIRD-ATTRACTING
CONTAINER PLANT

Description A variable species which grows from 1 to 4 m high. It has long narrow leaves which are notched at the ends and produces shining flower spikes with colour variations of gold, orange, red and brown with black styles. It has a long flowering season from autumn through to October, providing nectar for the birds and good cut flowers.

B. spinulosa var. *collina* (syn. *B. collina*), known as the hill banksia, differs in the leaves, which are usually broader and have recurved margins with prominent serrations for most of their length.

Dwarf and gold forms are also available.

Cultivation This hardy banksia will grow in most well-drained soils with good moisture. It will flower in filtered shade and can be grown under tall trees. It is frost-resistant.

Landscape Use This species will form an attractive rounded specimen shrub. It may be used as an informal hedge, or as

Banksia spinulosa var. *collina*

Banksia spinulosa

Bauera rubioides

B. rubioides (white form)

B. 'Ruby Glow'

a screen or windbreak. Dwarf forms may be grown in the rockery or in a large container.

BAUERA

BAUERACEAE

A small endemic genus of three species of low-growing shrubs, commemorating the name of Francis and Ferdinand Bauer, who assisted early explorers as botanical artists. These small plants are most attractive, with whorl-like leaves and white to magenta cup-shaped flowers, and are popular garden subjects. They are easy to grow, preferring a friable peaty soil in a semishaded moist situation. A spring pruning after flowering will help retain bushy growth. Relatively pest- and disease-free, baueras may occasionally be subject to scale which is easily controlled with white oil. Propagation is from half-ripened tip cuttings.

Bauera rubioides

WIRY BAUERA

Origin Qld, NSW, Vic., Tas., SA
Climate S, WT, M, CT, H
Shade None to filtered
FAST-GROWING
CONTAINER PLANT

Description A small to medium-sized spreading shrub which varies from almost prostrate, up to 3 m wide, to 2 m tall. The small soft leaves are arranged in whorls along the slender stems. It bears dainty bright pink or white flowers in profusion in spring and summer, but is seldom without blooms at other times.

B. rubioides var. *microphylla* is usually prostrate, with finer leaves and pale pink or white flowers.

'Ruby Glow' is a garden hybrid between *B. rubioides* and *B. sessiliflora*. It has dark ruby red flowers in spring and grows to a rounded 1 m.

Cultivation This pretty species prefers a position with adequate moisture in sun or partial shade. Protect plants and roots from strong drying winds. It is frost-tolerant.

Landscape Use This versatile plant may be clipped as an informal hedge or screen or grown in the shelter of trees in the bush garden. It looks particularly attractive when planted with ferns. The smaller varieties make delightful rockery or container plants.

Bauera sessiliflora
GRAMPIANS BAUERA; SHOWY BAUERA

Origin Vic.
Climate WT, M, CT
Shade Light to filtered
CONTAINER PLANT

Description An open shrub to 2 m high and 2 to 4 m across with dark green hairy leaves and masses of magenta flowers closely packed along the stems in spring and early summer.

A white-flowering form is sometimes available.

Cultivation This species is restricted to the Victorian Grampians where it is found in profusion along moist creek banks and shaded gullies. In cultivation it needs moist, well-drained soil and semishade. A good mulch will help to retain moisture during dry weather and a light pruning will keep the bush compact. It is frost-hardy.

Landscape Use Grow in groups for a pretty, natural effect in the garden. It can also be grown as a rockery or container plant.

Bauera sessiliflora

BEAUFORTIA
MYRTACEAE

This Western Australian genus of some 16 or more species is named in honour of Mary Somerset, Duchess of Beaufort, a patroness of botany in the early eighteenth century. The genus is closely allied to and closely resembles Melaleuca, *differing chiefly in the stamen arrangement of the bottlebrush flowers. They are highly ornamental shrubs, thriving in friable peaty or acid soil with excellent drainage. Light to heavy pruning can be carried out to encourage bushiness and more flowers. The fruit is a woody capsule and is retained on old stems for years.*

Propagation is from ripe seed, which is obtained from the mature capsules. Propagation may also be carried out from half-hardened tip cuttings.

Beaufortia schaueri
PINK BOTTLEBRUSH

Origin WA
Climate WT, M, CT
Shade None to light
BIRD-ATTRACTING
CONTAINER PLANT

Description A spreading shrub to 1 m tall with small narrow leaves and rounded bottlebrush flowers clustered along the branches in spring. These may be rose pink to rich mauve in colour.

Cultivation This species does best in a dry sunny position in light to heavy soil with good drainage. Tip pruning may be carried out to maintain shape. It will tolerate light frost.

Landscape Use A beautiful spreading shrub for the rockery. It may also be grown in a container.

Beaufortia schaueri

Beaufortia sparsa
SWAMP BOTTLEBRUSH

Origin WA
Climate WT, M, CT
Shade None to light
BIRD-ATTRACTING

Description An open, erect shrub to around 2 m high with dark green oval foliage crowded along the branches. It bears striking orange-red brush flowers, bundled around the stems, from late summer into late autumn. They provide beautiful cut flowers.

Cultivation Although known as the swamp bottlebrush, this species does best in a well-drained soil with plenty of water provided during dry spells. It will tolerate frost. Prune lightly to shape.

Landscape Use A very showy autumn-flowering plant that looks spectacular when planted in groups.

Beaufortia sparsa

BILLARDIERA
PITTOSPORACEAE

Billardieras are delicate twining plants found only in Australia and named after Jacques de Labillardière, an eighteenth to nineteenth-century French botanist who visited Australia with d'Entrecasteaux on the expedition in search of La Perouse. They have attractive bell-shaped or starry flowers followed by green, sometimes purple, berries. Some species have edible fruits that were a favoured food of Aborigines. The flowers and fruit are grown for their restrained growth habit and are a pretty addition to the garden where a light climber is needed. Propagation is best carried out from half-ripened tip cuttings, as seed is often unreliable.

Billardiera cymosa

(syn. *B. sericophora)*

SWEET APPLE BERRY

Origin NSW, Vic., SA
Climate WT, M, SA
Shade None to light
BIRD-ATTRACTING
CONTAINER PLANT

Description A shrubby, slender climber which will reach 2 m. It has pretty greenish-blue to mauve bell flowers borne in small clusters throughout most of the year, with the main flush in spring. The fruits are oblong, hanging red berries.

Billardiera cymosa

Cultivation This pretty plant, from dry inland areas, is hardy in cultivation and will tolerate most soils and situations. It is frost-resistant.

Landscape Use This non-invasive climber may be grown among other shrubs in the garden. It may also be grown in a large tub as a shrub or trained as a climber.

Billardiera erubescens

(syn. *Marianthus erubescens*)

RED BILLARDIERA

Origin WA
Climate WT, M
Shade None to light
BIRD-ATTRACTING
CONTAINER PLANT

Description An attractive climber to 5 m with dark green oval leaves and bright red tubular flowers produced in clusters over a long period in summer and into autumn.

Cultivation A hardy species in cultivation that grows well in either full sun or semishade. It likes moist, well-drained soils, but will tolerate dry periods.

Landscape Use An attractive slender climber which can be trained on a trellis. It can be encouraged to form a shrub in open situations or can be grown in tubs, where its twining habit can be seen to advantage.

Billardiera erubescens

Billardiera scandens

COMMON APPLE BERRY

Origin Qld, NSW, Vic., Tas., SA
Climate S, WT, M, CT, SA
Shade Light to filtered
BIRD-ATTRACTING
CONTAINER PLANT

Description This slender twining shrub will reach up to 5 m but develops a more shrubby habit in an open situation. The oval leaves with a wavy margin are often silky on the underside. Greenish yellow bell flowers appear all year and are

Billardiera scandens

followed by greenish edible berries with a sweet, acidic taste.

Cultivation This plant adapts to most situations and soils, including clay. It will grow in semishade and although it likes moist positions will withstand dry periods. It is frost-resistant.

Landscape Use A climber for the small garden, as it is non-rampant and produces flowers and fruits over a long period. It also makes an attractive container plant.

BLANDFORDIA

BLANDFORDIACEAE

A charming Australian genus of four species named after George Spencer-Churchill, Marquis of Blandford (1766–1840). Collectively known as Christmas bells, they are restricted to the east coast of Australia and Tasmania and are a favourite wildflower of many. They need a deep, well-drained but moist spot in the garden. They are slow-growing and look best when mass-planted in a deep rockery pocket or in a container. Propagation is from the brown woolly seed, sown when freshly released from the capsule. Seed germinates readily, but plants can take up to four years to flower.

Blandfordia grandiflora

(syn. *B. flammea)*

CHRISTMAS BELLS

Origin Qld, NSW
Climate S, WT, M
Shade None to filtered
CONTAINER PLANT

Description A lovely perennial plant with crowded grass-like leaves to 80 cm and flower stems to 80 cm with a bunch of three to ten large waxy bell-like flowers which vary from yellow to orange or red with yellow tips. Occasionally the whole flower is yellow. Flowers usually appear in summer, especially of course around Christmas time.

Cultivation This species usually grows in swampy areas, so it needs lots of moisture in full or partial sun. It is frost-resistant. It has thick fibrous roots which can spread to form long-lasting clumps, so it is best to plant it in a permanent place without disturbance.

Landscape Use A lovely specimen for a deep rockery pocket. It can also be grown as a container plant.

Blandfordia grandiflora

Blandfordia nobilis
CHRISTMAS BELLS

Origin NSW
Climate WT, M
Shade None to filtered
CONTAINER PLANT

Description A perennial plant with stiff grassy leaves to 60 cm crowded at the base of the flowering stem to 60 cm. The three to ten tubular bell flowers in a bunch come in tones of yellow, orange or red, or orange tipped with yellow. Flowers appear from November to January.

Cultivation This species requires a mild climate but will thrive in a moist, well-drained position in full or partial sun. It has thick fibrous roots which need to spread undisturbed.

Landscape Use Grow in a deep rockery pocket near a water feature, where the brightly coloured bells will contrast beautifully with the lush green of other moisture-loving plants. It can also be grown in a container.

Blandfordia nobilis

Blandfordia punicea
TASMANIAN CHRISTMAS BELLS

Origin Tas.
Climate WT, M, CT
Shade Light to filtered
CONTAINER PLANT

Description A perennial with tough, narrow leaves to 45 cm long curving out from the base of the flowering stem. The numerous flowers appear on a stout erect stem up to 1 m long. They are bell-shaped and pendulous, brilliant red with the inside of the flower and the reflexed tips bright yellow. Occasionally the whole flower is yellow.

Cultivation Plant in a deep soil with fairly constant moisture but good drainage. This species needs some shade. It is frost-resistant.

Blandfordia punicea

Landscape Use Grow in a deep rockery pocket with the protection of other plants. It can also be grown in a container.

BLECHNUM

BLECHNACEAE

A widely distributed genus of terrestrial ferns with about 18 species found in Australia. They are widespread from Tasmania to northern Queensland and are almost always in shaded, moist situations, and are commonly called water ferns. Many species are in cultivation and they make excellent pot plants as well as taking kindly to a shady spot in the garden with plenty of moisture. Propagation may be carried out by division of the rhizome.

Blechnum cartilagineum

GRISTLE FERN

Origin Qld. NSW, Vic., Tas.
Climate T, S, WT, M, CT
Shade Light to filtered

ORNAMENTAL FOLIAGE
CONTAINER PLANT
RAINFOREST PLANT

Description An erect or semierect fern with broad pinnate fronds to 1.5 m tall arising from a central clump. The new fronds are pink, changing to pale green as they mature, sometimes darker in shady locations.

Cultivation A very hardy fern in a variety of climatic conditions. It prefers moist, shaded positions, but stands periods of dryness.

Landscape Use This attractive fern will form large leafy clumps and will create a striking, tropical effect near water or next to a shady patio. It can also be grown in containers.

Blechnum nudum

FISHBONE WATER FERN

Origin Qld, NSW, Vic., Tas., SA
Climate T, S, WT, M, CT
Shade Light to filtered

ORNAMENTAL FOLIAGE
CONTAINER PLANT

Description This widespread fern often forms large colonies in its moist habitats, where it may develop a small trunk up to 30 cm high. The upright fronds, which form a spreading rosette, are up to 1 m tall and are fishbone-shaped.

Blechnum cartilagineum

Blechnum nudum

Cultivation This is a hardy fern for the garden, where it will thrive in moist, well-composted soils in sheltered situations. It is frost-hardy.

Landscape Use The graceful form of this fern can contribute to the shady rockery, fernery or water feature. It makes a good tub specimen.

Blechnum patersonii
STRAP WATER FERN

Origin Qld, NSW, Vic., Tas.
Climate T, S, WT, M, CT
Shade Filtered to full

ORNAMENTAL FOLIAGE
CONTAINER PLANT
RAINFOREST PLANT

Description This widespread fern has semierect, strap-like, dark green fronds up to 40 cm long. The fronds are reddish pink when young and can vary in shape from mainly undivided to pinnately lobed.

Cultivation This attractive, easy-to-grow fern requires well-composted soil in a protected moist position. It is frost-hardy.

Landscape Use An attractive foliage plant to grow at the shady edge of a water feature or rockery, or in the fernery. It also makes an attractive potted specimen.

Blechnum patersonii

Blechnum penna-marina
ALPINE WATER FERN

Origin NSW, Vic., Tas.
Climate WT, M, CT, H
Shade Filtered to full

CONTAINER PLANT

Description This is the smallest native species of *Blechnum*. It has dark green fronds up to 20 cm long with leathery stalks covered in minute reddish hairs. The narrow, branching rhizome is wiry and long-creeping, forming a low ground cover. It may become dormant during winter.

Cultivation This fern is found at very high altitudes and will tolerate extremely cold conditions, including snow. It will grow in warmer gardens in a moist, sheltered place in filtered to full shade.

Landscape Use An attractive little fern that will thrive at the edges of a pool, in moist wall crevices and rockery pockets or as a ground cover in moist seepage areas. Grow also in a container.

Blechnum penna-marina

BORONIA
RUTACEAE

A genus of some 95 Australian species named in honour of Francesco Borone, an Italian plant collector. The boronias are delightful shrubs, noted for their sweet fragrance, early spring blooms and aromatic foliage.

Boronias will grow in a lime-free soil that is well drained but never very dry. They prefer a cool root run and this can be achieved by providing a heavy mulch or by placing sandstone slabs around the root zone. Planting with other shrubs which provide shade or in a setting among rocks is also useful for keeping the root area cool. They will not tolerate drought or hot, drying winds and are relatively pest-free being subject only occasionally to scale.

Many species are small shrubs and can be grown as pot plants, where they may get the special attention they often demand. In fact, it was as pot plants that boronias were first widely cultivated in Europe shortly after their discovery.

Boronias are generally long-lasting as cut flowers, and taking the flower stems benefits the plants, as they need pruning back after blooming to prolong life and improve bushiness.

Propagation is from half-ripened tip cuttings.

Boronia anemonifolia
STICKY BORONIA

Origin Qld, NSW, Vic., Tas.
Climate S, WT, M, CT
Shade Light to filtered

AROMATIC FOLIAGE

Description This variable and widespread shrub to 1 m or more has strong-smelling, usually narrow, pinnate leaves with notched tips. The plant in full flower in spring is very showy: tiny pink or white starry flowers cover the bush.

B. anemonifolia var. *variabilis* is a broader leaved variety. The leaves have a strong unpleasant odour, but this form is considered hardier in cultivation.

Cultivation This boronia is best planted in a well-drained soil among other shrubs and trees which provide mottled shade and protection for the roots. The plant will tolerate frost.

Landscape Use This is a very floriferous species which makes a brilliant display, but because of the strong-smelling leaves it is not the boronia for planting near doors or windows or for cut flowers inside.

Boronia anemonifolia

Boronia clavata

Origin WA
Climate WT, M, CT
Shade Light to filtered
FAST-GROWING
FRAGRANT
AROMATIC FOLIAGE

Description An erect shrub to 2 m with aromatic, narrow pinnate leaves. The greenish yellow bell flowers have a light perfume and appear throughout the spring months.

Cultivation This boronia is considered one of the easiest to maintain in cultivation. It prefers a sheltered, well-drained position and is frost-resistant. Prune back after flowering.

Landscape Use This species is ideal for using in groups beneath taller plants. It can also be used as a light screen.

Boronia clavata

Boronia crenulata

Origin WA
Climate WT, M, CT
Shade Light to filtered
AROMATIC FOLIAGE
CONTAINER PLANT

Description A dense small shrub to 1 m with aromatic obovate leaves, and pretty pink star flowers from late winter to summer.

Cultivation This boronia is quite hardy in most soils, but requires some moisture and filtered shade. It is frost-resistant.

Boronia crenulata

Landscape Use This dainty plant with slightly pendulous branches is ideal for growing in a rockery pocket or in a tub near the house, where its delicate beauty can be fully appreciated.

Boronia deanei
DEANE'S BORONIA

Origin NSW
Climate WT, M, CT
Shade Light to filtered
AROMATIC FOLIAGE
CONTAINER PLANT

Description A small erect shrub to about 1 m with narrow, almost cylindrical foliage which is highly aromatic when crushed. It bears masses of pink star flowers during spring.

Boronia deanei

Cultivation Grow in a well-drained soil with an adequate supply of moisture and a cool root run. It is frost-resistant. Prune after flowering to promote new growth and vigour.

Landscape Use This boronia is popular in cultivation and is suited to growing beneath taller plants in the garden. It will make an attractive small hedge and looks good in a container.

Boronia denticulata

Origin WA
Climate WT, M, CT
Shade Light to filtered
FAST-GROWING
SPECIMEN PLANT
AROMATIC FOLIAGE
CONTAINER PLANT

Description This bushy species will form a rounded shrub to 1 m. It has light green, narrow, aromatic leaves with minute teeth, and pink starry flowers in loose clusters cover the bush in late winter to spring.

Cultivation This reasonably hardy species will grow in most garden conditions, including coastal ones if given protection. It is frost-resistant. It should be pruned after flowering to keep up bushy growth.

Landscape Use This free-flowering, compact shrub will fit beautifully into any garden situation, including a large rockery or a container.

Boronia floribunda
PALE PINK BORONIA

Origin NSW
Climate WT, M, CT
Shade Light to filtered
FRAGRANT
AROMATIC FOLIAGE
CONTAINER PLANT

Description A small spreading shrub to 1 m with reddish stems and aromatic pinnate foliage. The pale pink star flowers have a strong perfume and are produced in spring.

Cultivation Grow in an open but partially shaded position with excellent drainage. This species requires plenty of moisture and the root area must be protected from direct sun. Tip prune when young and prune back after flowering.

Landscape Use A pretty, wispy plant for growing among other shrubs or beneath

Boronia denticulata

Boronia floribunda

tall trees. It is a good container plant provided it is watered regularly.

Boronia fraseri
FRASER'S BORONIA

Origin NSW
Climate WT, M
Shade Light to filtered
AROMATIC FOLIAGE
CONTAINER PLANT

Description A small shrub to 2 m with divided leaves on attractive, reddish, angular stems. Clusters of pink star flowers appear in spring.

Cultivation This species will grow in most soils but likes a little moisture. This can be achieved by mixing in some peat at planting time. It prefers a partially shaded position and will tolerate frosts. Prune to shape.

Landscape Use This is an attractive species to grow among other shrubs in the garden or use as a low screening plant.

Boronia fraseri

Boronia heterophylla
RED BORONIA; KALGAN

Origin WA
Climate WT, M, CT
Shade Light to filtered
SPECIMEN PLANT
FRAGRANT
AROMATIC FOLIAGE
CONTAINER PLANT

Description This is a compact, bushy shrub to 2 m. It has slender, aromatic bright green leaves and bears magnificent hanging magenta bell flowers, lightly perfumed, in spring. These are ideal for picking and remain fresh over a long period. This species has been extensively grown commercially as a cut flower.

Cultivation An easily grown boronia provided it is protected from hot winds and the roots are kept cool and moist. It prefers a shaded position but will grow in full sun if the roots are covered. It will tolerate frost. Take cut flowers or prune soon after flowering.

Landscape Use A beautiful small plant deserving a place on its own or among shrubs in the garden. It is particularly impressive when grown in groups or as a low hedge. It can also be used effectively as a container plant.

Boronia heterophylla

Boronia ledifolia

B. ledifolia (double pink-flowered form)

Boronia 'Lipstick'

Boronia ledifolia

LEDUM BORONIA; SYDNEY BORONIA

Origin Qld, NSW, Vic.
Climate WT, M
Shade Light to filtered
AROMATIC PLANT
CONTAINER PLANT

Description A small, compact shrub to around 1 m with very aromatic leaves in threes. From late July to spring it produces masses of deep pink star flowers. These are beautiful as cut flowers.

There are a white-flowered form and a beautiful double pink-flowered form in cultivation, but these are not always available.

Cultivation Grow in a protected, moist but well-drained position. Mulch to provide a cool root run. Prune back after flowering to encourage vigour and compact habit.

Landscape Use A beautiful boronia for planting under trees where it will tolerate quite heavy shade. It also makes a good container plant.

Boronia *'Lipstick'*

Origin A natural hybrid from WA (*B. heterophylla* x *B. crassipes*)
Climate WT, M, CT
Shade Light to filtered
AROMATIC PLANT
CONTAINER PLANT

Description An upright open shrub to around 1 m high with slender aromatic leaves. Prolific pink bell shaped flowers are borne in early spring.

Cultivation For best results adequate moisture and good drainage are required. It prefers a partially shaded position and will tolerate frosts. Mulch with organic material to keep the roots cool and prune after flowering to promote vigour. *B.* 'Lipstick' is relatively hardy in eastern Australia. Cut flowers are long lasting indoors.

Landscape Use This is a beautiful boronia for those established gardens partly shaded by large trees. It can also be grown in a container.

Boronia megastigma

BROWN BORONIA

Origin WA
Climate WT, M, CT
Shade Light to filtered
FRAGRANT
AROMATIC PLANT
CONTAINER PLANT

Description This is the well-known, sweetly scented brown boronia, famous for the beautiful and unusual perfume of its rich brown and yellow bell flowers, which appear in late winter and spring. It grows to about 1.5 m and has fine light green foliage which has a spicy aroma.

B. megastigma 'Heaven Scent' is a neat compact form to 1 m high.

The following colour forms are sometimes available from nurseries. All are sweetly perfumed.

B. megastigma 'Chandleri' — maroon flowers with red inside petals.

B. megastigma 'Harlequin' — candy stripe red and yellow flowers.

B. megastigma 'Lutea' — yellow-green flowers and yellow-green foliage.

B. megastigma 'Virtuosa' — very dark brown flowers.

Boronia megastigma

B. megastigma 'Lutea'

B. megastigma 'Chandleri'

B. megastigma 'Harlequin'

Cultivation The brown boronia has not got a reputation for always being long-lived. It requires a continuously moist, well-drained, friable soil that is never allowed to become waterlogged. It will tolerate frost. Taking cut flowers or pruning will promote vigour and growth for another season and maintain shape.

Landscape Use This is a beautifully perfumed shrub for planting near walkways, doors and windows where the scent will truly fill the air. If you have had no luck with cultivating this charming plant, buy several in bud and treat it as an annual. Place containers in baskets and position on patios, verandas and courtyards, where it will diffuse its sweet fragrance for all to enjoy.

Boronia microphylla
SMALL-LEAVED BORONIA

Origin Qld, NSW
Climate S, WT, M
Shade Light to filtered

AROMATIC FOLIAGE
CONTAINER PLANT

Description A low twiggy shrub which may reach 1 m, but is usually smaller. It has neat, shiny pinnate leaves and showy rose pink star flowers in summer.

Cultivation This colourful plant prefers good drainage and a moist semishaded situation. It will tolerate frost.

Boronia microphylla

Landscape Use Grow in the garden foreground or in a rockery pocket where it can spread. It makes a good container plant.

Boronia mollis
SOFT BORONIA

Origin NSW
Climate WT, M, CT
Shade Light to filtered

SPECIMEN PLANT
AROMATIC FOLIAGE

Description This is a rounded shrub to 2 m high. The aromatic leaves are pinnate and their undersurfaces and the stem are covered with fine hairs. The deep pink flowers are produced in great

Boronia mollis

abundance for long periods from late winter through spring.

B. mollis 'Lorne Pride' is a form found at Lorne, near Laurieton, NSW. It has a denser, more compact shape to 1.5 m.

Cultivation A light, well-drained soil with a surface mulch is best for this lovely boronia. It needs some protection from drying winds and likes dappled shade. It will tolerate frost. Prune after flowering to keep rounded and bushy. *B. mollis* 'Lorne Pride' will accept more sun than most other boronias.

Landscape Use A beautiful free-flowering specimen for the bush garden under the shade of a sparse-leaved eucalypt. The plant is bushy to the ground and may be trimmed to form a low screen or hedge.

Boronia molloyae

(syn. *B. elatior*)

TALL BORONIA

Origin WA
Climate WT, M, CT
Shade Light to filtered

SPECIMEN PLANT
AROMATIC FOLIAGE
CONTAINER PLANT

Description This species forms a dense, much-branched shrub to 1.5 m. The dark green aromatic leaves are downy with tiny hairs, and glowing pendent pink flowers are carried on numerous side branches in spring and summer. The flowers are excellent for cutting, remaining fresh over a long period.

Boronia molloyae

Cultivation This species likes mottled shade and a well-drained soil. Mulch regularly, particularly in summer, to aid retention of moisture. It is moderately frost-resistant. Prune back after flowering to prolong life.

Landscape Use This highly ornamental plant can be grown among other shrubs, in groups, or in rows to form a pretty screen or hedge. It makes a good container plant for a shady corner.

Boronia muelleri

FOREST BORONIA; PINK BORONIA

Origin NSW, Vic.
Climate WT, M, CT
Shade Filtered to full

SPECIMEN PLANT
AROMATIC FOLIAGE

Description This pretty boronia varies in habit from a rounded 1.5 m in cultivation to a slender tall tree to 6 m in its natural habitat of damp, shaded gullies. The fragrant fern-like leaves are carried on arching branches, and white to deep pink flowers in large open sprays appear in profusion in spring.

Boronia muelleri

B. muelleri 'Sunset Serenade'

B. muelleri 'Sunset Serenade' is a selected compact form with masses of pink star flowers.

Cultivation This is a hardy boronia that does well in a shady, moist part of the garden with good drainage. It is frost-tolerant.

Landscape Use A highly decorative shrub which blends beautifully with tree ferns and other ferns in a shady corner.

Boronia pilosa
HAIRY BORONIA

Origin Vic., Tas., SA
Climate WT, M, CT
Shade Light to filtered

AROMATIC FOLIAGE
CONTAINER PLANT

Description A dense rounded shrub to 1 m with hairy pinnate foliage. Masses of pink star-shaped flowers are produced in spring.

B. pilosa 'Rose Blossom' is a small shrub to around 50 cm with double deep pink flowers in profusion from late winter. This cultivar is considered easier to maintain in cultivation than the typical form.

Cultivation Grow in a partially shaded position with plenty of moisture but excellent drainage. Keep the roots cool by providing a mulch. It is frost-resistant. Prune after flowering to promote new growth.

Landscape Use A very pretty boronia for edging, rockery or container.

Boronia pilosa 'Rose Blossom'

Boronia pinnata

Boronia pinnata
PINNATE BORONIA

Origin NSW
Climate WT, M, CT
Shade Light to filtered

SPECIMEN PLANT
FRAGRANT
AROMATIC FOLIAGE
CONTAINER PLANT

Description An upright, slightly arching species to 2 m having fragrant, soft, segmented leaves. Attractive, lightly scented rose pink star flowers appear towards the ends of branches in late winter through spring. Sprays of flowers may be cut for the house.

Cultivation This hardy species prefers a friable, well-drained soil in a sheltered, partially shaded position. The root area must be kept cool. It is relatively frost-tolerant. Trim lightly after flowering.

Landscape Use This eye-catching species may be grown among other shrubs, where it will get the protection it needs. It will grow well in a large tub.

Boronia purdieana

Origin WA
Climate WT, M
Shade Light to filtered

FRAGRANT
CONTAINER PLANT

Description A small bushy shrub to around 80 cm with small pinnate leaves that are often downy. The beautifully scented, pendent yellow bell flowers are produced in late winter and spring.

Boronia purdieana

Cultivation Grow in a light-textured, well-drained soil in a protected position. It is moderately frost-tolerant. Prune back after flowering.

Landscape Use A prolific flowerer for the rockery or container.

Boronia rosmarinifolia
FOREST BORONIA

Origin Qld, NSW
Climate S, WT, M
Shade Light to filtered

SPECIMEN PLANT
CONTAINER PLANT

Description A loosely branching shrub which grows between 50 cm and 2 m high. It has slender leaves and bears pale to deep pink flowers from winter through spring.

Cultivation This understorey plant of open forests prefers dappled shade in a well-drained situation. It is hardy in subtropical gardens and coastal areas with some protection. It is moderately frost-tolerant.

Landscape Use A lovely shrub for the large rockery or for among other shrubs in the broken shade of eucalypts. It is also suitable for growing in a large container.

Boronia rosmarinifolia

Boronia safrolifera
SAFROLE BORONIA

Origin Qld, NSW
Climate S, WT, M
Shade Light to filtered
AROMATIC FOLIAGE
CONTAINER PLANT
Description A slender small shrub which varies in height from 50 cm up to 2 m. It has strongly aromatic pinnate foliage and has pale pink to rosy purple star flowers in spring.

Boronia safrolifera

Cultivation Grow in a moist but well-drained position. Mulch to create a cool root area and tip prune regularly to maintain shape and vigour. It is frost-resistant.

Landscape Use An ornamental boronia for growing beneath taller plants or in a protected position in the rockery.

Boronia serrulata
NATIVE ROSE; SYDNEY ROCK ROSE

Origin NSW
Climate WT, M
Shade Light to filtered
SPECIMEN PLANT
FRAGRANT
AROMATIC FOLIAGE
CONTAINER PLANT
Description This lovely boronia forms an attractive upright shrub to 1 m high, with rich green, toothed rhomboidal leaves, and vivid pink cup-shaped flowers at the ends of the branches in spring. The flowers have a beautiful perfume and make delightful cut flowers.

Cultivation The native rose is found growing in the protection of large shrubs amongst outcrops of Hawkesbury sandstone and demands the excellent drainage and moist cool root run that this habitat provides. It is frost-hardy.

Boronia serrulata

Landscape Use Grow as a pretty border plant or among other shrubs. It grows particularly well in the filtered shade of a raised rockery and makes a beautiful container specimen.

Boronia thujona
BRONZY BORONIA

Origin NSW
Climate WT, M
Shade Light to filtered
SPECIMEN PLANT
AROMATIC FOLIAGE
Description A loosely branching shrub which grows to about 2 m in cultivation. It has attractive fern-like deep green foliage and wide, starry, pale pink flowers from spring to summer.

Cultivation This species is quite adaptable to cultivation provided the roots are kept cool in a reasonably well drained soil. It is frost-tolerant. Prune after flowering to encourage bushiness.

Landscape Use Grow among other shrubs in the bush garden. It makes an attractive light screen plant.

Boronia thujona

BORYA
LILIACEAE

Named after J.B. Bory de St Vincent, a nineteenth-century French naturalist. There are three endemic species of these interesting tufted perennials with white pincushion flowers. They are found growing in damp soils of rocky gullies where water may flow or be present for long periods. They are commonly called 'resurrection plants' because when the habitat dries out the plants turn brown to orange-red, but with the onset of rain they again turn green. These attractive plants thrive very well next to water, and make interesting container plants. Propagation is by division or from stems that have produced roots.

Borya septentrionalis
PORCUPINE BUSH; RESURRECTION PLANT

Origin Qld
Climate T, S, WT
Shade Light to filtered
CONTAINER PLANT
Description A variable perennial which may form dense tufts to 60 cm in diameter. The leaves are crowded and end in sharp points; heads of small white flowers appear on slender stems in winter and spring.

Cultivation Grow in a humus-enriched, well-drained soil in semishade. It does best in moist situations, but can tolerate some periods of dry. It is frost-tender.

Landscape Use Grow in a rockery near a water feature. It makes an interesting container plant and may be taken indoors.

Borya septentrionalis

BRACHYCHITON
STERCULIACEAE

A genus of approximately 30 species of trees mostly native to Australia. They are mainly from the warmer northern areas and are grown as ornamentals or as street trees for their beautiful form, handsome foliage and spectacular flowers. Although reasonably hardy, they require a warm climate to bring out the best display of flowers. The leaves are entire or lobed and, although the tree is evergreen when not in flower, it may drop its leaves prior to flowering, which is often irregular. Common to all Brachychiton *species are the thick, leathery, boat-shaped seed pods containing numerous hairy seeds.* Brachychiton acerifolius *can be a source of an additional garden pleasure as it is the foodplant of one of Australia's more spectacular butterflies, the Tailed Emperor,* Polyura pyrrhus. *Propagation is from fresh seed, which germinates readily, but is often slow. They can also be propagated from cuttings, particularly in the tropics where they will strike readily.*

Brachychiton acerifolius
FLAME TREE

Origin Qld, NSW
Climate T, S, WT
Shade None to filtered
SPECIMEN PLANT
RAINFOREST PLANT
Description A magnificent ornamental tree to 30 m. It has a strong smooth trunk and dense light green maple foliage. In areas with a dry winter and spring the tree completely dispenses with its leaves to make way for a spectacular display of rich scarlet flowers commencing in late spring. The bell-shaped flowers are produced in loosely hanging panicles for several months. It may be slow-growing when young and will take a few years to flower.

Brachychiton acerifolius (tree)

Cultivation Plant in deep soil in an open sunny position for the best colour display. This tree requires frost protection in early years. After flowering mulch with well-rotted compost and apply slow-release fertiliser.

Landscape Use This spectacular specimen tree is best planted alone to show off its handsome pyramidal form and magnificent flowering display — in a large garden or as a street or park tree.

B. acerifolius

Brachychiton bidwillii
LITTLE KURRAJONG

Origin Qld, NSW
Climate T, S, WT
Shade None to filtered
SPECIMEN PLANT
Description An erect shrub or small tree up to 5 m. It has attractive, deeply lobed leaves, which are usually dropped when the flowers appear, after which the new foliage comes. The large bell flowers, a lovely deep rose colour, appear in clusters in summer.

Cultivation Grow in a full sun in a warm, well-mulched, well-drained position. Although from tropical and subtropical areas, this species will tolerate dry periods.

Brachychiton bidwillii

Cultivation Grow in a deep, moist but well-drained situation with protection from frost in early years.

Landscape Use A beautiful specimen tree for the large garden or park.

Brachychiton rupestris
BOTTLE TREE

Origin Qld, NSW
Climate T, S, WT, SA
Shade None to light
SPECIMEN PLANT

Description This beautiful, usually deciduous tree reaches a height of 20 m and can form a rather dense canopy of dark green entire or lobed narrow leaves. Small white flowers appear in spring, but it is the marvellous trunk that is the feature of this tree, as it swells into a bottle-like shape. The trunk contains a lot of soft tissue and a good deal of water and has been fed to cattle during times of drought.

Cultivation This slow-growing but adaptable tree is suited to most soils and situations and will accept fairly dry conditions. It is frost-hardy.

Landscape Use A specimen tree for larger gardens or parks where there is plenty of room to display its curious bottle-shaped trunk.

Brachychiton rupestris

Landscape Use A small decorative tree for garden, park or street planting.

Brachychiton discolor
WHITE KURRAJONG; LACEBARK

Origin Qld, NSW
Climate T, S, WT, M, SA
Shade None to filtered
SPECIMEN PLANT
BIRD-ATTRACTING
RAINFOREST PLANT

Description A handsome tree to 30 m, but it is slow-growing and is usually much smaller in cultivation. The downy dark green leaves with broad pointed lobes are shed before flowering, when large pink bell flowers covered with felt are produced, during summer.

Brachychiton discolor

BRACHYCOME
ASTERACEAE
(The spelling 'Brachyscome' is also in use.)

A genus of some 60 species of pretty, daisy-like plants found in all States. They are small annual or perennial herbs with flowers in colours of white, pink, mauve or blue. Some have taken very kindly to cultivation and their uses are many: as a border, in a rockery, for the courtyard, in pots or as ground covers. They look particularly attractive when mass-planted and are especially useful to jolly along a newly planted native garden with instant colour. Propagation of annual species is from seed. Perennial species are best propagated from cuttings or by division of the clumps.

Brachycome angustifolia
STIFF DAISY

Origin NSW, Vic., Tas., SA
Climate S, WT, M, CT, H
Shade None to light
CONTAINER PLANT
Description This small, suckering, mat-forming plant to about 50 cm across and 30 cm tall has soft, narrow, light green leaves and has dainty mauve to pink daisies in spring and summer.

Cultivation This species prefers a moist, protected situation that never dries out. It may be used as a bog plant for poolside planting. It is frost-resistant.

Landscape Use Grow near a water feature or as a ground cover in moist seepage areas. Can be grown in a container.

Brachycome angustifolia

Brachycome formosa
(syn. *B. pilligaensis*)

Origin NSW
Climate S, WT, M, CT
Shade None to light
CONTAINER PLANT
Description A low-growing prostrate perennial with bluish green lobed leaves and large rosy mauve flowers throughout spring and summer.

Cultivation This is a pretty plant for most sunny positions with regular watering in dry periods. It is frost-resistant.

Landscape Use The suckering habit makes this plant ideal for the rockery and other areas where a ground cover is required. It looks good in a large shallow terracotta container.

Brachycome formosa

Brachycome iberidifolia
SWAN RIVER DAISY

Origin SA, WA, NT
Climate WT, M, SA
Shade None to light
Description This is a branching annual to about 30 cm with pinnate leaves, and

Brachycome iberidifolia

daisy flowers in white, rose or purple in summer. This species may be bought in seed packets and is available in various colours.

Cultivation In cooler climates the seeds may be sown in seedling trays and planted out in early spring for summer flowers. In warmer areas scatter seeds in the garden in June for a cheery display in spring and summer. They will renew themselves year after year.

Landscape Use Grow as a border or in masses in the garden or rockery.

Brachycome multifida
CUT-LEAF DAISY

Origin Qld, NSW, Vic.
Climate S, WT, M, CT
Shade None to light

Description A compact perennial to 40 cm high and 1 m wide with finely divided leaves and many white, pink or, most usually, mauve daisy flowers throughout the year.

B. multifida 'Break of Day' bears dark mauve flowers in profusion for most of the year.

B. multifida var. *dilatata* has more compact leaf segments and form.

B. x *multifida* 'Lemon Drops' is a newly released hybrid which bears masses

Brachycome multifida

B. multifida (pink form)

B. multifida var. *dilatata*

of pale lemon coloured flowers throughout the warmer months.

Cultivation This hardy shrub does well in most situations but needs good sun and drainage. It is a trailing plant with a suckering habit, allowing easy division. Prune back older branches and trim to shape. It is frost-tolerant.

Landscape Use An ideal plant for the border or the rockery, or as a ground cover. It is perfect for the small garden or courtyard, providing colour for most of the year. Grow several in pots (it looks beautiful with terracotta) and place around patios or near steps, decks and verandas. They gracefully spill over the pots and so can also be used in hanging baskets.

BRACHYSEMA

FABACEAE

A small genus of some 16 species found mainly in Western Australia, with a few species extending to the Northern Territory. They are pea-flowered semiclimbing or prostrate creepers, usually with bright red flowers and attractive variable foliage that is sometimes silvery beneath. Most species are frost-hardy and those with a low spreading habit are particularly useful as ground covers on banks and in rockeries. Scale, sooty mould and some leaf-eating caterpillars are the main pests to watch for on Brachysema *species. Propagation is from half-hardened tip cuttings. Alternatively grow from seed that has been either scarified or treated with boiling water and let stand overnight.*

Brachysema celsianum

(syn. *B. lanceolatum*)

SWAN RIVER PEA

Origin WA
Climate S, WT, M, CT
Shade None to light

FAST-GROWING
BIRD-ATTRACTING
CONTAINER PLANT

Description This low-growing shrub to 1 m high has an eventual spread of about 3 m. It has bright green lanceolate leaves with a silvery underside. Bright red pea flowers with a silvery calyx are clustered along arching stems in spring, attracting honeyeaters. After flowering the new growth is silvery grey.

Brachysema celsianum

Cultivation This hardy, popular species demands good drainage but is not fussy as to soil. It prefers full sun but will grow in partial shade. It will tolerate most frosts.

Landscape Use This attractive, versatile plant may be pruned to form an upright dome-shaped bush, or can be trained to climb a trellis or fence. It can be used as a low screen, an informal hedge or a dense ground cover on sloping banks.

Brachysema latifolium

BROAD-LEAVED BRACHYSEMA

Origin WA
Climate WT, M, CT
Shade None to filtered

BIRD-ATTRACTING
CONTAINER PLANT

Description A vigorous ground cover plant with a spread to 1 m. It has dark green oval leaves with a silky undersurface, and it produces orange-red pea flowers from autumn to spring.

Cultivation This hardy species does best in light shade in a well-drained position. It is moderately frost-resistant.

Landscape Use This dense ground cover is ideal for small areas between shrubs, on sloping banks or spilling over walls. It is also suitable for large containers and hanging baskets.

Brachysema praemorsum

Origin WA
Climate WT, M, CT
Shade Light to filtered

FAST-GROWING
BIRD-ATTRACTING
CONTAINER PLANT

Description A prostrate creeper with a spread to 1.5 m. It has attractive fan-shaped leaves and bears dark red pea flowers through spring and summer.

Brachysema latifolium

Cultivation Grow in a lightly shaded position in a well-drained soil. It is moderately frost-resistant.

Landscape Use This is a good soil-binding plant that will cover banks and large areas between shrubs in the garden. It is attractive in rockeries or in containers or hanging baskets.

Brachysema praemorsum

BRACTEANTHA

ASTERACEAE

This newly named Australian genus was once included in the complex Helichrysum *which has long been under botanical revision and is no longer considered applicable to native Australian species.* Bracteantha *means 'bract flower'. A characteristic of this genus is the stiff, showy, usually yellow bracts that surround the flower heads. There are five named species and several not yet named species of this genus of annuals or short-lived perennial plants. The horticulturally well-known* Helichrysum bracteatum *has been assigned to this genus. It is grown for its bright papery flowers prized for their long lasting qualities when picked. When using flowers for dried floral arrangements, it is best to cut them just before they are fully opened and hang them upside down in an airy shady place to dry. Flowers with delicate stems can be wired. Young plants should be protected from slugs and snails. Infestations of aphids may be treated with an application of garlic spray. Propagation is from half-ripened tip cuttings for perennials and cultivars. Annuals are grown by seed from early winter or later in frost-prone areas.*

Bracteantha bracteata

(syn. *Helichrysum bracteatum*)

GOLDEN EVERLASTING

Origin All States
Climate S, WT, M, CT, H
Shade None to light
BIRD-ATTRACTING
CONTAINER PLANT

Description Many forms of this plant are available, including prostrate to tall growers, and both perennials and annuals. The leaves of all varieties are soft and woolly, and in most varieties large golden flowers with shining papery bracts appear over a long period in spring and summer. Annuals with flowers of many colours, including maroon and purple, have been produced by nurserymen and are sold commercially as straw flowers. All are excellent cut flowers, either fresh or in dried arrangements.

B. bracteata 'Bright Bikini' is a showy annual to 40 cm high. It can be bought as mixed seedlings and transplants well. Flowers continue for many months and are white, pink, yellow and dark red.

B. bracteata 'Cockatoo' is a beautiful perennial to 50 cm high and 1 m across with grey-green felty leaves. The white paper flowers opening to pale lemon are produced from late winter well into spring. This tough and vigorous plant provides lots of cut flowers, which should be taken often to encourage a fresh crop.

B. bracteata 'Dargan Hill Monarch' is a robust perennial to 50 cm high and 1 m across with rosettes of large woolly green leaves, and very large golden paper daisies to 7 cm in diameter in spring and summer.

B. bracteata 'Diamond Head' is a compact dwarf perennial to only 20 cm high and 60 cm across when the plant is

Bracteantha bracteata 'Bright Bikini'

B. bracteata 'Cockatoo'

B. bracteata 'Dargan Hill Monarch'

B. bracteata 'Diamond Head'

B. bracteata 'Princess of Wales'

in flower. The papery yellow flowers are borne above the foliage from late spring through summer.

B. bracteata 'Princess of Wales' is a perennial to around 60 cm tall and 1 m across, with golden paper flowers produced on long stems from spring to autumn. This cultivar was selected at the Australian National Botanic Gardens in Canberra and named in honour of the Princess of Wales on the occasion of her visit in November, 1985.

Cultivation Grow in a fairly rich, light soil to feed the long season of growth and flowering. A sunny position, good drainage and good watering are necessary. Prune back old growth to improve vigour.

Landscape Use All varieties make spectacular summer border and bedding displays. The dwarf 'Diamond Head' is a beautiful rockery or container plant and may be grouped and used as a ground cover.

BUCKINGHAMIA

PROTEACEAE

Named after the third Duke of Buckingham, this genus has only one named species, the beautiful Buckinghamia celsissima, *which naturally occurs on the Atherton Tableland and in other tropical rainforest pockets in northern Queensland. It is an excellent specimen tree and has become one of the most widely grown plants in northern gardens, streets and parks. Propagation is from fresh seed, which germinates readily.*

Buckinghamia celsissima

IVORY CURL FLOWER

Origin Qld
Climate T, ST, WT, M
Shade None to filtered

FAST-GROWING
SPECIMEN PLANT
FRAGRANT
RAINFOREST PLANT

Description A medium-sized tree to 6 m in cultivation, but much taller in its rainforest habitat. It has lovely dark green glossy leaves and beautiful pendulous spikes of cream curly flowers during summer. The flowers are sweetly perfumed, especially early in the morning. Flowers usually appear three years after planting.

Cultivation A beautiful tree that likes the tropics but will still flower as far south as Melbourne. It prefers a sunny position in moist but well-drained rich soils. It is frost-tender when young.

Buckinghamia celsissima

B. celsissima

Landscape Use An ideal specimen, street or public garden tree.

CALAMUS

ARECACEAE

These tall climbing palms or rattans are found in tropical rainforests throughout the world, with several species being found in north-eastern Queensland and one in southern Queensland and northern New South Wales. They are all climbing plants armed with vicious spines which help them climb through other plants. The spines are extremely sharp and clinging, and a popular name for the plant is 'wait-a-while' because of their delaying effect when they anchor on clothing. The strong, flexible, fibrous stems, commonly known as rattans, have been used extensively for weaving and for making cane furniture and basketware in overseas countries. They have been used to a lesser extent in northern Queensland in the making of lobster pots, baskets and more recently bush furniture and crafts.

They are not widely cultivated in Australia, but one species, C. muelleri, *is sometimes available and is grown as an attractive rainforest and container plant. Propagation is from seed, which should be sown when fresh.*

Calamus muelleri

LAWYER CANE

Origin Qld, NSW
Climate T, S, WT
Shade Filtered to full

BIRD-ATTRACTING
CONTAINER PLANT
RAINFOREST PLANT

Description This hook-climbing palm reaches far into the canopy of rainforests. The slender stems are covered with sharp, spreading prickles and the palm-like leaves have scattered prickles on their margins. It bears masses of small flowers which are followed by round white seeds.

Cultivation Grow out of direct sunlight in a compost-enriched soil with plenty of moisture. It is frost-tender.

Landscape Use Grow in the 'rainforest' section of the garden. Although slow-growing, it should be positioned where the spines cannot be troublesome. It makes an interesting container plant, ideal for indoors or out.

Calamus muelleri

CALANTHE

ORCHIDACEAE

A genus of some 120 species of terrestrial and epiphytic orchids from tropical regions of the world, with one species occurring in eastern Australia. The name is derived from the Greek kalos, *beautiful, and* anthos, *flower, and many exotic species and cultivars are grown for their beauty and for the cut flower trade. Propagation is by division or from seed.*

Calanthe triplicata

(syn. *C. veratrifolia*)

CHRISTMAS ORCHID

Origin Qld, NSW
Climate T, S, WT, M
Shade Light to filtered

CONTAINER PLANT
RAINFOREST PLANT

Description This lovely orchid is usually found on the floor of rainforests with its roots spreading through the leaf litter. It has broad leaves up to 60 cm long and has many delicate white flowers borne on erect stems to 1.2 m in summer.

Cultivation In warm areas, this species will grow well in a well-drained, humus-enriched, shaded position in the garden. When grown in southern States, it requires the protection and warmth of a glasshouse. It needs to be grown in a large pot to accommodate its extensive root system and it enjoys a good orchid compost and a plentiful supply of water.

Landscape Use A beautiful orchid to grow among ferns and under tree ferns or other trees in the garden. An excellent container plant.

Calanthe triplicata

CALLICOMA

CUNONIACEAE

This genus, consisting of one species C. serratifolia, *is endemic to eastern Australia. Its common name, Black Wattle, comes from early days when settlers used the branches in 'wattle and daub' construction. The creamy flowers with long spreading stamens superficially resemble those of many* Acacia *species, although it is quite unrelated to that genus. It is an attractive small tree, popular in cultivation, and gets the name* Callicoma *from the Greek* kalos, *beautiful, and* kome, *hair, because of the plant's numerous fluffy flower heads.*

Propagation is from seed or half-ripened tip cuttings.

Callicoma serratifolia

BLACK WATTLE

Origin Qld, NSW
Climate T, S, WT, M
Shade Light to filtered

FAST-GROWING
SPECIMEN PLANT
RAINFOREST PLANT

Description A multistemmed tall shrub or small tree to 12 m, but usually much smaller in cultivation. It has attractive, deep green, shiny, serrated leaves that are woolly white on the underside. Masses of fluffy cream flower balls provide a lovely display in spring.

Cultivation This species grows rapidly and develops a lush appearance if planted in a rich, moist position with some protection from heat and wind. It is moderately frost-resistant.

Landscape Use A handsome specimen plant for form, foliage and flower.

Callicoma serratifolia

CALLISTEMON

MYRTACEAE

There are some 25 species of bottlebrushes endemic to Australia. They are found in all States, usually in damp areas such as swamp margins and around streams and rivers. They are among the most popular ornamental native plants cultivated in both Australian and overseas gardens. They are extremely hardy, long-lived and adaptable, and have bright, conspicuous flowers. In fact the botanical name is derived from kalos, *meaning beautiful, and* stemon, *a stamen, referring to the spikes of clustered flowers with conspicuous stamens. Bottlebrushes flower in late spring and through summer, and some species flower again in autumn. All species attract bees and nectar-feeding birds to the garden.*

Bottlebrushes range in height from dwarf to small trees. The narrow to lanceolate foliage is often leathery, with a prominent midrib. Often new foliage is richly coloured, usually pink or bronze, making a colourful display for many months of the year. In many species the oil in the leaves is aromatic when crushed.

Although the main flower is generally red, pink, cream or green, a large number of new cultivars have been produced, adding white, mauve, burgundy and purple to this range. Bottlebrushes are versatile and hardy and fit into most landscape situations. Many of the larger species can be used as small street trees by removing lower branches on the trunk and leaving the top to branch out.

All the species respond well to pruning in the final days of flowering. Removal of the flowerheads promotes a denser growth habit as well as extra flowers and increases the chances of twice-a-year flowering. Although bottlebrushes adapt to dry conditions, many enjoy moist soils and appreciate copious water during dry periods. They flower best in full sun.

Callistemons are subject to few pests and diseases, the main problem being occasional infestations of scale insects which can be easily controlled with white oil.

Propagation is from the fine seed, which is produced in numerous woody capsules along the stems. The best seed is obtained from the oldest seed capsules, and it should be placed in a paper bag to dry. Germination rate is usually high and it is best to sow the seed thinly to avoid overcrowding and weak seedlings in the seed bed. Selected forms and cultivars are grown from half-ripened tip cuttings. Some can prove difficult to strike, so a rooting hormone should be used.

Callistemon citrinus

(syn. *C. lanceolatus*)

CRIMSON BOTTLEBRUSH; LEMON-SCENTED BOTTLEBRUSH

Origin NSW, Vic.
Climate T, S, WT, M, CT
Shade None to filtered

FAST-GROWING
SPECIMEN PLANT
AROMATIC FOLIAGE
BIRD-ATTRACTING
CONTAINER PLANT

Description A widely cultivated species with a great variety of forms varying in height from 2 to 6 m. Leaves are flat, broad and leathery, often with a sharp point, and have a pungent lemon odour when crushed. The flowers are a rich red and are usually produced in great numbers from spring to December and often again in mid-autumn.

This species hybridises freely and many beautiful garden varieties have been distributed under this name.

C. citrinus 'Anzac' is a low-growing, compact form to 2 m with soft light green new foliage, and vigorous white bottlebrush flowers in spring and autumn.

C. citrinus 'Austraflora Firebrand' is a spreading, arching shrub to 1 m high and 2.5 m across with silvery pink new growth

Callistemon citrinus 'Anzac'

C. citrinus 'Austraflora Firebrand'

C. citrinus (crimson)

C. citrinus 'Endeavour'

C. citrinus 'Reeves Pink'

C. citrinus 'Western Glory'

and masses of red brushes in spring and autumn. Its sweeping habit makes it a particularly interesting specimen.

C. citrinus 'Endeavour' is a compact grower to 3 m with large flat leaves and masses of large brilliant red bottlebrush flowers, often borne in clusters during early spring and autumn, and making superb cut flowers. This is one of the best bottlebrushes and is widely cultivated overseas. It is also known as 'Splendens'.

C. citrinus 'Reeves Pink' is a much-branched shrub to 3 m with profuse clusters of rose pink flowers. This is one of the best pink-flowering varieties.

C. citrinus 'Western Glory' is a medium shrub to 3 m with masses of deep pink flowers tinged with lilac, produced in spring and often again in autumn.

Cultivation All of the described forms of *C. citrinus* are easy to obtain and may be planted in any position or soil, including really wet conditions or in seaside gardens with some protection from heavy salt winds. After flowering, prune just below the dead flower to promote attractive new growth and more flowers in the future. They are able to withstand heavy frosts.

Landscape Use *C. citrinus* and *C. citrinus* 'Endeavour' are probably the best of all the bottlebrushes for hedging. All forms of *C. citrinus* make lovely screen plants or beautiful specimens, and grow and flower well in tubs.

Callistemon comboynensis
CLIFF BOTTLEBRUSH

Origin Qld, NSW
Climate T, S, WT, M
Shade None to filtered

FAST-GROWING
SPECIMEN PLANT
BIRD-ATTRACTING
CONTAINER PLANT

Description In nature, this bottlebrush grows in pockets on open cliffs or on rugged mountains, where it is straggly and often almost prostrate, but in cultivation it becomes an extremely attractive spreading bushy shrub to 2.5 m high and up to 1.5 m across. It has fairly narrow leaves and new growth is a lovely copper colour. Rich orange-red flowers appear for most of the year, commencing in early spring.

Cultivation This hardy species will grow in almost any soil in full sun or semishade, although it does require better drainage than most other bottlebrushes. It is moderately frost-resistant.

Landscape Use Use as a specimen or among other shrubs. It is also suitable for planting in tubs.

Callistemon comboynensis

Callistemon *'Harkness'*
(sometimes listed as *C.* 'Gawler Hybrid')

Origin Garden hybrid from Gawler, South Australia
Climate T, S, WT, M, CT, SA
Shade None to filtered

FAST-GROWING
SPECIMEN PLANT
BIRD-ATTRACTING
CONTAINER PLANT

Description This spectacular bottlebrush is a shrub or small tree to 6 m. It has an attractive drooping habit, and has fairly narrow light green foliage which is greenish bronze when fresh. Superb brilliant red brushes with a soft appearance are produced in great profusion in spring, and again in autumn in good years. These provide beautiful flowers. It may take a couple of years to flower profusely.

Cultivation This hardy species grows well in all soils, including limy ones. It may be planted in coastal gardens with some protection and is frost-resistant in most areas. Prune lower branches, if desired, to form tree-like growth.

Landscape Use Grow as a specimen, screen plant or street tree with correct pruning. It also makes an attractive container plant.

Callistemon 'Harkness'

Callistemon *'King's Park Special'*

Origin Hybrid from King's Park, WA
Climate S, WT, M, CT, SA
Shade None to filtered

FAST-GROWING
SPECIMEN PLANT
BIRD-ATTRACTING
CONTAINER PLANT

Description A large, bushy shrub with a vigorous growth to around 4 m. The branches are slightly pendulous, with shiny dark green foliage. Masses of bright red brushes in groups appear in spring and early summer.

Cultivation This species is extremely hardy in all soils and conditions and will

Callistemon 'King's Park Special'

withstand dry periods as well as heavy frosts.

Landscape Use This is an excellent specimen or street-planting species. It can also be used as a screen and is very beautiful as a tub plant.

Callistemon macropunctatus

(syn. *C. coccineus*)

SCARLET BOTTLEBRUSH

Origin NSW, Vic., SA
Climate S, WT, M, CT, SA
Shade None to filtered

SPECIMEN PLANT
BIRD-ATTRACTING
DROUGHT-RESISTANT
CONTAINER PLANT

Description This spreading shrub to 3 m has leathery pointed foliage and a semidrooping habit. The attractive crimson brushes have yellow-tipped stamens and appear in late spring. If picked soon after opening, the flowers last well in water.

Callistemon macropunctatus

Cultivation Although this species likes a light soil in a moist situation, it is able to withstand long dry periods. It is moderately salt-tolerant and withstands frost. Prune after flowering to promote compact growth.

Landscape Use Grow as a screen or specimen plant. A good street plant in dry areas. It is also suitable for growing in a container.

Callistemon pachyphyllus

WALLUM BOTTLEBRUSH

Origin Qld, NSW
Climate T, S, WT, M
Shade None to filtered

FAST-GROWING
SPECIMEN PLANT
BIRD-ATTRACTING
CONTAINER PLANT

Description An erect, open shrub to around 3 m with thick, textured flat leaves. The terminal flower spikes are dark red and appear erratically most of the year, often starting while the plant is quite young.

C. pachyphyllus var. *viridis* is the green Wallum Bottlebrush, with narrow leaves and weeping pendulous branches. It develops into a bushy shrub to 2 m and bears marvellous apple green bottlebrushes in spring and autumn.

Pink and prostrate forms are also available from native plant nurseries in Queensland.

Callistemon pachyphyllus

Cultivation The Wallum Bottlebrush is found in swampy coastal heaths of northern New South Wales and southern Queensland and will tolerate fairly bad drainage. The green form prefers a well-drained but moist situation. Both are good for coastal gardens if not directly exposed to salt-laden winds. Prune after flowering to promote a denser growth habit.

Landscape Use Grow as a specimen or among other shrubs in the garden. The green form is particularly attractive in a large tub.

C. pachyphyllus var. *viridus*

Callistemon pallidus

LEMON BOTTLEBRUSH

Origin NSW, Vic., Tas.
Climate WT, M, CT, H
Shade None to filtered

SPECIMEN PLANT
FRAGRANT
AROMATIC FOLIAGE
BIRD-ATTRACTING
CONTAINER PLANT

Description An attractive, erect and spreading shrub to around 4 m high and up to 3 m across. The grey-green leaves are aromatic when crushed, and new growth is silky and is a delicate silvery pink. The fragrant lemon yellow flowers, which appear in dense clusters in spring and summer, are most attractive and bring honeyeaters to the garden.

This is a variable species and several different colour forms are available from nurseries.

Callistemon pallidus 'Austraflora Candle Glow' is a prostrate form to 1 m tall with a spread of 2.5 m.

Callistemon pallidus 'Clearview Father Christmas' is a low, spreading form which has white stamens tipped with red.

Cultivation A very adaptable species that will grow in most soils and conditions including very wet, shady, windy and cold. It is frost- and snow-resistant and may be planted in coastal gardens with some protection. Prune after flowering to keep shrub bushy.

Landscape Use This is an excellent species for use as a windbreak, hedge or screen. It makes a lovely specimen with its dainty yellow flowers, and looks good in a tub.

Callistemon pallidus

Callistemon *'Perth Pink'*

Origin Cultivar from WA
Climate WT, M, CT
Shade None to filtered

FAST-GROWING
SPECIMEN PLANT
BIRD-ATTRACTING

Description An attractive shrub to around 2 m with slender lanceolate leaves and pink new growth. The flowers are a deep pink and are produced in spring and again in autumn if conditions are right.

Cultivation This hardy shrub grows in most soils and conditions, but does respond well to summer watering. It is frost-tolerant. Prune after flowering to maintain a densely foliaged shrub.

Landscape Use A good pink-flowering specimen which will also form a very attractive screen or informal hedge. It also makes a pretty container plant.

Callistemon 'Perth Pink'

Callistemon pinifolius

Origin NSW
Climate WT, M, CT
Shade None to filtered

SPECIMEN PLANT
BIRD-ATTRACTING
CONTAINER PLANT

Description A handsome, variable species which grows to around 2 m. It has stiff, narrow, pine-like leaves and bears yellowish, apple green or rich red flowers in spring. All forms are beautiful, but it is the green colour form that has attracted the attention of gardeners, and provides stunning cut flowers for the house.

Cultivation A hardy species that does best in full sun in a moist position. It is frost-resistant. Prune after flowering to encourage an attractive bushy shape.

Landscape Use Grow as a specimen or among other shrubs for a refreshing green colour accent. It makes a particularly attractive container plant.

Callistemon rigidus
STIFF BOTTLEBRUSH

Origin Qld, NSW
Climate T, S, WT, M, SA
Shade None to filtered

SPECIMEN PLANT
BIRD-ATTRACTING
CONTAINER PLANT

Description An erect shrub to around 2 m with rigid, pointed leaves and dense spikes of crimson brushes with gold-tipped stamens. The flowers appear throughout summer.

Cultivation This adaptable, hardy species from damp coastal habitats is very useful for wet problem areas, as well as low rainfall gardens. It may also be grown in

Callistemon pinifolius

seaside gardens if not directly exposed to salt-laden winds. It is frost-resistant. Prune after flowering to maintain shape.

Landscape Use Grow as a fence cover, hedge or windbreak. It may also be grown in a large container.

Callistemon rigidus

Callistemon salignus

WILLOW BOTTLEBRUSH; PINK TIPS

Origin Qld, NSW, SA
Climate T, S, WT, M, CT, H
Shade None to filtered

FAST-GROWING
SPECIMEN PLANT
BIRD-ATTRACTING
ORNAMENTAL FOLIAGE
CONTAINER PLANT

Description Growing to around 8 m, this attractive weeping shrubby tree has beautiful papery bark. It has fairly narrow leaves and distinctive coppery pink new growth, often appearing twice a year. The flowers are usually creamy yellow, but attractive pink and red colour forms are also available. Flowering is usually in spring and early summer.

Callistemon salignus

Cultivation This is an extremely adaptable plant for a wide range of soils and situations. It will grow in moist or dry conditions or near the coast. It tolerates most frosts.

Landscape Use An exceptionally beautiful specimen for street planting, parks or gardens. It is suitable for shelter, screen, windbreak or hedge planting and looks particularly attractive in a very large tub.

C. salignus (pink form)

Callistemon sieberi

(syn. *C. pityoides*)

ALPINE BOTTLEBRUSH

Origin Qld, NSW, Vic.
Climate WT, M, CT, H
Shade None to filtered

SPECIMEN PLANT
BIRD-ATTRACTING
CONTAINER PLANT

Description This attractive, compact shrub to 1 m occurs naturally at high elevations. The leaves are needle-like, and new growth is silky. Small, dense creamy yellow brushes are borne at the ends of the branches in summer. A form from lower altitudes with spreading branches will reach a height of about 3 m or more.

Cultivation This adaptable species is very hardy in most situations. It prefers a moist soil but will do well in drier sites. It is frost-resistant and will tolerate snow. Prune back after flowering to encourage compact growth.

Callistemon sieberi

Landscape Use An ornamental plant to grow singly or as a little thicket of hedge. It grows well in a container.

Callistemon speciosus

(syn. *C. glaucus*)

ALBANY BOTTLEBRUSH

Origin WA
Climate WT, M, CT
Shade None to filtered

SPECIMEN PLANT
BIRD-ATTRACTING
CONTAINER PLANT

Description This beautiful species forms a stiffly spreading shrub to around 3 m. It has narrow leathery leaves with a prominent midrib and bears especially large, bright crimson bottlebrushes in spring and summer.

Cultivation A hardy shrub for most soils and situations, but thriving in swampy

Callistemon speciosus

or moist conditions in full sun. It is frost-resistant.

Landscape Use A magnificent specimen that is especially suited to growing in wet problem areas. It will grow well in a container, but must be kept well watered.

Callistemon subulatus

Origin NSW, Vic.
Climate S, WT, M, CT
Shade None to filtered

FAST-GROWING
SPECIMEN PLANT
BIRD-ATTRACTING
CONTAINER PLANT

Description A most attractive little spreading shrub about 1.5 m high and 1.5 m wide. The linear leaves are slightly hairy when young. Many compact dark red brushes appear on pendulous branches from late spring through summer, attracting a variety of honeyeaters.

Cultivation A very hardy plant which will grow in heavy or light soils, provided adequate moisture is available. It is frost-hardy. It benefits from a good pruning to promote growth and flowering.

Landscape Use A delightful shrub for the small garden or courtyard. It forms an attractive screen and is an excellent container plant.

Callistemon viminalis
WEEPING BOTTLEBRUSH

Origin Qld, NSW
Climate T, S, WT, M, CT, H
Shade None to filtered

FAST-GROWING
SPECIMEN PLANT
BIRD-ATTRACTING
CONTAINER PLANT

Description This gracefully weeping bottlebrush will grow to a small tree to around 5 m, although it can grow taller. It has a rough, scaly bark and particularly attractive light green foliage with bronze-coloured new growth. Masses of long-lasting red brushes appear in spring.

C. viminalis 'Captain Cook' is a hardy, popular shrub growing to a compact 1.5 m with long narrow leaves, weeping branches and masses of bright red brushes in spring.

C. viminalis 'Dawson River' is a slender weeping tree to 10 m high with crimson flower spikes 12 cm long.

C. viminalis 'Hannah Ray' is a small weeping tree to 5 m with attractive grey-green foliage and long crimson flower spikes in spring and sometimes again in autumn.

C. viminalis 'Little John' is a beautiful dwarf shrub to 1 m with attractive grey-green foliage and squat, dark red brushes with golden tips in spring.

Cultivation A very hardy species that will grow in most soils and conditions, including very wet to very dry. It will tolerate only moderate frosts.

Landscape use The tree forms of the Weeping Bottlebrush make outstanding specimen, street or park trees. They may also be grown in very large tubs as

Callistemon subulatus

Callistemon viminalis

C. viminalis 'Dawson River'

C. viminalis 'Captain Cook'

C. viminalis 'Hannah Ray'

courtyard specimens. 'Captain Cook' will fit snugly in any small garden and 'Little John' is an excellent rockery plant. Both dwarf forms look splendid in containers.

Callistemon *'Violaceus'*

Origin Cultivar
Climate WT, M, CT
Shade None to filtered
BIRD-ATTRACTING
CONTAINER PLANT
Description A medium-sized branching shrub to 3 m high. It has leathery leaves tapering to a point, and purplish red brushes in spring.

Cultivation This species is hardy in most soils and conditions. It is frost-resistant. Prune back after flowering to ensure prolific blooming and dense growth.

Landscape Use A decorative dense shrub which may be used as a feature, fence screen or hedge.

C. viminalis 'Little John'

Callistemon 'Violaceus'

Callistemon viridiflorus
GREEN BOTTLEBRUSH

Origin Tas.
Climate WT, M, CT
Shade None to filtered
BIRD-ATTRACTING
CONTAINER PLANT
Description A medium-sized erect shrub to around 3 m. It has narrow dark green leaves with a sharp tip and bears greenish yellow brush flowers in late spring and summer.

Cultivation This hardy species is suitable for growing in poorly drained areas in heavy or clay soils. It is frost-resistant. Prune back after flowering to encourage branching and a good crop of flowers.

Landscape Use A pretty shrub for the garden, as a screening plant or in a container.

CALLITRIS
CUPRESSACEAE

A beautiful genus of native conifers comprising about 16 species found in all parts, including the dry inland. They are commonly known as cypress pines and they make excellent ornamentals with an erect columnar shape, bright green or bluish foliage and attractive knobbly seed cones which provide food for cockatoos and parrots.

Cypress pines make good screens, windbreaks, or specimen, street or shelter trees. Some have the ability to withstand prolonged drought, making them valuable for planting in inland gardens and country properties. Growth rate is moderately fast and most species are tolerant of frost. The Callitris *sawfly larvae feed on most species of* Callitris *and may cause serious foliage damage.* *See page 9 for treatment.* *Propagation is from the small winged seeds obtained from the small round cones.*

Callistemon viridiflorus

Callitris columellaris

COASTAL CYPRESS PINE; BRIBIE ISLAND PINE

Origin Qld, NSW
Climate T, S, WT, M
Shade None to light
SPECIMEN PLANT
BIRD-ATTRACTING
CONTAINER PLANT

Description This species was once included with the widespread inland species that is now known as *Callitris glaucophylla. C. columellaris* is found in subtropical coastal areas of Queensland and northern New South Wales. It is an upright ornamental conifer to around 15 m with fine, dense, very dark green foliage.

Callitris columellaris

Cultivation This species occurs naturally in deep coastal sands and will grow in almost pure sand. It likes a well-drained position and is suitable for seaside gardens. It is frost-resistant.

Landscape Use A good specimen or shade tree and an excellent windbreak.

Callitris glaucophylla

(syn. *C. columellaris*)

WHITE CYPRESS PINE

Origin Qld, NSW, Vic., WA, NT
Climate S, WT, M, SA
Shade None to light
SPECIMEN PLANT
BIRD-ATTRACTING
DROUGHT-RESISTANT
CONTAINER PLANT

Description This species has for many years been known as the inland form of *C. columellaris*, and some nurseries and forestry departments still sell it under this name. It is a slender, erect tree with a variable height of up to 20 m and has very fine grey-green foliage on slender spreading branches. The small solitary cones rarely remain on the tree long after maturing. In some areas, such as the Pilliga State Forest, NSW, trees form almost pure stands and are valuable in timber production. The attractively grained timber is durable and resistant to termites and is used in flooring and furniture.

Cultivation An excellent species for growing in dry inland areas, where it will tolerate extended dry periods. It demands excellent drainage and is frost-resistant.

Landscape Use A good specimen, shade and shelter tree for private and public places in rural areas. It looks particularly

Callitris glaucophylla

attractive when planted in groves on country properties.

Callitris macleayana
STRINGYBARK CYPRESS PINE

Origin Qld, NSW
Climate T, S, WT, M
Shade Light to filtered

SPECIMEN PLANT
BIRD-ATTRACTING
CONTAINER PLANT
RAINFOREST PLANT

Description Occurring in a few rainforest pockets of the coastal ranges, this species may reach 20 m, but is usually much smaller in cultivation, where it forms a shapely columnar tree to around 10 m. It is distinguished by its fibrous bark and whorls of sharply-pointed foliage which goes coppery red in winter.

Cultivation This species is hardy under most conditions and thrives in moist soils with good drainage. It prefers some shade protection when young, but will adapt to full sun. It is frost-tolerant.

Landscape Use An excellent specimen as a background to shrubs or as groups in a large garden. It is rather slow-growing and makes an attractive container plant.

Callitris macleayana

Callitris oblonga
TASMANIAN CYPRESS PINE

Origin NSW, Tas.
Climate WT, M, CT, H
Shade None to filtered

SPECIMEN PLANT
BIRD-ATTRACTING
CONTAINER PLANT

Description A large shrub or small shapely tree to no more than 8 m tall. It has whorls of grey-green leaves and attractive small pointed cones.

Cultivation This hardy and adaptable plant does best in a well-drained position. It will withstand moderately dry conditions and is tolerant of heavy frosts. Shaping is acceptable although rarely necessary.

Landscape Use With its compact formal appearance, small stature and hardiness some growers consider this species one of the best native cypress pines. It is an ideal substitute for exotic conifers and will give visual variety to an informal garden. It also makes an excellent container plant.

Callitris rhomboidea
OYSTER BAY PINE; PORT JACKSON PINE

Origin Qld, NSW, Vic., Tas.
Climate S, WT, M, CT, H
Shade None to filtered

FAST-GROWING
SPECIMEN PLANT
BIRD-ATTRACTING
CONTAINER PLANT

Description An attractive, narrow plant up to 10 m with a slightly weeping habit in new growth. The foliage is deep green, neat and feathery.

Cultivation Grow in a well-drained position with plenty of moisture in summer. It may be grown in coastal gardens with some protection and will withstand moderately dry conditions. It is frost-tolerant.

Callitris oblonga

Callitris rhomboidea

Landscape Use A widely planted species which forms a graceful specimen tree. It is very useful for planting as a windbreak or screen and makes a very attractive container plant.

CALOSTEMMA

AMARYLLIDACEAE

An attractive Australian genus of four species of lily-like plants with strap-like leaves which may die down each year. The trumpet-shaped blooms are produced on erect leafless stems in round terminal clusters. These charming plants make a colourful show over many weeks. They are easy to grow and multiply readily. Propagation is from the fleshy seeds, which germinate very easily.

Calostemma luteum

YELLOW GARLAND LILY

Origin Qld, NSW, SA
Climate S, WT, M
Shade None to filtered
CONTAINER PLANT
Description A bulbous herb with tufts of long shiny dark green leaves, and clusters of funnel-shaped yellow flowers on erect stems to 60 cm from summer to autumn. The foliage dies down each year and usually reappears after the flowers.

Calostemma luteum

Cultivation A hardy plant that tolerates moist to dry soils, but must have good drainage and a sunny position. It is frost-resistant.

Landscape Use An attractive species when mass-planted in the garden or used as a rockery plant. It may also be grouped in large tubs.

Calostemma purpureum

GARLAND LILY

Origin NSW, Vic., SA
Climate WT, M
Shade None to filtered
CONTAINER PLANT
Description A bulbous herb with dark green leaves to 40 cm and clusters of pink to reddish purple trumpet-shaped flowers on erect stems to 60 cm from summer to

Calostemma purpureum

autumn. Foliage dies down each year and in some conditions may not appear again until after the flowering.

Cultivation A hardy plant that tolerates moist to dry soils, but must have good drainage and a sunny position. It is frost-resistant.

Landscape Use An attractive species when mass-planted in the garden or used as a rockery plant. It may also be grouped in large tubs.

CALOTHAMNUS

MYRTACEAE

A genus of Western Australian shrubs comprising about 36 species. They are rigid shrubs with pine-like foliage and prominent, mostly red flowers clustered around or along one side of the branches; hence they are often referred to as 'one-sided bottlebrushes'. Many of the species are cultivated and most are hardy and popular as specimens and as hedging shrubs. The flowers are most attractive to honeyeaters. Prune lightly after flowering or regularly throughout the year. Prune hard into the old wood only when regenerating an elderly leggy bush, as flowers are produced on older wood. Propagation is from seed, which is retained in tightly packed seed cases that remain on the plant indefinitely. Propagate also from half-ripened tip cuttings taken in summer.

Calothamnus quadrifidus (prostrate form)

Calothamnus quadrifidus

ONE-SIDED BOTTLEBRUSH; NET-BUSH

Origin WA
Climate WT, M, CT, SA
Shade None to filtered

FAST-GROWING
SPECIMEN PLANT
BIRD-ATTRACTING
CONTAINER PLANT

Description An upright, dense shrub reaching to around 2 m. It has greyish to deep green, pine-like foliage which may be covered in fine hairs. The prominent flowers composed of bundles of rich red stamens bloom from late spring and through summer. Some flowers appear throughout the year. An unusual yellow-flowered form is also in cultivation.

C. quadrifidus prostrate is a multibranched, low, spreading form to 60 cm with a spread of about 2 m.

C. quadrifidus

Cultivation This very hardy plant is the most popular species of the genus in cultivation. It will grow in most soils, will tolerate dry conditions and is suitable for coastal planting with some protection. It will withstand most frosts.

Landscape Use This ornamental species may be grown as an individual specimen or as a hedging or screening shrub. The prostrate form is very pretty at the front of a garden, or grown on a rocky slope and allowed to tumble over in a natural way.

Calothamnus rupestris

CLIFF NET-BUSH

Origin WA
Climate WT, M, CT
Shade None to filtered

SPECIMEN PLANT
BIRD-ATTRACTING
CONTAINER PLANT

Description A large, spreading shrub which may grow to around 2 m. It has thick, crooked branches crowded with needle leaves and bearing pinkish red bundles of claw flowers in spring.

Calothamnus rupestris

Cultivation A hardy shrub suited to light to medium soil in a well-drained open position. It will withstand dry conditions, will tolerate light frosts and is moderately resistant to salty sea winds.

Landscape Use An attractive ornamental as an individual, among other shrubs or as a windbreak.

Calothamnus sanguineus

BLOOD-RED NET-BUSH

Origin WA
Climate WT, M
Shade None to filtered

SPECIMEN PLANT
BIRD-ATTRACTING

Description This tall, spreading shrub growing to around 2.5 m has silky, but prickly, pine-like leaves. Bundles of blood red claw-like flowers may appear from late spring through to the following winter.

Cultivation This popular ornamental prefers an open, sunny, well-drained position in a light soil. It is moderately drought- and frost-resistant and will grow near the coast with some protection. Keep bushy with regular light pruning.

Landscape Use This shrub may be planted as a screen or windbreak. It will flower in semishade and may be planted beneath sparsely leaved trees in the garden.

Calothamnus sanguineus

Calothamnus villosus
SILKY NET-BUSH

Origin WA
Climate WT, M, CT
Shade None to filtered
SPECIMEN PLANT
BIRD-ATTRACTING

Description A handsome, densely hairy shrub reaching up to around 3 m. It has hairy, crowded pine-like leaves, and showy, rich red bundles of flowers through spring and summer with intermittent flowers throughout the year.

Cultivation This hardy plant withstands dry conditions and some coastal exposure. It will do well in most soils, but likes good drainage. It is moderately frost-resistant.

Calothamnus villosus

Landscape Use Plant as a single specimen, or as a fence screen, windbreak or hedge.

CALYTRIX
MYRTACEAE

This is a beautiful group of some 50 species of heath-like shrubs. Although they are found mainly in Western Australia, a few eastern species are well known in cultivation. They are ornamental medium-sized shrubs with fine aromatic foliage, and they are often referred to as fringe myrtles, as the calyx lobes terminate in bristle-like points. Masses of starry blossoms, often hiding the foliage, have many thread-like filaments arising from the flower centre. After flowering the persistent, richly coloured calyces remain on the bush for several weeks, giving an added decorative feature to these charming plants. In nature they are often found growing in groups, and they give far more impact when planted this way. Propagation is from half-ripened tip cuttings.

Calytrix alpestris
(syn. *Llotzkya alpestris*)
SNOW MYRTLE

Origin Vic., SA
Climate WT, M, CT, SA
Shade Light to filtered
AROMATIC FOLIAGE
CONTAINER PLANT

Description A compact shrub to 2 m high with hairy, aromatic leaves at right angles to the stems. Masses of white star flowers with pretty pink buds cover the bush in spring.

Cultivation This plant will thrive in a well-drained, moist position in light shade. A regular light pruning will maintain attractive shrubbiness. It is frost-resistant.

Calytrix alpestris

Landscape Use A very attractive garden shrub, especially in groups or as a low screen. A good compact container plant.

Calytrix sullivanii

Origin Vic.
Climate WT, M, CT
Shade Light to filtered
BIRD-ATTRACTING
CONTAINER PLANT

Description A compact, erect shrub to 2 m with crowded fresh green leaves. Masses of white starry flowers are produced in clusters at branch ends during spring.

Cultivation Grow in a lightly shaded position with good drainage. It is not fussy about soils and is very lime-tolerant. It will withstand frost and dry periods and may be grown in protected coastal gardens. Prune to shape.

Landscape Use An ornamental shrub which gives a good splash of white to the spring garden or rockery. It may be used as an attractive informal hedge or as a container plant.

Calytrix tetragona

Calytrix sullivanii

Calytrix tetragona
FRINGE MYRTLE

Origin Qld, NSW, Vic., Tas., SA, WA
Climate S, WT, M, CT, SA
Shade None to light
FAST-GROWING
AROMATIC FOLIAGE
CONTAINER PLANT

Description An upright, spreading plant which varies throughout its wide distribution from a dwarf to a medium shrub of around 2 m. The tiny, crowded leaves have a spicy lemon scent when crushed. The beautiful small flowers from pure white to shades of pink appear in masses near the ends of the branches in spring. After flowering the calyces with long curling threads remain on the plant for some weeks, turning a decorative purplish bronze. The flowers and later the colourful branches may be picked for indoors.

Cultivation An adaptable species which does best in a well-drained soil in sun or light shade. It is frost-resistant and is suitable for coastal gardens with some protection. A light pruning after flowering will maintain bushiness.

Landscape Use This shrub makes splendid garden decoration when mass-planted, as an informal hedge, or along a small garden walk. It makes a beautiful container plant.

CANAVALIA
FABACEAE

This genus of twiners and trailers is mainly found in tropical regions, with three species extending to the coasts of northern Australia, Queensland and New South Wales. The leaves are usually composed of three large leaflets and the showy pea flowers are white to purplish pink. The seed pods are large and fleshy. In some species both pods and seeds have a reputation for being poisonous in the raw state. Propagation is from the seed, which is first soaked in hot water and left to stand overnight.

Canavalia maritima
(syn. *C. rosea*)
MACKENZIE BEAN; COASTAL JACK BEAN

Origin Qld, NSW, WA, NT
Climate T, S, WT
Shade None to filtered
SALT-TOLERANT

Description A common sprawling creeper on coastal sand dunes and in inland areas. It has bright green trifoliate leaves and large pink pea flowers in autumn. The large bean-like pods contain seeds which were eaten by Aborigines after being thoroughly cooked.

Cultivation Grow in a warm, well-drained sunny position. It will tolerate

Canavalia maritima

extreme coastal exposure, but is a more attractive and vigorous plant if given some protection. It is frost-tender.

Landscape Use Grow as a ground cover for sloping banks or large areas. Ideal for low-maintenance areas of seaside gardens.

CARPOBROTUS

AIZOACEAE

A genus with representatives in many countries; Australia has some four species distributed chiefly along the seashore and one in inland areas. These prostrate succulents, popularly known as pigface, have fleshy three-sided leaves and showy purplish flowers. They develop roots at the leaf nodes along the stems and may spread over considerable areas in sand dunes. As well as having decorative foliage and flowers, they have excellent sand-binding qualities against erosion. The leaves and fleshy fruits of some species were eaten by Aborigines and explorers. Propagation is readily carried out from cuttings or from division of layers.

Carpobrotus glaucescens

Carpobrotus glaucescens

COASTAL NOONFLOWER

Origin Qld, NSW
Climate T, S, WT, M
Shade None to light

FAST-GROWING
SALT-TOLERANT
CONTAINER PLANT

Description A succulent, spreading plant up to 3 m wide with thick, fleshy, grey-green leaves, and large deep pink or purple flowers in spring and summer.

Cultivation Grow in a sunny, well-drained position. The plant occurs often in coastal sand dunes and as it develops roots at the leaf nodes along the stems it is ideal as a sand binder in seaside gardens.

Landscape Use A hardy ground cover suitable for areas of low maintenance. It will trail over rocks and may be grown in a container.

Carpobrotus modestus

INLAND PIGFACE

Origin Vic., SA, WA
Climate WT, M, SA
Shade None to filtered

DROUGHT-RESISTANT
CONTAINER PLANT

Description A succulent trailing plant to 3 m wide with bluish green, sometimes reddish, leaves and with small purple to magenta flowers in spring and summer.

Cultivation Although from inland areas, this species will grow almost anywhere in a well-drained soil. It will tolerate very dry conditions as well as frost.

Carpobrotus modestus

Landscape Use This is a decorative ground cover or rockery plant. It may also be grown in a container.

Carpobrotus rossii
KARKALLA

Origin Vic., Tas., SA, WA
Climate WT, M, CT, SA
Shade None to filtered

SALT-TOLERANT
CONTAINER PLANT

Description A prostrate creeper with stems covering an area of up to 2 m. It has triangular bluish leaves and has light purple flowers in summer. The fruit is a red, edible, fleshy berry that was relished by Aborigines.

Cultivation Widespread and common in coastal areas, this plant is ideal for growing in seaside gardens, where it is capable of covering a large area. It will withstand periods of dryness.

Landscape Use Grow as a ground cover, in rockeries or as a spillover plant on walls and banks.

Carpobrotus rossii

CASSIA
CAESALPINIACEAE

A large genus with representatives in tropical and temperate regions of the world, with some 40 species found in Australia. They vary from prostrate plants to medium-sized trees with pinnate leaves and showy, mostly yellow, buttercup flowers, often in large clusters. The fruits, which are bean-like, contain rows of seeds which are released when the outer covering of the pod dries and splits. Many exotic species are cultivated and some of our own cassias make delightful ornamental plants. As well as being fast growers, they are hardy plants and are conspicuous with their bright yellow flowers. Cassias are subject to borer attack which if left untreated could kill the plant. Propagation is from seed. Seeds have a hard coat and require abrasion or hot water treatment before sowing. Seedlings will not stand excessive humidity.

Cassia aciphylla

Cassia aciphylla
(syn. *C. revoluta*)
SPRAWLING CASSIA

Origin Qld, NSW, Vic.
Climate S, WT, M
Shade None to filtered

CONTAINER PLANT

Description An attractive small spreading shrub up to 1.5 m high and 1 m across with dark green pinnate leaves and clusters of yellow flowers in spring and summer.

Cultivation Grow in an open, sunny position with good drainage. It will tolerate some frost and may be pruned to maintain a compact habit.

Landscape Use A good foreground, rockery or container plant.

Cassia artemisioides
SILVER CASSIA

Origin NSW, SA, NT
Climate S, WT, M, SA
Shade None to filtered

SPECIMEN PLANT
FRAGRANT
DROUGHT-RESISTANT
ORNAMENTAL FOLIAGE
CONTAINER PLANT

Description A bushy shrub with a low, branching habit to around 2 m. It has beautiful silvery grey pinnate leaves and the bush is covered with fine silky-white down, which gives it the popular name of silver cassia. It flowers in late winter and spring, bearing short sprays of bright yellow buttercup flowers with a delicate perfume.

Cultivation This versatile shrub grows naturally in the dry inland and is perfect for the garden in low rainfall areas. It will also do well in coastal areas with some protection from salt-laden winds. It will grow in most soils, including limy ones, but needs very good drainage and a hot, sunny position. It needs protection from severe frosts. Prune after the main flush of flowers to keep compact growth.

Landscape Use An outstanding plant which provides a beautiful foliage contrast in the garden. It may be used as a specimen, low screen or windbreak. It is great for the small garden or in a container in the courtyard.

Cassia artemisioides

Cassia nemophila

(syn. *C. eremophila*)

DESERT CASSIA

Origin NSW, Vic., SA, WA, NT
Climate WT, M, SA
Shade None to filtered

DROUGHT-RESISTANT

Description This is an exceedingly variable species with several named varieties as well as a range of natural hybrids. It is a small to medium, rounded shrub to 2.5 m high, with finely divided leaves, either terete or flattened linear, which taper to a fine slightly hooked point. The small clusters of bright yellow flowers appear from late winter and through spring, almost completely covering the plant when it is in full flower.

Cassia nemophila

Cultivation This widespread species is hardy and attractive in most soils and conditions. It will tolerate drought and some coastal exposure with protection. It tolerates moderate frosts.

Landscape Use A good ornamental for inland gardens private and public gardens. It is very useful as a hedging or screening plant.

Cassia odorata

Origin Qld, NSW
Climate T, WT, M, SA
Shade None to filtered

FRAGRANT
CONTAINER PLANT

Description A rounded shrub to 2 m with attractive dark green fern-like leaves, and masses of yellow buttercup flowers in spring which on some bushes have a delicate perfume.

A prostrate form to 50 cm high is sometimes available.

Cultivation A popular garden shrub which adapts to a wide range of soils and conditions, but must have regular watering to bring it to perfection. It does not mind some shade and can be sited under any open-topped tree. It will tolerate moderate frost, especially if it has some protection.

Cassia odorata

Landscape Use This graceful plant is useful for softening architecture and walled areas such as courtyards. It may also be used as a privacy screen. The prostrate form is a charming shrub for the small garden or rockery. It may also be grown in a container.

CASTANOSPERMUM

FABACEAE

A genus with only one species, C. australe, *found in rainforests in eastern Australia. The name* Castanospermum *is from the Greek* castanos, *chestnut tree, and* sperma, *seed, referring to the large chestnut-like seed, and the plant is often known in cultivation as the Moreton Bay Chestnut. It is better known in the timber trade as Black Bean for its dark brown, attractive figured timber is highly regarded as a cabinet wood. Propagation is from seed, which germinates very easily when fresh.*

Castanospermum australe

BLACK BEAN; MORETON BAY CHESTNUT

Origin Qld, NSW
Climate T, S, WT, M
Shade None to filtered

SPECIMEN PLANT
BIRD-ATTRACTING
ORNAMENTAL FOLIAGE
CONTAINER PLANT
RAINFOREST PLANT

Description This is a very handsome tree with a beautiful dense canopy reaching to 15 m in cultivation. It has shining dark green leaves and brilliant red to orange-red pea flowers in sprays along the branches on the old wood. Flocks of honeyeaters, parrots and lorikeets are attracted to the flowers in spring. These are followed by large bean-like pods. The seeds are regarded as being poisonous.

Cultivation Black Bean is one of the best known rainforest species in cultivation as a street tree and in the garden. It prefers rich, well-drained soil and ample moisture, but is remarkably adaptable and can be grown in temperate areas. A light frost is tolerated.

Landscape Use A magnificent shade and specimen tree for parks, street and large gardens. Seedlings make excellent indoor foliage plants.

CASUARINA

CASUARINACEAE

Some former species of Casuarina *have been transferred to a new genus* Allocasuarina. *As many nurserymen and forestry departments still sell these plants under the name* Casuarina, *all species have been included here under this heading for convenience. These shrubs or trees have graceful fine branchlets or stems with inconspicuous leaves. Male and female flowers are separate, either on the same plant or on different plants, depending on the species. The male plant in bloom has a reddish or brown covering of minute individual flowers along the tips of the stems. The female plant has little red tassel-like flowers which catch the wind-borne pollen and produce the next season's cones. These cones are most attractive to seed-eating birds. Casuarinas have a distinctive Australian character and are exceptionally beautiful. Because of their hardiness they are very popular in cultivation. They are generally fast-growing and may be planted singly or in groups. As they will withstand harsh, windy conditions they are ideal for wind protection. Propagation is by seed which usually germinates readily.*

Casuarina cristata

BELAH

Origin Qld, NSW, Vic., SA, WA
Climate WT, M, SA
Shade None to light

FAST-GROWING
BIRD-ATTRACTING
DROUGHT-RESISTANT
ORNAMENTAL FOLIAGE

Description A medium-sized tree to around 12 m found in drier areas across the continent. It is pyramidal in growth and has grey-green branches. The male

Castanospermum australe

Casuarina cristata

and female flowers appear on separate trees.

Cultivation This hardy and adaptable species will grow in most soils and situations. It is ideally suited to dry areas but may also be used in protected coastal gardens. It is frost-resistant.

Landscape Use A very useful shade and shelter tree for around properties in the country. It is well-suited for windbreaks and the foliage is edible to stock.

Casuarina cunninghamiana

RIVER OAK

Origin NT, Qld, NSW
Climate T, S, WT, M, CT, H
Shade None to light

FAST-GROWING
SPECIMEN PLANT
BIRD-ATTRACTING
ORNAMENTAL FOLIAGE

Description A handsome tall tree found along river and stream banks, both on the coast and inland. It grows to around 20 m and has slender branchlets with a graceful, slightly drooping habit.

Cultivation A hardy and adaptable tree for most soils and most conditions except extreme cold and drought. It is frost-resistant.

Landscape Use A good specimen and screening tree. It is beautiful for avenue planting and is useful in erosion control. The fallen needles make an excellent mulch.

Casuarina decaisneana

(now *Allocasuarina decaisneana*)

DESERT OAK

Origin SA, WA, NT
Climate SA
Shade None to light

FAST-GROWING
DROUGHT-RESISTANT
ORNAMENTAL FOLIAGE

Description A tall, straight and fairly symmetrical tree to around 18 m. It has a spreading canopy of grey-green drooping foliage. The decorative cylindrical cones are the largest of all casuarina cones.

Cultivation This is a valuable tree for very dry inland conditions, where it will grow in very sandy soil. It is frost-resistant.

Casuarina cunninghamiana

Casuarina decaisneana

C. distyla

Landscape Use A handsome tree for large gardens, parks and streets.

Casuarina distyla

(now *Allocasuarina distyla*)
SHE-OAK

Origin Qld, NSW
Climate S, WT, M
Shade None to filtered

BIRD-ATTRACTING
SALT-TOLERANT
ORNAMENTAL FOLIAGE

Description A dense large shrub to 4 m with long, coarse grey-green, branchlets. At flowering time the male plants take on an attractive bronzy-red hue.

Cultivation This extremely hardy species will tolerate dry conditions and may be used in coastal gardens. It is frost-resistant.

Landscape Use A good casuarina for the smaller garden. It will form a good hedge and windbreak.

Casuarina distyla (male flowers)

Casuarina equisetifolia

HORSETAIL SHE-OAK; COASTAL SHE-OAK

Origin Qld, NSW, NT
Climate T, S, WT
Shade None to light

FAST-GROWING
SPECIMEN PLANT
BIRD-ATTRACTING
SALT-TOLERANT
ORNAMENTAL FOLIAGE

Description A beautiful coastal species found mainly in tropical and subtropical areas of Australia, and the one casuarina that extends to South-East Asia. It is a graceful tree to around 9 m with weeping silvery grey branches.

Cultivation An excellent species for seaside planting, where it will grow in very sandy soils and accept the full blast of salt-laden winds. It is an excellent soil binder and is used by councils in dune stabilisation and reclamation of land.

Landscape Use An attractive specimen for windbreaks and street tree for windy sea-fronts.

Casuarina equisetifolia

Casuarina glauca

SWAMP OAK

Origin Qld, NSW, Vic., WA
Climate T, S, WT, M, SA
Shade None to filtered

FAST-GROWING
BIRD-ATTRACTING
ORNAMENTAL FOLIAGE

Description This inhabitant of saline marshes is a handsome, tall, spreading tree to around 20 m high and about 10 m wide. It has slightly drooping branchlets that are often bunched in large plumes and are most ornamental.

Cultivation This species thrives in very wet coastal conditions and as it spreads by suckers it is an excellent soil or sand binder. It is adaptable to most soils, including salty ones, and will also withstand dry conditions. It is frost-resistant.

Casuarina glauca

Landscape Use An excellent shade and street tree that may also be used as a windbreak.

Casuarina littoralis

(syn. *C. suberosa*)
(now *Allocasuarina littoralis*)
BLACK SHE-OAK

Origin Qld, NSW, Vic., Tas.
Climate T, S, WT, M, CT
Shade None to light

FAST-GROWING
SPECIMEN PLANT
BIRD-ATTRACTING
ORNAMENTAL FOLIAGE

Description An upright, shapely tree to 10 m. It has dusky green branchlets with

Casuarina littoralis (fruit)

C. littoralis

a slightly drooping habit. The male trees are red-tipped in spring with masses of tiny flowers.

Cultivation This adaptable species is suited to any well-drained soil and position. It will tolerate dry periods and grows well in protected coastal gardens. It is frost-resistant.

Landscape Use An attractive specimen tree that can also be used as a windbreak in parks, roadsides and rural properties.

Casuarina paludosa

(now *Allocasuarina paludosa*)
SWAMP SHE-OAK

Origin NSW, Vic., Tas., SA
Climate WT, M, CT, H
Shade None to light

BIRD-ATTRACTING
ORNAMENTAL FOLIAGE

Description An attractive small bushy shrub which rarely exceeds 3 m. It has short rigid branchlets that are bronze-tipped when in flower.

Cultivation This very hardy species will thrive in most well-drained soils. It will withstand dry and protected coastal conditions and is tolerant of extreme cold and frost.

Landscape Use This casuarina is ideal for the small garden where space is of prime importance. It is also suitable as

Casuarina paludosa

a dense hedge or low windbreak in rural areas.

Casuarina stricta

(now *Allocasuarina verticillata*)
DROOPING SHE-OAK

Origin NSW, Vic., Tas., SA
Climate WT, M, CT, SA
Shade None to filtered

FAST-GROWING
SPECIMEN PLANT
BIRD-ATTRACTING
SALT-TOLERANT
ORNAMENTAL FOLIAGE

Description A shapely, spreading tree to 10 m high and 6 m across with long dark green drooping branchlets. Flowers are produced from autumn to spring and are followed by ornamental cones.

Cultivation A very hardy and adaptable species for most soils and conditions. It

Casuarina stricta (fruit)

will withstand periods of dryness and severe coastal exposure, and it will grow in poor coastal sands. It is frost-tolerant.

Landscape Use A versatile tree that may be used as a specimen, for shade and shelter, as a windbreak or in street planting. The foliage provides useful subsistence fodder.

Casuarina stricta

Casuarina torulosa

(now *Allocasuarina torulosa*)

FOREST OAK

Origin Qld, NSW
Climate T, S, WT, CT
Shade None to light

SPECIMEN PLANT
BIRD-ATTRACTING
ORNAMENTAL FOLIAGE
CONTAINER PLANT

Description A shapely erect tree to 15 m with slender drooping branchlets. Under certain conditions the branchlets are a lovely coppery colour, which gives the tree a most delightful appearance. It has an attractive trunk with rough corky bark.

Cultivation This hardy species will grow in most reasonably well drained soils. It will withstand dry periods, protected coastal conditions and frost.

Landscape Use A fine-foliaged tree for specimen planting in most gardens and parks. It makes an attractive container

Casuarina torulosa

plant but it takes years for the marvellous trunk to develop.

CERATOPETALUM

CUNONIACEAE

A small genus of five species occurring in rainforests and moist open forests of eastern New South Wales and Queensland. They are small to large trees with small, inconspicuous flowers. After flowering, the calyx enlarges and becomes a colourful pink or deep red. This feature is particularly noticeable in the celebrated New South Wales Christmas Bush, which is widely cultivated and is popular as a long-lasting flower at Christmas. The flowers of the Christmas Bush may be damaged by thrips before the calyx has time to redden. Severe infestations may be controlled by garlic spray. Scale insects may be found on the leaves and stems and may be treated with an application of white oil. Propagation is from the fine seed, which germinates easily when freshly collected.

Ceratopetalum gummiferum (calyx)

Ceratopetalum gummiferum

NSW CHRISTMAS BUSH

Origin NSW
Climate S, WT, M
Shade None to filtered

SPECIMEN PLANT
CONTAINER PLANT
RAINFOREST PLANT

Description A shrub or small tree to around 6 m with shiny green leaves with

C. gummiferum

C. gummiferum (flower)

bronze new growth. It bears masses of small starry white flowers in spring. When the flowers die, the remaining calyx turns red and enlarges, giving the impression that the plant has red flowers in summer. Cut branches are perfect for floral arrangements.

C. gummiferum 'Christmas Snow' is a variegated form with green and white foliage.

C. gummiferum 'White Christmas' is an interesting cultivar which has white calyces at maturity instead of the usual red.

Cultivation Christmas Bush requires a deep, well-drained soil with plenty of water over dry periods. It will grow in a semishaded position, but full sun is preferred for good colouring. Colour can also be improved by abundant water or by sprinkling a handful of sulphate of iron around the roots in spring. Prune to keep growth bushy. It will tolerate most frosts.

Landscape Use An outstanding ornamental with tidy habits, either as a specimen or as a hedge. The cultivars make attractive container plants.

CHAMELAUCIUM

MYRTACEAE

Of the some 20 species of this Western Australian genus, only one is widely cultivated, the Geraldton Wax Flower, C. uncinatum. *Several other species have been tried in cultivation; all are attractive shrubs with narrow leaves and white, pink or red stiff waxy flowers. Perfect drainage is required to avoid fungal attack and scale attack may be controlled with white oil. Propagation is from half-ripened tip cuttings.*

Chamelaucium ciliatum

Origin WA
Climate S, WT, M, SA
Shade None to filtered
CONTAINER PLANT
Description An attractive little tufted shrub to around 1 m high or less. It has linear leaves 1 cm long and pale pink, waxy flowers, ageing to deeper pink in spring. Cut sprays make long-lasting cut flowers.

Cultivation Grow in a very well drained open position with adequate watering over dry periods. Prune lightly to keep shape. It is frost-tolerant.

Chamelaucium ciliatum

Landscape Use This beautiful little plant is best planted in the rockery or a raised garden bed, where it gets the perfect drainage it demands. It can also be grown in a container.

Chamelaucium uncinatum

GERALDTON WAX

Origin WA
Climate S, WT, M, CT, SA
Shade None to light
FAST-GROWING
BIRD-ATTRACTING
Description An open, spreading shrub to 2 m high and 2 m across with narrow needle foliage and masses of pale pink waxy flowers in spring. These make excellent cut flowers of long-lasting beauty.

Beautiful white-flowered forms are available as well as many colourful cultivars. The following are two particularly good dark-coloured forms:

C. uncinatum 'Purple Pride' has dark red or purple flowers.

C. uncinatum 'University Red' has weeping needle foliage and dark red flowers.

Cultivation Grow in a light, well-drained soil. This is a plant from fairly dry areas and one that does not favour excess water.

Chamelaucium uncinatum

C. uncinatum (white-flowered form)

C. uncinatum (flower)

C. uncinatum 'Purple Pride'

Cheiranthera cyanea

It will grow well in protected coastal gardens and will tolerate most frosts. Cut flowers freely for decoration and prune well when flowering has finished.

Landscape Use A dainty open shrub for the garden, or as a fence screen or informal hedge.

CHEIRANTHERA

PITTOSPORACEAE

A small endemic genus of four species of small shrubs or lightly twining plants with vivid blue flowers that have prominent anthers. These sit up like fingers of a hand, giving these pretty plants the common name of finger flower. Propagation is from seed or half-ripened tip cuttings.

Cheiranthera cyanea

(syn. *C. linearis*)

FINGER FLOWER

Origin NSW, Vic., SA
Climate WT, M
Shade None to filtered

CONTAINER PLANT

Description A small shrub up to 50 cm high with slender spreading branches. It has fine, narrow leaves and produces deep violet-blue flowers with prominent yellow anthers during spring.

Cultivation Grow in a fairly sunny position with good drainage. It will withstand periods of dryness and is frost-resistant.

Landscape Use A very pretty little shrub for a small rockery pocket, or as a container or flowerpot plant.

CHORIZEMA

FABACEAE

This genus contains approximately 15 species and all are endemic to Western Australia except for one occurring in Queensland and New South Wales. The French explorer and botanist Labillardière is said to have named this plant from the Greek choros, *a dance, and* zema, *a drink, when his thirsty expedition party discovered this plant near a fresh waterhole. These shrubs are hardy and, with their masses of intensely coloured pea flowers, make very decorative garden plants. Chorizemas may be attacked by caterpillars and sap-sucking insects which can be controlled by garlic spray. Propagation is from seed after treatment in hot water, or from half-ripened tip cuttings.*

Chorizema cordatum

HEART-LEAVED FLAME PEA

Origin WA
Climate WT, M, CT
Shade Light to filtered

FAST-GROWING
CONTAINER PLANT

Description A low spreading shrub to 1 m high and up to 2 m across with heart-shaped leaves with spines and wavy margins. Spikes of vivid, bright orange and red, pea-shaped flowers appear for long periods from late winter.

Several colour forms are available from specialist nurseries.

Cultivation Moist soils are suited to this adaptable plant, but it requires good drainage. It is best planted with some shade, where flower colour becomes more intense. Left unpruned, it will become a semiprostrate scrambler, but if pruned after flowering and pinched back occasionally, it makes a neat compact

Chorizema cordatum

bush. It is moderately frost-resistant and may be grown near the coast with some protection.

Landscape Use This makes an outstanding understorey shrub for the garden. Its scrambling habit is good for ground cover work, and it looks striking if allowed to spill over banks, walls or rocks. It may be grown in large hanging baskets or tubs.

Chorizema dicksonii
YELLOW-EYED FLAME PEA

Origin WA
Climate WT, M
Shade Light to filtered
CONTAINER PLANT
Description A small, well-branched shrub to around 1 m or less. It has narrow oval leaves tapering to a point and has pea flowers of varying shades of red with a yellow base from late winter through spring.

Cultivation This understorey plant prefers partial shade in a well-drained soil with a good mulch. It needs protection from frost. Prune back after flowering.

Landscape Use A very good small ornamental for growing under taller shrubs or trees for a splash of bright colour. This is a good rockery or container plant.

Chorizema ilicifolium
HOLLY FLAME PEA

Origin WA
Climate WT, M, CT
Shade Light to filtered
FAST-GROWING
CONTAINER PLANT
Description A variable species which may be a semi-climber with long, slender branches or a short, erect shrub to around 2 m. The holly-like leaves have prickly teeth and the plant bears masses of orange and red pea flowers in spring.

Cultivation Grow in a lightly shaded position in a well-drained but moist soil with a good mulch. Prune after flowering. This species is frost-tender.

Landscape Use An attractive spillover plant to drape over walls, banks or rockery. It may be grown in a hanging basket or large container and is lovely for the small garden.

CHRYSOCEPHALUM
ASTERACEAE

A genus of seven small Australian sub-shrubs or perennials which were previously included under the revised Helichrysum. *Several new species are still to be segregated and named. The flower heads are usually arranged in terminal clusters and have small soft floral bracts. Most species are low spreading and make attractive rockery, ground cover or edging plants. They are moderately frost tolerant, but resent hot, humid weather with prolonged summer rain. Propagation is from half-ripened tip cuttings or by division of suckering forms.*

Chrysocephalum apiculatum
(syn. *Helichrysum apiculatum*)
COMMON EVERLASTING

Origin All States
Climate S, WT, M, CT, H, SA
Shade None to filtered
CONTAINER PLANT
Description There are many forms of this variable perennial and a number are available at nurseries. It varies in height from a prostrate layering variety to a rounded form to 30 cm tall by 1 m across. The green to silver-grey leaves with a small point at the tip are often covered with dense, woolly white hairs. Clusters of small golden flower heads are produced from spring to autumn.

Cultivation A hardy species that will grow in most soils and conditions,

Chorizema dicksonii

Chorizema ilicifolium

Chrysocephalum apiculatum

provided drainage is good. It likes lots of sun and is frost-resistant. Prune hard in late winter to encourage vigorous new growth.

Landscape Use A lovely spreading plant for the rockery, garden edge or container.

Chrysocephalum baxteri
(syn. *Helichrysum baxteri*)
WHITE EVERLASTING

Origin NSW, Vic., SA
Climate WT, M, CT
Shade None to light
CONTAINER PLANT

Description A low-growing shrub which forms a rounded clump to 30 cm high. It has narrow grey-green leaves and produces papery white flowers with yellow centres in spring and early summer.

Cultivation This species does best in a sunny, open position in any well-drained soil. It is frost-resistant.

Landscape Use A bright little plant for borders, rockeries or containers.

Chrysocephalum baxteri

Chrysocephalum ramosissimum
(syn. *Helichrysum ramosissimum*)
YELLOW BUTTONS

Origin Qld, NSW
Climate S, WT, M, SA
Shade None to light
CONTAINER PLANT

Description A low-growing prostrate suckering plant to 1 m across with narrow leaves lightly covered with soft woolly hairs. Bright golden ball flowers appear in small clusters in spring and summer. Cut flowers make a pretty, long-lasting nosegay for a small vase.

Cultivation This species will grow in most well-drained soils in open sunshine. It flowers best when adequate water is supplied. Collect seed after it has flowered and treat as an annual.

Landscape Use A beautiful ground cover plant for borders or rockery pockets. It also makes a pleasing container plant.

CISSUS
VITACEAE

A large group of some 350 vigorous climbing plants found throughout the world, with about 14 species occurring in a variety of habitats in Australia. Most have very attractive foliage and they are popular as indoor and container plants. Propagation is from seed from ripened fruit or from half-ripened tip cuttings, which should strike easily.

Cissus antarctica
KANGAROO VINE

Origin Qld, NSW
Climate T, S, WT, M
Shade Light to filtered
FAST-GROWING
BIRD-ATTRACTING
ORNAMENTAL FOLIAGE
CONTAINER PLANT
RAINFOREST PLANT

Description A vigorous woody climber with tendrils and bright green, heart-shaped leaves with toothed margins. It has attractive bronze new growth. The fairly insignificant greenish flowers are followed by round, blackish purple, edible fruits.

Cissus antarctica

Cultivation This species is one of the most popular under cultivation. It will grow well in shade and likes well-composted moist soil in a warm position. It may be pruned back to prevent unwanted growth.

Landscape Use Suitable for covering a pergola or fence or scrambling over the ground on sloping banks. It can be grown in containers and makes an excellent indoor plant for sunrooms in cooler climates.

CLEMATIS
RANUNCULACEAE

This large genus with cosmopolitan distribution has more than 250 species, widely cultivated for the beauty of their flowers and their graceful climbing habit. Many produce seed heads almost as delightful as their flowers. Australia has some six species, occurring in all States. They are quite spectacular in their natural surroundings when masses of frothy white flowers light up the bush with delicate beauty. Most species are happy in home gardens and make most attractive climbers for many situations. Propagation is from seed, which should be sown when fresh, or from stem cuttings from leaf nodes.

Clematis aristata
TRAVELLER'S JOY; OLD MAN'S BEARD

Origin Qld, NSW, Vic., Tas.
Climate T, S, WT, M, CT
Shade None to filtered
FAST-GROWING
FRAGRANT

Description A vigorous climber which may reach up to 10 m. It has light green entire or irregularly toothed leaflets. The masses of starry white flowers in spring are followed by the fluffy white seed heads, which persist for a long time, becoming fluffier as they mature. These last well into summer and are the reason why this climber is call Old Man's Beard. This species is variable and has many forms.

Cultivation Grow in a moist, sheltered position, giving a cool root run but not bad drainage. It should be in a position

Clematis aristata

where it can reach a sunny spot for best flowering. It is frost-resistant.

Landscape Use A beautiful quick cover for walls, pergolas and fences. It may also be grown among large shrubs and trees where it can climb and wander freely through the branches.

Clematis microphylla
SMALL-LEAVED CLEMATIS

Origin Qld, NSW, Vic., Tas., SA, WA
Climate T, S, WT, M, CT, SA
Shade None to filtered
FAST-GROWING
Description A slender, light-growing climber with small narrow leaflets. Masses of creamy white flowers in spring are followed by attractive fluffy white seed heads.

Cultivation This species will grow in full sun to semishade in any soil provided the drainage is good. It will tolerate dry conditions and will grow in coastal gardens with some protection. It is frost-resistant.

Landscape Use This is a well-behaved climber that looks particularly attractive when allowed to mingle with other shrubs and trees. It may be trained to cover fences and pergolas and works well as a ground cover.

COMMERSONIA
STERCULIACEAE

A genus of around ten species of shrubs or small trees, eight of which occur in Australia. Some are found in rainforest habitats. Being fast growers they are excellent for screening or as shelter plants for edging a rainforest garden. Propagation is from fresh seed or cuttings.

Commersonia bantramia
BROWN KURRAJONG

Origin Qld, NSW
Climate T, S, WT
Shade None to filtered
FAST-GROWING
RAINFOREST PLANT
Description A large shrub or small spreading tree with a suckering habit, to about 10 m. It has almost horizontal branches and large ovate leaves to 10 cm or more long. The slightly hairy leaves are dull green above and have finely toothed margins. Abundant creamy white flowers are borne along the branches in spring and summer. Flowers are followed by rounded spiny fruit.

Cultivation This ornamental species is easy to grow in frost-free areas. It will grow in a variety of soils, but requires good drainage. Prune annually to keep shapely.

Landscape Use This fast growing species can be used as a shelter plant for others. It can also be use as an effective screen or small shade tree.

CONOSTYLIS
HAEMODORACEAE

This genus, which is closely related to the kangaroo paws (Anigozanthos), *is also found in Western Australia. There are around 45 species of these attractive tufted plants which have tubular flowers, usually in dense woolly heads on the ends of stout stems. Flower colours are mostly yellow or cream. They are very ornamental and adapt well to cultivation and make excellent rockery and container plants. Similarly to the kangaroo paws, this genus may be subject to ink disease and species are best planted with very good drainage and plenty of air circulation.*

The best method of propagation is to divide clumps in winter and cultivate the divisions in pots until they are established.

Clematis microphylla

Commersonia bantramia

Conostylis aculeata

Origin WA
Climate WT, M, CT
Shade None to light
CONTAINER PLANT
Description A perennial clump with slightly spiny leaves to 30 cm. The woolly yellow flower heads are borne on stems which are shorter than the leaves, and appear in spring and summer.

This is an extremely variable species, and has a number of subspecies.

Cultivation This hardy species will grow in a variety of situations in sandy soil with good drainage. It is moderately frost-resistant.

Landscape Use This is an ideal rockery specimen. It can also be grown in a container.

Conostylis candicans

Conostylis aculeata

Conostylis candicans
GREY COTTONHEADS

Origin WA
Climate WT, M, CT
Shade None to light
CONTAINER PLANT
Description A small fluffy plant with leaves up to 50 cm covered in grey felt. The hairy yellow flowers are borne in dense heads on stems beyond the foliage, appearing in spring and summer.

Cultivation Grow in a well-drained, sunny position. It is moderately frost-tolerant.

Landscape Use Ideal for the garden, rockery or container. It is most striking when grown in massed clumps.

Conostylis seorsiflora

Origin WA
Climate WT, M, CT
Shade Light to filtered
CONTAINER PLANT
Description A mat-like perennial with a suckering habit, rarely exceeding 5 cm high. It has thin, flat leaves and solitary, yellow star-like flowers in spring.

Cultivation Grow in a lightly shaded position with good drainage. Water during dry periods. It is moderately frost-tolerant.

Conostylis seorsiflora

Landscape Use A little ornamental for growing as an edging, rockery or ground cover plant. It grows well in containers.

Conostylis setigera

Origin WA
Climate WT, M
Shade None to filtered
CONTAINER PLANT
Description A miniature tufting perennial growing to about 30 cm with strap-like leaves with rough margins. The yellow heads tinged with red appear in spring.
Cultivation This species will grow in most well-drained soils in a sunny position. It is slightly frost-tender.
Landscape Use Grow in clumps in the garden, in a rockery or in containers.

Conostylis setigera

Conostylis setosa

Origin WA
Climate WT, M
Shade Light to filtered
CONTAINER PLANT
Description A dwarf perennial with leaves to 30 cm, fringed with white bristly hairs. Flower stems are soft and woolly and flower heads are pinkish cream opening to creamy white in spring.

Conostylis setosa

Cultivation Grow in a position with some shade in a well-drained soil. It is frost-hardy.
Landscape Use A pretty plant for the small rockery pocket. It is also a good container plant.

CORDYLINE
ASTELEACEAE

A genus of palm-like plants that extends beyond Australia, with eight species being found in rainforests of eastern Australia. They are cultivated for their attractive, lush, sword-like leaves. They make excellent indoor or greenhouse plants, and help create an instant tropical atmosphere in sheltered warm gardens. Propagation is from seed or from large half-ripened cuttings or by division.

Cordyline petiolaris
BROAD-LEAF PALM LILY

Origin Qld, NSW
Climate S, WT
Shade Filtered to full
ORNAMENTAL FOLIAGE
CONTAINER PLANT
RAINFOREST PLANT
Description A slender, upright plant which may reach 4 m. It may consist of one single stem or form several stems from which wide, dark leaves radiate. It bears pale mauve flowers followed by pendulous clusters of bright red berries that remain on the plant for a long period.

Cordyline petiolaris

Cultivation This species does best in a sheltered, well-mulched position with filtered sun. It likes ample moisture, but must have good drainage. It is frost-tender.
Landscape Use An attractive foliage plant for growing near a water feature or for creating a lush tropical effect in the garden. A good container plant that is suitable for indoors.

Cordyline stricta
SLENDER PALM LILY

Origin Qld, NSW
Climate S, WT
Shade Filtered to full
ORNAMENTAL FOLIAGE
CONTAINER PLANT
RAINFOREST PLANT
Description A slender, erect-growing species to 3 m. Long, narrow, pendulous leaves are bunched at the ends of upright stems and delicate sprays of mauve flowers appear in summer. These are followed by blackish rounded berries.
Cultivation Grow in a sheltered garden situation in well-mulched soil with a plentiful supply of water, but good drainage. Remove the lower leaves as they wither to keep stems neat. If stems grow too high, they can be cut down to ground level and replacement stems will soon develop. It is slightly frost-tender.
Landscape Use A ornamental plant for growing in the shady tropical section of

Cordyline stricta

the garden among other palms and ferns. It is ideal for growing in narrow spaces near driveway, entrance or courtyard. An excellent container plant that does very well indoors.

CORREA
RUTACEAE

This is a small endemic genus of around 10 species with many distinct varieties. It is named in honour of the Portuguese botanist, José Correa de Serra. Correas are small shrubs mostly, with tubular bell flowers in various shades of red, green, yellow and white. They have become popular garden shrubs and bloom over a long period, with many species flowering in winter. They are very hardy and are frequently sought by honey-eating birds. Propagation is from half ripened tip cuttings.

Correas may be affected by scale which can be controlled by applications of white oil.

Correa alba
WHITE CORREA

Origin NSW, Vic., Tas., SA
Climate WT, M, CT
Shade None to filtered
BIRD-ATTRACTING
SALT-TOLERANT
CONTAINER PLANT
Description Attractive rounded shrub to 2 m with grey-green, almost rounded leaves and white, open, starry flowers mostly in autumn but with some flowers throughout the year.

C. alba var. *pannosa* is a low-growing form with small, rusty leaves.

Pink-flowering forms and prostrate forms are sometimes available.

Cultivation This is an extremely hardy shrub that does well in all soils with good drainage. It will grow in semishade, but flowers best in full sun. An excellent plant for seaside gardens, as it is very resistant to salt winds. It is frost-resistant.

Landscape Use This tough shrub is ideal as a lightly clipped hedge or screen in inhospitable exposed situations where other plants will not grow. It makes an attractive container plant.

Correa backhousiana

Origin Tas., Vic.
Climate WT, M, CT
Shade Light to filtered
BIRD-ATTRACTING
SALT-TOLERANT
CONTAINER PLANT
Description This rounded, many-branched shrub to 2 m has very dark green, oval foliage with a downy underside. The pendulous, cream to pale green bell-shaped flowers appear in

Correa backhousiana

Correa alba

winter and spring, attracting honeyeaters to the garden. Foliage and flowers may be picked for pleasant floral arrangements.

Cultivation A hardy plant which prefers some shade in the garden. It is frost-tolerant and will withstand salt-laden winds. Prune to shape.

Landscape Use May be grown as a screen or fence cover. It will form an attractive container plant.

Correa baeuerlenii
CHEF'S CAP CORREA

Origin NSW
Climate WT, M, CT
Shade Light to filtered
BIRD-ATTRACTING
CONTAINER PLANT
Description An erect, rounded shrub to 2 m with glossy, dark green lanceolate leaves. The unusual greenish yellow flowers have a broad flattened calyx resembling a chef's cap. Flowers occur in autumn and winter. Attractive cut foliage and flowers make good winter arrangements for indoors.

Cultivation This species grows well in most well-drained soils and situations. It prefers some shade and responds to watering in dry weather. Tip prune to keep growth bushy.

Landscape Use Grow among other shrubs or beneath trees in the garden. It is also suitable as a low screen and as a container plant.

Correa baeuerlenii

Correa decumbens

Origin SA
Climate WT, M, CT
Shade None to filtered
BIRD-ATTRACTING
CONTAINER PLANT
Description A prostrate, spreading shrub up to 3 m across with narrow, dark green leaves. The small red and green cigar-shaped flowers stand in an upturned position, looking completely different from the hanging bells of other correas. These appear mainly through summer.

Cultivation This hardy plant prefers a moist, well-drained position and some shade. It is frost-tolerant.

Correa decumbens

Landscape Use This species forms a good mat or ground-hugging plant, useful for covering banks, in the rockery or as an edging plant.

Correa 'Dusky Bells'

Origin Cultivar
Climate WT, M, CT, SA
Shade Filtered to full
BIRD-ATTRACTING
CONTAINER PLANT
Description A low, spreading shrub to 60 cm with bright green oval foliage and deep pink bell-shaped flowers from autumn through to spring. These attract honeyeaters and are suitable for picking.

Correa 'Dusky Bells'

Cultivation This adaptable cultivar has been in cultivation for a long time. It prefers a shaded position. It is frost-resistant.

Landscape Use An excellent winter-flowering species for the rockery, or as a ground cover or edging plant. It is an attractive container plant.

Correa glabra
ROCK CORREA

Origin Qld, NSW, Vic., SA
Climate WT, M, CT
Shade Light to filtered
BIRD-ATTRACTING
CONTAINER PLANT

Description A spreading shrub up to 2 m high and up to 3 m across with deep green rounded leaves and greenish bell flowers mainly through winter.

Cultivation An adaptable species for most soils in full sun or semishade. It will tolerate extended wet periods and may be grown in costal gardens with some protection. It is frost-resistant. Can be pinched back to keep compact shape.

Landscape Use Grow as a low screen or among other shrubs for the green winter flowers. It may also be grown as a background shrub, in a large rockery or in a container.

Correa glabra

Correa lawrenciana
MOUNTAIN CORREA

Origin NSW, Vic., Tas.
Climate WT, M, CT, H
Shade Light to full
BIRD-ATTRACTING

Description This tall shrub will grow up to 8 m, but in cultivation usually grows to around 3 m. It has dark green leathery leaves and yellow-green bell flowers with a velvety brown calyx. Main flowering is between autumn and spring and it is an excellent species for attracting honeyeaters.

This is an extremely variable species, with several varieties including *C. lawrenciana* var. *glandulifera* from northern NSW and south-east Queensland, which has small glandular calyx lobes and shiny leathery leaves.

Cultivation A hardy species that prefers a cool, moist, well-drained position with some shade. It will tolerate frost and snow.

Correa lawrenciana var. *glandulifera*

C. lawrenciana

Landscape Use A useful screen or fence cover for the cold climate garden.

Correa *'Mannii'*

Origin Cultivar
Climate WT, M, CT, SA
Shade Light to filtered
BIRD-ATTRACTING
CONTAINER PLANT
Description This cultivar is probably a hybrid between *C. pulchella* and *C. reflexa*. It is a compact shrub to 1 m, with oval to heart-shaped leaves and pinkish red bell flowers from autumn through to spring bringing honeyeaters to the garden.

Cultivation This hardy and adaptable species is suited to most soils. It prefers some shade and will grow in coastal gardens with some protection. It will tolerate frost. Regular light pruning maintains compact shape.

Landscape Use An ornamental plant for the small garden or rockery in a container.

Correa 'Mannii'

Correa pulchella

Origin SA
Climate WT, M, CT, SA
Shade None to filtered
BIRD-ATTRACTING
CONTAINER PLANT
Description There are many colour forms of this pretty shrub and they vary in size from prostrate to a neat spreading shrub up to 1 m high and up to 3 m across. The pendulous bell flowers, borne from autumn through to spring, may be pink, orange, red or occasionally white.

Cultivation This is a hardy species suited to almost any soil or situation provided drainage is good. It is suitable for growing in coastal gardens with some protection and is frost-resistant. Tip prune to help bushy growth.

Landscape Use An excellent plant for the rockery or the edge of a garden path or in a container.

Correa pulchella

Correa reflexa
COMMON CORREA

Origin Qld, NSW, Vic., Tas., SA, WA
Climate S, WT, M, CT, SA
Shade None to full
BIRD-ATTRACTING
CONTAINER PLANT
Description The most variable species of all the correas, ranging in size from prostrate to 3 m high and occurring in a

Correa reflexa 'Fat Fred'

C. reflexa

variety of habitats. The leaves vary from oval to linear and may be smooth to rough and slightly hairy beneath. Flowering time is from autumn through to spring and flowers are usually pendulous and tubular or bell-shaped. Flowers are yellow, green pink or red with yellow or green tips. They attract honeyeaters to the garden and last well when cut.

A number of forms and hybrids are in cultivation and are available from some nurseries.

Correa reflexa 'Fat Fred' is a particularly attractive large-flowered form, with broad red flowers with greenish yellow tips.

Cultivation This species prefers a well-drained, moist position with filtered sunshine. It is frost-resistant and moderately lime-tolerant. Tip prune after the main flowering period to encourage compact shape and increase the number of flowers produced.

Landscape Use Grow in a rockery, among other shrubs, in groups or in a container. The prostrate forms may be used as a ground cover.

CRINUM

AMARYLLIDACEAE

There are over 100 species of these lily-like plants distributed throughout the world, with some five species found in Australia. They have a clump-forming habit with leaves up to 1 m long and fleshy stems bearing umbels of numerous flowers. A number of exotic species and hybrids are commonly cultivated, as well as some Australian species. Watch for slugs and snails. Propagation is from fresh seed, which often germinates while the fruit capsule is still on the plant.

Crinum pedunculatum

SWAMP LILY; RIVER LILY

Origin Qld, NSW
Climate T, S, WT
Shade None to filtered
FRAGRANT
CONTAINER PLANT
RAINFOREST PLANT

Description A bulbous perennial with large fleshy strap-like leaves forming a large clump. The heads of numerous, white, perfumed flowers are carried on thick stalks up to 80 cm long. These appear during summer.

Cultivation A hardy and adaptable species that needs a moist position in either full sun or filtered shade. It will tolerate boggy conditions and can be grown in coastal gardens with some protection. It is moderately frost-resistant.

Landscape Use Grow in a wet place under trees. It makes an excellent feature plant at pool or pond edges and may be grown in a container.

Crinum pedunculatum

CROWEA

RUTACEAE

Named in honour of Dr James Crowe, an eighteenth-century English botanist, this attractive endemic genus has only three species. They are all in cultivation and make beautiful small flowering garden shrubs providing long-lasting cut flowers for the house. Propagation is by taking half-ripened tip cuttings.

Crowea angustifolia

Origin WA
Climate WT, M
Shade Light to filtered
FRAGRANT
AROMATIC FOLIAGE

Description A small shrub to 1 m or less, with linear, toothed leaves and white or pink star flowers with pink buds through spring.

C. angustifolia var. *dentata* is a more vigorous form and may reach 3 m. It has elliptic to oval, toothed leaves and white or pink star flowers with a soft perfume. This form is more widely cultivated than the typical form and is sold as *C. dentata.*

Crowea angustifolia var. *dentata*

C. angustifolia var. *dentata*

Cultivation Grow in a well-drained, well-mulched soil with some shade. Prune lightly to maintain bushy growth. It is frost-tender.

Landscape Use Grow among other shrubs or under trees.

Crowea exalata
SMALL CROWEA

Origin NSW, Vic.
Climate WT, M, CT
Shade None to filtered
AROMATIC FOLIAGE
CONTAINER PLANT

Description A spreading small shrub to about 1 m high and 1 m across with small, narrow leaves that have a spicy aroma when crushed. The waxy, bright pink star flowers appear along the stems in summer through to late autumn and are perfect for picking.

Various forms of this species are available, including prostrate and white-flowered forms.

C. exalata 'Austraflora Green Cape' is a prostrate, spreading form with bright green, blunt leaves and pale pink flowers. This is an excellent small spillover plant for the rockery or container.

Cultivation Grow in a well-drained, composted soil in a cool position with some shade. Water well during dry periods. It is resistant to frost. Prune after flowering to maintain bushy growth.

Crowea exalata

C. exalata 'Austraflora Green Cape'

C. exalata x *Crowea saligna*

Landscape Use A delightful plant for the rockery, beside a path or in the garden for a pretty splash of pink in autumn. It is also an excellent container plant for the courtyard.

Crowea *'Festival'*

Origin Cultivar
Climate WT, M, CT
Shade None to filtered
SPECIMEN PLANT
AROMATIC FOLIAGE
CONTAINER PLANT

Description A beautiful cultivar which forms a neat rounded shrub to 1 m. It has narrow leaves and bears masses of deep pink flowers from spring through to the end of autumn, providing a continuous source of cut flowers.

Cultivation A hardy plant that will do well in an open, sunny position or in partial shade. It needs a well-drained soil and a good mulch to keep the root system cool. It is frost-resistant. Prune by taking cut flowers or after flowering to maintain bushy growth.

Landscape Use A beautiful specimen for a large rockery or when planted in groups in the garden. It makes an outstanding tub plant.

Crowea 'Festival'

Crowea saligna

Origin NSW
Climate WT, M, CT
Shade Light to filtered
AROMATIC FOLIAGE
CONTAINER PLANT

Description A rounded bushy shrub to around 1 m. The shiny aromatic leaves may be elliptic to lanceolate, and waxy, star-like pink or, rarely, white flowers appear in summer and autumn and at other times.

Crowea 'Poorinda Ecstasy' is a hybrid between *C. exalata* and *C. saligna*. It has masses of pale pink flowers many times a year.

Cultivation This species requires a deep, rich soil with plenty of moisture, but good drainage. Prune to maintain bushy growth. It is frost-tender.

Landscape Use A lovely plant for growing with the protection of other shrubs or under trees. It is ideal for the rockery or containers.

Crowea saligna

CRYPTANDRA

RHAMNACEAE

An endemic group of bushy shrubs with about 40 species found in temperate parts of Australia. Only a few species are cultivated, and although the usually white flowers are small, they are produced in profusion, often in the winter months. Propagation is from half-ripened tip cuttings.

Cryptandra amara

BITTER CRYPTANDRA

Origin Qld, NSW, Vic., Tas., SA
Climate S, WT, M, CT, SA
Shade Light to filtered
CONTAINER PLANT
Description A small, variable shrub which may grow to around 1 m, but is usually smaller. It has small crowded

Cryptandra amara

leaves on interlacing branches and bears masses of tiny waxy white bells in winter and spring.

Cultivation An adaptable plant which will grow in most soils and conditions with good drainage and a little shade. Prune lightly to keep bushy. It is frost-tolerant.

Landscape Use A pretty spillover plant for the rockery or garden edge. It may also be grown in a container.

Cryptandra scortechinii

(syn. *Stenanthemum scortechinii*)

BALL CRYPTANDRA

Origin Qld, NSW
Climate S, WT, M
Shade None to filtered
CONTAINER PLANT
Description A dense, rounded shrub to 1 m with lanceolate pointed leaves. The lovely woolly heads of flowers appear in winter and spring. These provide good, long-lasting cut flowers.

Cultivation Grow in a well-drained soil in full sun or some shade. A light pruning will keep bush dense. It is frost-resistant.

Landscape Use An attractive plant among other shrubs, providing good white winter flowers. Its attractive form makes it a good feature plant for the larger part of the rockery or in a container.

Cryptandra scortechinii

C. scortechinii

CYATHEA

CYATHEACEAE

This large genus of some 800 species of tree ferns is widely distributed throughout the world, with about 12 species occurring in Australia. They are ferns with an erect trunk or caudex and large spreading fronds radiating from the crown. They make very beautiful garden subjects when protected from wind, heat and frost, and also make outstanding container specimens. When purchasing cyatheas, ensure that a root system exists, as, unlike Dicksonia *species, they do not like having their trunk severed during transplanting. It is normal for them to have their outer fronds removed. The young fronds should be curled, plump, firm and furry to the touch. When planting these ferns in the garden, a well-composted soil should be used and ample moisture applied until the plant is re-established. A good mulch of peatmoss or leaf mould will keep the roots cool and moist. All tree ferns are protected and should only be purchased if they bear an official numbered tag. Propagation is from spores.*

Cyathea australis

ROUGH TREE FERN

Origin Qld, NSW, Vic., Tas.
Climate T, S, WT, M, CT
Shade Light to filtered

SPECIMEN PLANT
ORNAMENTAL FOLIAGE
CONTAINER PLANT

Description A large-growing slender species to 10 m tall with large, finely divided, dark green fronds radiating from the crown.

The rough frond bases persisting towards the top of the trunk give this fern its common name.

Cultivation This widely distributed tree fern grows very easily and is very popular in cultivation. It likes a sheltered, moist position, but will tolerate full sun provided the roots are kept moist. It is slightly frost-tender and needs some protection.

Landscape Use Grow as a specimen or in groves with other shade lovers. It will create a beautifully cool, tropical effect near water or next to a shady patio. An outstanding container plant.

Cyathea cooperi

SCALY TREE FERN

Origin Qld, NSW
Climate T, S, WT, M
Shade Light to filtered

FAST-GROWING
SPECIMEN PLANT
ORNAMENTAL FOLIAGE
CONTAINER PLANT
RAINFOREST PLANT

Description This tall tree fern grows to a height of 10 m. The large, quickly growing fronds, up to 4 m long, are

Cyathea cooperi

Cyathea australis

covered with reddish brown hair and larger white scales at the base. The shed fronds leave neat oval scars on the trunk, sometimes referred to as coin spots.

Cultivation A widely cultivated tree fern that requires a deep, well-composted soil with plenty of moisture. It likes a sheltered position and can tolerate sun provided the roots are in a damp situation. A mulch with leaf mould will keep the roots cool and moist. It is frost tender.

Landscape Use An outstanding tree fern for planting under trees, either singly or in groups. Used to its best advantage, the large crown of gracefully arching fronds will soften architectural lines and provide filtered sunlight which is ideal for smaller ferns. It is an excellent container plant for courtyard gardens.

DAMPIERA

GOODENIACEAE

An endemic genus of over 60 species named after explorer William Dampier, who landed in Western Australia in 1688. These are dwarf or prostrate plants and are very showy when in flower, with masses of striking blue or purple flowers appearing over a long season. Many have a suckering habit and multiply readily by sending up suckers from underground roots, making them excellent ground covers or rockery plants. This also provides a ready means of propagation. Propagation is also from half-ripened tip cuttings.

Dampiera diversifolia

Origin WA
Climate S, WT, M, CT
Shade Light to filtered
CONTAINER PLANT

Description A low, spreading, multibranched plant up to 2 m across with small stem leaves and a suckering habit. Masses of brilliant purple-blue flowers smother the plant through spring.

Cultivation This species needs a well-drained, moist soil and a little shade. It is moderately frost-resistant.

Landscape Use A charming spreading plant for the rockery, sloping banks or stone walls where the plant may tumble over in a natural way. It may be grown in containers, being particularly suited to hanging baskets, where the cascading stems are shown to advantage.

Dampiera lanceolata

GROOVED DAMPIERA

Origin Qld, NSW, Vic., SA
Climate WT, M, SA
Shade None to light
CONTAINER PLANT

Description A small, erect or slightly drooping shrub up to 50 cm high with narrow, lanceolate leaves with a felty undersurface. The pretty, deep blue flowers appear in spring and early summer.

Cultivation This species from fairly dry areas requires a very well drained, light-textured soil. It is moderately frost-resistant.

Landscape Use A very pretty rockery or container plant.

Dampiera lanceolata

Dampiera diversifolia

Dampiera linearis
COMMON DAMPIERA

Origin WA
Climate WT, M, CT
Shade None to light
CONTAINER PLANT
Description A prostrate, suckering plant with a spread of up to 1 m diameter. The leaves vary from narrow to cuneate and may be covered with grey hairs when young. The bright blue to purple flowers appear mainly from late winter through to early spring.

Cultivation This adaptable species prefers good drainage in full sun or a little shade. It will withstand periods of dryness and is moderately frost-resistant.

Landscape Use A popular plant for the rockery, or as an edging or ground cover.

Dampiera linearis

Dampiera purpurea
(syn. *D. brownii*)

Origin Qld, NSW, Vic.
Climate S, WT, M
Shade None to filtered
CONTAINER PLANT
Description A small suckering plant with erect branches to 1 m. The whole plant is densely hairy, including the branches, leaves and buds. The purplish flowers are produced at the branch ends in spring.

This is a variable species and many forms are in cultivation.

Cultivation Grow in a well-drained soil with a little shade. It is moderately frost-tolerant. Prune after flowering to maintain compactness.

Landscape Use An attractive plant for colour as a border, in the rockery, between shrubs or in a container.

Dampiera purpurea

Dampiera rosmarinifolia
WILD ROSEMARY

Origin NSW, Vic., SA
Climate S, WT, M, CT, SA
Shade None to light
CONTAINER PLANT
Description A low, spreading, suckering plant to 2 m across with leaves similar to those of the common rosemary. Flowers appear in spring and occur in various shades of white, pink, mauve, purple and blue, but blue flowers are most common.

Cultivation An adaptable species that does well in most soils and conditions, provided the drainage is excellent. It will withstand periods of dryness and can be grown in coastal gardens, with some protection from salt winds. It is frost-tolerant.

Landscape Use This plant will form large patches and is an ideal ground

Dampiera rosmarinifolia

cover or rockery plant. It is a most attractive container plant.

Dampiera stricta
BLUE DAMPIERA

Origin Qld, NSW, Vic., Tas.
Climate S, WT, M, CT
Shade None to filtered
CONTAINER PLANT
Description An upright, spreading bush to around 50 cm high and 2 m across with linear leaves, and bearing sprays of flowers mainly from spring to summer, but with some at any time of the year. The flowers vary in colour from pale blue to deep purple-blue.

Cultivation An adaptable species that will do well in a wide range of conditions with good drainage. It will grow on the coast with some protection and is frost-tolerant.

Landscape Use This scrambling shrub is a natural for the bush garden or rockery, where it looks superb with flannel flowers, which bloom at the same time. Also a good container plant.

Dampiera trigona
ANGLED-STEM DAMPIERA

Origin WA
Climate WT, M, CT, SA
Shade None to filtered
CONTAINER PLANT
Description A small spreading plant to around 20 cm high and 60 cm across. The thin, almost grass-like, stems are scattered with tiny leaves and bear a profusion of striking blue flowers in spring and summer.

Cultivation This popular species is hardy and is adaptable to a wide range of conditions. It will grow in sun or semishade in most well-drained soils and will tolerate very sandy ones. It is moderately resistant to frost.

Landscape Use The long trailing stems make this a useful cascading plant for a rockery, container or hanging basket.

Dampiera trigona

Dampiera stricta

DARWINIA
MYRTACEAE

An endemic genus of about 40 species named after Dr Erasmus Darwin (1721–1802), grandfather of Charles Darwin. A large number of species occur in Western Australia and although they are very showy, very few have been successful in cultivation. They are shrubs with small crowded leaves and fall roughly into two groups: those with small leaf-like bracts surrounding the small flowers and those with large coloured petal-like bracts giving the head a bell-like appearance. A number of the beautiful Western Australian bell flowered darwinias are now available as grafted plants in limited quantities. They are grafted onto the more reliable and hardy Lemon-scented Darwinea (D. citriodora) *making them longer-lived in cultivation, especially in the eastern states. They make an attractive garden shrub, flowering over a long period and attracting nectar-feeding birds to the garden. Darwinias demand excellent drainage, but need some moisture until established. A good mulch around the root area will keep the roots cool and moist during summer. Scale insects may be found on the leaves and stems of darwinias and may be treated with an application of white oil. Propagation is from half-ripened tip cuttings.*

Darwinia citriodora

LEMON-SCENTED MYRTLE

Origin WA
Climate WT, M, CT
Shade None to light

AROMATIC FOLIAGE
BIRD-ATTRACTING
CONTAINER PLANT

Description A compact, rounded shrub which may reach 2 m high with a similar spread but is usually smaller. The oblong to lanceolate leaves are grey-green, colouring to a reddish bronze during autumn and winter, and are pleasantly aromatic when crushed. Small, tightly packed red and yellow flowers, each with a prominent style, are surrounded by reddish green leaf-like bracts. These appear over a long period from winter through to summer.

Cultivation This widely cultivated species is hardy and adaptable. It needs good drainage with some moisture and a little shade. A mulch applied around the root zone will keep roots cool and moist during summer. It is usually frost-tolerant and can be grown in coastal gardens with some protection. Tip pruning following flowering will keep the bush compact.

Landscape Use An attractive plant in form, foliage and flowers to be grown singly or as an attractive low screen or hedge. It may be trimmed to form a compact shrub in a large container.

Darwinia citriodora

Darwinia fascicularis

Origin Qld, NSW
Climate S, WT, M, CT
Shade None to light

BIRD-ATTRACTING
CONTAINER PLANT

Description A neat, rounded shrub which grows to around 1 m. It has narrow light green leaves crowded at the ends of branches and bears heads of small white flowers with protruding styles. The flowers turn to bright red with age. They are a particularly good source of nectar for honeyeaters and make good cut flowers.

D. fascicularis ssp. *oligantha* is a low, spreading shrub to 50 cm high and 1 m across. Its decumbent branches will layer readily when left in contact with soil.

D. fascicularis ssp. *oligantha*

Darwinia fascicularis

Cultivation A hardy and adaptable plant for most soils with good drainage. It is frost-hardy and will grow in semishade or in full sun with a cool root run. Prune lightly to keep a compact shape.

Landscape Use A good long-flowering plant to grow amongst other shrubs in the rockery, small garden or container.

Darwinia grandiflora

Origin NSW
Climate WT, M, CT
Shade Light to filtered

AROMATIC FOLIAGE
BIRD-ATTRACTING
CONTAINER PLANT

Description A low growing, self-layering shrub with a height up to 1 m with a similar spread. It has light green narrow aromatic leaves. The white to deep pink flower heads appear in winter and spring.

Cultivation A hardy species that enjoys a moist, well-drained position with a little shade. It is frost-hardy.

Landscape Use An attractive cascading plant for garden edges, spilling over rocks and walls and slopes; also suitable for containers, including hanging baskets.

Darwinia grandiflora

Darwinia lejostyla
(syn. *D. leiostyla*)

Origin WA
Climate WT, M, CT
Shade None to filtered

BIRD-ATTRACTING
CONTAINER PLANT

Description A low-growing shrub to 1 m with dense, needle-like foliage and masses of showy deep pink hanging bells in spring. Available as a grafted plant.

Cultivation A beautiful ornamental plant that needs excellent drainage and a warm, dry position with a cool root run. Tip prune to keep plant bushy.

Landscape Use A very showy plant for a well-drained rockery pocket. It forms a beautiful miniature tree in a container and is probably best grown this way in the eastern States.

Darwinia lejostyla

Darwinia nieldiana
FRINGED BELL

Origin WA
Climate WT, M
Shade None to light

BIRD-ATTRACTING
CONTAINER PLANT

Description A prostrate or dwarf shrub to 50 cm high and a width of up to 1 m. The spreading branches are crowded with small linear leaves, and pendent green flower heads ageing to red appear in spring and early summer.

Cultivation This shrub needs conditions as near as possible to those of its natural habitat — an airy, warm, open position in a light, well-drained soil away from areas of high humidity. It will tolerate some frosts.

Landscape Use A beautiful rockery subject and container plant.

Darwinia oxylepis

Origin WA
Climate WT, M
Shade None to light

AROMATIC FOLIAGE
CONTAINER PLANT

Description A small shrub to 1 m high with crowded aromatic pine-like leaves on upright branches. Large scarlet bell-shaped flowers are produced generously during spring. This beautiful species is available as a grafted plant.

Cultivation Provide excellent drainage, but a cool moist root run for best results. It needs lots of sun and is moderately frost tolerant. Prune lightly after flowering.

Landscape Use A highly ornamental foreground plant for the garden. It also makes an excellent container plant. Flowers are good for picking and last well in water.

Darwinia nieldiana

Darwinia oxylepis

Darwinia taxifolia

Darwinia purpurea
ROSE DARWINIA

Origin WA
Climate WT, M, SA
Shade None to light
CONTAINER PLANT

Description This attractive small species is not often seen in cultivation and is only occasionally available from native plant nurseries. It has spreading branches and grows to around 70 cm high. The tiny oblong leaves are crowded along the stems and deep purplish red flowers are produced during spring. Available as a grafted plant.

Cultivation This species occurs naturally on sandy soils and prefers a light-textured, very well drained soil with an adequate supply of moisture.

Landscape Use An attractive rockery or container plant.

Darwinia purpurea

Darwinia taxifolia

Origin Qld, NSW
Climate S, WT, M
Shade Light to filtered
BIRD-ATTRACTING
CONTAINER PLANT

Description A spreading small shrub to around 1 m high by a similar width. It has slightly fleshy, crowded, grey-green leaves, and clusters of white flowers ageing to red in spring and summer.

D. taxifolia ssp. *macrolaena* is a prostrate form with larger flower heads and deep pink bracts. This subspecies is sometimes sold as *D. grandiflora*.

Cultivation This species is suited to a well-drained position with a little shade. It is frost-hardy and may be pruned to keep bush shapely.

Landscape Use A attractive edging or rockery plant. The prostrate form may be used as a ground cover or a container plant.

DAVALLIA

DAVALLIACEAE

There are some 40 species in this genus. They are known as hare's foot ferns because the prominent creeping stems or rhizomes are covered in hair-like scales, giving them a furry appearance. They are widely cultivated and are popularly used as hanging basket subjects. Australia has three species. They are all epiphytes and grow on rocks or trees in rainforest areas and in moist situations, displaying beautiful finely divided triangular fronds. Propagation is by division of rhizomes.

Davallia pyxidata

HARE'S FOOT FERN

Origin Qld, NSW, Vic.
Climate T, S, WT
Shade Light to full

ORNAMENTAL FOLIAGE
CONTAINER PLANT

Description A very attractive fern with dark green, finely divided glossy fronds up to 1 m long and creeping rhizomes covered with brown scales.

Cultivation A hardy fern for the garden in warm climates, but usually grown in containers in a coarse, open potting mixture with plenty of moisture. It is frost-tender and may be grown in a bush house in cooler climates.

Landscape Use A beautiful fern to grow on large boulders in a protected warm garden. It is an excellent pot or hanging basket plant.

Davallia pyxidata

DAVIDSONIA

DAVIDSONIACEAE

A small Australian genus of two species of small trees one of which is the popular garden subject D. pruriens, *best known for its attractive purple edible fruit which resembles plums. Propagation is from fresh seed.*

Davidsonia pruriens

DAVIDSON'S PLUM

Origin Qld, NSW
Climate T, S, WT, M
Shade None to filtered

SPECIMEN PLANT
BIRD-ATTRACTING
ORNAMENTAL FOLIAGE
CONTAINER PLANT
RAINFOREST PLANT

Description A small slender tree to around 10 m but often less in an open position. It has large spreading pinnate leaves to almost 1 m in length with up to 15 soft hairy leaflets. Highly decorative flushes of pink new growth emerge from the crown of the plant. Panicles of small pinkish flowers in spring are followed in autumn by bunches of purple, plum-like edible fruit. The acid fruit makes a delicious jam, jelly or wine.

Cultivation This slow growing plant needs protection from harsh sun and strong winds until established. It does best in a humus-enriched, very well drained soil with ample water.

Landscape Use An attractive feature plant that can be grown among other small trees. Young plants in containers make excellent indoor plants where they will adapt to low light and low temperatures.

Davidsonia pruriens

DENDROBIUM

ORCHIDACEAE

A very large genus of about 1,400 species with representatives in Asia, Polynesia and the Australian region. The name is derived from the Greek dendron, *tree, and* bios, *life, as most species grow on trees. There are about 50 Australian species and many are in cultivation. They are mostly epiphytes and are extremely popular in cultivation, as they are generally adaptable, growing in sun or shade, potted in compost, or on rocks, slabs or trees, and they display most attractive fragrant flowers. Some hardy species from warm areas will thrive in southern States if protected from frosts and drying winds under bush house conditions. Species from northern Queensland — such as the Cooktown Orchid, Queensland's floral emblem — need the conditions of a heated glasshouse when cultivated in cooler parts. Plants store nutrients gathered through their aerial roots in thickened stalks or pseudobulbs. They have a winter rest period and should not be fed and require less water during this season. Propagation is by division of clumps and from the aerial shoots, complete with leaves, that develop on the pseudobulbs of some species. This is best done during the main growing period which is late spring and summer.*

Dendrobium beckleri
PENCIL ORCHID

Origin Qld, NSW
Climate T, S, WT, M
Shade Light to filtered
CONTAINER PLANT
RAINFOREST PLANT
Description An epiphytic orchid with long stems up to 90 cm and cylindrical, upright leaves that reduce in size along the stems. The plant remains compact, although the stems can sometimes hang over in great masses. White or cream flowers with purple stripes are produced on short flower spikes in spring.
Cultivation This species is found in open forest and is best grown in a position where it receives good light. It is hardy and will grow well in a warm, humid garden with some protection.
Landscape Use May be grown in a container or mounted onto a garden tree.

Dendrobium canaliculatum
TEA-TREE ORCHID; ONION ORCHID

Origin Qld, WA, NT
Climate T, S
Shade Light to filtered
FRAGRANT
Description A variable orchid with widespread distribution. It has small onion-shaped pseudobulbs and thin, fleshy leaves. Sweet-smelling sprays of many small white flowers tipped with yellow and purple on the throat are produced in spring.

Several forms of this species are in cultivation.
Cultivation This species grows naturally on paperbark trees in tropical areas and it may be mounted on small paperbark logs or hardwood slabs. Heat and glasshouse conditions are needed in temperate Australia. It requires continuous watering during summer but must be kept almost dry during the resting period.
Landscape Use This species may be grown outdoors in tropical and subtropical areas with lightly filtered sunlight to encourage it to flower.

Dendrobium x delicatum

Origin Qld, NSW
Climate S, WT, M
Shade None to light
FRAGRANT
CONTAINER PLANT
Description This attractive orchid is a natural hybrid between *D. speciosum* and *D. kingianum*. It forms large clumps of tapered pseudobulbs and deep green leathery leaves. The beautiful sprays of fragrant, waxy flowers may be white, cream or pink with mauve blotches. These appear in spring.
Cultivation A hardy species that is suitable for growing in a protected position in the

Dendrobium beckleri

Dendrobium canaliculatum

garden where it will receive ample sunlight. It needs plenty of water during the growing season, but should be kept reasonably dry during winter. If grown in a container, it needs a coarse potting mix with charcoal chunks added for good drainage.

Landscape Use This species may be grown in a rockery pocket or attached to rocks. It can also be grown in tubs or baskets or on slabs.

Dendrobium x *delicatum*

Dendrobium falcorostrum

BEECH ORCHID

Origin Qld, NSW
Climate S, WT, M
Shade Light to filtered

FRAGRANT
CONTAINER PLANT
RAINFOREST PLANT

Description A beautiful orchid almost exclusively found growing on beech trees in south-east Queensland and northern New South Wales. It has long, slender pseudobulbs and dark green leathery leaves. The short sprays of snowy white to cream waxy flowers are highly perfumed and appear in spring.

Cultivation This species thrives outdoors in temperate areas and needs cool conditions to stimulate flowering. It comes from areas where most rain falls in summer and conditions are cold and dry in the winter months and these conditions should be reproduced as closely as possible in cultivation. It forms large clumps and although it may be attached to a slab or suitable host, is best planted in pots with a suitable coarse mixture.

Landscape Use A delightful perfumed plant suited to containers that may be placed in a protected cool section of the garden or bush house.

Dendrobium gracilicaule

Origin Qld, NSW
Climate T, S, WT
Shade Light to filtered

FRAGRANT
CONTAINER PLANT
RAINFOREST PLANT

Description A profusely flowering species with numerous long slender pseudobulbs and short spikes of small, cup-shaped yellow flowers with red markings on the outside. The flowers are lightly perfumed and appear in spring.

Cultivation This is an extremely easy orchid to cultivate and will readily flower

Dendrobium gracilicaule

Dendrobium falcorostrum

and quickly form good-sized clumps. It will grow in a pot, on a slab, or attached to a tree or a rock. Water well during the growing season.

Landscape Use Hang this freely flowering species in partial shade on a tree in the garden.

Dendrobium kingianum
PINK ROCK ORCHID

Origin Qld, NSW
Climate S, WT, M
Shade Light to filtered
FRAGRANT
CONTAINER PLANT
RAINFOREST PLANT

Description A very variable species with numerous pseudobulbs of varying lengths and thin-textured, slender leaves. The beautiful perfumed flowers range in colour from deep rose to pale pink, but may rarely be pure white. They appear in short spikes of five or more blooms in late winter and spring.

A large number of selected cultivated forms of this species exist, as well as many hybrids with *D. kingianum* as one of the parents.

Dendrobium 'Bardo Rose' (*D. kingianum* x *D. falcorostrum*) is a particularly beautiful cultivar with highly perfumed flowers in shades of pale pink to deep pink.

Cultivation This adaptable orchid will grow very well outdoors in temperate areas with some protection and good light. It needs plenty of water during the growing season and drying out in winter. When grown in containers, it requires a good friable soil with plenty of leaf mould and good drainage.

Landscape Use A pretty, mat-forming species admirably suited to a rockery pocket under the lacy umbrella of tree ferns. It may be grown on slabs, but does best in containers such as pots or baskets.

Dendrobium kingianum

Dendrobium linguiforme
TONGUE ORCHID; THUMBNAIL ORCHID

Origin Qld, NSW
Climate T, S, WT, M
Shade Light to filtered
FRAGRANT

Description A beautiful little orchid with a mat-forming habit, the fleshy oval leaves being attached to its host. Dainty cream flowers appear in spring.

D. linguiforme var. *nugentii* is an attractive northern form with a rough texture to the leaves and smaller but more densely flowered sprays. It requires protection from frost in southern areas.

Cultivation This orchid is easily established and will slowly cover its host. Once established, it should not be disturbed and is best attached to a long-lasting host such as a large rock, a suitable tree or a piece of hardwood. In cool climates, it does best in a bush house with maximum light.

Landscape Use A striking specimen when attached to rock surfaces in the warm garden. It is not suitable for pots.

D. linguiforme var. *nugentii*

D. linguiforme

Dendrobium ruppianum
(syn. *D. fusiforme*)
OAK ORCHID

Origin Qld
Climate T, S, WT
Shade Light to filtered
FRAGRANT
CONTAINER PLANT
RAINFOREST PLANT

Description A large clumping species with numerous variable pseudobulbs that are narrow at both ends but swollen in

Dendrobium ruppianum

the middle. The numerous flowers are closely packed along the stems and are white or cream coloured with purple blotches. They are sweetly fragrant and appear in spring.

Cultivation This species will form very large clumps and is best mounted on a substantial, long-lasting host. If planting it in pots, fill these with pieces of charcoal, pieces of bark and leaf mould, as it does not thrive in a mass of compost. It requires humidity, a warm temperature, lightly filtered sunlight and a good air flow. This is one of the easiest tropical species to grow without heat and it will do well in the bush house as far south as Sydney.

Landscape Use In warm climates, this is spectacular specimen attached to a tree in the garden, where a well-grown plant produces an outstanding display of flowers.

Dendrobium speciosum
KING ORCHID; ROCK ORCHID

Origin Qld, NSW, Vic.
Climate T, S, WT, M
Shade Light to filtered
SPECIMEN PLANT
FRAGRANT
CONTAINER PLANT
RAINFOREST PLANT

Description A spectacular orchid with a wide distribution and a wide variety of plant and flower forms. The pseudobulbs are usually large and thick, tapering to a point, and vary in length from 10 cm to 100 cm. Two to five oval, thick leathery dark green leaves appear on the top of each pseudobulb. Large sprays of numerous fragrant flowers in varying shades of pure white, cream or yellow appear in spring.

D. speciosum var. *hillii* is a variety commonly found on trees, with straight, longer pseudobulbs and smaller, but more numerous, flowers.

Cultivation This very hardy plant will grow under most conditions in a protected garden. It may be grown attached to rocks with leaf mould, on trees, on hardwood slabs, in pots or in baskets. It requires ample sunlight and plenty of water during spring and summer. During the winter rest period, ensure that the plant gets good sunlight to encourage next season's flowering.

Landscape Use A beautiful perfumed specimen for the rockery, veranda, courtyard and garden.

Dendrobium striolatum
STREAKED ROCK ORCHID

Origin NSW, Vic., Tas.
Climate WT, M, CT
Shade Light to filtered
SPECIMEN PLANT
CONTAINER PLANT

Description A small, spreading orchid that is usually found growing on rocks, where it may form extensive clumps. It has upright, fleshy, cylindrical leaves which may be dark green or red. The fragrant flowers are cream, yellow or green with brown striping and a pure white labellum. They are borne singly, or occasionally in pairs, in spring.

Cultivation This species from temperate areas does very well in the garden or bush house in cool climates. It may be grown attached to a slab or rock or in a container with a coarse compost, but it needs ample sunlight to produce a good display of flowers.

Landscape Use Place plant near to paths, veranda or courtyard where the delicate beauty of the flowers can be fully appreciated.

Dendrobium striolatum

Dendrobium speciosum

DIANELLA
PHORMIACEAE

This genus of about 30 species is widely distributed beyond Australia and includes about 15 native species found in all States. They are known as flax lilies because they have very tough and fibrous strap-like leaves that may be easily split and plaited. Aborigines used the leaves of some species for basket weaving. The plants form attractive clumps with long stems of mainly blue flowers, and make good garden subjects in rockeries, near water features, in the bush garden or for softening paved and walled areas such as courtyards and driveways. Propagation is from fresh ripe seed or by division of existing plants.

Dianella caerulea
PAROO LILY

Origin Qld, NSW, Vic., Tas., WA, NT
Climate T, S, WT, M, CT
Shade None to filtered
CONTAINER PLANT

Description This plant forms clumps of erect, strap-like, dark green leaves to about 1 m. Numerous blue starry flowers are carried on wiry stems up to 1 m long in spring and early summer. These are followed by attractive blue or purple berries.

Cultivation This hardy species will grow in most well-drained soils and conditions, but flowers best in a sunny position. It is frost-resistant.

Landscape Use A decorative plant for the rockery or bush garden or near a water feature. It may be grown in a large tub.

Dianella caerulea

Dianella revoluta
SPREADING FLAX LILY

Origin Qld, NSW, Vic., Tas., SA, WA
Climate T, S, WT, M, CT, SA
Shade None to filtered
CONTAINER PLANT

Description A clumping species with almost flat, dull blue-green leaves with revolute margins. The numerous pale blue flowers are held high on dainty wiry stems up to 1 m. These appear in spring and early summer and are followed by dark blue berries.

Cultivation This species is easily grown in most soils and conditions, but is happiest with a little shade and some moisture. It is frost-resistant.

Dianella revoluta

Landscape Use This is an ideal plant for the rockery, or beside pools or streams in association with ferns. It may be grown in a large tub.

DICKSONIA
DICKSONIACEAE

Named after James Dickson, an early nineteenth-century British botanist and nurseryman, this genus of tree ferns comprises some 25 species with three found in Australia. They are extremely attractive large ferns with trunks either large or small and handsome spreading fronds radiating from the crown. They are very popular in garden design and available in many nurseries in a variety of heights, usually as sawn logs. The trunk will grow new roots from the cut in several weeks and new frond growth will reshoot quickly in warm months. It is important to water the trunk and fronds while the plant establishes its roots and to provide liberal watering during hot, dry weather. Dicksonias are protected and should only be purchased if they bear an official numbered tag. Propagation is from fresh spores.

Dicksonia antarctica

Dicksonia antarctica
SOFT TREE FERN

Origin Qld, NSW, Vic., Tas., SA
Climate S, WT, M, CT, H
Shade Light to filtered
SPECIMEN PLANT
ORNAMENTAL FOLIAGE
CONTAINER PLANT
RAINFOREST PLANT
Description This magnificent plant is widespread in moist forests from south-east Queensland south to Tasmania. The thick, woolly trunk is covered in reddish brown hairs and can grow up to 10 m tall. The soft fronds uncurl rapidly in warm weather, and many are produced in one season, providing a beautiful dense cover. In earlier days, the Aborigines ate the soft pithy tissue near the top of the trunk.

Cultivation Grow in a well-drained, well-mulched soil, preferably in a protected position. It is happiest in semishade, but will tolerate a fair amount of sun. In dry weather apply plenty of water to crown and trunk. Rotted leaf mould and peat can be used at the base to keep roots moist. Occasional grooming of old fronds will maintain neatness.

Landscape Use A beautiful, slow-growing species that makes an outstanding feature plant in the garden, rockery, near water or next to a shady patio. The trunk provides an excellent host for epiphytic orchids and ferns. As a potted plant use on a veranda, in a courtyard or indoors.

DILLYWYNIA
FABACEAE

An endemic genus, of some 20 species, found in all States and often referred to as 'eggs-and-bacon' in allusion to the bright yellow and reddish tints of the flowers. They are mainly small shrubs with heath-like foliage and they occur in large numbers in dry sclerophyll forests, often being the earliest wildflowers to bloom in the bush in late winter. They are usually very floriferous and make attractive ornamental garden plants. Scale insects may be found on the leaves and branches of dillwynias and may be treated with an application of white oil. Propagation is from fresh seed produced in pods each season. Seed germinates readily after treatment in hot water and leaving to stand overnight. Alternatively, propagate from half-ripened tip cuttings.

Dillwynia juniperina
PRICKLY PARROT PEA

Origin Qld, NSW, Vic.
Climate S, WT, M
Shade Light to filtered
BIRD-ATTRACTING
Description An erect, dense prickly shrub with spreading branches to about 2 m. The leaves are narrow, stiff and pointed and small clusters of yellow and red pea-shaped flowers appear from late winter through spring. The plant is a favoured nesting site for small birds.

Cultivation Grow in very well drained soil in lightly filtered sun. Prune after flowering to maintain shrubby growth.

Landscape Use An attractive, prickly ornamental shrub that can be grown as a low, impenetrable hedge.

Dillwynia juniperina

Dillwynia retorta

Origin Qld, NSW
Climate S, WT
Shade Light to filtered
BIRD-ATTRACTING
CONTAINER PLANT
Description A small rounded or upright shrub which may reach 2 m. The numerous narrow leaves are twisted, and many yellow flowers, often with red centres, are borne at the ends of branches in late winter through to spring.

Cultivation A well-drained position with lightly filtered sun is preferred. It is frost-resistant. Prune after flowering to keep the plant bushy.

Landscape Use A lovely species for the bush garden. With regular trimming it makes an excellent rockery or container plant.

Dillwynia retorta

DIPLOLAENA
RUTACEAE

This endemic genus contains six species, all of which occur in the south-west of Western Australia. They are small to medium-sized shrubs with soft, hairy foliage. The numerous flowers with prominent stamens are surrounded by petal-like bracts, the whole resembling an attractive single flower. These make excellent ornamental plants for the garden or for containers. They are not readily available, but can be obtained from some nurseries specialising in native plants. Propagation is from half-ripened tip cuttings. These will not stand excessive humidity and require careful watering.

Diplolaena angustifolia
YANCHEP ROSE; NATIVE ROSE

Origin WA
Climate WT, M, CT
Shade Light to filtered
CONTAINER PLANT
Description A small bushy shrub which grows to around 1.5 m and has narrow leaves which have a central groove and rolled edges. The pendent flower heads have striking red stamens framed by green, overlapping bracts. These appear in late winter and early spring.

Cultivation A beautiful plant that demands perfect drainage. It grows on sand and limestone near Perth and will do well in alkaline soil. It prefers semishade and regular tip pruning will maintain bushy growth. It is frost-tender.

Landscape Use It may be grown among other shrubs in the garden or in a container.

Diplolaena grandiflora

Origin WA
Climate WT, M
Shade Light to filtered

Description An upright but spreading shrub to around 2.5 m high with a similar width. It has oval woolly leaves and pendent flower heads with pink or red stamens surrounded by green bracts. The flowers appear in late winter and spring.

Cultivation An attractive species that grows well in warm conditions with excellent drainage. It prefers partial shade and is moderately tolerant to frost.

Landscape Use Grow in the protection of other shrubs and trees in the garden.

DODONAEA
SAPINDACEAE

This genus of approximately 60 species is mostly native to Australia. Species are commonly known as hop-bushes because early settlers used the fruits of some species as a substitute for hops in beer making. Most of these are shrubs or small trees of attractive appearance and decorative foliage, although the flowers are small and insignificant. It is the highly coloured inflated fruits that form the attraction of these plants, and since these remain for long periods, some species make excellent ornamental plants. The genus is represented

Diplolaena angustifolia

Diplolaena grandiflora

in all States, extending from moist coastal areas to the dry inland. They are hardy and adaptable in cultivation and some do very well in inland gardens. Sometimes these shrubs are attacked by scale insects, which can be controlled by using white oil. Propagation is from half-ripened tip cuttings.

Dodonaea boroniifolia
FERN-LEAF HOP-BUSH

Origin Qld, NSW, Vic.
Climate WT, M, SA
Shade None to filtered
BIRD-ATTRACTING
ORNAMENTAL FOLIAGE
Description A spreading sticky shrub up to 2 m with a similar width. The dark green pinnate leaves have up to 12 leaflets with a toothed tip. The flowers that appear in winter and spring are followed by large four winged capsules that mature to deep pink or red in summer.

Cultivation A popular and particularly showy species that does well in most well drained soils. It will tolerate periods of dryness and is frost-resistant. Prune regularly to promote bushy shape.

Landscape Use This is a very ornamental plant for growing as a feature or among other shrubs.

Dodonaea boroniifolia

Dodonaea cuneata

Dodonaea cuneata
WEDGE-LEAF HOP-BUSH

Origin Qld, NSW, Vic., SA
Climate S, WT, M, SA
Shade None to light
BIRD-ATTRACTING
Description This erect shrub grows to around 2 m. It has dark green wedge-shaped leaves, minute flowers and masses of attractive winged bronze-red fruit pods during spring and summer.

Cultivation An adaptable species that will grow in most soils with good drainage. It will tolerate periods of dryness and is frost-resistant. Regular tip pruning will maintain bushy growth.

Landscape Use A dainty plant for growing among other shrubs. It will also form an attractive low screen.

Dodonaea microzyga
BRILLIANT HOP-BUSH

Origin Qld, NSW, SA, WA, NT
Climate WT, M, SA
Shade None to light
DROUGHT-RESISTANT
CONTAINER PLANT
Description A spreading, sticky shrub that grows to around 1.5 m high with a similar width. The varnished leaves are composed of tiny leaflets. In spring and summer the bush is covered in crimson, winged fruits.

Cultivation This species from semiarid regions has adapted well to cultivation, particularly in areas of low rainfall. It needs good drainage and will grow in very sandy soils. Prune lightly to shape. It is frost-resistant.

Dodonaea microzyga

Landscape Use The bright red fruits make this a most attractive ornamental or hedge plant. It may also be grown in a large container.

Dodonaea triquetra
LARGE-LEAF HOP-BUSH

Origin Qld, NSW, Vic.
Climate WT, M
Shade Light to filtered
BIRD-ATTRACTING
Description An erect shrub to around 3 m which has large, lanceolate leaves up to 10 cm long. The inconspicuous flowers that appear in spring are followed by attractive pendent clusters of green fruits. The fruits are a favoured food of Wonga Pigeons.

Cultivation This species is widespread in coastal regions in dry and wet sclerophyll forests. It prefers some shade and a well-drained position. Prune lightly to shape.

Landscape Use An ornamental plant with green fruits for planting among other shrubs or as part of an understorey to light-canopied trees.

Dodonaea triquetra

Dodonaea viscosa
HOP-BUSH

Origin All States
Climate T, S, WT, M, CT, SA
Shade None to filtered
FAST-GROWING
DROUGHT-RESISTANT
Description This very variable species is widespread throughout Australia. It is a tall bushy shrub to around 3 m with shiny, sticky leaves and large clusters of

Dodonaea viscosa

papery, reddish, three-winged fruits in spring and summer.

D. viscosa var. *purpurea* is a purple-leaved form from New Zealand.

Cultivation This hardy species will tolerate a wide range of conditions, including very dry, some coastal exposure, wind and frost. It likes a sunny, well-drained position. A light trimming will keep the plant compact.

Landscape Use An ornamental species which makes an ideal windbreak or privacy screen. It has a neat habit and is good for planting in the public landscape, to soften architecture and as a street shrub.

DOODIA

BLECHNACEAE

A small genus of about ten species of terrestrial ferns with about six species occurring in Australia. They are hardy, attractive ferns and are suitable for gardens, rockeries, containers or baskets. Propagation is from spores or by division of clumps.

Doodia aspera
PRICKLY RASP FERN

Origin Qld, NSW, Vic.
Climate T, S, WT, M, CT
Shade Light to filtered
CONTAINER PLANT
RAINFOREST PLANT

Description This widespread fern is common in the eastern States and is found growing in fairly exposed situations as well as shaded gullies. It has a short, creeping rhizome and grows to about 50 cm tall. The upright fronds, which widen at the base, have serrated margins and a slightly rough texture. The immature fronds have an attractive rosy pink tinge.

Doodia aspera

Doodia caudata

Cultivation This fern is hardy in a variety of situations and will tolerate a fair amount of sun. It likes a moist but well-drained soil and is moderately frost-hardy.

Landscape Use A pretty fern for the garden edge or rockery pocket. It will grow in containers and makes a good basket subject.

Doodia caudata
SMALL RASP FERN

Origin Qld, NSW, Vic., Tas., SA
Climate T, S, WT, M, CT
Shade Light to filtered
CONTAINER PLANT
RAINFOREST PLANT

Description A widespread fern of eastern Australia. It is very variable, has an underground creeping rhizome and grows to around 30 cm tall. The narrow, soft fronds have a slightly weeping habit, the upper portion often extending into a long tail.

Cultivation A hardy fern that likes a protected position in the garden with good filtered sunlight. It likes a moist, well-composted soil, but will tolerate some dryness once established.

Landscape Use An attractive fern for the garden or rockery pocket. The slightly pendulous habit makes it an excellent plant for a container or basket.

Doodia media
COMMON RASP FERN

Origin Qld, NSW, Vic., Tas.
Climate T, S, WT, M, CT
Shade Light to filtered
CONTAINER PLANT

Description A common fern of the eastern States, often found growing in small colonies, where its underground creeping rhizome forms spreading clumps. It has dark green erect fronds up to 60 cm tall; new growth may be an attractive purplish pink.

Cultivation A hardy species that flourishes in a moist, sheltered part of the garden. It will grow satisfactorily in sunny location, but prefers lightly filtered sun.

Landscape Use An attractive fern for the garden or rockery pocket. It will grow well in a container.

Doodia media

DORYANTHES
DORYANTHACEAE

This endemic genus of two species is named from the Greek dory, *a spear, and* anthos, *a flower, referring to the very long, narrow flower stems. These large perennial plants form big clumps of erect sword-like leaves and bear showy red flowers in heads at the end of tall stalks. They are striking plants and are widely cultivated around Sydney in public gardens, industrial and council landscape, and large private gardens. Propagation is from seed taken in mid to late summer, which germinates readily, but growth is slow. Often it takes up to six or seven years before flowering commences. Clumps may also be divided.*

Doryanthes excelsa
GYMEA LILY; GIANT LILY

Origin NSW
Climate S, WT, M
Shade Light to filtered
SPECIMEN PLANT
BIRD-ATTRACTING
CONTAINER PLANT

Description This magnificent plant forms a dense rosette of large sword-shaped leaves up to 1.5 m long. The flower stalk, up to 5 m tall, carries a large, rounded cluster of deep red flowers which appear in spring and summer. These produce an abundant supply of nectar and attract many birds, including both honeyeaters and insectivorous birds. The tall flower stems are most striking in floral art.

Cultivation This species needs a deep, friable, well-drained soil with some shade. The flower stem is frost-tender, but the foliage is resistant. It appreciates

water in dry periods and may be grown in coastal areas with some protection. Established plants may be successfully transplanted.
Landscape Use This is a marvellous feature plant for larger areas. It is also suitable for growing in large, deep containers.

Doryanthes excelsa

Doryanthes palmeri
SPEAR LILY

Origin Qld, NSW
Climate S, WT, M
Shade Light to filtered
SPECIMEN PLANT
BIRD-ATTRACTING
Description This species forms a dense rosette of broad, bright green leaves up to 3 m long. The flower stalk, up to 5 m tall, carries numerous bright red, funnel-shaped flowers with white throats. These are arranged in elongated clusters and appear in spring. They are very attractive to honeyeaters.

Cultivation Grow in a moist, but well-drained, position with a little shade. The flower is frost-tender, but the foliage is resistant. It may be grown in protected coastal gardens.

Landscape Use This is a striking accent plant for the large garden or rockery. It may also be grown in a large, deep container.

DRYANDRA
PROTEACEAE

This genus is named after Jonas Dryander, an eighteenth-century Swedish botanist. These beautiful shrubs, numbering over 50 species, are restricted to the south-west of Western Australia. They range in size from prostrate shrubs to small trees, but the majority grow as small shrubs. Dryandras are related to banksias and in many respects closely resemble members of that genus. The highly decorative leaves vary greatly in shape, but are generally stiff, lobed or saw-toothed, and are often prickly. Flower colours are usually yellow, gold, orange and bronze, often strikingly iridescent. Individual flowers are grouped together in rounded heads with a collar of persistent bracts, sometimes in attractive contrasting colours. Dryandra flowers produce large quantities of nectar, which makes them a favourite with both honeyeaters and insect-eating birds. The blooms are long-lasting and are perfect for floral decoration, in both fresh and dried arrangements. Some species are cultivated for cut flower production.

Dryandras are truly beautiful shrubs to have in the garden, but most of those which are known in cultivation have not proved to be hardy, generally requiring special conditions for their success. One of the major problems is their susceptibility to the root rot fungus Phytophthora cinnamomi.

Doryanthes palmeri

Perfect drainage is essential and a raised garden bed will provide a means to help improve drainage.

They are most reliable in the Mediterranean-type climate of southern Australia with a dry summer season and they have been found very difficult to grow in the humid coastal areas of Queensland and New South Wales.

Dryandras usually grow in naturally low-nutrient soils and established plants do not require fertilising. A yellowing of leaves points to an iron deficiency and may be corrected by applications of iron chelates around the roots. They like a uniform soil temperature and benefit from a thick mulch of well-rotted compost of leaf litter, or the use of ground covers.

Dryandras are not readily available from nurseries as there is a shortage of seed and propagation from cuttings is not always successful. There are, however, some specialist nurseries that do stock them from time to time.

Propagation is from seed sown in autumn or spring and although this germinates quite well, young plants are prone to damping off and require careful watering. They will not stand excessive humidity.

Dryandra formosa
SHOWY DRYANDRA

Origin WA
Climate M, SA
Shade None to light
SPECIMEN PLANT
BIRD-ATTRACTING
ORNAMENTAL FOLIAGE
CONTAINER PLANT
Description A beautiful, erect, open shrub to around 5 m with attractive long

Dryandra formosa

narrow leaves which are deeply divided to the midrib. In late winter and spring, glowing yellow to orange flowerheads appear at the ends of the branches. Flowers are long-lasting and plants are cultivated for the cut flower industry. They produce nectar and attract honeyeaters to the garden.

Cultivation This species prefers a warm position in a very well drained, light-textured soil. It will grow in coastal gardens with some protection and is moderately frost-resistant. Prune or take cut flowers to prevent straggly growth.

Landscape Use This is an outstanding plant as a specimen shrub, as a fence screen or in a large tub.

Dryandra nivea
COUCH HONEYPOT

Origin WA
Climate M, CT
Shade None to light

BIRD-ATTRACTING
ORNAMENTAL FOLIAGE
CONTAINER PLANT

Description This lovely ground-hugging dryandra, 3 m wide, rarely reaches 1 m high. The finely divided leaves are dark green with a white undersurface and form an attractive feature of the plant. The golden brown flower heads are set among the leaves and are held close to the ground. These appear in late winter and spring.

Dryandra nivea

Cultivation This widespread dryandra is reasonably hardy in cultivation, but must have good drainage and a sandy, light-textured soil. It will withstand dry periods and is frost-resistant.

Landscape Use This is a marvellous plant for the rockery, where if set in an elevated position it will get the good drainage it demands, and its lovely foliage and flowers may be displayed to advantage. It is also a good container plant.

Dryandra praemorsa

Dryandra praemorsa
CUT-LEAF DRYANDRA

Origin WA
Climate WT, M, CT, SA
Shade Light to filtered

SPECIMEN PLANT
BIRD-ATTRACTING
ORNAMENTAL FOLIAGE
CONTAINER PLANT

Description A very attractive shrub which grows to around 3 m. The prickly leaves are deep green above and white beneath and look very much like holly leaves with blunt ends. The large, showy terminal flowers are bright yellow with prominent stamens and have a tinge of pink when in bud. They are borne in profusion in late winter and spring and are most attractive to honeyeaters. They make excellent cut flowers.

Cultivation This species has been grown successfully in the eastern States. It is reasonably hardy in a well-drained position with some shade. It is frost-resistant. Regular pruning will maintain bushiness.

Landscape Use Grow as a specimen or among other shrubs and trees in the garden. It may be grown as a screen or in a large container.

Dryandra quercifolia
OAK-LEAF DRYANDRA

Origin WA
Climate M
Shade None to light

SPECIMEN PLANT
BIRD-ATTRACTING
ORNAMENTAL FOLIAGE

Description This highly ornamental shrub grows to around 4 m. It has prickly, shiny leaves. The flowers, borne in autumn and winter, begin as metallic yellow-green buds and open to large yellow flowers heads of great beauty. The flowers are attractive from bud to dried stage, and are cultivated for the cut-flower trade. Many honey-eating birds are attracted to the nectar of this plant.

Cultivation This dryandra will grow in a well-drained, light-textured soil in full or partial sun. It will withstand dry periods and moderate frosts. Prune or cut the flowers to encourage compact bush.

Landscape Use Grow as a specimen or among other shrubs or trees in the garden.

Dryandra quercifolia

Dryandra sessilis

Dryandra sessilis
PARROT BUSH

Origin WA
Climate M, SA
Shade None to filtered

BIRD-ATTRACTING
ORNAMENTAL FOLIAGE

Description A medium to large rounded shrub to about 3 m or more high. It has dark green cuneate leaves to 5 cm long with prickly lobes. The creamy yellow flowerheads are produced in abundance in winter and spring.

Cultivation This species is reasonably hardy in areas with low humidity. It requires excellent drainage and a raised garden bed will produce this. It will withstand dry periods and is moderately frost tolerant. Regular light pruning when young will promote bushiness.

Landscape Use A showy plant for use as a feature. It works well as a prickly hedge or fence screen.

EINADIA
CHENOPODIACEAE

A genus of six species of shrubs or perennial herbs with four species native to Australia. They are mostly prostrate to scrambling twining plants and are found in all States from coastal to inland areas. They are valued in cultivation for their attractive grey-green foliage and ability to withstand long periods of dryness. Propagation is from half-ripened tip cuttings.

Einadia nutans
(syn. *Rhagodia nutans*)
NODDING SALTBUSH

Origin All States
Climate WT, M, CT, SA
Shade None to filtered

BIRD-ATTRACTING
SALT-TOLERANT
DROUGHT-RESISTANT
ORNAMENTAL FOLIAGE

Description A prostrate, spreading perennial with narrow grey leaves on long trailing stems. The insignificant flowers are followed by bright red or yellow berries which are a source of food for a variety of birds in inland areas.

Cultivation This very adaptable species will grow in most soils in full or partial sun. It is resistant to drought and frost

Einadia nutans

Elaeagnus triflora

and will withstand extreme coastal exposure.

Landscape Use A marvellous silvery ground cover or cascading plant for a rocky slope.

ELAEAGNUS

ELAEAGNACEAE

A genus of about 45 species found mainly in the Northern Hemisphere with one species extending to Australia. A few exotic species are cultivated for their ornamental foliage, but the Australian species is grown in tropical and subtropical gardens also for its highly perfumed flowers. Propagation is from fresh seed, layers or cuttings.

Elaeagnus triflora

(syn. *E. latiflora*)

MILLAA MILLAA

Origin Qld
Climate T, S, WT
Shade None to light

FAST-GROWING
FRAGRANT
BIRD-ATTRACTING
ORNAMENTAL FOLIAGE
RAINFOREST PLANT

Description This is a scrambling shrub with many long stems which may find support on surrounding trees and shrubs or form a fairly dense thicket. It has decorative ovate leaves with a silvery underside and silvery new growth. The small white flowers have a jasmine-like scent which fills the garden on warm sunny days. These are followed by red edible fruits.

Cultivation This species requires a moist, but well-drained, protected position. It is frost-tender.

Landscape Use This rampant grower is best planted away from other shrubs and trees. It may be trained to form a bush or to cover a fence.

ELAEOCARPUS

ELAEOCARPACEAE

This large genus of some 200 species is native to tropical and warm regions, with about 25 species being found in Australia, chiefly in rainforest areas. They are mostly tall shrubs or trees and are very attractive when in flower. The flowers are followed by decorative coloured fruits which are enjoyed by many species of native birds. Propagation is from seed cuttings.

Elaeocarpus reticulatus

(syn. *E. cyaneus*)

BLUEBERRY ASH

Origin Qld, NSW, Vic., Tas.
Climate S, WT, M, CT, H, SA
Shade None to filtered

SPECIMEN PLANT
FRAGRANT
BIRD-ATTRACTING
RAINFOREST PLANT

Description This small tree with a straight, smooth trunk grows to around 8 m in cultivation. The dark green leaves are shiny with serrated margins, and dainty fringed, bell-shaped flowers appear in great profusion in summer. These have a delicate perfume and are usually white, but some plants produce flowers of a pale pink shade. The flowers are followed by a good crop of small shiny blue berries which are a favoured food of parrots and cockatoos. Flowers, fruit and foliage are attractive in floral arrangements.

A pink-flowering form known as 'Prima Donna' is also available.

Cultivation This widespread species is a popular garden subject in many areas. It prefers a moist, well-drained soil and flowers best in a sunny position. It may be grown in a protected seaside position as well as inland, provided

Elaeocarpus reticulatus

E. reticulatus 'Prima Donna'

summer watering is assured. It is frost-tolerant.

Landscape Use This is an outstanding small specimen and shade tree. It may be planted in rows and trimmed to form a hedge or fence screen.

EPACRIS

EPACRIDACEAE

This genus of some 40 species extends to New Zealand and New Caledonia, but eastern Australia has about 35 species native to a variety of habitats. They are mostly small heath-like shrubs with small, prickly leaves and with attractive tubular flowers clustered along the ends of the stems. Many have a long flowering period and all are useful in attracting native birds. Some have become popular garden subjects and a few are available through general nurseries and those specialising in native plants. Epacris are subject to attack by scale and sooty mould which manifest themselves in the branches which become dark, almost black in appearance. Applications of white oil will be an effective control. Propagation is from seed in late spring or early summer or from half-ripened tip cuttings.

Epacris impressa

COMMON HEATH

Origin NSW, Vic., Tas., SA
Climate WT, M, CT
Shade Light to filtered
BIRD-ATTRACTING
CONTAINER PLANT

Description An attractive small shrub which usually grows around 1 m high. It has dark green, sharp-pointed leaves and carries clusters of narrow bell flowers along the stems. Flowers appear over a long period during late winter and spring and vary in colour from white to several shades of pink and red. They are a popular source of nectar for a variety of honeyeaters and provide good cut flowers. This beautiful wildflower is the floral emblem of Victoria.

Epacris impressa

Cultivation This species prefers a moist, well-drained soil with some shade. It is frost-resistant and will grow in protected coastal gardens. Prune after flowering to promote compact growth.

Landscape Use An ideal subject for the rockery or container. It makes a beautiful display when planted en masse in the bush garden.

E. impressa

Epacris longiflora

Epacris longiflora
FUCHSIA HEATH

Origin Qld, NSW
Climate WT, M, CT
Shade Light to filtered
BIRD-ATTRACTING
CONTAINER PLANT

Description This open shrub which grows to around 1 m high with a similar spread, has triangular leaves tapering to a sharp point. Throughout most of the year it produces beautiful narrow tubular bell flowers. These are coloured rich crimson with white tips, and are suspended along slender branches; they are most attractive to honeyeaters.

Cultivation This species does best in a moist but perfectly drained soil. It needs partial shade and a position where the roots are kept cool. It is frost-tolerant and may be grown in protected coastal gardens. This is a sprawling plant and regular pruning will encourage it to become more compact if this is desired.

Landscape Use A beautiful plant for the rockery where its scrambling habit may be used to advantage. When planted in groups as an understorey plant in the bush garden it will provide a bright splash of colour throughout the year. It also makes an attractive container plant.

Epacris microphylla
CORAL HEATH

Origin Qld, NSW, Vic., Tas.
Climate S, WT, M, CT, H
Shade Light to filtered
BIRD-ATTRACTING
CONTAINER PLANT

Description This dwarf, upright plant with a wide distribution will grow up to 1 m. It has very small, prickly leaves and small white flowers, often with pink buds, clustered along the upper stems from autumn through to spring.

Cultivation This species will grow in most soils and situations, including extremely wet ones, providing drainage is adequate. It prefers partial shade and is frost- and snow-tolerant.

Landscape Use An attractive plant for the rockery or near a pond. It may be grown in a tub, where its erect habit can be softened by planting the ground cover

Epacris microphylla

Pratia pedunculata, a pretty moisture-conserving plant that enjoys the same conditions.

Epacris pulchella
CORAL HEATH; WALLUM HEATH

Origin Qld, NSW
Climate S, WT, M, CT
Shade Light to filtered
BIRD-ATTRACTING
CONTAINER PLANT

Description An upright shrub which may reach 2 m, but is usually smaller. It has sharp-pointed foliage and pink or sometimes white tubular flowers packed at the top of stems. They bloom in

Epacris pulchella

autumn, winter or spring and make pretty, long-lasting cut flowers.

Cultivation This species prefers a light-textured soil in a moist, partially shaded position. It is frost-tolerant. Prune after flowering to encourage compact growth.

Landscape Use A showy species for the rockery or container.

Epacris reclinata
SANDSTONE HEATH

Origin NSW
Climate WT, M, CT, H
Shade Light to filtered
BIRD-ATTRACTING
CONTAINER PLANT

Description A small erect shrub to around 1 m with tiny ovate spreading leaves. The attractive pendent bell flowers are pink or red and appear from late autumn through to spring.

Cultivation This species is from the higher parts of the Blue Mountains in New South Wales, where it occurs in moist situations on sandstone. It should never be allowed to dry out but at the same time should have good drainage. It will withstand quite heavy shade and is frost-resistant. Prune after flowering to encourage compact growth.

Landscape Use Grow with the protection of other plants or in a sheltered part of the rockery. It is a good container plant.

Epacris reclinata

EREMAEA
MYRTACEAE

A small genus of some eight species of attractive flowering shrubs found only in Western Australia. They are generally compact shrubs with flowers rather similar to Melaleuca *with intensely coloured staminal bundles forming brush-like flowers. All species are worthy of cultivation, but success has been varied. They are generally free of pests and diseases except for Cinnamon Fungus which attacks the roots in poorly drained soils.* Eremaea beaufortioides *has proved the most reliable and is the species most commonly available. Propagation is from seed collected about 12 months after flowering or from half-ripened tip cuttings.*

Eremaea beaufortioides
ROUND-LEAVED EREMAEA

Origin WA
Climate WT, M
Shade None to light
BIRD-ATTRACTING
CONTAINER PLANT

Description This shrub, which grows to around 1.5 m, has small, ovate, overlapping leaves. The bundles of vivid orange flowers are produced at the ends of the branches in spring.

Cultivation Grow in a light-textured soil with excellent drainage. It likes plenty of sun and will withstand dry periods. In areas of high humidity grow in an elevated open position to ensure good air movement. Regular light pruning will encourage compact growth. It is moderately frost-resistant.

Landscape Use An outstanding ornamental plant when in flower, for the foreground of the garden or in an elevated part of a large rockery. It makes a beautiful container specimen for the courtyard.

Eremaea beaufortioides

Eremaea pauciflora

Origin WA
Climate WT, M, SA
Shade None to light
BIRD-ATTRACTING
CONTAINER PLANT

Description A bushy shrub to around 1 m with hairy, narrow leaves. The bright orange flowers are produced at branch ends in late spring.

Eremaea pauciflora

Cultivation Grow in a sunny, open position in a light-textured soil with very good drainage. it will withstand dry periods and is frost-resistant. Regular light pruning will maintain compact growth.

Landscape Use The combination of soft foliage and colourful flowers make this an attractive shrub for the garden or container.

EREMOPHILA

MYOPORACEAE

A large genus of some 180 species of beautiful shrubs. The name Eremophila *is derived from the Greek word* eremos, *a desert, and* philo, *to love, referring to the semiarid and arid habitats of many of the species. Few plants of the interior are more attractive. They range in size from prostrate or low-growing shrubs to quite tall open shrubs or small trees. There is great variation in foliage; some have dark green sticky leaves, while the leaves of others bear a dense covering of wool or a coating of scales. The shape of the flower is tubular and colour may be white, yellow, violet, purple, pink or red, sometimes with a spotted interior. In some species attractive calyx lobes become enlarged after the flower dies. Many species attract nectar-feeding birds.*

Eremophilas make highly ornamental garden shrubs and many species are now available at nurseries and are proving adaptable in cultivation even in climates foreign to them. They are becoming very popular shrubs in dry-country areas and many thrive in alkaline soils with very dry atmospheric conditions and low rainfall. Some species will grow in temperate areas and for those that do not like humidity a built-up bed of good garden soil and excellent drainage in an open sunny position with plenty of air movement has proved successful. A number of species are now available as grafted plants making those from dry areas easier to grow in higher rainfall areas. They are grafted onto the more reliable Myoporum montanum *and other inland species of* Myoporum. *The most common pest of eremophilas is scale which can be controlled with applications of white oil. Seasonal infestations of caterpillars and flea beetles should also be watched out for with some species. Some damage to leaves and branches can also be caused by fungi which cause browning of leaves followed by defoliation. Affected plants should be removed or treated with a fungicide as a matter of urgency. Propagation is usually by taking half-ripened tip cuttings or, in some species hardwood cuttings. Seed is often very slow or difficult to germinate. While some species strike readily, others may be very slow and benefit from a treatment of low-strength rooting hormone.*

Eremophila bignoniiflora

BIGNONIA EMU-BUSH; EURAH

Origin Qld, NSW, Vic., SA, WA, NT

Climate WT, M, SA

Shade None to light

BIRD-ATTRACTING

DROUGHT-RESISTANT

Description A tall, weeping shrub or small tree from 3 to 7 m high. The narrow pale green leaves up to 18 cm

Eremophila bignoniiflora

long are slightly sticky and the pale cream pendulous flowers occur mostly in winter and spring. These are followed by succulent fruits which are enthusiastically devoured by emus.

Cultivation As this species is found in heavy clay soils of river and creek flood plains in arid areas, it is perfect for growing in heavy soils in dry inland gardens. It responds to pruning, which makes for an attractive rounded shrub. It is moderately frost-resistant.

Landscape Use A very graceful plant for dry areas which makes and excellent screen or windbreak.

Eremophila bowmanii

BOWMAN'S EMU-BUSH

Origin Qld, NSW
Climate WT, M, SA
Shade None to light

DROUGHT-RESISTANT
ORNAMENTAL FOLIAGE
CONTAINER PLANT

Description A lovely silvery grey shrub to 2 m high, covered with soft woolly hairs. The linear leaves are silvery to blue-green, and tubular lavender or blue flowers are produced in winter and spring. Available as a grafted plant.

Cultivation This is a particularly attractive plant worthy of cultivation in gardens with a low rainfall. It requires a well-drained, light-textured soil and an open sunny position. It is drought- and frost-resistant.

Landscape Use A very pretty plant for the rockery or garden, providing a striking foliage contrast. It does well in a container.

Eremophila calorhabdos

RED ROD; SPIKED EREMOPHILA

Origin WA
Climate WT, M, CT, SA
Shade None to light

BIRD-ATTRACTING
DROUGHT-RESISTANT
CONTAINER PLANT

Description A slender, upright shrub to around 2 m tall. It has crowded ovate leaves with toothed margins, and carries pink or red tubular flowers clustered along the stems during spring and summer. Honeyeaters are attracted to the flowers. Grafted plants are sometimes available.

Cultivation This species has adapted well to cultivation and will grow in a variety of climatic conditions, including temperate, providing drainage is good. It prefers a sunny, warm position and is frost- and drought-resistant.

Landscape Use Grow in a rockery or raised garden bed. It makes an attractive container plant.

Eremophila christophori

Origin NT
Climate WT, M, SA
Shade None to light

BIRD-ATTRACTING
DROUGHT-RESISTANT

Description An erect shrub to around 2 m which is found growing naturally at the base of rocky hillsides and along creeks in

Eremophila bowmanii

Eremophila calorhabdos

central Australia. It has bright green leaves crowded along the branches, and bears pale to dark blue tubular flowers over a long period during winter and spring. This beautiful plant has been cultivated mostly by enthusiasts and is available only from a few specialist nurseries.

Cultivation This species has been successfully grown in warm temperate and Mediterranean climates as well as in its natural arid zone. It demands excellent drainage, and needs plenty of sun and air movement in humid areas. It responds to regular light pruning to encourage bushy growth. It is moderately frost-resistant.

Landscape Use Grow in a built-up garden or in a larger part of the rockery.

Eremophila christophori

Eremophila decipiens
SLENDER FUCHSIA

Origin SA, WA
Climate M, SA
Shade None to filtered
BIRD-ATTRACTING
DROUGHT-RESISTANT
CONTAINER PLANT

Description A small, spreading shrub to 1 m high and a similar width, with narrow lanceolate leaves. Branches and leaves are sometimes sticky. The bright orange flowers are held out from the foliage on curved flower stems. Flowers appear in late winter and spring.

Cultivation A hardy species in cultivation. It needs very good drainage and seems to do best in a built-up garden bed. Once established it is drought- and frost-resistant. Tip prune regularly or prune immediately after flowering to encourage compact growth.

Landscape Use For a raised garden bed, rockery or container.

Eremophila decipiens

Eremophila densifolia

Origin WA
Climate WT, M, CT, SA
Shade None to filtered
BIRD-ATTRACTING
DROUGHT-RESISTANT

Description A small, spreading shrub to no more than 50 cm high and about 3 m wide. It has crowded narrow leaves and carries mauve to purple flowers towards the end of the stems during winter and spring.

Cultivation This species does well in most soils provided drainage is good.

Eremophila densifolia

It is more tolerant of shade in temperate areas than most other eremophilas. It has rather a large spread and may be cut back if desired. It is moderately frost-tolerant.

Landscape Use Grow in the rockery, where the procumbent branches may be displayed to advantage. It is also a useful ground cover.

Eremophila drummondii

Origin WA
Climate WT, M, SA
Shade None to light
DROUGHT-RESISTANT
CONTAINER PLANT

Description A medium upright shrub to around 2 m, with many slender branches covered with sticky narrow leaves. Mauve or blue tubular flowers are produced in abundance along the branches during late winter and spring.

Cultivation This species will tolerate most soil types provided drainage is very good. It is usually slow-growing, but it is quite hardy and will tolerate frost and drought. A regular light pruning will keep compact growth.

Landscape Use An ornamental plant for the garden or a large container.

Eremophila drummondii

Eremophila gilesii
DESERT FUCHSIA

Origin Qld, NSW, SA, WA, NT
Climate M, SA
Shade None to light
DROUGHT-RESISTANT
CONTAINER PLANT

Description A small, slightly spreading shrub to around 1 m and to 3 m high.

Eremophila gilesii

Eremophila glabra

The branches and the narrow grey-green leaves are hairy and the showy tubular flowers may be pink, blue, or light or deep purple and have a hairy exterior. These make a beautiful floral display during winter and spring and in good conditions there will be some flowers all year round. Grafted plants are sometimes available.

Cultivation This extremely common species of arid regions of inland Australia is best suited to gardens in low rainfall areas. It grows in a variety of soils but needs excellent drainage. It is drought-resistant and moderately frost-resistant.

Landscape Use The low, spreading habit of this ornamental plant makes it ideal for the rockery or the front of the garden. It is also suitable for growing in a container.

Eremophila glabra
COMMON EMU-BUSH; TAR BUSH

Origin Qld, NSW, Vic., SA, WA, NT
Climate WT, M, CT, SA
Shade None to light

BIRD-ATTRACTING
DROUGHT-RESISTANT
CONTAINER PLANT

Description This very variable species has many forms in cultivation, ranging from a low prostrate form to 3 m wide with a dense covering of short hairs to an erect shrub about 1.5 m high with hairless leaves. All forms are often sticky to the touch, particularly on young growth. Most are long-flowering, from spring through to autumn; the yellow, orange or red tubular flowers are most attractive to honeyeaters.

An ornamental form, popular in cultivation, is the 'Murchison River' variety, with silver foliage and bright red flowers. Grafted plants of this variety are sometimes available.

Another popular variety is a prostrate form with yellow flowers and dark green oval leaves.

Cultivation Many forms have adapted very well to cultivation and will grow in a variety of soils with good drainage. They will withstand drought and some frost. Some forms are suitable for coastal planting with some protection. Pruning is recommended to encourage bushy growth.

Landscape Use Size will determine the position in the garden. The prostrate forms are good ground cover or rockery plants and most low-growing forms make beautiful container plants.

Eremophila laanii

Origin WA
Climate WT, M, SA
Shade None to light
DROUGHT-RESISTANT
CONTAINER PLANT
Description A many-branched shrub which may reach 3 m, but is usually smaller in cultivation. The light green leaves are slightly hairy and the tubular flowers, which are white, pink, or deep pink, appear during late winter and spring.

Cultivation This species has adapted well to cultivation and will grow in a variety of soils, including limy ones, provided the drainage is good. It will withstand drought and frost. Prune lightly to encourage bushy growth.

Landscape Use This is a very pretty species for the garden. The white form may sucker and form thickets and can be utilised as a screen.

Eremophila laanii

Eremophila latrobei

CRIMSON TURKEY BUSH

Origin Qld, NSW, SA, WA, NT
Climate M, SA
Shade None to light
BIRD-ATTRACTING
DROUGHT-RESISTANT
CONTAINER PLANT
Description A slender, variable shrub which may reach 2 m. The linear to oblong leaves vary from dark green and smooth to grey and coated with hairs. Deep pink or red tubular flowers are produced from winter to spring.

Cultivation There are several attractive forms of this lovely species in cultivation. Grafted plants are also available. It prefers a hot, fairly dry climate and needs good drainage. It is moderately frost-resistant. Tip prune when young and immediately after flowering to encourage compact growth.

Landscape Use Grow in a raised garden bed or in a container.

Eremophila latrobei

Eremophila macdonnellii

Origin Qld, NSW, SA, NT
Climate M, SA
Shade None to light
DROUGHT-RESISTANT
CONTAINER PLANT
Description A low, bushy shrub to around 1 m high and up to 5 m wide with small narrow leaves, and very showy deep purple flowers in spring and summer. There are several different forms of this ornamental species from inland Australia, including a grey-foliaged form and a prostrate form with slender, hairy green leaves.

Cultivation This species is ideally suited to gardens in low rainfall areas. It will grow in a variety of soils with very good drainage, and responds well to pruning. It will tolerate drought and frost.

Landscape Use A showy plant for the sunny rockery or the border of the garden, where it may happily spread and the beautiful flowers may be displayed to advantage. All forms are excellent container plants.

Eremophila macdonnellii

Eremophila maculata

SPOTTED EMU-BUSH; NATIVE FUCHSIA

Origin Qld, NSW, Vic., SA, WA, NT
Climate WT, M, CT, SA
Shade None to light
BIRD-ATTRACTING
DROUGHT-RESISTANT
CONTAINER PLANT
Description A very variable shrub which may be prostrate or may grow up to 3 m tall and to a similar width. It has narrow ovate leaves and tubular flowers with the lower lip deeply cut and curled back. The flowers usually have spotted throats and may be white, pink, red, yellow or orange; they occur over a long period during winter and spring. This species is extremely attractive to a variety of native birds.

E. maculata 'Aurea' is a popular yellow-flowering form. It is a compact shrub growing to around 1 m.

Cultivation This is the most commonly cultivated eremophila and it is the most reliable. It will grow in most well-drained soils in full or partial sun. It is suitable for coastal planting with some protection and is drought- and frost-resistant. A regular light pruning will encourage bushiness.

Eremophila maculata

E. maculata 'Aurea'

Landscape Use This ornamental, free-flowering plant will attract many birds to the garden. The prostrate forms may be used as a foreground shrub or in the rockery. Most of the low-growing forms make excellent container plants.

Eremophila merrallii

Origin WA
Climate M, SA
Shade None to light
BIRD-ATTRACTING
DROUGHT-RESISTANT
CONTAINER PLANT

Description A small, dense shrub to around 50 cm with crowded hairy grey-green foliage. Tubular mauve flowers are produced towards the ends of the branches in spring and summer.

Cultivation This species prefers a warm, fairly dry climate and a well-drained position. In its natural habitat it grows in stony clay-loam. It is moderately frost-resistant. Prune after flowering to encourage compact growth.

Eremophila merrallii

Landscape Use Pretty foliage and flowers make this lovely small shrub ideal for the garden foreground, rockery or container.

Eremophila nivea

Origin WA, SA
Climate WT, M, SA
Shade None to light
ORNAMENTAL FOLIAGE
CONTAINER PLANT

Description A dense, rounded shrub which may grow to around 2 m. The branches, new growth and greyish leaves are covered in white hairs, giving the bush a beautiful silvery woolly appearance. The pretty lilac flowers are a perfect accompaniment; they appear during spring. Grafted plants are sometimes available.

Eremophila nivea

Cultivation This species adapts well to cultivation and will grow in light to heavy soil with good drainage. It responds to light pruning from an early age and appreciates watering during extended dry periods. It is moderately frost-resistant.

Landscape Use This beautiful silver-foliaged plant will provide year-round contrast in the garden. It looks most striking when planted en masse and is a beautiful feature for the rockery. When kept lightly trimmed it is an excellent container plant.

Eremophila pachyphylla

Origin WA
Climate M, SA
Shade None to light
BIRD-ATTRACTING
DROUGHT-RESISTANT
CONTAINER PLANT

Description An erect shrub to around 2 m with shiny narrow leaves with a curved tip. Masses of pale mauve tubular flowers are produced along the branches in late winter and spring.

Cultivation Growing naturally in sandy or brown clay soils, this species needs full sun in a well-drained position and does best in a built-up garden bed. It is moderately frost-resistant. Tip prune

Eremophila pachyphylla

regularly or prune immediately after flowering to encourage compact growth.

Landscape Use A very pretty flowering eremophila for the dry-country garden. It does well as a container plant.

Eremophila racemosa
(syn. *E. bicolor*)

Origin WA
Climate WT, M, SA
Shade None to light
CONTAINER PLANT

Description A small, erect shrub which may grow up to 2 m and has narrow pale green leaves. The colourful tubular flowers, which are orange-yellow in bud, open to pinkish red, giving the plant the appearance of having many different colours at the one time. Flowers are produced throughout spring.

Cultivation This very adaptable species is popular in cultivation. It prefers a sunny, well-drained position and is resistant to drought and frost. Regular light pruning is recommended to encourage bushiness.

Landscape Use This is a colourful feature plant for the garden or rockery. It looks very good in a container in a sunny courtyard.

ERIOSTEMON
RUTACEAE

An endemic genus of some 32 species of ornamental flowering shrubs known as wax flowers. They are small to fairly large shrubs whose alternate leaves have conspicuous oil glands, which in some species are highly aromatic. The starry flowers with five waxy petals vary in colour from white and pink to mauve and are produced over a long period during winter and spring. These plants are commonly cultivated in the eastern States, where E. myoporoides *has been a garden favourite for many years. Eriostemons are not prone to many pests or diseases although scale insects will attack under certain conditions and will be noticeable on branches and the undersides of leaves. Applications of white oil will be a sufficient control of this pest. Propagation from seed is often difficult and most species are propagated from half-ripened tip cuttings.*

Eremophila racemosa

Eriostemon australasius
(syn. *E. lanceolatus*)
PINK WAX FLOWER

Origin Qld, NSW
Climate S, WT, M
Shade None to light
CONTAINER PLANT

Description An upright shrub to around 2 m high with narrow, leathery, grey-green leaves. Profuse large pink, waxy, star-like flowers appear over a long period during late winter and spring. These are long-lasting when cut for indoors. This species is not always

Eriostemon australasius

readily obtainable because of propagation difficulties.

Cultivation This very beautiful wildflower is generally considered tricky in cultivation. It must have perfect drainage and a cool root run, provided by a good mulch or the protection of low-growing plants. It will withstand dry periods and is moderately frost-resistant. Tip prune after flowering.

Landscape Use A lovely addition to the bush garden or for growing in a large container.

Eriostemon buxifolius

Eriostemon buxifolius
BOX-LEAF WAX FLOWER

Origin NSW
Climate WT, M
Shade Light to filtered
CONTAINER PLANT
Description A small, rounded shrub to around 1.5 m with crowded, flat, leathery leaves. The white star-like flowers, pink in bud, are produced during late winter and spring.

E. buxifolius ssp. *obovatus* has similar flowers, but differs in having oval leaves with warty margins.

Cultivation Naturally growing on the sandstone of the Sydney region, this species needs very well drained soil in a partially shaded position. Some protection for the root system should be provided. It is frost-tolerant. Tip prune to encourage compact growth.

Landscape Use A pretty, profusely flowering shrub for the garden or container.

Eriostemon difformis

Eriostemon myoporoides

Eriostemon difformis
SMALL WAX FLOWER

Origin Qld, NSW, Vic.
Climate WT, M
Shade None to light
CONTAINER PLANT
Description A small shrub to around 1 m with many small, thick, narrow leaves. Clusters of small pink or white flowers are produced at the ends of the branches during winter and spring.

Cultivation Found growing naturally on the plains and slopes of the Great Dividing Range, this species will grow in an open, warm position with very good drainage. A surface mulch will keep the root area cool. It is moderately frost-resistant. Regularly trim to keep the bush shapely.

Landscape Use A graceful small shrub for the small garden, rockery or container.

Eriostemon myoporoides
LONG-LEAF WAX FLOWER

Origin Qld, NSW, Vic.
Climate S, WT, M, CT, H, SA
Shade None to filtered
FAST-GROWING
AROMATIC FOLIAGE
BIRD-ATTRACTING
CONTAINER PLANT
Description A medium-sized shrub to around 2 m which is dense in growth down to ground level. The aromatic leathery leaves are very variable in length. The pink buds along the stems open to beautiful white star-shaped flowers throughout winter and spring. These make delightful sprays of cut flowers. The species is extremely variable and six subspecies are recognised. Many forms have been selected and some ornamental cultivars are available.

Cultivation This reliable shrub is the most commonly grown *Eriostemon*. It is extremely adaptable and may be grown in almost any position in the garden, from full sun to semishade. It will grow in most soils provided the drainage is good. It is frost-resistant. Prune lightly after flowering to maintain bushy habit.

Landscape Use A very easily maintained shrub for the garden, planted either singly or in groups. It may be used as an informal hedge or screen along walls or fences. It makes a shapely container plant.

Eriostemon obovalis
NORTHERN FAIRY WAX FLOWER

Origin NSW
Climate WT, M
Shade Light to filtered
CONTAINER PLANT
Description A small shrub to 1 m with broad, leathery, heart-shaped leaves. Showy, waxy white flowers are produced along the stems during winter and spring.

Cultivation Grow in a well-mulched soil with good drainage. It is tolerant of dry conditions but a surface mulch and thorough soaking during hot dry weather are appreciated. It is moderately frost-resistant. A light regular trimming or pruning after flowering will keep the bush shapely.

Landscape Use A lovely, free-flowering shrub for the garden, rockery or container.

Eriostemon spicatus

Eriostemon obovalis

Eriostemon spicatus
SPIKED WAX FLOWER

Origin WA
Climate WT, M
Shade None to light
CONTAINER PLANT
Description A small shrub up to 1 m with narrow glandular foliage. The pinkish mauve flowers are produced in loose sprays during winter and spring.

Cultivation Grow in a open, sunny position with very good drainage. A surface mulch will keep the root area cool. This species will withstand dry spells, but a thorough soaking during hot dry weather is appreciated. Prune immediately after flowering to encourage compact growth.

Landscape Use A good rockery or container subject.

Eriostemon verrucosus
FAIRY WAX FLOWER

Origin Vic., Tas., SA
Climate WT, M, CT
Shade None to filtered
AROMATIC FOLIAGE
BIRD-ATTRACTING
CONTAINER PLANT
Description A small open shrub to around 1.5 m high and a similar width, with many branchlets, often with an arching habit. The ovate, grey-green leaves are glandular and aromatic. The waxy white or pink flowers grow from the leaf axils along the branches. As there may be flowers at all stages from small bud to fully open, the flowering season is long during late winter and spring.

Eriostemon verrucosus

'Semmons Double Wax Flower' is an outstanding multi-petalled form from near Bendigo, Victoria. It has long, weeping branches and beautiful large waxy white or pink flowers with three rows of petals.

Cultivation This species will grow in most well-drained soils, but does appreciate abundant leaf mould in and on the soil. It is tolerant of dry periods,

E. verrucosus (multi-petalled form)

E. verrucosus (multi-petalled form)

but benefits from summer watering. It is frost-resistant. Tip prune when young and prune rather hard after flowering to maintain shape and vigorous growth.

Landscape Use A beautiful plant for the garden, rockery or container.

EUCALYPTUS

MYRTACEAE

This large genus of over 500 species, as well as many hybrids, dominates the Australian landscape. The name is derived from the Greek eu, *well, and* kalypto, *to cover, referring to the cap of the calyx which covers the flower stamens before they open.*

Eucalypts are adaptable to a wide range of climatic conditions and have found an appreciative home in many countries of the world, including North Africa, Europe, Israel and many parts of North America. In California they have been established for so long that they are regarded as native trees.

Eucalypts offer a vast selection of plants for all purposes including timber production, oil distillation, large landscape design, shade, shelter and soil protection. They provide a haven and food for birds and mammals and many are noted for the beauty of their flowers, foliage, capsules and bark and for their interesting forms. Many are useful for honey production and others provide excellent fuel. They vary in height from towering forest giants to the dwarf, spectacular-flowered mallees. The wide range of species available means that there is a eucalypt for every garden; however, it should be remembered that many grow into trees too big for the suburban garden and they often have extensive root systems. Smaller species should be chosen to eliminate the complications of branch overhang and drop, pipe damage and litter fall in gutters. A few species may be used as container plants, in which situation they flower quite satisfactorily.

Many of the eucalypts perform a valuable service in holding the soil and preventing erosion by wind and water. Mallee species hold the sand in the dry inland. The main distinguishing character of mallees is their lignotuber, which is a swollen mass of woody tissue that occurs at ground level, from which a number of thin stems arise. Many of the small ornamentally flowering mallees are from drier regions of Western Australia and may be difficult to cultivate in coastal eastern Australia. Most of these appreciate dry summers and care must be taken to select a dry, well-drained spot with good air circulation. Many of the mallee species, which have multiple trunks in natural conditions, frequently develop only one stem under cultivation. Some mallees are straggly or develop crooked trunks. These different shapes are visually pleasing and should be encouraged, as they contribute much to the character of ornamental planting.

In rural districts eucalypts are one of the most important elements in country garden design. They are used to protect paddocks from wind, to provide shelter for the stock, as a safeguard against soil erosion and to provide shade, shelter and beauty around the homestead.

Eucalypts are fast-growing and long-lived and demand little or no attention.

Seasonal infestations of beetles and leaf-chewing caterpillars cause most noticeable damage to eucalypts but rarely are these so severe as to cause permanent damage. Scale insects and lerps, which are sap sucking, can be more serious as they can limit growth and, in some cases, kill plants if allowed to flourish. However, both are a food source for native birds and much natural control is achieved by them.

Propagation is by seed, which germinates readily. In some species such as E. ficifolia *and* E. sideroxylon *flower colour may not always come true from seed.*

Eucalyptus alpina
GRAMPIANS GUM

Origin Vic.
Climate M, CT, H
Shade None to light
BIRD-ATTRACTING
Description This is a small tree or shrub to around 3 m high. It has fibrous bark, broad, leathery leaves and very warty flower buds opening to cream flowers in summer to early winter.

Cultivation This is a hardy plant, suited to moist soils and situations. It occurs naturally along the high peaks of the Grampians and has developed a resistance to harsh winds, frosts and snow.

Eucalyptus alpina

Landscape Use This is a valuable screen or shelter plant in cold climate areas.

Eucalyptus amplifolia
CABBAGE GUM

Origin Qld, NSW
Climate WT, M, CT, H
Shade None to light
BIRD-ATTRACTING
Description This is a medium-sized to tall tree which may reach 15 m. It has a smooth trunk which may either develop into a short bole or divide close to the ground into several large ascending stems. It has long lanceolate leaves and produces tight clusters of white flowers during summer.

Eucalyptus amplifolia

Cultivation This tree is found growing mainly on heavy soils, often with poor drainage, and is suitable for wet or swampy sites. It will withstand frost and some snow in the higher areas.

Landscape Use This ornamental tree is too large for the average garden, but is an ideal shade or shelter tree for rural areas with heavy frosts.

Eucalyptus blakelyi
BLAKELY'S RED GUM

Origin Qld, NSW, Vic.
Climate WT, M, SA
Shade None to light
SPECIMEN PLANT
BIRD-ATTRACTING
Description A medium-sized tree to 16 m with a graceful crown and a mostly smooth, mottled bark. It has long grey-green leaves and clusters of white flowers during spring and summer. The koala feeds on the leaves of this species and it is a good honey producer. It yields a good, red, hard timber suitable for fencing.

Cultivation This species will thrive in most soils and under cultivation can be a most ornamental tree. It will withstand frost, dry conditions and wind.

Landscape Use This is a suitable species for windbreaks, shade or shelter on rural properties.

Eucalyptus blakelyi

Eucalyptus botryoides
BANGALAY; SOUTHERN MAHOGANY

Origin NSW, Vic.
Climate WT, M
Shade None to light
FAST-GROWING
BIRD-ATTRACTING
Description A shapely medium-sized tree to 20 m with a brown, fibrous, persistent bark. It has slender glossy green leaves and produces clusters of small white flowers during summer.

Cultivation This is a very hardy and useful tree, suited to damp situations along the coast, where it will resist a considerable amount of salt spray and wind. It will grow in heavy soils and will tolerate soil salinity. It is frost-resistant.

Landscape Use This is an excellent shade tree for parks, industrial sites or rural gardens.

Eucalyptus botryoides

Eucalyptus caesia
GUNGURRU

Origin WA
Climate WT, M, SA
Shade None to light
FAST-GROWING
SPECIMEN PLANT
BIRD-ATTRACTING
DROUGHT-RESISTANT
CONTAINER PLANT
Description This graceful weeping small tree to 8 m is a most beautiful ornamental eucalypt. It has a slender habit, blue-green foliage and powdery white pendulous branches. The attractive reddish bark curls to reveal a smooth green colour beneath. Deep pink flowers hang in loose clusters during winter and spring, followed by silvery bell-shaped capsules.

E. caesia 'Silver Princess', an extremely beautiful cultivar grows to 10 m. It has very pendulous branches and larger leaves, flowers and fruits. The magnificent flowers are a deep pinky-red.

Cut flowers, foliage and capsules of both forms are excellent for floral decoration and the flowers attract honeyeaters to the garden.

Cultivation This adaptable species will grow in well-drained sandy soil, and in some clayey soils. In cultivation the branches may grow very long and leggy, and will not withstand winds.

A regular light pruning in early years will help to establish a better balanced root system. This species is moderately frost-resistant and, although it survives drought, appreciates watering during dry periods. It resents excessive humidity.

Landscape Use This lovely small eucalypt may be planted as a specimen or in a group in the garden. It is a beautiful street or park tree and may be grown in a large container.

Eucalyptus caesia

Eucalyptus calophylla
MARRI

Origin WA
Climate WT, M, CT
Shade None to light
SPECIMEN PLANT
BIRD-ATTRACTING
Description This medium-sized to tall tree grows to around 9 m to 20 m high. It has rough, flaky bark and broad glossy leaves to 18 cm long. It has a dense rounded crown and in summer produces large clusters of usually white flowers. A beautiful pink flowering form is available from most native plant nurseries. Flowers are followed by large decorative urn-shaped fruits.

Cultivation This species prefers a moist, but well drained position. It will grow in most soils and is moderately frost hardy.

Landscape Use The birds love this tree. It makes an outstanding shade tree for large gardens and rural properties.

Eucalyptus calophylla

Eucalyptus calycogona
SQUARE-FRUITED MALLEE; GOOSEBERRY MALLEE

Origin Vic., SA, WA
Climate WT, M, SA
Shade None to light
BIRD-ATTRACTING
DROUGHT-RESISTANT
Description A shapely mallee or thin tree which may reach 10 m. It has smooth pale grey bark with some persistent rough bark at the base of the main branches. It has narrow green leaves and abundant

white, sometimes tinged with pink, blossoms during spring.

Cultivation A hardy small tree that will grow in very sandy soil in dry areas. It is frost-resistant.

Landscape Use This species is suitable for ornamental planting and makes a good windbreak. Its small habit makes it ideal for street planting.

Eucalyptus calycogona

Eucalyptus camaldulensis

Eucalyptus camaldulensis
RIVER RED GUM

Origin Qld, NSW, Vic., SA, WA, NT
Climate WT, M, SA
Shade None to light

FAST-GROWING
BIRD-ATTRACTING
DROUGHT-RESISTANT

Description This well-known inland species is a large, spreading, stately tree growing to around 30 m high and about 30 m wide. The attractive bark is creamy white, patterned with brown and pinkish red patches. It has a dense crown of slender lanceolate leaves and bears small creamy white flowers during summer. The timber is red, hard and durable and is used in heavy construction and flooring. This is a variable tree and appears in quite a number of different forms. Several varieties are available from nurseries and forestry departments and advice should be sought on trees suited to local conditions.

Cultivation The River Red Gum is widespread along watercourses throughout drier inland Australia and will accept heavy clay soils and soil that remains waterlogged after heavy rain. It will also tolerate drought and frost. It will withstand hard pruning, but it may drop large branches, so it should not be planted too close to the house.

Landscape Use This is an ideal tree for rural properties, giving shade and shelter to stock as well as fodder during periods of drought.

Eucalyptus campaspe
SILVER-TOPPED GIMLET

Origin WA
Climate M, SA
Shade None to light

SPECIMEN PLANT
BIRD-ATTRACTING
DROUGHT-RESISTANT

Description A small tree to around 10 m, sometimes branched very low on the trunk. The bark is smooth and copper-coloured with slight fluting or twisting on the trunk and some branches. It has a rounded crown of grey-green leaves and produces creamy white flowers in spring and summer.

Eucalyptus campaspe

Cultivation This species will grow in most soils, including clay and saline soils. It is resistant to drought and frost. It may be pruned lightly.

Landscape Use This is a useful ornamental small tree for streets and parks in areas with low rainfall. It is also suitable for planting as a windbreak or as a shade tree.

Eucalyptus cinerea
ARGYLE APPLE; MEALY STRINGYBARK

Origin NSW, Vic.
Climate WT, M, H
Shade None to light

SPECIMEN PLANT
BIRD-ATTRACTING
ORNAMENTAL FOLIAGE

Description A small to medium-sized ornamental tree which grows to around 12 m. The rounded juvenile foliage is an attractive blue-grey colour and is often retained throughout the life of the tree. The adult leaves, which become elongated, are also blue-grey. The buds are borne in threes in the axils of the leaves and open to small white flowers in spring or early summer.

Cultivation This species will grow in most soils in a well-drained position. It is relatively slow-growing at first, but once established the tree grows vigorously, sometimes assuming a pleasing twisted shape. With judicious pruning a very dense crown of foliage may be produced. It is native to cool fairly dry climates and is suited to areas of low rainfall; it is extremely hardy to frost.

Landscape Use This lovely tree has the habit of retaining the lower branches even as an old tree, which makes it an ideal screen or windbreak tree. It has been used successfully as a street tree in a number of areas, including Canberra. Its interesting form and decorative silver foliage make it one of the most ornamental of small trees for specimen planting.

Eucalyptus cinerea

Eucalyptus citriodora

Eucalyptus citriodora
LEMON-SCENTED GUM

Origin Qld
Climate T, S, WT, M
Shade None to light

FAST-GROWING
SPECIMEN PLANT
AROMATIC FOLIAGE
BIRD-ATTRACTING

Description This graceful, slender tree to around 20 m has a long straight trunk with a beautiful smooth white or pink bark. It has an open crown of delightfully lemon-scented long narrow leaves and bears clusters of white flowers in winter.

Cultivation Well known in cultivation, this adaptable species will grow in a variety of soils. It will tolerate dry or wet conditions, but not severe frost. It may be grown in coastal gardens with some protection.

Landscape Use This is a particularly beautiful specimen tree which creates a dramatic effect in any landscape. The leaves provide only light shade, so it does not inhibit the growth of other plants.

Eucalyptus cordata
HEART-LEAVED SILVER GUM

Origin Tas.
Climate WT, M, CT, H
Shade None to light

BIRD-ATTRACTING
ORNAMENTAL FOLIAGE

Description A tall shrub to medium-sized tree to 20 m or more high. It is valued for its extremely attractive silvery-grey, heart-shaped juvenile leaves which persist on most trees. The adult lanceolate leaves are seen only on the tops of tall mature trees. Profuse creamy-white flowers are produced in spring. The cut foliage is used for floral decoration.

Cultivation This species is ideal for planting in cool areas where it will withstand heavy frosts. It is suitable for most soils but must have good drainage.

Landscape Use This decorative foliaged tree is best grown in parks, large gardens or rural properties because of the size to which it eventually grows.

Eucalyptus cordata

E. cordata (leaves)

Eucalyptus curtisii
PLUNKETT MALLEE

Origin Qld
Climate S, WT, M
Shade None to light
SPECIMEN PLANT
BIRD-ATTRACTING

Description This is a slender-stemmed mallee or small tree which may reach 7 m high. The smooth bark is shed in long thin strips to leave a silvery grey surface. The mature lanceolate leaves are shiny green above and pale underneath. It bears large clusters of creamy white flowers at the ends of the branches in summer.

Cultivation This adaptable species is hardy in a wide range of conditions. It prefers a well-drained soil, but will tolerate periods of wetness as well as dry spells. It is frost-resistant.

Landscape Use This is an excellent ornamental tree for the small garden. It may also be used as a windbreak.

Eucalyptus curtisii

Eucalyptus elata
(syn. *E. andreana, E. lindleyana*)
RIVER PEPPERMINT

Origin NSW, Vic.
Climate WT, M
Shade None to light
SPECIMEN PLANT
BIRD-ATTRACTING

Description This is a medium-sized tree which grows to around 15 m or more high. It has rough bark at the base and smooth white bark on the upper trunk and branches. The open crown provides a light shade of long, narrow, drooping leaves. Clusters of cream flowers are produced in abundance in winter and spring.

Cultivation This hardy tree prefers moist but well-drained soils. It is frost-hardy.

Landscape Use This most ornamental weeping tree is suited to specimen planting and can also be used as a windbreak, or as a street tree where wires are absent.

Eucalyptus elata

Eucalyptus eximia
YELLOW BLOODWOOD

Origin NSW
Climate WT, M, CT
Shade None to light
FAST-GROWING
SPECIMEN PLANT
FRAGRANT
BIRD-ATTRACTING

Description A small to medium-sized tree to around 15 m. It has persistent scaly yellow-brown bark and most attractive curved bluish-green leaves up to 20 cm long. It bears showy perfumed creamy flowers in spring followed by urn-shaped fruits. Friarbirds and many other nectar eaters are attracted to the flowers.

Cultivation This species is confined to the coastal sandstone of temperate New South Wales and is ideal for growing in difficult poor soil; it may be used in coastal gardens with some protection. It is slightly frost-tender, particularly when young.

Landscape Use An ornamental tree suitable for specimen planting or for use as a windbreak.

Eucalyptus eximia

Eucalyptus ficifolia
RED FLOWERING GUM

Origin WA
Climate WT, M, CT
Shade None to light
SPECIMEN PLANT
BIRD-ATTRACTING

Description This well-known eucalypt is widely planted throughout the world. It is a small, rough-barked tree which grows to around 10 m. It has a dense, rounded crown and in summer produces a profusion of flowers; these are often brilliant red, but the colour varies and

Eucalyptus ficifolia

may be white, any shade of pink, salmon or red. The flowers are followed by large, decorative, urn-shaped fruits. Both flowers and fruits are excellent for floral arrangements.

Cultivation This species prefers a well-drained position with a light-textured soil. It thrives in coastal areas with protection. It prefers a frost-free situation, especially when young.

Landscape Use This is a beautiful specimen tree used either singly or in groups. It is ideal for street planting and for shade and ornament in parks.

Eucalyptus forrestiana
FUCHSIA GUM

Origin WA
Climate WT, M, CT, SA
Shade None to light

SPECIMEN PLANT
BIRD-ATTRACTING
DROUGHT-RESISTANT

Description This ornamental small tree or mallee grows up to 5 m high. The smooth grey bark peels off in long strips to expose fresh light brown bark. The very attractive bright red pendulous flower buds are present for a long period and are the feature of this species. Yellow flowers appear during summer, followed by ribbed fruits that are dull red, ageing to brown. The buds, flowers and fruits are all excellent in floral arrangements.

E. forrestiana ssp. *stoatei* (syn. *E. stoatei*) has bright red multi-grooved flower buds.

Cultivation This widely cultivated species is suitable for most soils. It is tolerant of salty conditions and may be planted in coastal areas with some protection. It is resistant to drought and is moderately frost-tender when young. It will not tolerate excessive humidity.

Landscape Use This species has been successfully planted as a small street tree, hedge and low windbreak in many drier parts of Australia. It is highly ornamental for the small garden. Can be trained as a single-trunked small tree.

Eucalyptus globulus
TASMANIAN BLUE GUM

Origin Vic., Tas.
Climate WT, M, CT, H
Shade None to light

FAST-GROWING
BIRD-ATTRACTING

Description This large forest tree up to 30 m is the floral emblem of Tasmania. It has a tall straight trunk with grey-blue

Eucalyptus forrestiana

Eucalyptus globulus

bark which is shed in long ribbons. The attractive blue-grey juvenile leaves are rounded and stem-clasping. These are replaced by elongated dark glossy green leaves. The creamy flowers, which are quite large, appear in winter and spring. Many native birds are attracted to the nectar and fruits of this species.

E. globulus var. *compacta*. This is a smaller-growing form to 10 m. It has a dense, compact habit and retains its lower branches. The juvenile foliage is used in floral arrangements.

Cultivation This species prefers deep, well-drained soils, but will grow in most heavy soils. It may be used in coastal areas with protection and is frost-resistant.

Landscape Use This tree is best suited to large parks and gardens because of the size to which it eventually grows. It may be used as a tall windbreak in rural areas.

Eucalyptus grossa
COARSE-LEAVED MALLEE

Origin WA
Climate M, SA
Shade None to light

BIRD-ATTRACTING
DROUGHT-RESISTANT

Description This species is mostly a mallee-like low shrub to 3 m, but may grow as a small straggly tree to 6 m. It has rough grey bark and leathery, broad, shining green leaves. The young branches and flower buds are reddish. Large, crowded, ornamental yellow or yellow-green flowers appear in spring.

Cultivation This adaptable species will grow in most soils provided the drainage is good. It is drought-resistant, is tolerant of saline conditions and, although it is slightly frost-tender when young, is able to withstand frosts when established.

Landscape Use This species is suitable for use as a dense hedge or low windbreak if pruned and trained. It is used as a street plant in drier inland areas and makes an interesting ornamental plant for the garden.

Eucalyptus grossa

Eucalyptus gunnii
CIDER GUM

Origin Tas.
Climate WT, M, CT, H
Shade None to light

FAST-GROWING
BIRD-ATTRACTING
ORNAMENTAL FOLIAGE

Description This is a tall, straight tree to 20 m. It has a smooth grey to pinkish bark and beautiful, rounded grey juvenile foliage with silvery pink shoots. White flowers appear in summer. The juvenile foliage is used extensively in the florist industry.

Eucalyptus gunnii

Cultivation This species is widely cultivated in Great Britain and is ideal for planting in cold climates, as it is extremely frost-resistant and will tolerate snow. It does well in a wet position and will grow in heavy soils.

Landscape Use This is a good shade tree and may be used for screening or as a windbreak.

Eucalyptus haemastoma
SCRIBBLY GUM

Origin NSW
Climate WT, M
Shade None to light

SPECIMEN PLANT
BIRD-ATTRACTING

Description This is a small to medium-sized tree which may reach 20 m. It grows rather crookedly and has a satiny white trunk that is characteristically marked by

Eucalyptus haemastoma

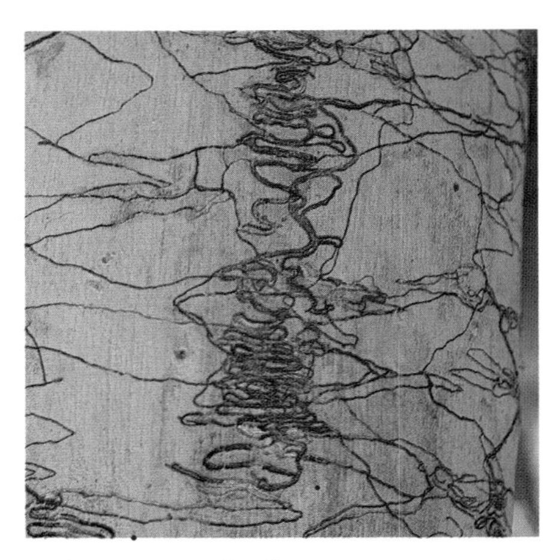

E. haemastoma (bark)

zigzag lines made by insect larvae. It has a light crown of grey-green leaves and bears small creamy flowers in spring.

Cultivation This species is ideal for growing in areas with infertile soil in a mild climate. It requires good drainage and is frost-resistant.

Landscape Use This graceful tree has a tendency to produce a number of trunks and makes an interesting feature plant.

Eucalyptus kruseana
KRUSE'S MALLEE

Origin WA
Climate WT, M, SA
Shade None to light

SPECIMEN PLANT
BIRD-ATTRACTING
DROUGHT-RESISTANT
ORNAMENTAL FOLIAGE

Description This rather straggly, but delightful, small mallee usually grows to around 3 m. The smooth bark is copper-coloured and the round silvery-blue leaves provide good contrast. The greenish yellow flowers which form between the leaves appear in autumn and winter.

Cultivation This species does best in a light-textured soil with good drainage. It is drought- and frost-resistant, but may be frost-tender when young. It will stand light pruning.

Landscape Use This species is cultivated in many dry inland towns and is a useful small street tree. It may be used as a feature plant in the small garden.

Eucalyptus kruseana

Eucalyptus lehmannii
BUSHY YATE

Origin WA
Climate WT, M, SA
Shade None to light

FAST-GROWING
SPECIMEN PLANT
BIRD-ATTRACTING
SALT-TOLERANT
DROUGHT-RESISTANT

Description This is a dense, rounded mallee or small tree growing to around 6 m. It has smooth grey-brown bark and branches from near ground level. The large clusters of green flowers from late winter to summer are preceded by fused clusters of red finger-like buds. These are followed by large spiky fruits. The buds, flowers and fruit provide excellent material for floral and dried arrangements.

Cultivation This hardy and adaptable species will grow in most well-drained soils. It is drought-resistant, will tolerate exposed coastal conditions and is frost-resistant once established.

Landscape Use The natural bushy habit of this species makes it an ideal windbreak or screen. It also makes a decorative feature plant.

Eucalyptus lehmannii

Eucalyptus leucoxylon
YELLOW GUM

Origin Vic., SA
Climate WT, M, CT, SA
Shade None to light

FAST-GROWING
SPECIMEN PLANT
BIRD-ATTRACTING
DROUGHT-RESISTANT

Description A medium-sized tree which in some areas may reach 15 m. The upper trunk has a smooth white surface with a persistent fibrous base. It has a light open crown of blue-green leaves and bears flowers, usually in threes, which may be white, pink or red. These appear over a long period from autumn to summer and are highly attractive to a number of native birds.

A pink-flowering form is often sold as *E. leucoxylon* 'Rosea'.

E. leucoxylon ssp. *megalocarpa* grows to around 9 m and has larger seed vessels. The flowers are usually large and often a striking deep pink, but cream flowers also occur.

Cultivation This species is very hardy in a range of soils, including limestone. It is tolerant of drought, wind and frost and may be grown in coastal gardens with some protection.

Landscape Use This is an excellent specimen tree for suburban gardens. It is

Eucalyptus leucoxylon

suitable for windbreaks, shade and honey production.

Eucalyptus macrocarpa
MOTTLECAH

Origin WA
Climate WT, M, SA
Shade None to light
SPECIMEN PLANT
BIRD-ATTRACTING
DROUGHT-RESISTANT
Description A sprawling mallee up to 3 m with powdery grey young branches. The large leathery leaves are silvery grey, and beautiful large red flowers up to 10 cm wide occur in late winter and spring. These are followed by attractive large woody fruits, the largest among the eucalypts.

Cultivation This species does best in a light-textured soil with good drainage and a sunny, dry position. It is drought-resistant and is moderately frost-resistant when mature. Lightly prune the young plant to help develop a dense shrub.

Landscape Use A highly ornamental plant for an open position in the garden. Branches have a tendency to tumble over and become horizontal; this is visually pleasing and should be encouraged, and used to advantage, rather than being discouraged by heavy staking.

Eucalyptus maculata
SPOTTED GUM

Origin Qld, NSW, Vic.
Climate S, WT, M
Shade None to light
FAST-GROWING
BIRD-ATTRACTING
Description This is a tall tree to 30 m with a very straight trunk and smooth bark shed in irregular patches to give an attractive greyish brown mottled effect. It has a crown of slightly glossy leaves and bears small white flowers in winter. Koalas feed on the foliage of this species.

Eucalyptus maculata

Cultivation This tree will do well in most well-drained soils. It is a coastal tree and will tolerate moderate exposure, but is also hardy in dry areas. It is moderately frost-resistant.

Landscape Use This is a rather large tree for the average garden, but it looks beautiful in public gardens and parks where its attractive form may be appreciated. It is suitable for windbreaks with a subsidiary underplanting and produces a good hardwood timber.

Eucalyptus macrocarpa

Eucalyptus mannifera *ssp.* maculosa
BRITTLE GUM

Origin NSW, Vic.
Climate WT, M, CT, H
Shade None to light
FAST-GROWING
SPECIMEN PLANT
BIRD-ATTRACTING
Description A medium-sized, sometimes multistemmed, tree which may reach a height of 20 m. The white bark is most striking, often mottled with patches of grey and pink. It has a rather sparse crown of narrow, usually drooping, foliage, and small white flowers appear in autumn.

Cultivation This species will grow in a wide range of soil types, but requires good drainage. It is frost- and snow-tolerant and will withstand extended dry periods.

Landscape Use As the common name suggests, this tree has a tendency to drop branches and care should be taken when planting it near dwellings. It is a beautiful, graceful tree for parks and street planting and has been used extensively in Canberra.

Eucalyptus mannifera ssp. *maculosa*

Eucalyptus melliodora
YELLOW BOX

Origin Qld, NSW, Vic.
Climate WT, M, CT, H, SA
Shade None to light
FAST-GROWING
FRAGRANT
BIRD-ATTRACTING

Description A handsome, wide-spreading medium tree to around 20 m, with variable bark which may be fibrous and persistent or completely smooth. It has wide-spreading, drooping bluish grey foliage and bears masses of creamy honey-scented flowers in spring and summer. It is regarded as one of the best honey producers of all of the eucalypts. During flowering, the trees are visited by large numbers of honeyeaters. Koalas feed on the foliage.

An ornamental pink-flowering form is sometimes available.

Cultivation This species is adaptable to many situations and soils. It will withstand dry periods and is frost-resistant.

Landscape Use This is an excellent shade tree for rural areas. It is also suitable for windbreaks.

Eucalyptus melliodora

Eucalyptus microcorys
TALLOWWOOD

Origin Qld, NSW
Climate T, S, WT
Shade None to filtered
FAST-GROWING
BIRD-ATTRACTING

Description This handsome tree of variable height may reach 30 m. It has soft, fibrous ginger-coloured bark and a dense crown of light green leaves, and has a horizontal branching habit. Small white flowers appear from winter through to early summer. This tree produces the beautiful yellowish brown tallowwood, popularly used as an attractive flooring material. Koalas feed on the foliage.

Eucalyptus microcorys

Cultivation This species does best in good soils in areas with a high rainfall. It will tolerate shade when young, but is frost-tender.

Landscape Use The low-branching habit makes this species ideal for windbreaks. It is too large for the average garden, but is a fine shade tree for homestead groves and parks.

Eucalyptus nicholii
NARROW-LEAVED PEPPERMINT

Origin NSW
Climate WT, M, CT, H
Shade None to light

FAST-GROWING
SPECIMEN PLANT
AROMATIC FOLIAGE
BIRD-ATTRACTING
CONTAINER PLANT

Description A small to medium-sized graceful weeping tree to 20 m with a fibrous persistent brown bark. It has a rounded, compact crown of narrow light green leaves, often plum-coloured when young and smelling of eucalyptus-menthol when crushed. Many small white flowers appear in autumn.

Cultivation This fast-growing, adaptable tree will grow in moist soils with good drainage. It is hardy to frost and will tolerate dry periods. Can be pruned hard to encourage shrubby growth.

Landscape Use A most ornamental tree for the spacious suburban garden. It forms an ideal windbreak and shade tree in rural areas and is an excellent street tree. It is well worth growing as a large tub plant for courtyards and patios.

Eucalyptus nicholii

Eucalyptus pilularis

Eucalyptus pilularis
BLACKBUTT

Origin Qld, NSW
Climate S, WT
Shade None to light

FAST-GROWING
BIRD-ATTRACTING

Description A medium to large tree, reaching to 40 m, with a rough fibrous bark on the lower trunk and smooth bark higher up and on the branches. It has an open crown and an erect branching habit. Small white flowers appear in summer. This species produces a good hardwood timber and koalas feed on the foliage.

Cultivation This fast-growing tree thrives in light-textured, well-drained soils in areas with good rainfall. It is suitable for planting in coastal areas with some protection. It will tolerate mild frosts.

Landscape Use A good park tree, and fast shelterbelt or windbreak tree if underplanted with smaller trees or shrubs.

Eucalyptus polybractea
(syn. *E. fruticetorum*)
BLUE MALLEE

Origin NSW, Vic.
Climate WT, M, SA
Shade None to light

AROMATIC FOLIAGE
BIRD-ATTRACTING

Description This species is a small mallee to around 7 m which typically develops a number of stems from one rootstock. It has rough persistent bark and narrow bluish grey leaves, which are highly aromatic and produce a high quality essential oil. The small white flowers are produced during autumn and are a good source of honey.

Cultivation This species does well in medium to heavy soils. It will tolerate very dry conditions and is frost-resistant. It may be pruned back very hard to encourage bushy growth.

Landscape Use A ideal species for low shelter and windbreak planting in low rainfall areas.

Eucalyptus polybractea

Eucalyptus preissiana
BELL-FRUITED MALLEE

Origin WA
Climate WT, M, SA
Shade None to light

SPECIMEN PLANT
BIRD-ATTRACTING

Description A small, many-stemmed mallee which grows to around 3 m. It has a straggly, open habit and smooth grey bark. The youngest branches are red. The thick leathery leaves are bluish green, and showy, colourful deep yellow flowers appear mainly during spring. These are followed by marvellous bell-shaped fruits. The flowers are perfect for cutting and the fruits are ideal dried arrangements.

Cultivation This adaptable species will grow in most soils and is suitable for many areas in southern Australia. It will grow in coastal gardens with some protection and does not mind extended dry periods. It is moderately frost-resistant, but needs protection the first winter. Prune to encourage compact growth.

Landscape Use This is a most ornamental small species for the garden. It forms a bushy shrub with multiple stems and may be used as a low windbreak.

Eucalyptus preissiana

Eucalyptus pyriformis
PEAR-FRUITED MALLEE

Origin WA
Climate WT, M, SA
Shade None to light

BIRD-ATTRACTING
DROUGHT-RESISTANT

Description A well-branched, spreading mallee to around 5 m high, with smooth grey bark. The young stems are often shining red. It has thick green-grey leaves and bears very attractive, extremely large (up to 10 cm wide), red, yellow or cream coloured flowers during late winter and spring. The large, ribbed, top-shaped fruits are most decorative.

Cultivation This species requires deep soil with good drainage. It is resistant to drought and is moderately frost-resistant, but needs protection when young. It will withstand hard pruning and will subsequently make bushy growth.

Landscape Use A most ornamental shrub for the garden, with attractive buds, flowers and fruits. When pruned it is suitable for use in hedges or windbreaks.

Eucalyptus risdonii

Eucalyptus risdonii
RISDON PEPPERMINT

Origin Tas.
Climate M, CT, H
Shade None to light

SPECIMEN PLANT
BIRD-ATTRACTING
ORNAMENTAL FOLIAGE

Description A small to medium-sized tree which may reach 12 m. It has smooth light grey bark and unusual silver juvenile leaves which become fused together along the stems. Adult leaves are not often developed. The white flowers are most frequently formed in the axils of juvenile leaves.

Cultivation This species is endemic to south-eastern Tasmania and is able to withstand periods of wetness, frost and light snow.

Landscape Use This is a beautiful silver foliage specimen for cold areas. It is suitable for use as low shelter or as a windbreak.

Eucalyptus pyriformis

Eucalyptus robusta
SWAMP MAHOGANY

Origin Qld, NSW
Climate S, WT, M
Shade None to light

FAST-GROWING
BIRD-ATTRACTING
SALT-TOLERANT

Description A medium-sized tree to around 15 m with coarse fibrous bark. It has a dense crown of thick dark green leaves and bears white flowers during winter. Koalas feed on the foliage.

Cultivation As the common name implies, this species inhabits swampy areas and is a most valuable plant for use in heavy, sodden soils. This is one of the few eucalypts that will tolerate severe coastal exposure. It is also frost-resistant.

Eucalyptus robusta

Landscape Use This is a good dense-crowned tree for parks and picnic spots, roadside landscaping, windbreaks, shelterbelts and industrial sites.

Eucalyptus rossii
INLAND SCRIBBLY GUM

Origin NSW
Climate WT, M, CT, H
Shade None to light
SPECIMEN PLANT
BIRD-ATTRACTING
Description A medium-sized tree which grows to around 15 m, with a lovely smooth white trunk which bears insect scribbles. It has a fairly dense crown of narrow grey-green leaves and produces small creamy white flowers in summer.

Cultivation This species does well in light-textured soils with good drainage. It will withstand dry periods and is frost-resistant.

Landscape Use This handsome species is a good shade tree, best suited to large properties and public parks. It is closely related to *E. haemastoma* but will tolerate harsher conditions.

Eucalyptus rossii

Eucalyptus saligna
SYDNEY BLUE GUM

Origin Qld, NSW
Climate S, WT, M
Shade None to light
FAST-GROWING
BIRD-ATTRACTING
Description A handsome tall straight tree to around 30 m or more high with beautiful, smooth bluish white bark. It has long dark green leaves and bears clusters of white flowers during summer. The tree is an excellent timber and honey producer and koalas feed on the foliage.

Cultivation This rapid-growing tree thrives in deep, well-drained soils in areas with good rainfall. It does well near the coast and is moderately frost-resistant once established.

Landscape Use An ornamental tree for parks, picnic spots, avenues and large spaces where its beautiful form may be appreciated.

Eucalyptus saligna

Eucalyptus scoparia
WALLANGARRA WHITE GUM

Origin Qld, NSW
Climate WT, M, CT, H
Shade None to light
FAST-GROWING
SPECIMEN PLANT
BIRD-ATTRACTING
Description A small tree to around 12 m with a slender, smooth white trunk. It has an open crown of graceful weeping branches and has narrow shiny green leaves. Small creamy white flowers appear in summer.

Cultivation This species is best suited to light-textured soils. It will tolerate dry conditions, is frost-resistant and will withstand light snow.

Landscape Use A beautiful and graceful specimen for any garden. It can be used as a windbreak and shelterbelt in rural areas.

Eucalyptus scoparia

Eucalyptus sideroxylon
MUGGA, RED IRONBARK

Origin Qld, NSW, Vic.
Climate WT, M, CT, H, SA
Shade None to light
SPECIMEN PLANT
BIRD-ATTRACTING
Description A medium-sized tree to around 15 m with marvellous, deeply

furrowed dark brown bark which persists to the lower branches. It has a wide crown of soft grey-green foliage and bears clusters of pendent flowers in autumn and winter. Some forms produce cream flowers, but the colour generally varies through pale pink to bright red. This species produces a very durable heavy timber and is a good honey tree. Many native birds are attracted to the flowers and fruits, and koalas feed on the foliage.

E. sideroxylon 'Rosea' is a pink-flowered form available through many nurseries.

Cultivation This widespread ironbark is extremely hardy in a wide range of conditions. It will grow in most well-drained soils and will tolerate extended dry periods and hot summers. It also tolerates a considerable amount of frost.

Landscape Use This is an extremely ornamental tree for use as an individual specimen or in groups. It makes a good windbreak if planted reasonably close and an excellent shade tree for streets and parks.

Eucalyptus sideroxylon

E. sideroxylon (bark)

Eucalyptus tetragona
TALLERACK; WHITE MARLOCK

Origin WA
Climate M, SA
Shade None to light
BIRD-ATTRACTING
ORNAMENTAL FOLIAGE

Description A rather open, straggly but attractive mallee which grows to around 5 m. It is distinguished by having squarish glaucous stems, very mealy, almost white leaves and four-sided, bell-shaped flower buds which open to pale cream flowers in late spring and summer. These are followed by groups of squarish grey fruits. All these features are excellent in indoor arrangements.

Cultivation This species prefers a light-textured, well-drained soil. It will tolerate very dry conditions and may be grown in seaside areas with some protection. It is moderately frost-resistant, but needs protection in the young stages.

Landscape Use An ornamental garden shrub which may be used as a 'silver' feature or in contrast with darker-foliaged plants. It forms a good low shelter and windbreak.

Eucalyptus tetraptera
SQUARE-FRUITED MALLEE

Origin WA
Climate WT, M, SA
Shade None to light
BIRD-ATTRACTING
CONTAINER PLANT

Description A very straggly mallee which may grow to 3 m, with robust, smooth grey stems. It has large, thick lanceolate leaves and large glossy red buds with pink or red stamens. These are followed by bizarre, hefty-looking square grey fruits.

Cultivation This species does best in light sandy soils with good drainage.

Eucalyptus tetragona

Eucalyptus tetraptera

It will grow in coastal areas with protection and will tolerate extended dry periods. It is moderately frost-resistant. Pruning will encourage a more shapely habit.

Landscape Use An interesting eucalypt for ornamental planting. It may be trained along a fence or grown in a large tub.

Eucalyptus torquata
CORAL GUM

Origin WA
Climate WT, M, SA
Shade None to light

FAST-GROWING
SPECIMEN PLANT
BIRD-ATTRACTING
DROUGHT-RESISTANT
CONTAINER PLANT

Description This is one of the most ornamental and popular small eucalypts in cultivation. It grows to around 10 m and has a rounded crown of blue-grey leaves that contrast sharply with the deep grey bark of the trunk and the base of the branches. The distinctive buds hang in clusters and are shiny red, almost wax-like, with pointed caps; they open to fluffy red, pink or sometimes white flowers. These appear in spring and summer and at other times through the year and they are followed by attractive bunches of brown fruits. Buds, blossoms and fruits are excellent for indoor arrangements.

Cultivation This species is suitable for light to medium soils and is resistant to drought. It is salt-tolerant and may be grown in coastal gardens with some protection. It is moderately frost-resistant. Light pruning may be beneficial.

Landscape Use A most decorative tree for specimen planting. As branches are borne close to the ground it provides a fine windbreak. It has been used successfully as a street tree in a number of dry inland towns, including Bourke, Kalgoorlie and Alice Springs. It will flower quite well when grown in large tubs.

Eucalyptus woodwardii
LEMON-FLOWERED GUM

Origin WA
Climate WT, M, SA
Shade None to light

SPECIMEN PLANT
BIRD-ATTRACTING
DROUGHT-RESISTANT
ORNAMENTAL FOLIAGE

Description A medium-sized tree which may grow to 15 m high. It has grey-green lanceolate leaves and frosty-grey stems. The decorative green pointed buds open to brilliant lemon-yellow flowers in winter and spring. These are followed by frosty grey, bell-shaped fruits.

Cultivation This popular street tree of inland towns of southern Australia does well in areas with low rain fall and extreme summer temperatures. It will grow in sandy or heavy soils with good drainage. Protect from strong winds and lightly prune when young to shape. It is moderately frost-resistant.

Landscape Use An extremely ornamental tree for specimen planting in inland gardens. It flowers well when young and in some places produces flowers throughout the year.

Eucalyptus torquata

Eucalyptus woodwardii

EUTAXIA
FACACEAE

A small endemic genus of about eight species of pea-flowered shrubs found mostly in Western Australia. They produce a showy spring display of flowers and are becoming popular in cultivation. White fly is the main pest attacking this genus but little serious damage is caused beyond a yellowing of the leaves and plants generally recover from such infestations. Propagation is from half-ripened tip cuttings or from seed soaked in boiling water and left to stand overnight.

Eutaxia cuneata

Origin WA
Climate WT, M, CT
Shade None to filtered
FAST-GROWING
CONTAINER PLANT

Description A small shrub which grows to around 1 m. It has small dark green opposite leaves, and attractive orange-yellow flowers suffused with red that appear from winter to early spring.

Cultivation Grow in a light to medium soil with good drainage. It does best in an open position but will tolerate some shade. It is frost-resistant. Prune after flowering to shape.

Landscape Use A pretty winter-flowering shrub for the garden foreground, rockery or container.

Eutaxia cuneata

Eutaxia obovata

Origin WA
Climate WT, M, CT
Shade None to light
FAST-GROWING
CONTAINER PLANT

Description A small bushy shrub to 1 m. It has small pointed lanceolate leaves and in spring, bears masses of yellow and red pea flowers along the branch ends.

Cultivation A reliable shrub in most well-drained soils. It is suitable for protected coastal gardens and is frost-resistant. Prune after flowering to shape.

Landscape Use An attractive compact shrub for the rockery or container.

Eutaxia obovata

Faradaya splendida

FARADAYA

VERBENACEAE

A tropical genus of climbing plants with one native species, F. splendida, *found in northern Queensland rainforests. Propagation is from fresh seed or half-ripened tip cuttings which will strike fairly readily.*

Faradaya splendida

Origin Qld
Climate T, S
Shade None to filtered

FAST-GROWING
FRAGRANT
RAINFOREST PLANT

Description A very vigorous climbing plant that scrambles up the tallest trees in its rainforest habitat. It has large, oval, shiny green leaves and clusters of perfumed white flowers followed by large glossy white edible fruits.

Cultivation Grow in a humus-enriched soil with plenty of moisture. This plant likes hot, humid conditions and is frost-tender.

Landscape Use The beautiful display of flowers and their lovely fragrance make this climber ideal for large areas in the garden. It is perfect for training over fences and pergolas, but keep it away from other trees and shrubs.

FICUS

MORACEAE

Of the 800 species of figs distributed worldwide, there are approximately 35 species that occur in warmer regions of Australia. They are mainly large trees from the rainforest and, although too large for most gardens, make superb shade trees for parks and large open areas. The fruits resemble those of the edible fig in general structure and attract many fruit-eating birds and bats. When young many species make excellent, leafy container plants and can tolerate low light levels when brought indoors. Gardeners should not be tempted to plant outgrown container specimens in the average suburban garden as the extensive root systems can damage pipes, paths, foundations of houses and swimming pools. Lerps and fig-leaf beetles may be seasonal pests which cause defoliation and fungi may cause some leaf disfigurement but, generally, figs are relatively pest-free. Propagation is carried out from cuttings, seed and aerial layers.

Ficus benjamina

WEEPING FIG

Origin Qld
Climate T, S, WT
Shade None to full

FAST-GROWING
BIRD-ATTRACTING
CONTAINER PLANT
RAINFOREST PLANT

Description This is a shapely, spreading tree to around 20 m. It has slender, drooping branches with small bright green leaves and small reddish fruits borne in pairs.

Cultivation This species thrives in a humus-enriched soil with plenty of moisture. It is frost-tender and needs protection from harsh winds.

Landscape Use This is a beautiful weeping shade tree for large gardens or parks. Young trees make excellent container plants in frost-free areas or brought indoors.

Ficus benjamina

Ficus coronata

SANDPIPER FIG

Origin Qld, NSW, Vic., NT
Climate T, S, WT
Shade None to filtered

BIRD-ATTRACTING
CONTAINER PLANT
RAINFOREST PLANT

Description A medium-sized tree which may reach 8 m. It has very rough leaves and Aborigines used these for the final sanding of their weapons. When ripe the fruits are a dark purple and they are said to have the best flavour of any of the native figs.

Cultivation Grow in a rich soil with plenty of moisture in summer. It is frost-tender. As a container plant it may need pruning to maintain shape.

Landscape Use An attractive species for parks and large gardens. It makes a good container plant for patios or indoors.

Ficus coronata

Ficus macrophylla

MORETON BAY FIG

Origin Qld, NSW
Climate T, S, WT, M
Shade None to filtered

FAST-GROWING
SPECIMEN PLANT
BIRD-ATTRACTING
CONTAINER PLANT
RAINFOREST PLANT

Description A most beautiful, stately tree which grows to a height of 40 m. It has a massive buttressed trunk, large spreading branches and a dense canopy. The large glossy green leaves have a rusty brown undersurface. Under some conditions it may develop characteristic hanging aerial roots. Lorikeets and native pigeons feed on the clusters of purplish figs.

Cultivation This species will grow in most soils in low frost regions. It will grow in coastal areas with protection.

Ficus macrophylla

Landscape Use A magnificent shade tree for parks and large, open areas. When young it is suitable for containers and is a successful indoor plant.

Ficus rubiginosa
PORT JACKSON FIG; RUSTY FIG

Origin Qld, NSW
Climate T, S, WT, M
Shade None to filtered

FAST-GROWING
SPECIMEN PLANT
BIRD-ATTRACTING
CONTAINER PLANT
RAINFOREST PLANT

Description This very large, broad, spreading tree may reach 20 m. It has a habit similar to *F. macrophylla* but has smaller elliptical leaves, dark green and glossy with a rusty undersurface, and produces small figs.

F. rubiginosa 'Variegata' with large gold and green variegated foliage is used extensively as a tub plant.

Cultivation Plant in a medium-rich soil with plenty of moisture. It may be planted in coastal areas. Some protection from frost is needed when young.

Landscape Use A beautiful shade tree for coastal parks and large gardens. When young it is suitable as a container plant for indoors and courtyards.

Ficus rubiginosa (leaves)

FLINDERSIA
FLINDERSIACEAE

This is a mainly tropical genus with some 15 species occurring in Australia. The genus commemorates Matthew Flinders and includes a number of valuable timber trees which are used in the building

F. rubiginosa

industry. Most species make handsome shade trees and bear clusters of small flowers and unusual woody fruits. Propagation is from the large winged seeds, which germinate readily when sown while fresh.

Flindersia australis
CROWS ASH; AUSTRALIAN TEAK

Origin Qld, NSW
Climate T, S, WT, M
Shade None to light
SPECIMEN PLANT
RAINFOREST PLANT

Description A tall, straight, semideciduous tree growing up to 20 m, with a scaly, mottled grey bark. It forms a dense canopy of pinnate leaves and may shed all its foliage. When this occurs the tree then becomes covered in sprays of small white flowers. The unusual woody seed capsules open out into a five-pointed star and are often used in dried arrangements. This is one of the most widely used rainforest timbers, as it is very strong and durable.

Flindersia australis

Flindersia schottiana

Cultivation This species prefers a rich, moist soil but needs good drainage. It is frost-tender.

Landscape Use Usually too large for average gardens, this species makes an excellent park or street tree where wires are absent.

Flindersia schottiana
BUMPY ASH; CUDGERIE

Origin Qld, NSW
Climate T, S, WT
Shade None to light
SPECIMEN PLANT
FRAGRANT
RAINFOREST PLANT

Description A tree which may reach 20 m. The tall straight trunk has irregular swellings or bumps which give rise to one of its common names. It forms a rounded canopy of large pinnate leaves and bears large clusters of small white flowers that are sweetly fragrant, in late spring. The woody, prickly fruits open into a five-pointed star. The pale timber is used for flooring and other indoor work.

Cultivation Grow in rich soil in a well-drained position with plentiful supply of water. It is moderately frost-resistant.

Landscape Use An attractive shade tree for parks and large gardens.

FRANKENIA
FRANKENIACEAE

A large genus of some 80 species of annuals and small shrubs from temperate regions of the world. Approximately 50 species occur in Australia, mainly on saltpans in drier areas. They make good rockery or seaside plants and one species F. pauciflora, *has been in cultivation for some time. Propagation is easily carried out by division.*

Frankenia pauciflora
COMMON SEA HEATH

Origin All States
Climate S, WT, M, CT, SA
Shade None to light
SALT-TOLERANT
CONTAINER PLANT

Description A prostrate, mat-like plant with a layering habit. It has small, light grey-green leaves, and small pink or white flowers in late summer.

Cultivation This hardy small plant will grow in most soils, including sandy and salty. It is ideal for exposed seaside gardens and is frost-resistant.

Landscape Use A useful sand binder or ground cover when planted in groups. It is a good rockery and container subject.

Frankenia pauciflora

Geijera parviflora

GEIJERA
RUTACEAE

A small genus of trees and shrubs with four or five species native to Australia. It is the beautiful Wilga G. parviflora *that is most often cultivated. Propagation of this genus is difficult but the best results have been obtained using fresh seed.*

Geijera parviflora
WILGA

Origin Qld, NSW, Vic., SA
Climate WT, M, SA
Shade None to light

AROMATIC FOLIAGE
DROUGHT-RESISTANT
CONTAINER PLANT

Description A comparatively small weeping tree to 12 m with a very shapely, heavy crown of pendulous leaves, which almost sweep the ground. The tree is loved by stock, which constantly graze upon the lower leaves, producing a very neat trimmed effect. The small cream flowers are produced in loose panicles in late winter.

Cultivation This tree is extremely hardy in warm, well-drained situations. It resists drought after the first year and is frost-tolerant.

Landscape Use This is an ideal tree for low windbreaks, and for shade, shelter and beauty around the homestead in rural areas. It is a perfect street or avenue tree and may be grown in a large tub for the courtyard.

G. parviflora (leaves)

GEITONOPLESIUM
GEITONOPLESIACEAE

A genus of one species, G. cymosum, *found in coastal rainforest edges of eastern Australia. It is a small climber suited to a shady position in the garden. Propagation is from fresh seed which can be scarified to speed up germination.*

Geitonoplesium cymosum
SCRAMBLING LILY

Origin Qld, NSW, Vic.
Climate S, WT, M
Shade Light to filtered

FAST-GROWING
ORNAMENTAL FOLIAGE
CONTAINER PLANT
RAINFOREST PLANT

Description A slender twining plant with wiry green stems and alternate glossy leaves with parallel veins. The small white, green-tipped flowers in spring are followed by shiny blue-black berries.

Cultivation Grow in a humus-enriched soil which is cool, moist and well drained. It requires some protection as it is slightly frost-tender and it may need to be given some support by tying.

Landscape Use A pretty, leafy climber for a shady fence. It makes a good indoor plant and looks most attractive in a large hanging basket.

GERANIUM
GERANIACEAE

A very large genus found in temperate regions of the world, with approximately 10 species extending to Australia. They are mostly slender, spreading perennials with deeply lobed

Geitonoplesium cymosum

leaves, and they are grown for their dainty white or pink flowers. Propagation is from cuttings or by division.

Geranium solanderi
(syn. *G. pilosum*)
AUSTRAL CRANESBILL

Origin All States
Climate S, WT, M, CT
Shade None to filtered
CONTAINER PLANT
Description A small perennial spreading to 1.5 m with rounded, light green, lobed leaves, and pale pink flowers during spring and summer.

Cultivation Grow in a medium soil in a moist position with good drainage. It likes a little shade and is frost-tolerant.

Landscape Use This is an excellent small ground cover for growing near path edges, in a rockery pocket where it will spread and tumble over, or in pots or hanging baskets.

GLEICHENIA
GLEICHENIACEAE

There are approximately 16 species of coral ferns, with six being found in Australia. They are terrestrial ferns, often forming dense clumps in moist, swampy areas. Members of the genus are most attractive, having light green forked fronds, divided many times and resembling forms of coral. Propagation is from spores or by division of rhizomes.

Gleichenia dicarpa
POUCHED CORAL FERN

Origin Qld, NSW, Vic., Tas.
Climate T, S, WT, M, CT
Shade Light to filtered
BIRD-ATTRACTING
ORNAMENTAL FOLIAGE
CONTAINER PLANT
Description This is a beautiful fern with a long creeping rhizome and upright fronds on branches up to 2 m that are divided many times. It forms a delightful thicket and provides an important nesting site for fairy wrens.

Cultivation This species needs an acid soil, plenty of sun and must be kept moist at all times. Large plants resent disturbance, but transplanting is successful when the plant is very small.

Landscape Use A spectacular fern for

Geranium solanderi

Gleichenia dicarpa

growing in a spacious moist position in the garden, where it will form large thickets. It adds grace to a water feature and may be grown in a container provided the roots are kept wet.

GOODENIA

GOODENIACEAE

There are over 100 species of Goodenia, *found in all States. They are small herbs or shrubs producing pretty, mainly yellow flowers and are ideal edging or rockery plants. Scale insects are an occasional problem on goodenias but are easily controlled with applications of white oil. Seasonal infestations of white fly are less easily controlled but rarely cause severe damage. Where growth of prostrate plants is dense or compact, grey mould may be present. Severe infestation will need treatment from a suitable fungicide. Propagation is from cuttings, or in some species by division.*

Goodenia hederaceae

IVY GOODENIA

Origin Qld, NSW, Vic.
Climate S, WT, M
Shade Light to filtered
CONTAINER PLANT
Description A small spreading plant to 20 cm high and 50 cm wide which sometimes suckers from trailing stems.

Goodenia hederaceae

It has ivy-like, rounded dark green leaves with a silvery underside and bears bright yellow to orange flowers in spring and summer.

Cultivation A widespread species that will grow in most soils with some moisture. It needs some shade and is frost- and snow-tolerant.

Landscape Use A very pretty trailing plant for the rockery, container or hanging basket.

Goodenia ovata

HOP GOODENIA

Origin Qld, NSW, Vic., SA
Climate S, WT, M, SA
Shade Light to filtered
FAST-GROWING
CONTAINER PLANT
Description A semierect shrubby species which may reach 1.5 m high and 3 m

Goodenia ovata

wide, with light green, ovate, toothed leaves, and large yellow flowers in spring and summer.

Cultivation This very common species of south-east Australia is usually found in wet forests and does best with some shade and moist soil in cultivation. It is frost-hardy, adaptable to most soils and may be grown in coastal gardens with some protection.

Landscape Use A free-flowering species for the foreground of the garden under other shrubs and trees. Its tendency to trail makes it useful for covering a sloping bank or spilling over rocks. It may also be grown in a container.

Goodenia rotundifolia
STAR GOODENIA

Origin Qld, NSW
Climate S, WT, M
Shade None to light
CONTAINER PLANT

Description A prostrate plant trailing to 1.5 m wide with rounded lobed leaves, and yellow flowers on short stalks in spring and summer.

Cultivation Grow in a well-drained, humus-enriched soil. It is frost-resistant.

Landscape Use This species will form attractive clumps and is ideal as a ground cover or rockery plant. It may also be grown in a container.

Goodenia rotundifolia

GOSSYPIUM
MALVACEAE

A genus of shrubs from the warmer parts of the world which includes the economically important cotton species.

Gossypium sturtianum

There are several Australian species which make attractive garden plants with flowers that resemble those of Hibiscus. *Propagation is from seed collected in summer or from cuttings.*

Gossypium sturtianum
STURT'S DESERT PEA

Origin Qld, NSW, SA, WA, NT
Climate M, SA
Shade None to light
DROUGHT-RESISTANT

Description This is the floral emblem of the Northern Territory. It is an erect shrub to around 2 m with broad, black-dotted greyish leaves, and handsome hibiscus-like mauve flowers with maroon centres in winter and spring.

Cultivation Once established this species does well in hot, dry positions with full sun. It is frost-tender. Prune back after flowering.

Landscape Use A very pretty plant for inland gardens and parks.

GRAPTOPHYLLUM
ACANTHACEAE

A genus of 10 tropical and subtropical species of which four are endemic to Australia. They are mostly dense erect shrubs which can grow quite tall. Attractive glossy foliage and showy bird-attracting flowers make them good specimen plants. Propagation is from half-ripened tip cuttings.

Graptophyllum excelsum
SCARLET FUCHSIA

Origin Qld
Climate T, S, WT
Shade None to filtered
SPECIMEN PLANT
BIRD-ATTRACTING
ORNAMENTAL FOLIAGE
CONTAINER PLANT

Description A bushy erect shrub to 3 m with dark green shiny obovate leaves to

Graptophyllum excelsum

4 cm long and masses of deep red tubular flowers in spring.

Cultivation This species is the most popular in cultivation and does very well in most warm frost-free areas. It does best with good drainage, lots of sun and regular pruning to keep shapely.

Landscape Use Its erect habit and ability to withstand hard pruning makes this a good shrub for planting in narrow gardens or as a hedge. It is also a useful container plant.

GREVILLEA

PROTEACEAE

With over 250 species and countless cultivars, grevilleas are probably one of the most widely known and widely grown of Australian native plant groups. The genus is named after Charles Francis Greville, a patron of botany and once vice-president of the Royal Society of London during the nineteenth century. All species are native to Australia except for a few which occur on nearby islands.

As true members of the plant family Proteaceae, which shows great diversity of form, grevilleas differ very much in appearance and habit. Even within a species a number of different forms may occur. Many grevilleas have high horticultural value and they are popular as garden subjects because of their striking forms, bright flowers, ornamental foliage and ability to attract birds. They range in size from quite tall rainforest trees such as the well-known silky oak, G. robusta, *to prostrate ground covers like the lovely* G. laurifolia. *However, it is mainly the dwarf to medium-sized shrubby species that have found great popularity in our gardens. Most are easily grown, but in general they flower best in sunny positions. Many bloom in late winter and spring and some flower continuously throughout the year. Many species have considerable potential for use in floral arrangements, and they provide a constant source of fresh flowers and decorative foliage for this purpose. When picking grevillea flowers choose those that have not yet opened their styles as these will last much longer in water.*

Grevilleas are most valuable plants for attracting nectar-feeding birds to the garden. Almost all species provide nectar, but birds will especially flock to the toothbrush-type flowers such as those of G. banksii, G. hookerana *and* G. robusta, *to name a few. Consider placing a grevillea in a sunny spot near a window, balcony or sun deck where you can comfortably watch the live entertainment of the many honey seekers that will feed and frolic on the nectar-rich flowers.*

Grevillea acanthifolia

Some of the most beautiful species are low-growing or procumbent. These may be planted in borders, rockeries and containers. Some grow erect; others will happily cascade over rocks, steps, banks and retaining walls. Some ground covers will turn an unsightly bank into a beautiful display of colour and greenery or may be used as a living mulch in situations where it is necessary to shelter the root systems of other plants.

There is an outstanding range of spreading medium-sized grevilleas that reach about 3 m. These are ideal as rapid screening, hedge or low windbreak plants. Pruning to shape makes a compact bushy shrub. In fact, regular pruning of all grevilleas is recommended, especially after peak flushes of flowers. The flowering will be enhanced, and the plant will display healthy regrowth and more vigour.

The extraordinary diversity of grevilleas has encouraged many plant breeders to experiment with them. Grevilleas hybridise very readily and some excellent long-flowering cultivars have become available, among them ' Poorinda Royal Mantle', 'Robyn Gordon', 'Sandra Gordon' and 'Misty Pink'.

Propagation is from cuttings. Grevilleas can be propagated from seed collected in early summer, but as seed is often difficult to collect and as grevilleas hybridise very readily in favourable garden conditions, it is best to take half-ripened tip cuttings in late summer. All hybrids and cultivars must be propagated by cuttings to obtain progeny true to type.

Grevilleas are not often seriously troubled by pests and diseases but a few to watch out for are moth borers, leaf-eating caterpillars and larvae, scale insects and bugs like crusader bug. The popular 'Robyn Gordon' is subject to a leaf spot during humid weather.

Grevillea acanthifolia

Origin NSW
Climate WT, M, CT, H
Shade Light to filtered
SPECIMEN PLANT
BIRD-ATTRACTING

Description This is generally an upright, spreading shrub growing to around 2 m or more in height. It has deeply divided leaves that are rather prickly and toothbrush flowers of a deep mauve or pinkish colour, which occur through spring and summer and irregularly at other times. Cut flowers and foliage are exceptionally good for indoors.

A lower growing, almost prostrate, form to 1 m high and 4 m wide is also in cultivation.

Cultivation This species is hardy and adaptable in cultivation, but favours the damper situations. It will tolerate fairly heavy shade and is frost-resistant.

Landscape Use This is a most attractive specimen for the garden. The low-growing form may be used as an edging plant or in a large rockery.

Grevillea alpina
MOUNTAIN GREVILLEA

Origin NSW, Vic.
Climate WT, M, CT, H
Shade Light to filtered
BIRD-ATTRACTING
CONTAINER PLANT
Description This is one of the most variable species of all, ranging from semiprostrate to 2 m, with variable, mostly soft green, sometimes leathery, linear to oval leaves. Small clusters of spidery flowers appear for a long period between winter and summer in colour combinations of white, pink, yellow, apricot and red. Honeyeaters are attracted to the flowers.

Cultivation Most forms of this species do very well under garden conditions. It will grow in most soils in a well-drained location and will tolerate moist, dry or cold conditions. It is frost-resistant.

Landscape Use A pretty grevillea with a form for every garden situation: as an edging plant, among other shrubs, in the rockery or in a container.

Grevillea alpina

Grevillea anethifolia
SPINY CREAM SPIDER FLOWER

Origin NSW, SA, WA
Climate WT, M, SA
Shade None to light
BIRD-ATTRACTING
DROUGHT-RESISTANT
Description A small, rather erect shrub to 1.5 m high. The leaves are divided into very narrow segments tipped with a fine point. Loose clusters of small creamy white flowers are borne in the leaf axils in spring.

Cultivation This species, which occurs in mallee communities in western New South Wales, will tolerate very dry conditions. It needs good drainage and is frost-resistant.

Landscape Use In nature this species forms dense clumps and it is ideal for planting as an impenetrable hedge in rural areas.

Grevillea anethifolia

Grevillea aquifolium
VARIABLE PRICKLY GREVILLEA

Origin Vic., SA
Climate WT, M, CT, H, SA
Shade None to filtered
FAST-GROWING
BIRD-ATTRACTING
ORNAMENTAL FOLIAGE
CONTAINER PLANT
Description Usually an upright but spreading plant up to 3 m high with a variable spread. The attractive, holly-like leaves are grey-green and hairy. The bright red toothbrush flowers, which bloom freely from late winter through spring, are most attractive to honeyeaters.

Grevillea aquifolium

Prostrate forms, including an attractive ground-hugging form known as *G. aquifolium* 'Carpenters Rock' are also available.

Cultivation A hardy, fast-growing species that does well in most soils with good drainage. It will tolerate considerable shade, frost and very dry conditions.

Landscape Use A beautiful plant, with exceptional foliage, for use as an understorey plant in the garden or as a fence screen. The prostrate forms are ideal edging plants, ground covers or large trailing rockery specimens.

Grevillea asplenifolia

(syn. *G. asplenifolia* var. *shepherdii*)

Origin NSW
Climate S, WT, M, CT
Shade None to filtered

FAST-GROWING
BIRD-ATTRACTING

Description A handsome spreading shrub to around 3 m high and 3 m or more wide with very long narrow leaves that are rarely toothed. The red toothbrush flowers appear throughout the year, but particularly in spring. Many native birds are attracted to the flowers. Foliage and flowers are good for indoor arrangements.

Cultivation This species will grow in a variety of soils with good drainage. It will tolerate very cold conditions and is frost-resistant. Pruning after flowering will promote vigour and more flowers.

Landscape Use This unusual shrub needs plenty of room to grow into a shapely bush. It is ideal for rapid screening or windbreaks.

Grevillea asplenifolia

Grevillea 'Austraflora Canterbury Gold'

Grevillea 'Austraflora Canterbury Gold'

Origin Cultivar (*G. juniperina* prostrate yellow form x *G. victoriae* var. *leptoneura*)
Climate S, WT, M, CT
Shade None to filtered

BIRD-ATTRACTING
CONTAINER PLANT

Description A prostrate, spreading shrub with a dense habit and a spread up to 2 m across. The stems are covered in soft hairs and the glossy dark green leaves have a silky underside. Good displays of pale gold flowers appear mostly in spring, but some flowers are found in all seasons.

Cultivation A hardy cultivar that grows best in a well-drained, sunny position. It will adapt to some shade and is frost-resistant. Prune lightly to shape.

Landscape Use This is an ideal ground cover for large areas. It is excellent for council planting where visibility is to be maintained, for instance in median strips and car parks. It looks beautiful spilling over dry stone walls and large containers.

Grevillea australis

ALPINE GREVILLEA

Origin NSW, Vic., Tas.
Climate WT, M, CT, H
Shade None to filtered

FRAGRANT
BIRD-ATTRACTING
CONTAINER PLANT

Description There are several forms of this grevillea and whilst it is found in alpine regions it is by no means confined to these altitudes. It is a small to medium shrub up to 2 m high, with linear dark green leaves, and small perfumed white flowers in spring and summer.

Grevillea australis

A prostrate form from Tasmania is also available. It will spread to about 60 cm across.

Cultivation This species will grow in a variety of soils, including heavy and moist ones. It is very hardy to frost and is snow-tolerant.

Landscape Use Although the flowers are rather unexciting compared to those of other grevilleas, this is a good little bird-attracting plant for the very cold garden.

It is a good container and rockery subject, and the prostrate form may be used as a ground cover.

Grevillea banksii

RED SILKY OAK; BANKS'S GREVILLEA

Origin Qld
Climate S, WT, M
Shade None to light
FAST-GROWING
SPECIMEN PLANT
BIRD-ATTRACTING
ORNAMENTAL FOLIAGE

Description A marvellous tall-growing shrub which may reach 5 m, but usually reaches only 3 m in cultivation. It has quite large leaves which are deeply divided and dark green in colour. It bears many large red or creamy white flowers held well above the bush for most of the year. These are most attractive to nectar-feeding birds, and rosellas and other parrots feed on the fruits. Cut foliage and flowers are beautiful for indoors.

Attractive prostrate forms with either cream or red flowers are available from some nurseries.

Cultivation Grow in a well-drained sunny position. This species tolerates humidity and may be grown in coastal gardens with protection from salt-laden winds. It is susceptible to heavy frosts. Prune regularly to encourage a neat rounded shape.

Landscape Use An excellent specimen plant which can also be grown as a fence or privacy screen. Prostrate forms are suitable for the rockery, banks, retaining walls and large containers.

G. banksii (creamy-white form)

Grevillea banksii

Grevillea barklyana

Origin NSW, Vic.
Climate S, WT, M, CT
Shade NSW form: None to light
Victorian form: None to heavy
FAST-GROWING
BIRD-ATTRACTING

Description There are two distinct subspecies.

G. barklyana ssp. *barklyana* from deep mountain gullies of Gippsland, Vic. can reach a height of up to 8 m high and 3 m wide. It has deeply lobed leaves to 25 cm long and attractive bronzy red new growth. The pink toothbrush flowers to 10 cm appear in winter and spring.

G. barklyana ssp. *macleayana* from the Jervis Bay region of NSW is a branching shrub to 2 m high and up to 3 m wide with dull green entire leathery leaves to 10 cm long and deep pink toothbrush flowers from late winter to summer. This subspecies is the most commonly cultivated.

Cultivation The Gippsland form thrives in cooler conditions and will accept quite heavy shade and frost.

The Jervis Bay form may be grown in coastal gardens with some protection. It needs full sun and is fairly frost-tolerant. It benefits from pruning to encourage bushiness.

Landscape Use The Jervis Bay form needs plenty of room for it to develop into an attractive ornamental plant. The Gippsland form, being rather weak-rooted, is better planted amongst other plants of similar height where it will be protected from strong winds.

Grevillea barklyana

Grevillea baueri

Origin NSW
Climate S, WT, M, CT, H
Shade None to light
FAST-GROWING
BIRD-ATTRACTING
CONTAINER PLANT

Description This small shrub up to 1 m high has closely packed, oblong leaves, often with bronze tips. Deep pink spider flowers appear in winter and spring.

Several forms of this species are found in cultivation and flower colours vary from cream through pink to crimson.

Cultivation A hardy shrub that will accept most soils with good drainage. It prefers full sun and adequate water during summer. It is frost-tolerant.

Grevillea baueri

Tip prune or cut sprays for indoor flowers to keep bush shapely.

Landscape Use An attractive small plant for garden, rockery or container. It may be trimmed to form a pretty miniature hedge.

Grevillea beadleana

Origin NSW
Climate S, WT, M
Shade None to filtered

FAST-GROWING
BIRD-ATTRACTING
ORNAMENTAL FOLIAGE

Description A bushy shrub to 2 m high with a similar spread. It has soft deeply lobed dark green leaves up to 12 cm long covered with soft hairs. Dark red toothbrush flowers are produced in winter and spring and at other times. Recently described in 1986, this species is doing well in cultivation and is now available at some native plant nurseries.

Cultivation It requires a well-drained sunny position and will withstand frost and periods of dryness. Tip pruning is recommended when young to encourage compact growth.

Landscape Use An attractive foliaged plant suitable as a low screen or among other shrubs. Foliage and unopened flowers are suitable for picking for indoor decoration.

Grevillea beadleana

Grevillea 'Boongala Spinebill'

Grevillea *'Boongala spinebill'*

Origin Cultivar (possible parents *G. bipinnatifida* x *G. caleyi*)
Climate S, WT, M, CT
Shade None to light

SPECIMEN PLANT
BIRD-ATTRACTING
ORNAMENTAL FOLIAGE

Description A dense, spreading shrub which grows to 2 m high with a similar spread, with deeply divided foliage and reddish new growth. The large dark red toothbrush flowers in spring and summer and at other times attract honeyeaters.

Cultivation Grow in a sunny, well-drained position with some moisture. It will grow in coastal areas with some protection and is moderately frost-resistant. Prune to maintain shape.

Landscape Use A long-flowering plant to use as a feature or among other shrubs.

Grevillea brachystylis

Origin WA
Climate WT, M
Shade None to light

CONTAINER PLANT

Description A small shrub to around 60 cm high with hairy linear leaves to 10 cm or more long with curled margins.

Grevillea brachystylis

The conspicuous bright red, slightly pendent flowers are covered in hair and have interesting blue style tips. Flowers appear throughout most of the year with the main flush in spring and summer. There is also a prostrate form in cultivation.

Cultivation Grow in a well-drained sunny position. Provide plenty of water during dry summers. It will tolerate light frosts. Regular tip pruning is recommended to keep the plant shapely.

Landscape Use A showy small plant suited to the rockery, garden edge or container.

Grevillea buxifolia
GREY SPIDER FLOWER

Origin NSW
Climate WT, M, H
Shade None to filtered
BIRD-ATTRACTING

Description A common grevillea around Sydney, this open, rounded shrub grows to 1.5 m high. It has crowded oval leaves which are softly hairy, and carries terminal heads of grey woolly spider flowers for most of the year. These lovely flowers last well indoors and look excellent in pastel arrangements.

Cultivation A hardy shrub that likes a light-textured soil with good drainage. It will grow in coastal areas with some protection and is frost-resistant. Prune or pick flowers to maintain compact growth.

Landscape Use A delightful plant to grow among other shrubs for subtle colour contrast. It goes particularly well with wattles and is ideal for the bush garden. It can be used as a fence or privacy screen.

Grevillea buxifolia

Grevillea caleyi
CALEY'S GREVILLEA

Origin NSW
Climate WT, M, CT
Shade None to light
BIRD-ATTRACTING
ORNAMENTAL FOLIAGE

Description A large, spreading shrub to 3 m high and with a similar spread. It has deeply divided leaves and has attractive new growth that is soft to the touch and is coloured pink. The abundant deep pink or red toothbrush flowers are produced from late winter to

Grevillea caleyi

summer, and are a good source of nectar for the birds.

Cultivation This is a hardy plant for a deep, well-drained position. It likes plenty of sun and adequate moisture. It may be used in a protected coastal position and is frost-resistant. Trim regularly to encourage compact growth.

Landscape Use This is a large shrub that needs plenty of room to spread. It can be trained to grow along a fence and can be used as a windbreak.

Grevillea *'Canberra Gem'*

Origin Cultivar (*G. juniperina* x *G. rosmarinifolia*)
Climate WT, M, CT, H
Shade None to light
BIRD-ATTRACTING

Description This popular cultivar has a rounded, compact habit to around 2 m x 2 m. It has fine needle leaves and bears clusters of pendent deep pink or red spider flowers during winter and spring.

Cultivation Grow in an open, sunny and well-drained position. It is frost-resistant. Prune to maintain an attractive rounded shape.

Landscape Use A good showy shrub for general garden purposes. It is an ideal hedge plant.

Grevillea 'Canberra Gem'

Grevillea *'Clearview Robin'*

Origin Cultivar
Climate WT, M
Shade None to light
FAST-GROWING
BIRD-ATTRACTING

Description A compact, rounded shrub to 2 m. It has attractive grey-green pointed leaves, and deep pink to red hanging spider flowers from late winter to spring.

Cultivation This hardy species will tolerate fairly heavy soils with good drainage. It will withstand dry conditions and frost-resistant. Prune after flowering to maintain shape.

Landscape Use Grey foliage and bright red flowers make this a most attractive shrub for the garden or as a fence screen.

Grevillea 'Clearview Robin'

Grevillea *'Coastal Glow'*

(syn. *G.* 'Frampton's Hybrid')

Origin Cultivar
Climate S, WT, M
Shade None to filtered
BIRD-ATTRACTING
SALT-TOLERANT

Description A spreading medium shrub to 3 m high and wide with attractive dark green entire leaves to 20 cm long. Plentiful deep pink toothbrush flowers throughout the year attract honey-eating birds.

Cultivation This species is suited to a sunny or partially shaded position with good drainage. It will withstand salt-laden winds and is reliable in subtropical areas. It is also moderately frost-tolerant. Regularly prune to encourage bushiness.

Grevillea 'Coastal Glow'

Landscape Use A good screening or hedge plant for seaside gardens.

Grevillea crithmifolia

Origin WA
Climate WT, M, SA
Shade None to light
BIRD-ATTRACTING
CONTAINER PLANT

Description A compact, rounded shrub to 2 m with light green needle leaves divided into three segments. Clusters of showy white flowers develop from pink buds in winter and spring. A selected prostrate form with pale pink flowers is also in cultivation.

Cultivation This hardy plant will grow in most well-drained garden conditions. It withstands dry periods, some coastal exposure and frost. Prune to maintain density.

Landscape Use A good dense plant for low screens and hedges. The prostrate form is suitable for edging and rockeries.

Grevillea crithmifolia

Grevillea *'Crosbie Morrison'*

Origin Hybrid (*G. lavandulacea* x *G. lanigera*)
Climate WT, M, CT, SA
Shade None to light
CONTAINER PLANT

Description A small bushy shrub to 1.5 m. It has dark green pointed foliage and has bright crimson spider flowers in winter and spring.

Cultivation A hardy species for a sunny, well-drained position. It will withstand dry conditions and is moderately frost-resistant. Prune after flowering to shape and to encourage a good crop of flowers.

Landscape Use A good shrub for a small garden or container for a colourful display of winter flowers.

Grevillea 'Crosbie Morrison'

Grevillea curviloba

(previously sold as G. biternata *or* G. tridentifera *'Prostrate Form')*

Origin WA
Climate WT, M, CT, SA
Shade None to filtered

FAST-GROWING
FRAGRANT
BIRD-ATTRACTING

Description There are different forms of this shrub, but the most popular variety is a vigorous semiprostrate form which will cover an area 4 m across. It has bright green three-lobed leaves and produces masses of creamy clusters of sweetly perfumed flowers in late winter and spring.

Grevillea curviloba

Cultivation Grow in a sunny, well-drained position. It may be grown in coastal gardens with some protection and moderately frost-resistant. The plant responds well to pruning and if an occasional branch tends to grow vertically it may be cut off at the base.

Landscape Use A valuable ground cover for covering large areas or spilling over retaining walls.

Grevillea dielsiana
DIEL'S GREVILLEA

Origin WA
Climate WT, M, SA
Shade None to light

BIRD-ATTRACTING
ORNAMENTAL FOLIAGE

Description A most attractive multibranched shrub to around 2 m with varnished, prickly foliage. The pendent pink and yellow flowers have an apricot waxy appearance and are very numerous during spring and early summer.

A scarlet-flowering form is also available.

Grevillea dielsiana

Cultivation Grow in a deep, well-drained soil in a sunny open position. It is moderately frost-resistant. It may become straggly unless constantly pruned, which is a good excuse to use the foliage indoors.

Landscape Use An unusual and decorative shrub and one which should be shown off.

Grevillea diffusa *ssp. diffusa*

(syn. *Grevillea capitellata*)

NODDING SPIDER FLOWER

Origin NSW
Climate WT, M, CT, H
Shade None to filtered
BIRD-ATTRACTING
CONTAINER PLANT

Description A small spreading shrub to around 1 m high and with a similar spread. Leaves are variable and are narrow to oblong, from 1 to 6 cm long. The dainty, pendent dark red flowers appear in winter and spring.

Cultivation Grow in a light soil in a partially shaded, well-drained position. It may be grown in protected coastal gardens and is frost-resistant when mature. Trim lightly to maintain a compact habit.

Landscape Use A pretty plant for edging or to grow near steps where the nodding flowers may be seen to advantage. It will happily cascade over walls, rocks or containers.

Grevillea diffusa

Grevillea diminuta

Origin NSW
Climate WT, M, CT, H
Shade Light to filtered
BIRD-ATTRACTING
CONTAINER PLANT

Description A small, rather spreading shrub to around 50 cm high, with a spread of 1 m. It has soft oval foliage and bears pendent clusters of rusty red spider flowers in spring.

Cultivation Grow in a well-drained soil in either a sunny or a semishaded position. It will tolerate frost and light snow. Tip prune regularly to shape.

Landscape Use A dainty edging or rockery plant. It looks particularly attractive in a container.

Grevillea diminuta

Grevillea *'Evelyn's Coronet'*

Origin Cultivar (*G. buxifolia* x *G. lavandulacea*)
Climate S, WT, M
Shade None to light
FAST-GROWING
BIRD-ATTRACTING

Description A most attractive bushy cultivar to around 2 m having shiny green narrow leaves with a woolly underside, and plum-coloured new growth. The lovely woolly pinkish grey spider flowers appear throughout the year and are attractive to nectar-seeking birds. Pick bunches for the house.

Cultivation Grow in a sunny, well-drained position. It does well in

Grevillea 'Evelyn's Coronet'

subtropical gardens and is frost-resistant. Occasional pruning will maintain shape.

Landscape Use An ornamental bushy shrub that is ideal for general garden purposes. It will form an attractive hedge.

Grevillea floribunda

Origin Qld, NSW
Climate WT, M, CT, H, SA
Shade None to filtered
BIRD-ATTRACTING
CONTAINER PLANT

Description An erect but spreading shrub to around 1.5 m with longish

Grevillea floribunda

grey-green leaves. The pendent leaves are green and yellow with short brown hairs that give them a rusty felted appearance. They appear during winter and spring and are attractive to honeyeaters.

Cultivation Grow in a sunny position in well-drained soil. This hardy plant will tolerate dry periods and is frost-resistant. It may be grown in protected coastal gardens. Prune to shape.

Landscape Use An unusual flowering plant for the garden, rocky slope or container.

Grevillea x gaudichaudii

Origin NSW
Climate S, WT, M, CT, H
Shade None to filtered

FAST-GROWING
BIRD-ATTRACTING

Description This naturally occurring hybrid between *G. acanthifolia* and *G. laurifolia* is found in the Blue Mountains of New South Wales. It is well-established in cultivation as a ground cover plant and will spread up to 3 m or more across. It has deeply lobed dark foliage and dark red new growth. Wine-coloured toothbrush flowers cover the prostrate branches during late spring and early summer.

Cultivation This hybrid will grow in most well-drained soils. It likes an open sunny position and plenty of room to display itself. It is used successfully as a ground cover plant where it is necessary to shelter the root systems of other plants. It is frost-resistant and requires very little pruning apart from control of unwanted branches.

Landscape Use An excellent ground cover for growing over large areas of rocky slopes, banks, retaining walls, boulders and garden edges. It is ideal for public planting where low cover is needed.

Grevillea glabrata

Grevillea x *gaudichaudii*

Grevillea glabrata

Origin WA
Climate WT, M
Shade None to filtered

FAST-GROWING
BIRD-ATTRACTING
ORNAMENTAL FOLIAGE

Description A tall, bushy shrub to around 3 m high with a slightly weeping spread of up to 4 m. It has lovely prickly, fan-shaped grey-green foliage and bears masses of small lacy white flowers for much of the year.

Cultivation A hardy plant that suits most soils in a sunny, well-drained position. It will tolerate dry spells, some humidity and is frost-resistant. It can be kept very compact by persistent pruning.

Landscape Use A dense, fast-growing shrub useful as a fence or as a privacy screen, hedge or windbreak.

Grevillea hilliana
HILL'S SILKY OAK

Origin Qld, NSW
Climate T, S, WT
Shade Light to filtered

SPECIMEN PLANT
BIRD-ATTRACTING
ORNAMENTAL FOLIAGE
RAINFOREST PLANT

Description A rainforest tree to around 15 m, but lower and spreading in cultivation. The attractive shiny green leaves, either entire or lobed, have a silvery undersurface. Long slender sprays of creamy white flowers are produced in summer.

Cultivation Grow in a protected position in well-composted soil with good drainage. It is moderately frost-tolerant when mature.

Landscape Use A neat, compact tree that may be used as a feature or, if space

Grevillea hilliana

Grevillea 'Honey Gem'

permits, in conjunction with other rainforest trees.

Grevillea *'Honey Gem'*

Origin Cultivar (*G. banksii* x *G. pteridifolia*)
Climate T, S, WT, M
Shade None to light

FAST-GROWING
SPECIMEN PLANT
BIRD-ATTRACTING

Description A marvellous shrubby cultivar which grows to around 6 m. It has finely dissected dark green foliage on long branches, with bronze new growth. Masses of large orange flowers appear throughout the year, with the main flush in early spring. These are laden with honey and attract many varieties of nectar-feeding birds to the garden. The flowers and foliage make spectacular floral arrangements.

Cultivation An outstanding plant that does well in Queensland gardens. It needs a well-drained, sunny position. It is able to withstand strong winds and is moderately frost-resistant. Prune hard after flowering to promote vigorous new growth and further flowering.

Landscape Use A fine specimen, screen or hedge plant.

Grevillea hookerana *hybrid*

(sometimes sold as G. *'Red Hooks')*

Origin Cultivar
Climate S, WT, M, CT
Shade None to filtered

FAST-GROWING
SPECIMEN PLANT
BIRD-ATTRACTING
ORNAMENTAL FOLIAGE

Description A favourite in cultivation, this graceful spreading shrub often with horizontal branches will grow to around 3 m high with a similar spread. It has decorative light green divided leaves up to 20 cm long. New growth is often bronze. The brilliant red toothbrush flowers commence in spring and appear well into summer, much to the delight of many varieties of nectar-seeking birds.

Cultivation Grow in a well-drained, sunny position. It will grow near the coast and will tolerate dry conditions, but it is slightly frost-tender. May be trimmed to shape.

Grevillea hookerana

Landscape Use A fine specimen plant. It makes an excellent screen, hedge or windbreak.

Grevillea insignis
WAX GREVILLEA

Origin WA
Climate WT, M, SA
Shade None to light
BIRD-ATTRACTING
ORNAMENTAL FOLIAGE
Description A spreading medium-sized shrub up to 3 or 4 m tall. It has prickly grey-green, holly-like leaves and plentiful clusters of pinky red waxy flowers in winter and spring.

Cultivation This beautiful grevillea grows best in an open sunny aspect with excellent drainage. It will withstand dry periods and is moderately frost hardy. Lightly prune to shape when young and after peak flushes of flowers to promote healthy new growth.

Landscape Use This is a good specimen, screen or hedge plant for dry country gardens. The foliage is useful for indoor arrangements.

Grevillea intricata

Origin WA
Climate WT, M, SA
Shade None to filtered
BIRD-ATTRACTING
Description A dense bushy shrub to 2 m high with a spread to 4 m across. It has almost terete, finely divided pointed leaves which are densely interwoven. Masses of creamy-white candle-like flowers are produced in winter and spring.

Cultivation An attractive and reliable shrub for areas with low rainfall. Grafted plants, available in Queensland nurseries, are more suited to subtropical regions. It requires plenty of sun, good drainage and a spacious position to spread. It will tolerate light frosts. Prune to keep shapely.

Landscape Use A branches are dense to ground level, this species makes a fine hedging or screening plant.

Grevillea insignis

Grevillea intricata

Grevillea *'Ivanhoe'*

Origin Cultivar (*G. longifolia* x *G. caleyi*)
Climate S, WT, M, CT
Shade None to light
FAST-GROWING
SPECIMEN PLANT
BIRD-ATTRACTING
Description A very dense, spreading shrub to around 3 m high and 3 m wide. It has attractive deeply divided foliage with a bronze flush when young. The red toothbrush flowers appear for most of the year and will attract the honeyeaters.

Grevillea 'Ivanhoe'

Cultivation A hardy and vigorous plant that does well in a sunny, well-drained position. It will grow in coastal gardens with some protection and is frost-resistant. Prune lightly to shape.

Landscape Use A very useful specimen or screen plant.

Grevillea johnsonii

Origin NSW
Climate WT, M, CT, SA
Shade None to filtered
SPECIMEN PLANT
BIRD-ATTRACTING
Description A beautiful, slightly weeping, dense shrub to 3 m with long, fine, divided needle foliage. Loose clusters of pinkish red flowers are produced from late winter through the spring months. An excellent fast-growing hybrid known as *G. johnsonii* x *G. longistyla* is also available. It bears masses of showy red waxy flowers and is more suitable for growing in subtropical and warm temperate regions.

Grevillea johnsonii

Cultivation Grow in a well-drained soil in full sun or partial shade. It is moderately frost-resistant. Prune to maintain shape.

Landscape Use Attractive at all times, this shrub is outstanding when in flower and may be used as a feature. It will form a beautiful screen.

Grevillea juncifolia
HONEYSUCKLE GREVILLEA

Origin Qld, NSW, SA, WA, NT
Climate M, SA
Shade None to light
BIRD-ATTRACTING
DROUGHT-RESISTANT
Description A bushy shrub or small tree to around 4 m. It has long, narrow greyish leaves and numerous rich orange flowers that produce copious nectar and are most attractive to honeyeaters. It is a popular honey plant used by Aborigines.

Cultivation This species occurs in inland areas and responds well to cultivation in dry conditions. It is moderately frost-resistant. Prune immediately after flowering to encourage compact growth.

Landscape Use An excellent shrub for use as a feature in inland gardens.

Grevillea juncifolia

Grevillea juniperina
JUNIPER GREVILLEA

Origin NSW
Climate S, WT, M, CT, H, SA
Shade None to light
BIRD-ATTRACTING
CONTAINER PLANT
Description A tall, rounded shrub to 2 m with dark green, needle-like foliage on arching branches. Clusters of yellow, orange-red or red spider flowers appear from late winter through spring. This is a valuable shrub for honeyeaters, providing shelter and food.

Grevillea juniperina

G. juniperina (red prostrate form)

This is one of the most variable species and many forms are in cultivation and available from nurseries. The prostrate forms are especially popular for rockery and ground cover use and may have yellow, apricot or red flowers.

Cultivation All forms are hardy in a well-drained position in most climates and soils. They will grow well in full sun or partial shade and are frost-resistant. Prune to desired shape.

Landscape Use The upright form is suitable as a hedge or low screen. It can be prickly to walk past so be careful where you plant it. Prostrate forms are

G. juniperina var. *trinervis*

G. juniperina (yellow prostrate form)

ideal for cascading over rockeries, slopes, walls and containers.

Grevillea lanigera
WOOLLY GREVILLEA

Origin NSW, Vic.
Climate WT, M, CT, H
Shade None to filtered
BIRD-ATTRACTING
CONTAINER PLANT

Description A bushy, rounded shrub to 1.5 m with narrow, woolly greyish leaves. The clusters of red and cream spider flowers are produced in late winter and spring.

There are several forms of this variable grevillea in cultivation, including a low-growing dwarf form.

G. lanigera 'Mt Tamboritha' is a lovely prostrate spreading form with soft grey foliage and pink and cream flowers.

Cultivation This grevillea does well in most soils in full sun or partial shade.

Grevillea lanigera

G. lanigera 'Mt Tamboritha'

It will withstand very cold conditions and is frost-tolerant.

Landscape Use As this grevillea will flower quite well in shade it is ideal for growing as an understorey plant. It forms an attractive screen or low hedge. Low forms are excellent rockery specimens.

Grevillea laurifolia

Origin NSW
Climate S, WT, M, CT, H
Shade None to filtered
BIRD-ATTRACTING
CONTAINER PLANT

Description A prostrate, mat-forming plant with a spread of 3 m or more in diameter. It has oval, rather leathery leaves and bronze new growth. The dark red flowers appear in spring and summer.

Cultivation Grow in a sunny, well-drained position with some moisture. Growth is slow at first, but once established it will cover over 3 m in

Grevillea laurifolia

diameter. It is frost-resistant. Prune lightly to keep tidy.

Landscape Use An excellent ground cover for sloping banks, retaining walls and large containers.

Grevillea lavandulacea
LAVENDER GREVILLEA

Origin NSW, Vic., SA
Climate WT, M, CT, H, SA
Shade None to filtered
BIRD-ATTRACTING
CONTAINER PLANT

Description This is an extremely variable species, ranging from an almost prostrate plant to a bushy shrub just over 1 m. Foliage is also variable, but some forms have narrow blue-grey leaves similar to those of lavender. The flowers are mostly pink or red and appear during winter and spring. They are rich in nectar and are most attractive to honeyeaters.

G. lavandulacea 'Billy Wing' is a low-growing semi-prostrate plant with greyish green leaves and deep pink flowers. A compact form to 60 cm is also in cultivation.

G. lavandulacea 'Black Range' has an upright but spreading habit to around 1.5 m. It has prickly foliage and an abundance of glowing pink flowers.

G. lavandulacea 'Tanunda' grows to around 1 m with attractive silver-grey leaves and massed clusters of deep pink flowers during winter and spring.

G. lavandulacea 'Billy Wing'

G. lavandulacea 'Black Range'

G. lavandulacea 'Tanunda'

G. lavandulacea 'Victor Harbour'

G. lavandulacea 'Victor Harbour' is a small upright shrub with green foliage and brilliant red hanging spider flowers.

Cultivation Grow in a well-drained, light-textured soil. Most forms prefer full sun, but will grow in partial shade. They are frost-resistant and some forms will tolerate very cold conditions. Regular pruning will promote compact growth.

Landscape Use All forms are decorative for general garden purposes. Low-growing forms are excellent rockery or container plants. 'Billy Wing' is a beautiful edging plant.

Grevillea longifolia
FERN-LEAF GREVILLEA

Origin NSW
Climate WT, M, CT, H
Shade None to filtered

FAST-GROWING
SPECIMEN PLANT
BIRD-ATTRACTING
ORNAMENTAL FOLIAGE

Description A large, spreading grevillea to around 3 m high with similar spread. The dark green serrated leaves up to 8 cm long have a bronze tinge when young and the undersides are covered with silky brown hairs. Deep pink or red toothbrush flowers cover the bush during winter and spring and are a valuable source of nectar for honeyeaters. Cut foliage and flowers are good for indoor arrangements.

Cultivation Grow in a lightly shaded, well-drained position. It likes plenty of moisture and is resistant to frost and cold conditions. The plant responds well to pruning after flowering.

Grevillea longifolia

Landscape Use A most ornamental species for feature planting. Its density makes it an ideal screen or windbreak plant.

Grevillea longistyla

Origin Qld
Climate S, WT, M
Shade None to light

FAST-GROWING
SPECIMEN PLANT
BIRD-ATTRACTING

Description An upright shrub to around 3 m. It has very narrow bright green leaves which may be entire or divided. The deep pink or red flowers with a long red style are produced in loose clusters at branch ends from late winter to early summer.

Grevillea longistyla

Cultivation Grow in a well-drained, sheltered position in full sun. It requires good watering during summer and, although frost-hardy at maturity, is slightly tender when young. Prune lightly after flowering.

Landscape Use A lovely feature plant. Its slender, upright habit makes it a good fence screen in narrow places.

Grevillea *'Mason's Hybrid' ('Ned Kelly')*

Origin Cultivar (related to *G.* 'Robyn Gordon')

Climate S, WT, M, CT

Shade None to light

BIRD-ATTRACTING

Description A spreading shrub which grows to around 2 m high and with a similar spread. It has bright green, deeply lobed foliage and bears orange-red flowers all year, with several peaks of dense flowering.

Cultivation A hardy and reliable plant in most soils in a sunny, open position. It will withstand dry periods and is very frost-tolerant. Regular pruning will maintain shape and vigour.

Landscape Use A lovely compact feature plant with flowers top to bottom. It will form a good hedge and screen.

Grevillea 'Masons Hybrid' (Ned Kelly)

Grevillea *'Misty Pink'*

Origin Cultivar (*G. banksii* x *G. sessilis*)

Climate T, S, WT, M

Shade None to light

FAST-GROWING
SPECIMEN PLANT
BIRD-ATTRACTING

Description A very vigorous bushy shrub which grows up to 3 m. It has beautiful

Grevillea 'Misty Pink'

silvery green lobed leaves, and these complement the plentiful large pink flowers that appear for most of the year, with peaks in spring and autumn. Honeyeaters and parrots are attracted to this lovely shrub and it provides excellent fresh cut flowers.

Cultivation This hardy plant will grow in most soils with good drainage. It needs an open, sunny position and will tolerate both dry and moist conditions. It will withstand frost and may be grown in cold climate areas. Prune off old flower heads and seed heads to promote vigour and further flowering.

Landscape Use A spectacular feature shrub that can be used as a screen or hedge with appropriate pruning.

Grevillea *'Moonlight'*

Origin Cultivar (*G. banksii* x *G. whiteana*)

Climate S, WT

Shade None to light

SPECIMEN PLANT
FRAGRANT
BIRD-ATTRACTING
ORNAMENTAL FOLIAGE

Description An upright shrub to 4 m tall with dark green finely divided foliage with a silvery underside. Large creamy-white toothbrush flowers, up to 12 cm long, are produced mainly in winter and spring, but can be seen at other times.

Cultivation Grow in a sunny well-drained position. Provide plenty of moisture in hot dry periods. It will tolerate light frost.

Grevillea 'Moonlight'

Landscape Use This is an excellent screening plant. The foliage and flowers are very good for indoor decoration. For longer vase life pick the flowers before the styles open.

Grevillea mucronulata

Origin NSW

Climate WT, M

Shade Light to filtered

BIRD-ATTRACTING

Description A small, slightly open shrub to around 1.5 m high. The dark green oval leaves have recurved margins and end in a short point. Green spidery flowers produced freely in winter and spring are especially attractive to nectar-feeding birds.

Cultivation Good drainage and some shade are this dainty plant's main requirements. It is moderately frost

Grevillea mucronulata

hardy. A regular pruning will encourage a shapely bush.

Landscape Use An excellent bird-attracting species for growing beneath trees in bush gardens or large rockeries.

Grevillea muelleri

Grevillea muelleri

Origin WA
Climate WT, M, CT
Shade None to filtered

BIRD-ATTRACTING
CONTAINER PLANT

Description A small upright shrub to around 50 cm. The narrow, rigid leaves may be entire or three-lobed at the ends, and creamy yellow flowers are clustered along the branches in late winter and spring.

Cultivation Grow in a well-drained soil in either full sun or partial shade. It is frost-resistant. Prune lightly to maintain a rounded shape.

Landscape Use A neat shrub for the garden foreground or the rockery. It is a good container grevillea.

Grevillea nudiflora

Origin WA
Climate WT, M, SA
Shade None to filtered

BIRD-ATTRACTING
SALT-TOLERANT
CONTAINER PLANT

Description An unusual, low-growing, dome-shaped shrub up to 70 cm high, with bright green narrow leaves. The small bright red flowers are borne on long trailing leafless branches which radiate from the main section of the plant. Flowers appear throughout the year, with a main flush in spring.

Cultivation Grow in a well-drained, sunny or partially shaded position. It will withstand fairly dry conditions and may be grown in exposed coastal gardens, as it will stand salt spray and strong winds. It is moderately frost-resistant.

Landscape Use An interesting plant that looks very good cascading over rocks, steps, retaining walls, banks and containers.

Grevillea nudiflora

Grevillea petrophiloides

Origin WA
Climate M, SA
Shade None to light

FAST-GROWING
SPECIMEN PLANT
BIRD-ATTRACTING
DROUGHT-RESISTANT

Description This is a beautiful spreading shrub to around 2 m. It has long green leaves divided into terete segments and unusual sprays of pink flowers that are shaped like bottlebrushes. They are produced at the branch ends over a long period during winter and spring.

Cultivation Grow in a very well drained soil in a sunny open position. This species prefers a dry climate and resents humidity. It is moderately frost-resistant and will tolerate hard pruning.

Landscape Use A lovely flowering plant which may be used as a feature. Flowers are suitable for picking.

Grevillea *'Pink Parfait'*

Origin Cultivar (related to *G.* 'Misty Pink')
Climate T, S, WT
Shade None to light

BIRD-ATTRACTING
ORNAMENTAL FOLIAGE

Description A tall, bushy shrub to around 3 m. It has deeply lobed silvery green leaves with a coating of dense hairs. The prolific large flowers to 18 cm long are a vivid pink and occur all year round.

Grevillea 'Pink Parfait'

Cultivation A very free-flowering grevillea for subtropical gardens. It needs a well-drained, sunny position. Prune well after flowering peaks to shape the bush and encourage future flowering. Extra water in dry times promotes good flowering.

Landscape Use A very showy plant that looks very good in group planting. It forms an excellent screen. Foliage and flowers are excellent in indoor arrangements.

Grevillea *'Poorinda Beauty'*

Origin Cultivar (*G. alpina* x *G. juniperina*)
Climate WT, M, CT
Shade None to filtered
FAST-GROWING
BIRD-ATTRACTING
CONTAINER PLANT
Description A compact, rounded shrub to around 2.5 m. It has fine, soft leaves and bears tight clusters of rich orange-red flowers through winter and spring.

Cultivation Grow in a sunny, well-drained position. It will tolerate fairly dry conditions and is moderately frost-resistant. Prune to maintain a bushy habit.

Grevillea 'Poorinda Beauty'

Landscape Use A good winter-flowering cultivar for planting with other shrubs or as a neatly trimmed hedge.

Grevillea *'Poorinda Blondie'*

Origin Cultivar (*G. hookerana* seedling)
Climate S, WT, M
Shade None to filtered
FAST-GROWING
BIRD-ATTRACTING
Description A vigorous tall spreading shrub to around 3.5 m high with a spread of 4 m or more across. It has deeply lobed dark green foliage and throughout late winter and spring bears

Grevillea petrophiloides

Grevillea 'Poorinda Blondie'

masses of dull yellow toothbrush flowers that are most attractive to honeyeaters.

Cultivation Grow in a sunny, well-drained position. It will tolerate humid as well as fairly dry conditions and is moderately frost-resistant. Prune to shape after flowering.

Landscape Use A marvellous screening plant for a roomy position.

Grevillea *'Poorinda Diadem'*

Origin Cultivar ('Poorinda Leane' seedling)
Climate WT, M
Shade None to light
FAST-GROWING
BIRD-ATTRACTING
Description A bushy erect shrub which reaches to around 2.5 m. It has shiny green elliptic leaves with a silky underside and masses of light golden-apricot flowers cover the bush in spring.

Cultivation Grow in a well-drained, sunny position. It will grow in heavy soils and will tolerate fairly dry conditions. It is moderately frost-resistant.

Landscape Use A beautiful flowering shrub for use as a specimen or for privacy or fence screening.

Grevillea 'Poorinda Diadem'

Grevillea *'Poorinda Royal Mantle'*

Origin Cultivar (*G. laurifolia* x *G. willisii*)
Climate T, S, WT, M, CT, H
Shade None to filtered
FAST-GROWING
BIRD-ATTRACTING
Description This very popular ground cover will eventually form a dense mat up to 4 m or more across. It has irregularly lobed leaves and attractive reddish new growth. The large dark red toothbrush flowers, borne on short branches during winter and spring, are most attractive to honeyeaters.

Grevillea 'Poorinda Royal Mantle'

Cultivation Grow in a well-drained soil in full sun or partial shade. It is frost-resistant and will tolerate dry conditions, but flowering is improved with extra water during summer. Give it plenty of room to spread and prune to tidy or to remove any unwanted branches.

Landscape Use An exceptional ground cover suitable for covering large areas. It looks beautiful as an edging plant, or spilling down rocky slopes and retaining walls. When grafted, using *G. robusta* as the rootstock, it makes a spectacular weeping standard.

Grevillea *'Poorinda Tranquillity'*

Origin Cultivar (*G. alpina* x *G. lavandulacea*)
Climate S, WT, M, CT
Shade None to filtered
FAST-GROWING
BIRD-ATTRACTING
CONTAINER PLANT
Description A small erect shrub to around 1 m. It has attractive grey-green leaves with a white woolly underside and bears many pastel pink flowers all through winter months.

Grevillea 'Poorinda Tranquillity'

Cultivation Grow in a well-drained soil in full or partial sun. It will tolerate frost. Prune back after flowering to encourage bushy growth.

Landscape Use A beautiful pink-flowering shrub for winter; ideal for foregrounds, in rockeries or in large containers.

Grevillea pteridifolia
GOLDEN GREVILLEA

Origin Qld, WA, NT
Climate T, S, WT
Shade None to light
FAST-GROWING
BIRD-ATTRACTING
SALT-TOLERANT (prostrate form)
Description A tall shrub or small tree with an open habit to 5 m. It has finely divided silvery foliage and spectacular

orange toothbrush flowers from autumn to spring. Flowers attract quite a variety of native birds, including lorikeets and honeyeaters.

G. pteridifolia prostrate form from Cooktown is available from Queensland nurseries. It spreads to around 3 m and has slightly broader bright green foliage and bright orange toothbrush flowers. This form is sometimes sold under the cultivar name 'Mandarin Mantle'.

Cultivation Grow in a sunny, well-drained position. Best suited to warmer climates, it may be grown in protected coastal gardens, but is slightly frost-tender. It does not like strong winds, so prune off any gangly branches to promote vigour. The prostrate form may be grown in exposed coastal situations.

Landscape Use This shrub is vary sparsely branched and is best grown in groups or among other trees and shrubs. The prostrate form makes an ideal foreground or rockery plant.

Grevillea pteridifolia

G. pteridifolia (prostrate form)

Grevillea quercifolia

Grevillea quercifolia
OAK-LEAF GREVILLEA

Origin WA
Climate WT, M
Shade Light to filtered

BIRD-ATTRACTING
CONTAINER PLANT

Description A small scrambling shrub to around 1 m high and 1 m wide. The interesting leaves have prickly lobes. Erect pink-purple flowers with twisted styles appear during spring.

Cultivation Grow in a well-drained soil. This plant is from south-western forests of Western Australia and prefers some shade. It is moderately frost-resistant and will tolerate dry periods.

Landscape Use A most unusual grevillea for the garden foreground, rockery or container.

Grevillea robusta
SILKY OAK

Origin Qld, NSW
Climate T, S, WT, M, CT, SA
Shade None to filtered

FAST-GROWING
SPECIMEN PLANT
BIRD-ATTRACTING
DROUGHT-RESISTANT
ORNAMENTAL FOLIAGE
CONTAINER PLANT
RAINFOREST PLANT

Description A tall, shapely tree to around 30 m with a rough bark. The beautiful large divided leaves have a grey-green undersurface and may be semideciduous in some areas. New growth is an attractive bronze colour. The long bright orange flowers appear in huge numbers in late spring and summer. Rich in nectar, they attract a variety of birds. This species produces a fine cabinet timber.

Cultivation This rainforest tree has adapted well to cultivation. It will grow in most well-drained soils and once

Grevillea robusta

established will tolerate very dry conditions and frost. It may be grown in coastal gardens with some protection. Prune to shape.

Landscape Use A beautiful ornamental tree for large specimen planting. It is used extensively in streets and parks and is an ideal shade tree for schoolyards and industrial sites.

When young it makes an ornamental container plant for courtyards and indoors. When it has outgrown the container do not be tempted to plant it in a small garden. This tree is for a large area only and is a dreadful drain clogger.

Grevillea *'Robyn Gordon'*

Origin Cultivar (*G. banksii* x *G. bipinnatifida*)
Climate T, S, WT, M, CT
Shade None to filtered

FAST-GROWING
SPECIMEN PLANT
BIRD-ATTRACTING
CONTAINER PLANT

Description This now famous cultivar, which is available from most nurseries, originally arose as a spontaneous hybrid in the garden of David Gordon, Glenmorgan, Queensland. It is a low, spreading shrub reaching a height of around 1.5 m and a spread of about 2 m with dark green lobed leaves with a silky undersurface. Profuse slightly hanging coral red flowers appear almost continuously throughout the year, with peaks in spring and autumn. These provide a constant source of nectar for honeyeaters.

Grevillea 'Robyn Gordon'

Cultivation This very popular cultivar is grown in gardens throughout Australia. It is hardy and adaptable to a wide climate range and soil types and has proved to be relatively frost-hardy. It needs a well-drained situation in any open sunny position. Prune regularly to maintain shape.

Landscape Use A magnificent plant for many landscaping purposes. It makes a beautiful specimen shrub and an excellent informal hedge and may be grown in a large tub. Its hardiness and continuous flowering make it ideal for municipal and street planting.

Grevillea rosmarinifolia
ROSEMARY GREVILLEA

Origin NSW, Vic.
Climate S, WT, M, CT, H
Shade **None to light**

FAST-GROWING
BIRD-ATTRACTING
CONTAINER PLANT

Description A dense-growing, spreading shrub up to 2 m high and 2 m wide. It has dark green needle foliage and carries spidery red and cream flowers for most of the year, with a main display in spring. There are many forms of this shrub available, including several good low-growing forms. It is also the parent of many hybrids.

G. rosmarinifolia 'Pink Pixie' is a compact rounded shrub to 50 cm high with light green leaves and masses of pink spider flowers during winter and early spring.

G. rosmarinifolia 'Lutea' is a rounded shrub to 2.5 m. Abundant yellow spider flowers are produced in late winter and spring.

G. rosmarinifolia 'Nana' is a low, spreading shrub to 50 cm high with

Grevillea rosmarinifolia

G. rosmarinifolia 'Pink Pixie'

G. rosamarinifolia 'Lutea'

G. rosmarinifolia 'Nana'

narrow dark green foliage and pink flowers.

Cultivation A very hardy shrub that will grow in most well-drained soils and conditions. Once established it will tolerate dryness, frost, some snow and semiexposed coastal conditions. Can be pruned hard to shape.

Landscape Use This species makes an excellent dense screen or hedge. The low-growing forms may be used as edging, rockery or container subjects.

Grevillea saccata
POUCHED GREVILLEA

Origin WA
Climate WT, M, SA
Shade None to light

BIRD-ATTRACTING
CONTAINER PLANT

Description A small compact shrub to around 30 cm high with crowded linear leaves that are quite woolly when young. Conspicuous bright red flowers are borne in winter and early spring. Although rare in its natural habitat, this species is available in some specialist nurseries.

Cultivation It requires full sun, good drainage and a light tip pruning when young to promote bushy growth. It will withstand moderate frosts but resents humidity.

Landscape Use A bright little edging, rockery or container plant.

Grevillea saccata

Grevillea *'Sandra Gordon'*

Origin Cultivar (*G. pteridifolia* x *G. sessilis*)
Climate T, S, WT, M
Shade None to light

FAST-GROWING
SPECIMEN PLANT
BIRD-ATTRACTING

Description A tall open shrub to around 4 m or more, with grey-green divided foliage and bronze new growth. The bright yellow toothbrush flowers appear mainly during spring but again in autumn. They are rich in nectar and attract lorikeets as well as a variety of other nectar-feeding birds. Cut flowers last well indoors.

Cultivation Grow in a sunny, well-drained position. It is moderately frost-tolerant and may be grown in coastal areas with some protection. It needs to be thoroughly pruned after flowering to produce a stronger, more compact plant.

Landscape Use A prolifically flowering plant which may be used as a feature.

Grevillea 'Sandra Gordon'

Grevillea sericea
PINK SPIDER FLOWER

Origin NSW
Climate S, WT, M, CT
Shade None to filtered

BIRD-ATTRACTING
CONTAINER PLANT

Description A small erect shrub to around 1.5 m. It has narrow dark green leaves with a silky undersurface and produces an abundance of spidery pink flowers for most of the year, with the main display in spring. A form from Collaroy Plateau near Sydney has very pretty deep pink flowers. A white-flowering form is also available.

Grevillea sericea

G. sericea (Collaroy Plateau form)

Cultivation A hardy shrub for a well-drained sunny position. It will tolerate frost and is suitable for coastal planting with some protection. Prune to encourage compact growth.

Landscape Use A very pretty shrub for the garden or in a large container.

Grevillea *'Shirley Howie'*

Origin Cultivar (*G. diffusa* x *G. sericea*)
Climate T, S, WT
Shade None to light

BIRD-ATTRACTING
CONTAINER PLANT

Description A small rounded shrub up to 1.5 m. It has dark green linear leaves and bears masses of vibrant pink spider flowers throughout the year.

Cultivation This Queensland cultivar is most reliable in tropical and warm temperate climates in a well-drained, sunny position. It is resistant to frost and may be grown in coastal gardens with some protection. Prune to shape.

Landscape Use A lovely feature plant when in flower, for the small garden or container.

Grevillea speciosa *ssp.* speciosa

(syn. *G. punicea*)

RED SPIDER FLOWER

Origin NSW
Climate T, WT, M, CT
Shade None to filtered

FAST-GROWING
BIRD-ATTRACTING

Description A variable shrub from 1 to 3 m tall with dark green elliptical to ovate leaves with a silky undersurface and ending in a small point. Pendent bright red spider flowers appear in late winter, spring and summer. There are a two further subspecies that are popular in cultivation.

G. speciosa ssp. *dimorpha* (syn. *G. dimorpha*) from the Grampians, Vic. is a small dense shrub to around 1 m high with two distinctive forms based on leaf width: one has elliptical leaves to 2 cm wide and the other has extremely fine, almost needle-shaped leaves. The bright red flowers appear along the stems in autumn, winter and spring.

G. speciosa ssp. *oleoides* (syn. *G. oleoides*) from NSW is an upright shrub to about 2 m high with narrow dark green lanceolate leaves covered with soft silvery hairs on the undersurface. Rich red flowers are borne along the stems in leaf axils in late winter and spring.

Grevillea speciosa

Cultivation All forms are well adapted to cultivation requiring good drainage and a sunny to partly shaded position. Plants are frost resistant and benefit from regular pruning to shape.

Landscape Use All subspecies are very useful long-flowering bird-attracting shrubs.

Grevillea stenomera

Origin WA
Climate S, WT, M
Shade None to light

FAST-GROWING
BIRD-ATTRACTING
CONTAINER PLANT

Description A dense, spreading shrub to around 2 m high and 2 m wide with narrow grey-green foliage. Pendent clusters of red or pink waxy flowers appear in winter and spring.

Grevillea stenomera

G. stenomera (prostrate form)

A prostrate form with a spread to 1.5 m is also available. It has bright green foliage and red spider flowers.

Cultivation This species is best suited to winter rainfall regions, however grafted plants are available in Queensland nurseries. Grow in a well-drained sunny position. It may be grown in protected coastal gardens and is frost-resistant. Prune to shape.

Landscape Use Ideal as a screen or informal hedge. The prostrate form may be used as a ground cover or as a container plant.

Grevillea *'Superb'*

Origin Cultivar (*G. bipinnatifida* x *G. banksii* white form)
Climate T, S, WT, M
Shade None to light

FAST-GROWING
SPECIMEN PLANT
BIRD-ATTRACTING
CONTAINER PLANT

Description A small, rounded shrub to 1 m. The dark green, lobed foliage is very similar to that of *G.* 'Robyn Gordon', as the two crosses have the same parent species. The flowers are also similar, but are a beautiful salmon colour. These appear almost continuously throughout the year.

Cultivation This cultivar is hardy and adaptable to a wide range of soils and climatic conditions. It needs a well-drained position and lots of sun. It is resistant to light frosts. Prune regularly to maintain shape.

Landscape Use A beautiful plant as a specimen or low hedge. It may be grown in a large container for a courtyard or patio.

Grevillea synapheae

CATKIN GREVILLEA

Origin WA
Climate WT, M
Shade None to filtered

BIRD-ATTRACTING
CONTAINER PLANT

Description A low-growing, spreading shrub to around 1 m across. The leaves are usually three-lobed, and creamy yellow flower heads are clustered at the ends of long stalks in spring.

Cultivation Plants tend to be short lived and grafted plants are available. Grow in

Grevillea 'Superb'

Grevillea synapheae

a light-textured, well-drained soil in full sun or part shade. It is frost-tolerant. Prune to shape.

Landscape Use An ornamental ground cover for the garden foreground or for the rockery, where it will trail attractively over rocks.

Grevillea thelemanniana

SPIDER NET GREVILLEA

Origin WA
Climate S, WT, M
Shade None to filtered

BIRD-ATTRACTING
CONTAINER PLANT

Description This species is very variable in habit, but it is usually the prostrate forms that are popular in cultivation. There are both green and grey foliage forms. The green form is slightly more upright and generally more compact, while the grey form has long prostrate stems. The red waxy flowers appear during spring and summer and sometimes again in late autumn.

Cultivation Both forms like a sunny, well-drained position. While the green leaf form is generally hardier, the grey form is the more desirable, but definitely more frost-tender. Prune to shape.

Landscape Use An attractive ground cover for edging, for the rockery, or to grow cascading over walls, banks or containers.

Grevillea thelemanniana (grey form)

Grevillea thelemanniana *ssp.* obtusifolia

(syn. *G. obtusifolia*)

Origin WA
Climate S, WT, M, CT
Shade None to light

Description This is a variable plant which may be prostrate and hugging the ground or erect to 3 m high and to a similar width. It is the densely spreading prostrate form that is most often seen in cultivation and is available from nurseries. It has shining green entire leaves with a blunt tip and bears pendulous clusters of deep red flowers in winter and spring.

Cultivation A hardy plant that will grow in most well-drained soils in a sunny position. It is frost-tolerant.

Landscape Use Use as a lush ground cover, in a rockery, or spilling from a container.

Grevillea thelemanniana ssp. *obtusifolia*

Grevillea thyrsoides

Origin WA
Climate WT, M, SA
Shade None to light

ORNAMENTAL FOLIAGE
CONTAINER PLANT

Description This beautiful and very rare species in nature is now available at some native plant nurseries. It is a prostrate or dwarf shrub with a spread to 1.5 m with attractive grey-green hairy leaves divided into narrow leaflets. The hairy reddish-pink toothbrush flowers are borne on trailing leafless branches, sometimes along the ground beyond the plant. Flowers are produced mostly in spring and summer, but can be seen at other times.

Cultivation Provide excellent drainage in a sunny open position. It is moderately

Grevillea thyrsoides

frost tolerant but should be grown as a grafted plant in humid areas. Lightly prune from early days to encourage dense growth in the centre of the plant.

Landscape Use Grow in an elevated position in the garden such as rockery, raised garden bed, retaining wall or container where it will receive perfect drainage.

Grevillea triloba

Origin WA
Climate WT, M, CT, H, SA
Shade None to light
FAST-GROWING
FRAGRANT
BIRD-ATTRACTING
Description A vigorous, dense shrub to around 2.5 m in height and diameter.

Grevillea triloba

It has pointed three-lobed leaves which are a lovely soft grey-green when young. Masses of perfumed white flowers cover the bush in late winter and spring.

Cultivation Grow in a light-textured, well-drained soil, in full sun if possible. It will withstand dry periods and is frost-resistant. Will tolerate hard pruning.

Landscape Use An excellent background or screening shrub.

Grevillea tripartita

Origin WA
Climate WT, M, CT, SA
Shade None to light
BIRD-ATTRACTING
Description An erect-growing shrub to around 2.5 m high. The sharp grey-green leaves are divided into three leaflets, and large showy flowers are produced along the branches. These are red and yellow with a very long style; they appear in late winter and spring and are most attractive to a variety of nectar-feeding birds.

Cultivation This species requires good drainage in an open, dry situation. It is frost-resistant. Lightly prune from early days to encourage growth.

Landscape Use An attractive and unusual grevillea for the garden.

Grevillea tripartita

Grevillea venusta
BYFIELD SPIDER FLOWER

Origin Qld
Climate T, S, WT
Shade None to filtered
FAST-GROWING
BIRD-ATTRACTING
Description A dense medium shrub up to 4 m. It has large, entire or deeply

Grevillea venusta

lobed dark green leaves with copper-coloured new growth. The unusual green and orange spidery flowers, with a long style, are borne in loose clusters during winter and spring.

Cultivation Grow in a well-drained soil in full sun or partial shade. It is suitable for protected coastal gardens and is fairly frost-resistant. Prune to shape.

Landscape Use A graceful shrub with a lush appearance, suited to use as a background or screening plant.

Grevillea vestita

Origin WA
Climate WT, M, CT
Shade None to light
FAST-GROWING
BIRD-ATTRACTING

Description A dense, spreading shrub to around 2 m high and 3 m across, with lovely grey-green wedge-shaped leaves that are lobed near the tip. Masses of feathery white flowers appear in the leaf axils and at branch ends in winter and spring.

Cultivation A hardy species that will grow in most well-drained soils and in most situations. It is frost-tolerant. Prune to shape.

Landscape Use A beautiful screening or background shrub.

Grevillea vestita

Grevillea victoriae

ROYAL GREVILLEA

Origin NSW, Vic.
Climate WT, M, CT, H
Shade None to filtered
FAST-GROWING
BIRD-ATTRACTING

Description An upright, compact shrub to around 2 m high and 2 m in diameter. It has beautiful grey-green leaves with silvery undersides that complement the pendent clusters of rusty red flowers appearing in winter and spring.

Cultivation Grow in a well-drained soil in either full sun or partial shade. It will tolerate very cold conditions, withstanding heavy frosts and snow. Prune to shape.

Landscape Use A particularly attractive shrub for the cold climate garden. It is a good screening plant.

Grevillea victoriae

Grevillea whiteana

(syn. *G.* sp. 'Coochin Hills')
(Also known as *G.* 'Honeycomb')

COOCHIN HILLS OAK

Origin Qld
Climate S, WT, M
Shade None to light
FAST-GROWING
FRAGRANT
BIRD-ATTRACTING
ORNAMENTAL FOLIAGE

Description A tall erect shrub to around 5 m high with attractive long leaves that are pinnately divided into elongated linear lobes. The leaves are dark green with a silky white under surface. The creamy-yellow flowers appear in winter and spring.

Cultivation Grow in a well-drained soil in a sunny position protected from strong winds. It is moderately frost-resistant. Prune or take generous sprays

Grevillea whiteana

of flowers and foliage for the house, to keep shapely.

Landscape Use A most ornamental plant that needs room in the garden to display itself properly.

Grevillea *'White Wings'*

Origin Cultivar
Climate S, WT, M, CT
Shade None to light
FAST-GROWING

Description A dense shrub to 2 m with a spreading habit to 3 m or more across. It has divided prickly foliage and produces masses of delicate white flowers in winter and spring.

Cultivation Grow in a sunny, well-drained position. This hardy plant will tolerate dry conditions and is frost-resistant. Prune regularly to keep shapely.

Grevillea 'White Wings'

Landscape Use This very fast-growing shrub may be trained as a hedge or to screen a fence, but is also good when allowed to tumble over a retaining wall, rocks or a sloping bank.

Grevillea wilsonii
WILSON'S GREVILLEA

Origin WA
Climate WT, M, SA
Shade None to light
SPECIMEN PLANT
BIRD-ATTRACTING

Description A many-stemmed, rounded shrub to 1.5 m high and across with prickly, deeply divided foliage. The profuse bright red flowers appear at the ends of the branches in spring and summer.

Cultivation Grow in a very well drained, sunny position. It prefers dry conditions and is frost-resistant. Grafted plants should be grown in humid areas. Prune to shape.

Landscape Use An outstanding ornamental shrub to use as a specimen or to plant en masse.

Grevillea wilsonii

GUICHENOTIA
STERCULIACEAE

A small genus of six species native to Western Australia. They are small woody shrubs with a downy covering. The lantern-shaped flowers have virtually no petals, but the calyx is usually brightly coloured. Propagation is from half-ripened tip cuttings or from seed.

Guichenotia ledifolia

Origin WA
Climate WT, M, CT, SA
Shade None to filtered
CONTAINER PLANT

Description A dense, rounded shrub to almost 1 m. It has grey-green linear leaves and bears small mauve lantern-shaped flowers in groups of four to five in late winter and spring.

Cultivation Grow in a well-drained soil. It is frost-hardy and will withstand extended dry periods. It is suitable for coastal planting with some protection. A light pruning after flowering will keep the bush shapely.

Landscape Use Use as a garden shrub or grow in a container.

Guichenotia ledifolia

Guichenotia macrantha

Origin WA
Climate WT, M, CT, SA
Shade None to filtered
CONTAINER PLANT

Description A dense, rounded shrub to 1 m. It has narrow pale grey leaves and produces showy deep pinkish purple bell-shaped flowers from August through to summer. Cut foliage and flowers make pretty sprays for indoors.

Cultivation This species will grow in most soils, including salty ones and those containing some lime, but it needs good drainage. It will withstand dry periods and frost and may be grown in coastal areas with some protection. Prune lightly after flowering.

Guichenotia macrantha

Landscape Use An attractive rockery plant, garden shrub or container plant.

HAKEA
PROTEACEAE

This genus is limited to Australia and contains more than 140 species of shrubs and small trees, some of which are well known in cultivation. Hakeas were named in honour of Baron Christian Ludwich von Hake, an eighteenth-century German patron of botany.

Some hakeas are called needle bushes because their leaves are cylindrical and sharply pointed like needles. Others are willow-leaved, some have long, flat, narrow leaves and others such as H. victoriae *have rounded leathery leaves. Some have flower clusters similar to those of* Grevillea, *while others have tight balls of flowers that give the plant the name 'pincushion'. However, all hakeas can easily be identified by the large woody seed cases, which usually persist on the plant until dried or burnt, when they open to release two winged seeds.*

Hakeas are among Australia's most hardy and attractive plants, with ornamental foliage, conspicuous flowers and interesting fruits. The flowers are most attractive to nectar-feeding birds, and the prickly foliage of some species provides a haven for small birds. Cockatoos include the seeds of some in their diet.

Almost all hakeas prefer a well-drained soil, and can usually tolerate a certain amount of dryness during the summer months. All species will tolerate pruning and some of the prickly species will trim into a fine hedge.

Some species of Hakea *which originate in areas with a dry climate may succumb to the Cinnamon Fungus,* Phytophthora cinnamomi, *in periods of high humidity. Grafted plants are available and should be considered for humid areas in eastern Australia.*

Propagation is most successful from seed. The seed is easily collected and germination is usually reliable, but can take up to ten weeks. Hakeas do not appear to hybridise as easily as grevilleas, and colour forms usually do come true from seed.

Hakea bucculenta
RED POKERS

Origin WA
Climate M, SA
Shade None to light

SPECIMEN PLANT
BIRD-ATTRACTING

Description A large, erect, slightly open shrub to 4 m high, with narrow grass-like leaves up to 15 cm long. Spectacular orange-red tapering flower spikes borne on old wood appear in late winter and spring.
Cultivation This species likes a light-textured soil with excellent drainage. It will tolerate dry conditions and is moderately frost-resistant, but resents humidity. Grafted plants are available.

Landscape Use This most ornamental bird-attracting shrub may be used as a specimen or fence screen.

Hakea bucculenta

Hakea cinerea
ASHY HAKEA

Origin WA
Climate WT, M, SA
Shade None to light

SPECIMEN PLANT
BIRD-ATTRACTING

Description An upright, robust shrub to around 2.5 m tall, with stiff, dull blue-green foliage. The clusters of yellowish flowers borne in the upper branches mature to an attractive orange shade. They appear from late winter to October.

Cultivation Grow in a light, well-drained soil in full sun. It will tolerate dry conditions and is moderately frost-resistant. From early days prune lightly to shape.

Landscape Use This attractive shrub may be used as a feature or windbreak.

Hakea corymbosa
CAULIFLOWER HAKEA

Origin WA
Climate WT, M, CT, SA
Shade None to light

SPECIMEN PLANT
BIRD-ATTRACTING

Description A dense, compact shrub to around 1.5 m in cultivation. It has very stiff prickly-pointed leaves, and produces lime green flowers at the top of the shrub in late winter and spring. The flowers are rich in nectar and attract honeyeaters.

Hakea cinerea

Cultivation This species has adapted well to cultivation. It grows well in full sun and prefers a light, well-drained soil. It will withstand fairly dry conditions and is frost-resistant.

Landscape Use An ornamental shrub for use as a feature or as a low prickly hedge.

Hakea cucullata
SCALLOPS

Origin WA
Climate M
Shade None to light

FAST-GROWING
BIRD-ATTRACTING
ORNAMENTAL FOLIAGE

Description An erect, branching shrub which may reach 3 m or more high.

Hakea corymbosa

Hakea cucullata

Its attractive cup-shaped leaves surround the deep pink flowers, which appear in winter and early spring. Foliage and flowers make interesting floral arrangements.

Cultivation Grow in a very well drained, light to medium soil. It appreciates some water during dry periods and is moderately frost-tolerant. Prune lightly from an early age to encourage branching.

Landscape Use The attractive foliage and flowers make this a beautiful feature plant. It may also be used a a screening plant.

Hakea eriantha
TREE HAKEA

Origin Qld, NSW, Vic.
Climate WT, M
Shade None to filtered
BIRD-ATTRACTING
Description A small bushy tree to around 4 m in cultivation. It has dark green, lanceolate leaves to 12 cm long and bears small silky white flowers growing on the branchlets without stalks. The rather large, smooth fruits attract cockatoos.

Cultivation This hakea of eastern coastal forests will tolerate more shade and moisture than most other species. It will grow in most soils and is frost-resistant.

Landscape Use This leafy plant is useful as a fence screen, hedge or windbreak.

Hakea francisiana

Origin SA, WA
Climate WT, M, SA
Shade None to light
SPECIMEN PLANT
BIRD-ATTRACTING
Description A tall erect shrub to 5 m high with flat silvery green linear leaves up to 26 cm long. The beautiful deep pink or red spikes of flowers, to 10 cm long, are produced in winter and spring.

Hakea francisiana

Cultivation This species will grow in most soils, provided drainage is excellent. It requires full sun and is frost hardy. Grafted plants are more reliable in coastal eastern Australia. Prune from an early age to shape.

Landscape Use An extremely decorative, bird attracting, shrub for ornamental planting. Cut flowers last well in water if picked before the styles open.

Hakea gibbosa
HAIRY HAKEA

Origin Qld, NSW
Climate S, WT, M
Shade None to full
FAST-GROWING
BIRD-ATTRACTING
Description A dense, erect shrub to 3 m high. It has bright green needle-like foliage that is quite soft and silky when young. The small clusters of creamy white flowers in winter and spring are followed by decorative woody fruits that persist on the plant for long periods. The shrub provides good protection for nesting birds and the flowers provide nectar for the residents.

Cultivation A hardy species that does well in well-drained, sunny or shady positions. It will withstand dry periods and is frost-resistant. Lightly prune sparse wood to encourage compact growth.

Landscape Use An attractive shrub for foliage, flowers and fruits. It is very prickly and should not be grown where

Hakea eriantha

Hakea gibbosa

it can be brushed against. A good screen or windbreak plant.

Hakea laurina
PINCUSHION HAKEA

Origin WA
Climate WT, M, CT
Shade None to light

FAST-GROWING
SPECIMEN PLANT
BIRD-ATTRACTING

Description An old favourite in cultivation, this shrub or small tree may reach 6 m. It has long, flat, deep green foliage and wonderful rounded ball flowers that are bright crimson, with thin, creamy-coloured styles protruding from them like short pins. These appear in good numbers in autumn and winter and make lovely cut flowers They are rich in nectar and are a valuable source of food for honeyeaters.

Cultivation Grow in a well-drained soil in full sun. It is best in an open situation, but should have protection from strong winds, as it is rather prone to being blown over. It should be planted when very young to allow the root system to develop fully. It may be grown in protected coastal positions and is usually frost-resistant, but new growth may be damaged by frost. It dislikes excessive humidity. Prune and shape as required.

Landscape Use A very decorative shrub for ornamental planting. It is useful for street, hedge, screening and windbreak planting.

Hakea laurina

Hakea lissocarpha
HONEYBUSH

Origin WA
Climate WT, M
Shade None to filtered

FAST-GROWING
FRAGRANT
BIRD-ATTRACTING

Description This is a small, spreading shrub to around 1 m high, with pointed divided leaves. The numerous spreading branches make a fairly dense cover about 1.5 m across. The numerous sweetly scented flowers borne in winter are usually white, but are sometimes tinged pink.

Cultivation Grow in a well-drained soil in full or partial sun. It will withstand periods of dryness and is frost-resistant. Prune to shape.

Landscape Use A prolific winter-flowering shrub. It will form a splendid low impenetrable hedge.

Hakea lissocarpha

Hakea multilineata
GRASS-LEAF HAKEA

Origin WA
Climate WT, M, CT, SA
Shade None to light

FAST-GROWING
SPECIMEN PLANT
BIRD-ATTRACTING

Description An erect plant to 5 m tall, with one or two developed main trunks and with very long, narrow leaves. Dense spikes of rosy pink flowers are produced throughout the bush in winter and spring. These are most attractive to honeyeaters, and cockatoos feed on the seed.

Cultivation This species will grow in most soils, provided the drainage is excellent. It does best in warm, dry positions and is frost-resistant. Grafted plants are more reliable in eastern Australia.

Landscape Use This shrub makes a spectacular addition to the garden. It may also be used as a privacy or fence screen.

Hakea multilineata

Hakea myrtoides
MYRTLE HAKEA

Origin WA
Climate WT, M
Shade None to light

CONTAINER PLANT

Description A small, spreading shrub to around 40 cm high and 60 cm wide. The leaves are small and broad with long points, and deep pink flowers appear

Hakea myrtoides

along the branches in winter and early spring.

Cultivation Grow in a light-textured soil with excellent drainage. It likes full sun and is frost-resistant. Grafted plants are available.

Landscape Use This is a very pretty cascading plant, ideal for the rockery or container.

Hakea petiolaris
SEA-URCHIN HAKEA

Origin WA
Climate WT, M, CT
Shade None to light
FAST-GROWING
SPECIMEN PLANT
BIRD-ATTRACTING

Description An upright shrub or small tree to around 5 m high in cultivation. The broad, ovate leaves are a lovely grey-green colour and the flowers are dull red pincushions with creamy styles. The flowers are produced along the branches during autumn and winter and are most attractive to honeyeaters.

Cultivation This species will grow in most soils, provided the drainage is good. It may be used in partly protected coastal gardens and will withstand periods of dryness. It is frost-resistant. Lightly prune from an early age to shape.

Landscape Use An attractive, off-season flowering shrub with silvery foliage that can be used as a feature or for coastal planting. It will form a good screen.

Hakea petiolaris

H. petiolaris

Hakea propinqua

Origin NSW
Climate WT, M, CT, H
Shade None to filtered
BIRD-ATTRACTING

Description There are two distinct forms of this attractive hakea.

The coastal form is a weeping small tree to 4 m with branches almost to the ground. It has soft terete leaves to 8 cm and bears white flowers massed along the branches in autumn and winter.

The tablelands form is a low-growing, rigid shrub to 2 m high with needle-like leaves arranged around red stems. It has small, creamy flowers in winter and spring.

Both forms have attractive, prominent, warty fruits which persist for some years. Small species of birds nest in the foliage.

Cultivation A hardy species that will grow in most soils with good drainage. It is frost-resistant.

Landscape Use The coastal form has a graceful, soft appearance and may be used as a feature or background shrub. The lower growing tablelands form will form a good prickly hedge.

Hakea propinqua

H. propinqua (tablelands form)

Hakea purpurea
CRIMSON HAKEA

Origin Qld, NSW
Climate S, WT, M, SA
Shade None to light
BIRD-ATTRACTING

Description A fairly dense, erect shrub to 2.5 m tall, with sharp, needle-like foliage. The showy bright crimson flowers are borne along the stems during winter months and sometimes well into spring.

Cultivation A favourite and adaptable species suited to a wide range of climatic conditions. It does best in an open, sunny, well-drained position. It will withstand dry periods and is frost-resistant. Prune to shape.

Hakea purpurea

Landscape Use An attractive winter-flowering shrub which looks best in groups.

Hakea sericea
(syn. *H. acicularis*)
SILKY HAKEA

Origin NSW, Vic., Tas.
Climate S, WT, M, CT, H, SA
Shade None to filtered
FAST-GROWING
FRAGRANT
BIRD-ATTRACTING
Description An erect shrub growing to around 3 m, with very prickly, needle-like leaves. It has slightly pubescent branches and young shoots and bears clusters of white, often tinged with delicate pink, flowers along the main stems for long periods during winter and spring. The attractive woody fruits persist on the bush for years. Small species of birds nest in the protective foliage and the flowers provide food for honeyeaters. A very attractive, deep pink flowering form is also in cultivation.

Cultivation A very hardy plant suited to a variety of situations. It does best in well-drained soils and is tolerant of dry periods and frost. Prune to shape.

Landscape Use A very attractive fence screen or prickly hedge. It is a beautiful shrub for natural or bush gardens, but is best kept away from pathways and positions where it will be brushed against.

Hakea sericea

Hakea suaveolens
SWEET-SCENTED HAKEA

Origin WA
Climate WT, M, CT, SA
Shade None to filtered
FRAGRANT
BIRD-ATTRACTING
SALT-TOLERANT
Description A rounded shrub to about 3 m tall and wide. It has narrow, divided foliage with sharp, pointed leaf segments. Sweetly scented white flowers are scattered throughout the bush during autumn and winter.

Cultivation This hardy shrub is adaptable to a variety of soil types and conditions. It is very successful in seaside gardens, where it will tolerate exposure. It will withstand dry periods and heavy frost. Prune to encourage dense growth.

Landscape Use This is an excellent hedge, boundary and screen plant, particularly in coastal areas.

Hakea teretifolia
(syn. *H. pugioniformis*)
DAGGER HAKEA

Origin Qld, NSW, Vic., Tas.
Climate S, WT, M, CT, H
Shade None to filtered
BIRD-ATTRACTING
Description A spreading or erect shrub up to 3 m. It has very prickly, hard, stiff leaves, and produces profuse white flowers along the stems during spring and summer. The unusual narrow fruits are dagger-shaped.

Cultivation A hardy shrub that will do well in most well-drained soils and in most situations. It is frost-resistant.

Landscape Use A very prickly shrub best planted out of harm's way. It is a good plant as a hedge or prickly screen.

Hakea teretifolia

H. sericea (pink-flowering form)

Hakea suaveolens

Hakea trineura

Origin Qld, NSW
Climate S, WT, M
Shade None to light

BIRD-ATTRACTING
ORNAMENTAL FOLIAGE

Description A tall shrub or small tree to 6 m high with leathery oblong leaves to 12 cm long. New growth is rusty coloured. Masses of orange-red flowers dangle from the old wood in late winter and spring.

Cultivation This is a most attractive and reliable hakea for coastal eastern Australia. Good drainage and plenty of sun are its requirements. It is moderately frost tolerant.

Landscape Use Although it may take up to three years to flower, this species makes a lovely screening plant. Attractive new rusty growth is good for picking.

Hakea trineura

Hakea verrucosa

WARTY-FRUITED HAKEA

Origin WA
Climate WT, M, CT, SA
Shade None to light

BIRD-ATTRACTING
CONTAINER PLANT

Description A spreading, rounded shrub to 2 m high with a similar width. It has thick, needle-like leaves, and delicate deep pink flowers hang softly along the stems during the winter months. This species provides both nesting sites and a source of food for honeyeaters.

Cultivation A hardy shrub in most soils and conditions, provided the drainage is good. It will tolerate periods of dryness and may be grown in protected gardens. It is moderately frost-resistant.

Landscape Use A good winter-flowering shrub which may be used as a feature in a safe garden position. It may be used as a lightly trimmed hedge.

Hakea verrucosa

Hakea victoriae

ROYAL HAKEA

Origin WA
Climate WT, M, SA
Shade None to light

SPECIMEN PLANT
BIRD-ATTRACTING
ORNAMENTAL FOLIAGE

Description This species is probably the most spectacularly foliaged of all native plants. It is an upright shrub to 3 m high

Hakea victoriae

with large, variegated, scalloped leaves enclosing the long stems. The floral leaves produced each season deepen in colour as they age, changing from yellow to orange and finally to a rich red. The green of the other leaves at the base of the plant darkens to deeper shades with age. Small cream and pink flowers are cupped at the base of the leaves during the winter months. Plants are available from some specialist nurseries.

Cultivation Grow in a very well drained soil in a hot, open sunny position. It will withstand periods of dryness, protected coastal positions and light frosts.

Landscape Use A magnificent plant that should be used as a feature. Cut branches of foliage make wonderful long-lasting indoor arrangements.

HALGANIA

BORAGINACEAE

A small endemic genus of about 20 species of small shrubs which occur mainly in drier areas, one species of which has found its way into cultivation. Halgania cyanea *is colourful when in flower and has a low spreading habit, making it ideal as an edging or rockery plant. Propagation is from division or half-ripened tip cuttings.*

Halgania cyanea

Halgania cyanea

ROUGH HALGANIA

Origin Qld, NSW, Vic., SA, WA, NT
Climate WT, M, SA
Shade None to light

CONTAINER PLANT

Description A dwarf, spreading shrub to 40 cm high and up to 1 m across, with dull green, toothed leaves. The flowers are deep blue or purple and occur throughout the year, with the main flush in spring.

Cultivation A hardy plant for most soils with good drainage. Although it will withstand dry periods, it flowers best when adequate water is provided. It is frost-resistant.

Landscape Use A very colourful cascading plant for the rockery or a container.

HARDENBERGIA

FABACEAE

A small, well-known genus of three species found in all States. These attractive climbers with rich purple, pink or white pea-shaped flowers are an absolute delight when encountered in the bush in early spring and make extremely ornamental garden plants. Care must be taken with drainage as plants may succumb to Cinnamon Fungus, Phytophthora cinnamomi. *Propagation is from firm tip cuttings or seed, which should be covered with boiling water and left for 24 hours before sowing.*

Hardenbergia comptoniana

NATIVE LILAC; WILD SARSAPARILLA

Origin WA
Climate WT, M
Shade None to filtered

FAST-GROWING
CONTAINER PLANT

Description A moderately vigorous climber to 5 m with dark, shiny leaves each consisting of three leaflets. It produces masses of long sprays of deep purple flowers in late winter and spring.

Cultivation This hardy plant will grow in most soils with good drainage. Although an inhabitant of forest areas, it likes good sunlight for vigour and flowering. It will withstand dry periods and is moderately frost-resistant. Prune back unwanted branches.

Hardenbergia comptoniana

Landscape Use A beautiful climbing plant that may be trained to cover fences and pergolas, or allowed to spill over banks, walls or containers.

Hardenbergia violacea

(syn. *H. monophylla*)

FALSE SARSAPARILLA; PURPLE CORAL PEA

Origin Qld, NSW, Vic., Tas., SA
Climate T, WT, M, CT, H, SA
Shade None to filtered

FAST-GROWING
CONTAINER PLANT

Description This very hardy twining plant varies from a climber to a prostrate shrub which may spread to 1 m or more. The single leaves may be anything from quite narrow to broadly ovate with conspicuous veins. The clusters of flowers are usually purple, but white and pink forms also occur.

H. violacea 'Happy Wanderer' is a vigorous climbing form with larger flowers.

Cultivation This species will grow in most soils with good drainage. It likes a fairly sunny position and will withstand dry periods and some frost.

Landscape Use Use as a ground cover for scrambling over banks, rocks and walls.

Hardenbergia violacea

Harpullia pendula

The climbing forms may be trained to cover fences and pergolas.

HARPULLIA

SAPINDACEAE

A genus of some 37 species, eight of which are found in rainforests and their fringes in Queensland and northern New South Wales. They vary from understorey shrubs to tall trees, and a few species are cultivated in high rainfall areas. Harpullia pendula *has been used successfully for many years in Queensland cities as a shade tree in parks, gardens and streets. Propagation is from fresh seed, which germinates readily.*

Harpullia pendula

TULIPWOOD

Origin Qld, NSW
Climate T, S, WT
Shade None to filtered

FAST-GROWING
SPECIMEN PLANT
RAINFOREST PLANT

Description A medium-sized tree to 12 m, with a dense, rounded canopy of light green foliage. The small yellowish green flowers are insignificant, but they are followed by colourful orange fruits.

Cultivation This tree will grow in most soils and positions, provided there is plenty of moisture. It dislikes heavy frost. Pruning is seldom necessary.

Landscape Use An ornamental shade tree useful for specimen or street planting. It is seldom that the roots cause any drainage problems.

HELICHRYSUM AND HELIPTERUM

Botanical revision of Australian members of the large daisy family, Asteraceae has placed species of Helichrysum *and* Helipterum *in various other genera. Following is a list of popular ornamental species with their old and new names for easy cross-reference. They are included in this book under their new names.*

OLD NAMES NEW NAMES

HELICHRYSUM APICULATUM=
Chrysocephalum apiculatum

HELICHRYSUM BAXTERI=
Chrysocephalum baxteri

HELICHRYSUM BRACTEATUM=
Bracteantha bracteata

HELICHRYSUM DIOSMIFOLIUM=
Ozothamnus diosmifolius

HELICHRYSUM RAMOSISSIMUM=
Chrysocephalum ramosissimum

HELIPTERUM ALBICANS=
Leucochrysum albicans

HELIPTERUM ANTHEMOIDES=
Rhodanthe anthemoides

HELIPTERUM ROSEUM=
Rhodanthe chlorocephala ssp. *rosea*

HELIPTERUM MANGLESII=
Rhodanthe manglesii

HEMIANDRA

LAMIACEAE

A small endemic genus of some eight species found only in Western Australia. One attractive species, H. pungens, *is popular as a ground cover and rockery plant. Propagation is from half-ripened tip cuttings or by seed, which germinates easily.*

Hemiandra pungens

SNAKEBUSH

Origin WA
Climate WT, M, CT, SA
Shade None to light
CONTAINER PLANT

Description There are several forms of this plant, but it is the prostrate form that is usually available and is popular in cultivation. It is a small spreading shrub to 1 m across with rigid pointed foliage, and masses of pretty mauve flowers with pink-spotted throats in spring and summer.

Cultivation Grow in a sunny position with perfect drainage. It prefers a light soil and needs protection from wind and frost. It will withstand extended dry periods.

Landscape Use A very pretty cascading plant for a small rockery pocket or a container.

Hemiandra pungens

HIBBERTIA

DILLENIACEAE

This genus is named after George Hibbert, a distinguished English patron of botany during the eighteenth and nineteenth centuries. Although it extends beyond Australia, most of the 150 species are endemic, with representatives being found in all States. Most are small, shrubby plants or, occasionally, climbers. They are noted for their bright, usually yellow flowers which resemble a buttercup with a cluster of yellow stamens in the centre. There are many attractive species available for cultivation, and as many are dwarfs they make ideal rockery subjects, where they get the excellent drainage they demand. Some species of Hibbertia *may succumb to the Cinnamon Fungus* Phytophthora cinnamomi *during wet spells and periods of high humidity. Propagation is from half-ripened tip cuttings.*

Hibbertia cuneiformis

CUT-LEAF GUINEA FLOWER

Origin WA
Climate WT, M
Shade None to filtered
FAST-GROWING

Description This erect shrub to 2.5 m is one of the tallest hibbertias. It has toothed, deep green leaves, and large bright yellow flowers in spring and summer.

Hibbertia cuneiformis

Cultivation This species is suited to most soils with good drainage. It is moderately frost-resistant and may be grown in protected coastal gardens.

Landscape Use Grow among other shrubs for a splash of yellow flowers.

Hibbertia dentata

TRAILING GUINEA FLOWER

Origin Qld, NSW, Vic.
Climate S, WT, M, CT, H
Shade Light to heavy
FAST-GROWING
CONTAINER PLANT

Description A most attractive trailing plant to 1 m or more with oval, toothed foliage that develops bronze tints in the winter months. The numerous bright yellow flowers appear in winter and carrying through to spring and summer.

Cultivation This species will grow in most soils with good drainage. It likes some shade and will flower well with very little sunlight. It needs shelter from heavy frost. Adequate water should be provided during dry spells. Prune lightly to encourage dense growth.

Landscape Use A non-vigorous twining plant that may be trained as a climber or used as a ground cover. It looks superb trained over a support in a large tub.

Hibbertia dentata

Hibbertia empetrifolia
(syn. *H. astrotricha*)

SCRAMBLING GUINEA FLOWER

Origin NSW, Vic., Tas.
Climate S, WT, M, CT, H
Shade Light to filtered
FAST-GROWING
CONTAINER PLANT

Description A wiry-branched shrub that may spread along the ground to 2 m or scramble up into neighbouring shrubs to 1 m or more. It has small dark green leaves and produces a profusion of deep yellow flowers in spring and through summer.

Cultivation One of the most reliable hibbertias in cultivation. It prefers good drainage, some shade and shelter and adequate water, although it will withstand some dry conditions. It is frost-resistant.

Landscape Use A lovely informal plant for the bush garden, where it may happily climb and cascade over other plants. It may be trained to cover walls or fences, or used as a ground cover or trailing plant on a rocky slope.

Hibbertia miniata

Hibbertia empetrifolia

Hibbertia miniata

ORANGE GUINEA FLOWER

Origin WA
Climate M
Shade Light to filtered
CONTAINER PLANT

Description This is a rare species in the field and it is only occasionally available from some specialist native plant nurseries. It has been included here because it is considered by some to be one of the most beautiful of the hibbertias. It is a small shrub to 40 cm high with broad linear leaves, and lovely apricot-coloured flowers from early spring.

Cultivation Grow in a light-textured soil with very good drainage. It requires adequate moisture and is moderately frost-tolerant.

Landscape Use An attractive rockery or container plant.

Hibbertia obtusifolia

HOARY GUINEA FLOWER

Origin Qld, NSW, Vic., Tas.
Climate S, WT, M, CT
Shade Light to filtered
CONTAINER PLANT

Description It is the prostrate form of this species that is usually found in

Hibbertia obtusifolia

cultivation. It is a spreading small shrub to 1 m across with oval leaves, and masses of bright yellow flowers in spring and summer.

Cultivation Grow in a light, well-drained soil. It requires adequate moisture and is moderately frost-resistant.

Landscape Use A softening, cascading plant for edging, ground cover, rockery or container.

Hibbertia pedunculata

Origin Qld, NSW, Vic.
Climate WT, M, CT, H
Shade None to light
CONTAINER PLANT
Description A semiprostrate plant, with a spread of up to 60 cm with stems rooting at the nodes. It has narrow dark green leaves and bears masses of bright yellow flowers held above the leaves in spring and summer and at times throughout the year.

Cultivation A hardy, long-lived species that does best in light soils with good drainage. It will grow in protected coastal gardens as well as in the mountains and is frost-resistant.

Landscape Use An ideal rockery plant. Its spreading habit makes it a most attractive ground cover.

Hibbertia pedunculata

Hibbertia procumbens
SPREADING GUINEA FLOWER

Origin Vic., Tas.
Climate S, WT, M, CT, H
Shade None to filtered
CONTAINER PLANT
Description A prostrate, mat-forming plant that may cover an area of 1 m across. It has small dark green leaves and produces numerous golden yellow flowers in spring and summer.

Cultivation This species likes good drainage in a sheltered, moist position. It will tolerate wet conditions and is frost-resistant.

Landscape Use A very attractive ground cover or rockery plant. It will softly trail over edges, steps, stones and containers.

Hibbertia procumbens

Hibbertia scandens
(syn. *H. volubilis*)
CLIMBING GUINEA FLOWER

Origin Qld, NSW, NT
Climate T, S, WT, M, CT, SA
Shade None to heavy
FAST-GROWING
SALT-TOLERANT
CONTAINER PLANT
Description A vigorous climbing or trailing plant to 2 m or more with broad dark green leaves and fleshy stems. It has large, showy buttercup flowers from spring through summer and at times throughout the year.

Cultivation This is an extremely hardy and adaptable plant that will grow in most areas, except where frosts are heavy. It grows well in sandy soil and may be grown in exposed seaside gardens. Prune to shape, to control or to make growth denser.

Landscape Use A versatile plant that may be used as a fence or pergola cover; trained over a support to form a shapely rounded bush, or as a ground cover to spread over large areas, including waterfronts and banks. It will quickly cover a wire support in a container. It has a very vigorous habit and is best kept away from small shrubs and young trees.

Hibbertia scandens

Hibbertia sericea
SILKY GUINEA FLOWER

Origin Qld, NSW, Vic., Tas., SA
Climate S, WT, M, CT, H
Shade Light to filtered
CONTAINER PLANT
Description A small shrubby plant to around 50 cm high, with soft hairy young branches and foliage. The bright yellow flowers are borne at branch ends during spring and summer.

Cultivation Grow in a light to medium, well-drained soil. It will tolerate dry conditions and is frost-resistant.

Hibbertia sericea

Hibbertia serpyllifolia

Landscape Use A delightful small plant for the rockery or container.

Hibbertia serpyllifolia

Origin NSW, Vic., Tas.
Climate WT, M, CT
Shade None to light
CONTAINER PLANT
Description A prostrate plant with a spread of up to 1 m. It has crowded short blunt shining leaves and produces bright yellow stalkless flowers throughout the year.

Cultivation Grow in a well-drained position with lots of sun and plenty of moisture. It is frost-resistant. Tip prune regularly.

Landscape Use A good rich green spreading plant that will trail over garden edges, rocks or containers.

Hibbertia stellaris
STAR GUINEA FLOWER

Origin WA
Climate WT, M
Shade Light to filtered
CONTAINER PLANT
Description A small, dainty shrub to 30 cm with fine bronze-tipped foliage. It bears beautiful apricot flowers over a long period from spring to autumn.

Hibbertia stellaris

Cultivation This species does best in a very well drained, but fairly moist, position. It prefers some shade and is moderately frost-resistant.

Landscape Use A very pretty plant that has a longer life in a container.

Hibbertia stricta
ERECT GUINEA FLOWER

Origin Qld, NSW, Vic., SA
Climate S, WT, M, CT
Shade Light to filtered
CONTAINER PLANT
Description An upright small shrub to 50 cm with a spreading habit. It has narrow linear leaves and produces bright yellow flowers throughout the year, with a main flush in spring.

Hibbertia stricta

Cultivation A hardy species that does well in most well-drained soils and in most positions. It is moderately frost-resistant.

Landscape Use A good rockery or container plant.

HIBISCUS
MALVACEAE

A large genus of about 300 species mostly native to the tropics, with about 40 species extending to Australia. A large number of exotic species and hybrids are widely grown, and a few beautiful native species have been cultivated. Most species are shrubs or small trees that produce showy flowers freely over a long period. Propagation is from seed, which germinates readily, or by taking half-ripened tip cuttings.

Hibiscus heterophyllus
NATIVE ROSELLA

Origin Qld, NSW
Climate S, WT
Shade None to light
FAST-GROWING
Description A tall, open shrub or small tree to 5 m. The leaf shape may be entire or deeply lobed. Large white to pastel pink flowers with a dark red centre are produced in summer. A yellow-flowered form with a dark red centre is also available.

Cultivation A reliable and beautiful shrub that requires a well-drained, sunny position. It will tolerate dry conditions, but is moderately frost-resistant. Tip prune regularly to maintain a compact appearance.

Landscape Use A delightful feature or background shrub.

Hibiscus heterophyllus

Hibiscus splendens

Hibiscus splendens
PINK HIBISCUS

Origin Qld, NSW
Climate S, WT
Shade Light to filtered
FAST-GROWING
Description A spreading, open shrub with large downy leaves that may be lobed or entire. The large light to deep pink flowers with a crimson centre appear from spring to summer.

Cultivation Grow in a well-drained, warm position and ensure adequate water during dry summers. Prune after flowering to encourage compact growth.

Landscape Use A most attractive species when in flower as a background to smaller shrubs.

HICKSBEACHIA
PROTEACEAE

A genus of two species. H. pinnatifolia, *a rainforest inhabitant of Queensland and northern New South Wales is the most commonly grown species. It is a striking small tree with pinnately lobed leaves and bright red fruit, and makes an ideal specimen plant in warm coastal areas. It is available from Queensland nurseries and those specialising in rainforest plants. Propagation is from fresh seed.*

Hicksbeachia pinnatifolia
RED BOPPLE NUT

Origin Qld, NSW
Climate S, WT
Shade None to filtered
SPECIMEN PLANT
FRAGRANT
ORNAMENTAL FOLIAGE
CONTAINER PLANT
RAINFOREST PLANT
Description An unusual small slender tree to 10 cm with a beautiful crown of dark green pinnately lobed leaves and with dark red new growth. The purple and gold sprays of scented flowers appear only on the mature wood, often low on the main branches and on the trunk in spring. Brilliant red fruits hang in clusters in summer. These each contain a single, edible nut.

Cultivation Grow in a well-composted soil with plenty of moisture. It will grow in full sun or some shade and will grow indoors. It is frost-tender.

Landscape Use An outstanding small specimen tree. It makes an excellent

Hicksbeachia pinnatifolia

container plant when young and may be taken indoors.

HOMORANTHUS

MYRTACEAE

A small endemic genus of about seven species, closely related to Darwinia. *They are small shrubs with handsome foliage and are most attractive when planted in group displays. Although the flowers are small, they are rich in nectar and attract nectar-feeding birds. Propagation is from half-ripened tip cuttings.*

Homoranthus darwinioides

(syn. *Rylestonea cernua*)

Origin NSW
Climate S, WT, M
Shade None to filtered

AROMATIC FOLIAGE
BIRD-ATTRACTING
CONTAINER PLANT

Description A small shrub to 80 cm high, with arching branches and grey-green aromatic foliage. The pendulous, fringed flowers are pink, yellow and green and occur in summer and autumn.

Cultivation A hardy shrub for a sunny or partially shaded, well-drained position. It will tolerate some dryness and is frost-resistant.

Landscape Use A pretty, long-flowering shrub for a container or rockery.

Homoranthus darwinioides

Homoranthus flavescens

Origin Qld, NSW
Climate S, WT, M, CT
Shade None to filtered

FRAGRANT
BIRD-ATTRACTING
CONTAINER PLANT

Description An almost prostrate shrub to 40 cm high with layered, horizontal branches to 1 m across. It has crowded, light grey-green foliage and produces masses of tiny yellow upright flowers along the branches in spring and summer. These are very rich in nectar and have a honey fragrance.

H. virgatus is very similar but taller, growing up to 1 m high. The tiny yellow flowers have a mousy-honey scent.

Cultivation A hardy shrub that does well in most soils and situations. It is frost-resistant.

Homoranthus flavescens

H. virgatus

Landscape Use A beautiful symmetrical shrub that may be used as a feature where any low-growing plant is required. It is a marvellous rockery or container plant and may be used as an undershrub below tall trees. It is ideally suited to municipal planting where visibility is needed, such as in parking areas and on street corners.

HOVEA

FABACEAE

An Australian genus of about 20 species of small to medium shrubs, occurring in all States. They are often found in forests and present a lovely sight when in bloom with bright blue or purple pea-shaped flowers. They are mostly undershrubs, and in cultivation they enjoy similar conditions of some shade and a cool root run provided by leaf litter or a heavy mulch. Propagation is from seed soaked in hot water for 24 hours.

Hovea acutifolia

NORTHERN HOVEA

Origin Qld, NSW
Climate S, WT
Shade Light to filtered
FAST-GROWING
CONTAINER PLANT
Description An open shrub to 2 m, with branching stems and olive green lanceolate leaves with a velvety brown undersurface. Masses of purple pea flowers are carried along the stems in late winter and early spring.

Cultivation Grow in a partially shaded position with plenty of moisture and a good mulch. It may be grown in protected coastal gardens and is moderately frost-resistant.

Hovea acutifolia

Landscape Use A lovely species for planting among other shrubs and trees. A pretty container plant for a shady courtyard.

Hovea chorizemifolia

HOLLY-LEAVED HOVEA

Origin WA
Climate WT, M
Shade None to filtered
CONTAINER PLANT
Description An erect shrub with a few branches, to around 1 m high. It has prickly, holly-like leaves and bears rich purple pea flowers in late winter and spring.

Cultivation Grow in a very well drained, light-textured soil. Mulch well around the root area. It is frost-resistant.

Landscape Use An interesting foliage plant for a well-drained rockery or container.

Hovea chorizemifolia

Hovea elliptica

TREE HOVEA

Origin WA
Climate WT, M
Shade Light to filtered
CONTAINER PLANT
Description A slender, open shrub of the karri and jarrah forests of WA which may reach 3 m. It has elliptical leaves up to 8 cm long and bears purple pea flowers in the leaf axils in spring.

Hovea elliptica

Cultivation Grow in a well-drained soil in a partially shaded position. It prefers a light soil with a good mulch. It is moderately frost-resistant.

Landscape Use This species likes some protection in the garden and is best planted among other shrubs. It may be grown in a large container.

Hovea linearis

(syn. *Hovea heterophylla*)

COMMON HOVEA

Origin Qld, NSW, Vic., Tas., SA
Climate S, WT, M, CT
Shade None to filtered
CONTAINER PLANT
Description A dwarf species which grows to around 50 cm. It has oval to narrow

Hovea linearis

leaves and produces lilac flowers in clusters from the leaf axils in late winter and spring.

Cultivation Grow in a full sun or in a half-shaded position with good drainage. It is frost-resistant.

Landscape Use A pretty wildflower for the rockery or container.

Hovea pungens
DEVIL'S PINS

Origin WA
Climate WT, M, SA
Shade Light to filtered
CONTAINER PLANT
Description An erect bush to around 1.5 m high with prickly, narrow dark green leaves. Masses of violet pea flowers are produced along the branches in late winter and spring.

Cultivation Grow in a well-drained soil in a partially shaded position with a cool root run provided by a good mulch. It is moderately frost-resistant.

Landscape Use Grown among other shrubs, this plant is most attractive when in flower.

Hovea pungens

Hovea trisperma
COMMON HOVEA

Origin WA
Climate WT, M, CT
Shade Light to filtered
CONTAINER PLANT
Description A small shrub to 50 cm high, with narrow lanceolate leaves. It bears many violet pea flowers through the winter months.

Cultivation This widespread understorey shrub of woodlands and forests in Western Australia prefers a half-shaded position with very good drainage. It is frost-resistant.

Landscape Use A good winter-flowering shrub for under tall trees, in the rockery or in a container.

Hovea trisperma

HYMENOSPORUM
PITTOSPORACEAE

A genus of only one species, the beautiful native frangipani, H. flavum, *a slender tree which is cultivated for its large, fragrant, creamy flowers. Propagation is from seed which germinates easily.*

Hymenosporum flavum
NATIVE FRANGIPANI

Origin Qld, NSW
Climate T, S, WT, M
Shade None to filtered
FAST-GROWING
SPECIMEN PLANT
FRAGRANT
RAINFOREST PLANT
Description An erect, slender tree to 10 m, but often taller in its rainforest habitat. It has shiny, dark green leaves and highly perfumed creamy white flowers which darken with age.

Cultivation Grow in a well-composted soil in a warm, sheltered position. It needs plenty of moisture and once established is moderately frost-resistant.

Landscape Use A beautiful small specimen tree which is also used as a street tree in warmer parts of Australia.

Hymenosporum flavum

HYPOCALYMMA

MYRTACEAE

A small genus of some 13 species, all endemic to Western Australia. They are beautiful shrubs, with masses of dainty sprays of flowers which liven up the bush and roadsides in late winter and spring. A few species make very desirable ornamental subjects and are very suitable for cutting for indoor decoration. Propagation is from half-ripened tip cuttings.

Hypocalymma angustifolium

WHITE MYRTLE

Origin WA
Climate WT, M, SA
Shade Light to filtered
AROMATIC FOLIAGE
CONTAINER PLANT

Description A small bushy shrub to 1 m in diameter with narrow, aromatic foliage. The white and deep pink blossoms are closely set along the graceful drooping branches. They appear in profusion during late winter and early spring and are lovely for cutting.

There is a pretty all-white flowering form also in cultivation.

Cultivation Grow in a very well drained light soil. It needs protection from strong winds and extreme heat, and is best grown in a sheltered position with a good mulch to provide a cool root run. It is moderately frost-resistant. Lightly trim regularly to maintain compact growth.

H. angustifolium (white-flowering form)

Hypocalymma angustifolium

Landscape Use A graceful small shrub that is happiest when planted with the protection of other shrubs. It is ideal for the bush garden and looks good in a container.

Hypocalymma cordifolium

Origin WA
Climate WT, M, CT
Shade Light to filtered
CONTAINER PLANT

Description A compact small shrub to 90 cm high with stem-clasping heart-shaped leaves on red stems. Numerous small white flowers appear in spring.

H. cordifolium 'Golden Veil' is an attractive, almost prostrate, variegated form available from nurseries.

Cultivation Grow in a very well drained soil in partial shade. Provide adequate water during dry periods. It is moderately frost-resistant. Trim lightly to shape.

Landscape Use Although the flowers are not prominent, the foliage makes the bush handsome at all times. It is an excellent rockery or container plant.

Hypocalymma cordifolium

Hypocalymma robustum

SWAN RIVER MYRTLE

Origin WA
Climate WT, M, SA
Shade Light to filtered
FRAGRANT
CONTAINER PLANT

Description An erect shrub to 1 m with stiff narrow leaves. Masses of rich pink double flowers, resembling peach blossoms, are borne along the stems in spring.

Cultivation This particularly attractive plant is more difficult in cultivation than the other species mentioned. It needs excellent drainage in a light soil and the roots must be kept cool. It will tolerate will tolerate light frosts.

Landscape Use A lovely small shrub for the garden or container. Flowers are excellent for picking.

Hypocalymma robustum

Hypocalymma xanthopetalum

Origin WA
Climate WT, M
Shade None to light
CONTAINER PLANT
Description A small rounded shrub to 60 cm with oval stem-clasping leaves. Bright yellow flowers are tightly clustered along the stems during winter and spring.

Hypocalymma xanthopetalum

Cultivation Grow in a warm, dry position with perfect drainage. It will tolerate light frosts. Trim to shape after flowering.

Landscape Use A neat, rounded bush for the rockery or container.

INDIGOFERA

FABACEAE

This very large genus found in warmer parts of the world gets its name from the dark blue dye indigo, which is obtained from the leaves of two exotic species. There are approximately 30 Australian species, one of which, the common bushland species I. australis, *has found its way into cultivation. This charming plant is very hardy in cultivation and may be pruned to form an attractive rounded shrub. Propagation is from cuttings or seed soaked in hot water overnight before sowing.*

Indigofera australis

AUSTRAL INDIGO

Origin All States
Climate S, WT, M, CT, H
Shade Light to filtered
FAST-GROWING
FRAGRANT
Description An upright, open shrub to 2 m tall with attractive feathery blue-green foliage. Loose mauve sprays of pea flowers appear in late winter and spring. A rare white form is sometimes cultivated.

Cultivation This hardy shrub will grow in most well-drained soils. It is suitable for semishade and is frost-resistant. It may be left unpruned to form a slender open shrub, or be trimmed from an early stage to become a more compact balanced shrub.

Landscape Use A dainty shrub for background or under tall trees. A natural for the bush garden.

ISOPOGON

PROTEACEAE

An Australian genus of about 35 species, of which most are found in Western Australia. They are ornate and attractive shrubs with handsome foliage, prominent flowers which form dense rounded heads, generally yellow or pink, and distinctive rounded knob-like fruits that give members of this genus the common name of drumsticks. The fruit is retained on the bush and may be gathered to collect seed, which falls easily from the cones when they are left in a warm place. Propagation is from cuttings or seed, which may be rather slow to germinate.

Isopogon anemonifolius

BROAD-LEAF DRUMSTICKS

Origin NSW
Climate S, WT, M
Shade None to light
BIRD-ATTRACTING
ORNAMENTAL FOLIAGE
Description An upright shrub up to 2 m tall, with deeply divided flattened leaves that have an attractive reddish tinge during

Indigofera australis

Isopogon anemonifolius

the cooler months. Compact yellow flower heads appear at the ends of branches in spring and summer and are followed by rounded seed cones. Foliage, flowers and cones are all attractive and long-lasting in floral arrangements. Insectivorous birds are attracted to the flowers.

Cultivation Grow in a well-drained, light soil with plenty of sun. Although this species will withstand dry periods adequate water will ensure good flowering. It is frost-resistant.

Landscape Use An attractive shrub for the garden or the large rockery.

Isopogon anethifolius
NARROW-LEAF DRUMSTICKS

Origin NSW
Climate S, WT, M, CT
Shade None to light
SPECIMEN PLANT
BIRD-ATTRACTING
ORNAMENTAL FOLIAGE

Description An upright, spreading shrub which may reach 2 m high and 2 m across. It has finely divided terete foliage and reddish stems and bears prominent heads of yellow flowers in spring and summer. These are most attractive to insectivorous birds. The flowers are followed by persistent rounded seed cones. Foliage, flowers and cones are excellent in indoor arrangements.

Cultivation A hardy shrub for a well-drained, sunny to partially shaded position. Provide adequate water during dry periods. It is frost-resistant.

Landscape Use A very attractive hardy feature or screening plant.

Isopogon anethifolius

Isopogon cuneatus
DRUMSTICKS

Origin WA
Climate WT, M
Shade None to light
BIRD-ATTRACTING

Description An erect, much-branched shrub to 2 m or possibly 3 m with smooth, lanceolate leaves to 10 cm long. The large terminal mauve-pink flower heads appear on strong upright stems in early spring. These are very good for picking.

Cultivation Grow in a well-drained soil in a dry sunny position. Avoid overwatering during the summer months. Prune after flowering to encourage new growth and improve the following year's flowering. It is moderately frost-resistant.

Isopogon cuneatus

Landscape Use A tall, showy background shrub. Cut flowers last well when picked.

Isopogon dawsonii
NEPEAN CONE BUSH

Origin NSW
Climate WT, M, CT
Shade Light to filtered
BIRD-ATTRACTING
Description A tall, many-branched shrub to 3 m or more high with flat, divided leaves. The pale yellow flower heads tinged with pink are silky-haired and are produced in late winter and spring. They are followed by silky grey fruiting cones.

Cultivation A hardy shrub that will grow in most well-drained soils. It will grow in dry shady positions and is frost-resistant.

Landscape Use An unusual and decorative background shrub.

Isopogon dawsonii

Isopogon dubius
(syn. *I. roseus*)
ROSE CONE BUSH

Origin WA
Climate WT, M, CT
Shade None to light
BIRD-ATTRACTING
Description An upright shrub to around 1 m with prickly, flat, deeply segmented leaves. The bright rose pink flowers appear in early spring.

Cultivation This species has been in cultivation for a long time and does well in the eastern States. It requires excellent drainage and will tolerate dry conditions. It is moderately frost-resistant.

Isopogon dubius

Landscape Use An attractive shrub either singly or in groups. Flowers are good for picking.

Isopogon formosus
ROSE CONE FLOWER

Origin WA
Climate M
Shade None to light
SPECIMEN PLANT
BIRD-ATTRACTING
Description This handsome shrub may be bushy or upright to around 1.5 m high. It has prickly, finely divided foliage

Isopogon formosus

and bears large deep pink flower heads in late winter and spring which attract insectivorous birds.

Cultivation This very beautiful species does not do well in the eastern States. It requires excellent drainage in a light-textured soil. It is moderately frost-resistant.

Landscape Use An outstanding feature plant for those who can grow it successfully. Flowers are good for picking.

Isopogon trilobus
BARREL CONE FLOWER

Origin WA
Climate WT, M
Shade None to light
BIRD-ATTRACTING
Description A dense upright shrub to around 1 m. It has irregularly lobed wedge-shaped leaves and produces silky yellow flower heads at the ends of branches during spring. The flowers are followed by attractive velvety grey fruiting cones.

Cultivation This species requires very good drainage in a light-textured soil. It will withstand periods of dryness and is moderately frost-resistant.

Landscape Use An attractive shrub for the small garden. Flowers and cones last well when picked.

Isopogon trilobus

ISOTOMA
LOBELIACEAE

This small genus has about 10 Australian species and one extending to other tropical areas. They are small bushy herbs with masses of pretty white, blue or pink star flowers and they make an attractive display when planted as a border or in a rockery. The succulent stems produce an irritating milky sap which is harmful to the eyes and may cause a skin irritation. Propagation is from seed which should be sown in mid-winter.

Isotoma axillaris
ROCK ISOTOME

Origin Qld, NSW, Vic.
Climate S, WT, M
Shade None to light
CONTAINER PLANT
Description A small bushy perennial to around 30 cm with light green lobed leaves. The masses of flat star-like flowers of a clear blue or occasionally pink occur in summer.

Cultivation Grow in a well-drained, sunny position. As this species is frost-

Isotoma axillaris

tender it can be treated as an annual in cold climates.

Landscape Use A pretty, soft-looking plant for the border, rockery or container.

IXODIA
ASTERACEAE

There are presently two endemic species in this genus of small shrubs that bear clusters of small papery white flowers. Ixodia achilleoaides *is grown commercially for its excellent cut flowers which last up to four weeks in water, or which can be hung upside down to dry. For drying they are best picked on a dry day before most of the buds have fully opened. Propagation is easiest from half-ripened tip cuttings.*

Ixodia achilleoides
IXODIA, MOUNTAIN DAISY

Origin SA
Climate WT, M, CT
Shade None to light
FAST-GROWING
CONTAINER PLANT
Description A small upright shrub to 1 m or more high with angled sticky stems and flat dark green linear, or narrow lanceolate leaves. The tight clusters of small, papery white daisy-like flowers are borne at branch ends mostly in late spring and summer.

Cultivation Grow in a well-drained sunny position and provide plenty of water during dry times. It is moderately frost-resistant. Tip prune when young and throughout its life to encourage bushy growth.

Landscape Use An excellent cottage-garden and picking plant. Ixodia is also suitable for large rockeries, borders and containers.

Ixodia achilleoides

JACKSONIA
FABACEAE

An endemic genus of about 50 species, most of which occur in Western Australia. They are attractive pea-flowered shrubs or small trees but only one, J. scoparia, *is common in cultivation. Propagation is from seed, which should be soaked in hot water and left to stand overnight.*

Jacksonia scoparia
DOGWOOD

Origin Qld, NSW
Climate S, WT, M
Shade None to filtered
FRAGRANT
ORNAMENTAL FOLIAGE
Description A tall, slender, branching shrub or small tree to 5 m high. It has weeping grey-green leafless stems and produces lightly fragrant pale orange pea flowers along the ends of the stems during spring.

Cultivation A hardy and adaptable plant for a well-drained position. It tolerates dry conditions and will withstand most frosts.

Landscape Use An attractive tall foliage plant for the small garden or to use as a background shrub.

Jacksonia scoparia

JASMINUM
OLEACEAE

A large genus of some 300 species of mostly exotic climbers and shrubs cultivated for centuries for their fragrant flowers. Australia has approximately 12 species which are climbers or semishrubs. Propagation is from fresh seed or half-ripened tip cuttings.

Jasminum suavissimum
SWEET JASMINE

Origin Qld, NSW
Climate S, WT, M
Shade None to light
FAST-GROWING
FRAGRANT
CONTAINER PLANT
Description A light climber or semishrub with twining branches and narrow linear leaves. It bears clusters of perfumed creamy white flowers in spring and summer.

Cultivation This species prefers a moist, well-drained, sunny position. It is moderately frost-resistant.

Landscape Use This jasmine may be trained to form a shrubby dense plant or given support to climb on a trellis or fence. It is not vigorous and may be grown in a container.

Jasminum suavissimum

KENNEDIA

FABACEAE

Named after John Kennedy, a London nurseryman, this genus of approximately 15 species is endemic to Australia and is found in all States. It comprises climbing or prostrate plants with alternate leaves divided into three leaflets and with showy pea flowers in colours of pink, red, purple or black and yellow. They are widely cultivated as ornamental ground covers and climbers, and make excellent rockery and container plants. Some species can be very fast-growing and may invade other shrubs and trees, so care should be taken when selecting species. Kennedia glabrata, K. macrophylla *and* K. retrorsa *are all rare and endangered species in the field. All species attract insectivorous birds to the garden. Propagate from seed, which requires soaking in hot water for 24 hours before sowing.*

Kennedia glabrata

Origin WA
Climate WT, M
Shade None to filtered
FAST-GROWING
FRAGRANT
BIRD-ATTRACTING
CONTAINER PLANT
Description A prostrate species with a spread of up to 2 m. It has small shiny leaves and bears lightly perfumed prominent red flowers in late spring and summer.

Kennedia glabrata

Cultivation Grow in a well-drained position in either full or filtered sun. It likes some moisture and is frost-tender.

Landscape Use An attractive, leafy, non-vigorous ground cover that will cascade well over slopes, steps, walls and garden edges.

Kennedia macrophylla

Origin WA
Climate WT, M
Shade None to light
FAST-GROWING
BIRD-ATTRACTING
Description A vigorous climbing or scrambling plant that will quickly cover an area 4 m in diameter. It has large, rounded light green leaflets and produces brilliant scarlet flowers, held well out from the foliage, in late spring and summer.

Cultivation This species prefers full sunlight or light shade and grows in most well-drained soils. It needs protection from heavy frost.

Landscape Use This vigorous species can be used to cover a large area either on the ground or as a climber. It is useful in soil erosion control, but it should not be planted too close to other trees or shrubs as it will scramble through the branches.

Kennedia microphylla

Origin WA
Climate WT, M, CT
Shade None to filtered
BIRD-ATTRACTING
CONTAINER PLANT
Description A small prostrate species that will form a neat mat up to 1 m

Kennedia macrophylla

Kennedia microphylla

across. It has tiny oval leaflets and produces many small red flowers on short stems during the spring months.

Cultivation Grow in a sunny, well-drained position. It needs protection from frost.

Landscape Use This is a very good kennedia for the small garden, as it can be relied upon to remain modest. It is a pretty edging, rockery or container plant.

Kennedia nigricans
BLACK CORAL PEA

Origin WA
Climate WT, M, SA
Shade None to filtered

FAST-GROWING
BIRD-ATTRACTING

Description A very strong climbing plant that will cover an area of up to 6 m diameter. It has large dark green leaflets and bears unusual black and yellow flowers in spring.

Cultivation This species will grow in most well-drained soils in full or partial sun. It may be grown in protected coastal gardens and is moderately frost-resistant. After flowering prune back any twiggy branches and unwanted growth.

Landscape Use This outrageous climber should only be grown where it has room to spread away from other plants. It is ideal for covering back fences or old sheds, for stabilising sloping banks, or for growing as a robust ornamental at the beach house.

Kennedia prostrata
RUNNING POSTMAN

Origin NSW, Vic., Tas., SA, WA
Climate S, WT, M, CT, SA
Shade None to filtered

FAST-GROWING
BIRD-ATTRACTING
CONTAINER PLANT

Description A creeping ground cover with a neat spread of up to 2 m. It has small wavy leaflets and produces many brilliant red flowers from late winter through to early summer.

Cultivation This species will grow in most well-drained soils in full or partial sun. It can be grown in protected coastal gardens and will withstand periods of dryness. It requires protection from heavy frost. Trim lightly to promote healthy new growth.

Kennedia prostrata

Kennedia nigricans

Landscape Use A dainty ground cover that can be relied upon to stay on the ground. It is a very pretty rockery or edging plant and looks good spilling over a container.

Kennedia retrorsa

Origin NSW
Climate WT, M
Shade None to filtered

FAST-GROWING
BIRD-ATTRACTING

Description This dense ground cover will spread up to 4 m. It has dark green crinkled leaflets and bears bright pink-purple pea flowers in late winter, spring and summer.

Cultivation Grow in a sunny or partially shaded position in a moist, but well-drained soil. It will tolerate dry conditions and is frost-resistant.

Landscape Use A most ornamental species for ground cover work when given plenty of room to spread. It can also be trained as a climber on a strong support.

Kennedia retrorsa

Kennedia rubicunda
DUSKY CORAL PEA

Origin Qld, NSW, Vic.
Climate S, WT, M
Shade None to light

FAST-GROWING
BIRD-ATTRACTING

Description A vigorous climbing or scrambling plant with a spread of up to 5 m or more. It has large dark green leaflets and bears large deep red pea flowers in spring and early summer.

Cultivation This species will thrive in most well-drained soils in either full sun or partial shade. It will withstand dry conditions and is suitable for coastal

Kennedia rubicunda

planting when sheltered from strong salty winds. It will withstand light frosts. Severe pruning may be necessary to control growth.

Landscape Use This extremely vigorous species must not be grown near other shrubs or trees as it will invade and smother them. It will quickly climb a fence, pergola or trellis and may be used as a ground cover for a steep bank or rocky slope.

Kennedia stirlingii

Origin WA
Climate WT, M
Shade Light to filtered

FAST-GROWING
BIRD-ATTRACTING

Description A prostrate leafy plant with a spread of up to 2 m. It has light green leaflets and produces orange-red pea flowers in spring and summer.

Cultivation Grow in a lightly shaded position with good drainage. It is frost-tender. Prune back to remove unwanted growth and to encourage dense cover.

Landscape Use This species has lush foliage and makes an attractive ground cover for a large area free of shrubs.

Kennedia stirlingii

KUNZEA

MYRTACEAE

An Australian genus of about 30 species named after Gustav Kunze (1793–1851), a German physician and botanist. Plants vary in size from prostrate forms to tall shrubs with aromatic foliage and bear often brightly coloured flowers with a large number of fluffy conspicuous stamens. They make hardy, ornamental plants with attractive foliage and showy flowers. Some species provide food for honeyeaters and insectivorous birds. Propagation is from half-ripened tip cuttings.

Kunzea affinis

Origin WA
Climate WT, M, SA
Shade None to light

AROMATIC FOLIAGE
BIRD-ATTRACTING
CONTAINER PLANT

Description A many-stemmed shrub up to 1.5 m high. It has small, narrow aromatic leaves and bears clusters of deep pink flowers along the stems during spring.

Cultivation Grow in a very well drained, light-textured soil. It is frost-resistant. Prune after flowering to shape and to encourage vigour and future flowers.

Landscape Use A very pretty shrub for the garden or container.

Kunzea affinis

Kunzea ambigua

WHITE KUNZEA; TICK BUSH

Origin NSW, Vic., Tas.
Climate S, WT, M, CT
Shade None to filtered

FAST-GROWING
FRAGRANT
AROMATIC FOLIAGE
BIRD-ATTRACTING

Description A tall upright or spreading shrub which may reach 3 m. The narrow, heath-like leaves are aromatic and the arching branches are covered with masses of creamy-white honey-scented flowers during the spring months. It attracts colourful beetles,

Kunzea ambigua

K. ambigua (pink-flowering form)

and a variety of birds feed on the nectar and on visiting insects.

An attractive pink-flowering form with a more open habit is also in cultivation.

Cultivation A hardy shrub that does well in most well-drained soils in full sun or partial shade. It will withstand dry periods and may be grown in protected coastal gardens. It is frost-resistant. Prune to shape and to encourage compact growth.

Landscape Use An attractive shrub that makes a good show when in flower. It may be used as a feature, background, hedge or screening plant.

Kunzea *sp. 'Badja Carpet'*

Origin NSW
Climate WT, M, CT, H
Shade None to light

FAST-GROWING
AROMATIC FOLIAGE
BIRD-ATTRACTING

Description A prostrate shrub with spreading reddish stems to around 2 m across. It has small, rounded glossy leaves and bears masses of fluffy white flowers along the branches in summer.

Cultivation Grow in a well-drained soil in a sunny position. Prune to shape and to tidy after flowering. It will tolerate heavy frosts.

Landscape Use An excellent ground cover with dense fresh green foliage, suited to covering banks or cascading over retaining walls and sleepers.

Kunzea sp. 'Badja Carpet'

Kunzea baxteri

SCARLET KUNZEA

Origin WA
Climate WT, M
Shade None to light

FAST-GROWING
SPECIMEN PLANT
AROMATIC FOLIAGE
BIRD-ATTRACTING

Description An open, spreading shrub reaching about 3 m with attractive crowded foliage on drooping branches. The spectacular crimson flower spikes appear in late winter and continue through spring, and may appear again in autumn. Honeyeaters, parrots and insectivorous birds are attracted to the flowers and fruits.

Cultivation A hardy plant for a well-drained, sunny position. It prefers a light soil and may be grown in coastal gardens with some protection. It will withstand strong winds and is frost-resistant. Prune to maintain bushy growth. In cultivation it is slow to come into flower.

Landscape Use An outstanding shrub as a feature or screen.

Kunzea baxteri

Kunzea capitata

HEATH KUNZEA; PINK BUTTONS

Origin Qld, NSW
Climate S, WT, M
Shade None to filtered

AROMATIC FOLIAGE
BIRD-ATTRACTING
CONTAINER PLANT

Description A small erect shrub to 1 m with narrow foliage that is downy when young. Bright terminal heads of pinkish mauve flowers appear in spring and summer. These are good for picking. A white form is also in cultivation.

Cultivation A hardy and adaptable shrub that will grow in full or partial sun. It likes a moist but well-drained soil and is frost-resistant. Prune after flowering to shape.

Kunzea capitata

Landscape Use A long-flowering shrub for the garden foreground, rockery or container.

Kunzea pulchella
GRANITE KUNZEA

Origin WA
Climate WT, M, SA
Shade None to light

SPECIMEN PLANT
BIRD-ATTRACTING

Description A medium shrub to 2.5 m high with arching branches and grey-green silky obovate leaves to 1 cm long. Showy scarlet flowers are borne in clusters during spring and early summer.

Cultivation Grow in a well-drained soil in a sunny position. Lightly prune to shape when young and immediately after flowering. It will tolerate moderate frosts.

Landscape Use An ornamental, bird-attracting plant that can be used as a feature or screen.

Kunzea pulchella

Kunzea recurva

Origin WA
Climate WT, M
Shade None to light

FAST-GROWING
AROMATIC FOLIAGE
BIRD-ATTRACTING

Description An erect, rounded shrub to 2 m with small stem-clasping leaves. Bright pinkish mauve rounded flowers, tipped with gold, occur at branch ends during spring.

K. recurva var. *montana*, with dense heads of yellow flowers, is also in cultivation.

Cultivation A hardy shrub that prefers a light to medium well-drained soil. It will withstand periods of dryness, wet conditions, and protected coastal conditions. It is frost-resistant.

Landscape Use An attractive shrub that can be used as a feature or be trimmed to form a neat screen.

Kunzea recurva

LAGUNARIA
MALVACEAE

A genus with only one species, L. patersonii, *an attractive flowering tree indigenous to Queensland and also to Norfolk and Lord Howe Islands. It is an excellent species for coastal planting, as it is very resistant to salt winds. The fruiting capsule contains numerous fine splinter-like hairs that penetrate the skin and can cause irritation. Care should therefore be taken when removing the seeds. Propagation is from seed, which germinates easily.*

Lagunaria patersonii
(syn. *Fugosia patersonii*)
NORFOLK ISLAND HIBISCUS; PYRAMID TREE

Origin Qld, Norfolk Island
Climate T, S, WT, M
Shade None to light

FAST-GROWING
SPECIMEN PLANT
BIRD-ATTRACTING
SALT-TOLERANT

Description An upright, dense-crowned tree to around 10 m, but habit varies depending on conditions. It has oval light green leaves and produces pink hibiscus-like flowers over a long period during summer and autumn. These appear in great numbers and attract varieties of nectar-feeding birds.

Cultivation Grow in a well-drained, sunny position. It is suited to all soils, including alkaline ones, and is able to withstand strong salt-laden winds. It will tolerate periods of dryness and is moderately frost-resistant when mature.

Lagunaria patersonii

visited by native birds. Flowers are good for picking.

Cultivation Grow in a well-drained, sunny position. Growth may be fairly slow and flowering may take some time. An application of blood and bone will promote more rapid growth. The plant is frost-resistant.

Landscape Use A beautiful plant for an informal or bush garden. It will form an excellent hedge or fence screen.

Lambertia inermis
CHITTICK

Origin WA
Climate WT, M
Shade None to light
FAST-GROWING
BIRD-ATTRACTING
Description An erect bushy shrub to 3 m. It has shiny obovate leaves that are not

Landscape Use A beautiful tree for seaside gardens. It is an excellent street and shade tree and may be used in mild inland areas.

LAMBERTIA
PROTEACEAE

A small genus of 11 endemic species, all found in Western Australia except for one species, L. formosa, *from New South Wales. They are rounded shrubs, mostly with stiff prickly foliage and showy yellow, orange or red flowers which are most attractive to a variety of native birds. Flowers are followed by an unusually shaped, horned woody capsule resembling an animal's head. This is particularly obvious in* L. formosa, *which is sometimes called Mountain Devil. Propagation is from seed, which germinates readily.*

Lambertia formosa
HONEY FLOWER; MOUNTAIN DEVIL

Origin NSW
Climate WT, M, CT, H
Shade None to light
BIRD-ATTRACTING
Description A bushy erect shrub to around 3 m high. It has a number of stems arising from the ground and has dark green narrow leaves tapering to a point. The beautiful bright red flowers appear through most of the year. They are rich in nectar and are constantly

Lambertia formosa

prickly, and produces heads of cream or orange flowers during spring and summer.

Cultivation Grown in a light, well-drained soil. It will withstand dry periods and is frost-resistant. Prune to shape.

Landscape Use An attractive large dense shrub that can be used in place of or covering a fence. This species flowers well when quite young.

Lambertia inermis

Lambertia multiflora
MANY-FLOWERED HONEYSUCKLE

Origin WA
Climate WT, M
Shade None to light
BIRD-ATTRACTING
Description An erect shrub to 1.5 m high with flat narrow leaves and with red or yellow flowers throughout the year.

Cultivation Grow in a light-textured, well-drained soil in full sun. It is moderately frost-resistant.

Landscape Use A long-flowering shrub that suits a raised garden bed or a large rockery.

LECHENAULTIA
GOODENIACEAE

This genus of about 20 endemic species is named after a French botanist, Leschenault de la Tour, who collected plants in Australia in the early 1800s. Most of these beautiful semiwoody plants are confined to Western Australia. They produce brilliantly coloured flowers, often over a long period, and make striking rockery or container plants. Many species are only short-lived but are easily propagated by half-ripened tip cuttings, which usually strike readily.

Lechenaultia biloba
BLUE LECHENAULTIA

Origin WA
Climate WT, M, CT, SA
Shade None to light
CONTAINER PLANT

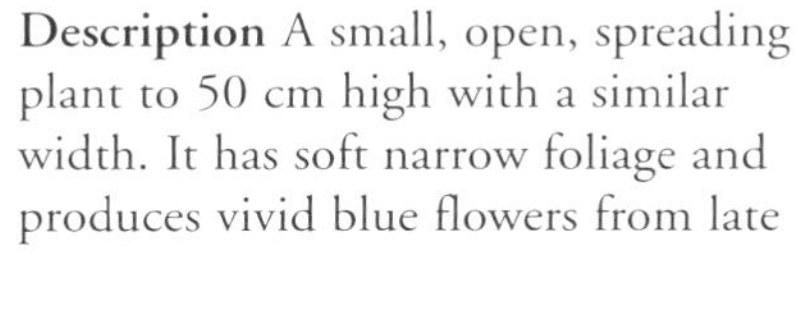

Description A small, open, spreading plant to 50 cm high with a similar width. It has soft narrow foliage and produces vivid blue flowers from late winter through to summer. The colour can vary from light blue to a rich deep blue. A white form exists.

L. biloba 'White Flash' is an attractive bicoloured form with a white centre and deep blue surround.

Cultivation This species requires excellent drainage in a light sandy soil. It needs protection from strong winds, but is frost-resistant. A light pruning after flowering will encourage compact growth and provide cuttings, which strike readily.

Landscape Use This lovely plant is best suited to a rockery, raised garden bed or container, where it will get the perfect drainage it demands.

Lambertia multiflora

Lechenaultia biloba

L. biloba 'White Flash'

Lechenaultia formosa
RED LECHENAULTIA

Origin WA
Climate WT, M, CT, SA
Shade None to light
CONTAINER PLANT
Description A small, spreading plant to around 30 cm high and 1 m across, with

Lechenaultia formosa

fine soft foliage. Many colour forms and cultivars are available and they include intense shades of yellow, orange, pink and red as well as combinations of these colours. Flowering is mainly through winter and spring.

L. formosa 'Sunrise' is one of the many colourful cultivars available. The brilliant orange and red flowers appear throughout the year with a main flush in spring.

Cultivation Grow in a light sandy soil with excellent drainage ad lots of sun for best flowering displays. It is frost-tolerant. Prune lightly to encourage vigour and compact growth.

Landscape Use A beautiful little plant that will trail in the rockery, container or hanging basket.

Lechenaultia laricina

Origin WA
Climate WT, M, SA
Shade None to light
CONTAINER PLANT

Description A dense, spreading small shrub to 50 cm high with crowded small leaves. The bright orange-red flowers are produced through the summer months and into autumn.

Cultivation Grow in a sandy soil in a built-up bed with perfect drainage. It requires full sun and is frost-resistant. Prune lightly to encourage vigour and compact growth.

Landscape Use Ideal for the rockery, raised garden or container.

L. formosa 'Sunrise'

Lechenaultia laricina

LEEA

VITACEAE

A genus of some 70 species found in tropical parts of the world with two species extending to rainforests in northern Queensland. Leea indica *has become a popular foliage plant in Queensland gardens and is available from nurseries in that State as well as from rainforest plant specialists. Propagation is from fresh seed.*

Leea indica

BANDICOOT BERRY

Origin Qld
Climate T, S, WT
Shade Filtered to full shade

FAST-GROWING
ORNAMENTAL FOLIAGE
CONTAINER PLANT
RAINFOREST PLANT

Description An open, spreading shrub to around 3.5 m with shiny bright green pinnate leaves. The small white flowers are followed by showy clusters of dark red fruits in autumn.

Cultivation This fast-growing shrub prefers a moist, well-drained soil in a shady position sheltered from frost.

Landscape Use A handsome shrub for a shady part of the garden. It grows well as an indoor pot plant.

Leea indica

LEPIDOZAMIA

ZAMIACEAE

This genus comprises two species of palm-like plants found in coastal forests of northern New South Wales and Queensland. They are very slow-growing plants and their dark green glossy foliage makes them good ornamental specimens for large containers. Propagation is from seed.

Lepidozamia peroffskyana

(syn. *Macrozamia denisonii*)

PINEAPPLE PALM

Origin Qld, NSW
Climate T, S, WT
Shade Filtered to full

ORNAMENTAL FOLIAGE
CONTAINER PLANT
RAINFOREST PLANT

Description A very slow-growing palm-like plant with long dark green shiny fronds, up to 2 m in length.

Lepidozamia peroffskyana

Cultivation Grow in a sheltered, frost-free position. It requires some shade and plenty of moisture.

Landscape Use A beautiful plant for the garden that has become popular as a long-lived indoor plant. It is suitable for air conditioned rooms.

LEPTOSPERMUM

MYRTACEAE

A genus of around 80 species of shrubs and small trees which occurs mainly in Australia, but also extends to New Zealand and Malaysia. The approximately 60 species native to Australia are collectively known as tea-trees because the leaves of some species were used as a tea substitute by early settlers. They were among the first native plants to be cultivated and they are still popular garden subjects. They have attractive open five-petalled flowers in white and many shades of pink which are usually produced in profusion over many months. Tea-trees are a hardy group of shrubs and many species make excellent hedges, shelters or windbreaks. The leaves and branches of tea-trees may be attacked by web-building insects. If the mass of webbing cannot be removed by pruning it will be necessary to spray with an insecticide before the plant is defoliated and dies. Tea-tree scale may attack some plants and is best treated immediately before the associated sooty mould appears. Propagation is from seed or half-ripened tip cuttings.

Leptospermum epacridoideum

Origin NSW
Climate S, WT, M, CT
Shade None to filtered

FAST-GROWING
CONTAINER PLANT

Description A bushy shrub to 2 m with small, dark, oval leaves. The dainty white flowers are produced at branch ends in spring and summer.

Cultivation A reliable shrub that will grow in most soils and situations, including those that are wet for extended periods. It will grow in coastal gardens with some protection and is moderately frost-hardy.

Landscape Use This species can be planted to form a screen or hedge and grows well in a large container.

Leptospermum juniperinum

Leptospermum juniperinum

PRICKLY TEA-TREE

Origin Qld, NSW, Vic., SA
Climate S, WT, M, CT
Shade None to filtered

FAST-GROWING
BIRD-ATTRACTING

Description A variable shrub which grows to around 3 m. It has light green pointed leaves and bears masses of white flowers in spring.

L. juniperinum var. *horizontalis* is a low, spreading form to 50 cm high and a width of up to 3 m, with white flowers covering the horizontal branches in spring.

Cultivation Grow in a moist, sunny position. It is frost-resistant *L. juniperinum* var. *horizontalis* may be used in protected coastal gardens. Prune to shape.

Landscape Use The upright form makes an excellent windbreak and the low, spreading form can be used as a dense ground cover.

Leptospermum laevigatum

COASTAL TEA-TREE

Origin NSW, Vic., Tas., SA
Climate S, WT, M, CT
Shade None to light

BIRD-ATTRACTING
SALT-TOLERANT

Description A bushy shrub to 3 m or more high with grey-green obovate

Leptospermum epacridoideum

Leptospermum laevigatum

leaves. Masses of white flowers cover the bush in spring and early summer.

Cultivation This hardy species does well in most well-drained soils. Its natural habitat is coastal dunes making it ideal for exposed coastal situations where it will withstand salt-laden winds. It is frost-tolerant. Prune to shape.

Landscape Use A good protective screen and windbreak in seaside gardens.

Leptospermum lanigerum
WOOLLY TEA-TREE

Origin NSW, Vic., Tas., SA
Climate WT, M, CT, H
Shade None to heavy
BIRD-ATTRACTING

Description This variable shrub to around 3 m may be slender and erect or bushy and weeping. It has silky grey-green foliage and produces woolly buds that open to large white flowers in late spring and summer.

L. lanigerum var. *macrocarpum* is a low, spreading species to 1 m high with a similar spread. It has smooth green foliage and large white or pink flowers with waxy green centres.

Cultivation This species will grow in most moist soils, including those permanently wet. It will withstand very cold conditions, including heavy frost and snow.

Landscape Use A good hedge or screening plant for the cold climate garden. *L. lanigerum* var. *macrocarpum* is an attractive rockery subject.

Leptospermum lanigerum var. *macrocarpum*

L. lanigerum

Leptospermum petersonii
(syn. *L. citratum*)
LEMON-SCENTED TEA-TREE

Origin Qld, NSW
Climate T, S, WT, M, CT
Shade None to light
FAST-GROWING
AROMATIC FOLIAGE
BIRD-ATTRACTING

Description A dense-growing large shrub or small tree to 4 m high. It has attractive narrow, lemon-scented leaves and produces prolific white flowers in summer.

Cultivation This fast-growing species will do well in most well-drained soils. It may be used in protected coastal gardens, but is slightly frost-tender. Prune to promote bushy habit. This provides an opportunity to collect the leaves, dry them, and use them in a potpourri. Fresh or dried leaves can be used to add a lemon flavour to tea.

Landscape Use A lovely, slightly weeping species for use as a specimen in the garden. It makes a good screen or windbreak and has been used successfully as a small street plant.

Leptospermum petersonii

Leptospermum polygalifolium
TANTOON

Origin Qld, NSW
Climate T, S, WT, M, CT
Shade None to filtered
FAST-GROWING
BIRD-ATTRACTING
CONTAINER PLANT

Description This medium bushy shrub will grow to 4 m. It has thick, angular branches that have a semisweeping habit,

Leptospermum polygalifolium var. *grandiflora*

L. 'Cardwell'

and light green oblong leaves. Prolific white flowers cover the bush in late spring and summer. There are numerous forms of the species in cultivation.

L. polygalifolium var. *grandiflora*, to 3 m, has glossy dark green leaves, and large white flowers in spring.

L. 'Cardwell' is a beautiful small weeping shrub to 1.5 m. It has light green leaves, and masses of white flowers along arching branches in winter and spring.

L. 'Pacific Beauty', to 1.5 m high and 2 m across, has a low spreading habit, and bears a prolific crop of white flowers in spring.

L. 'Pink Cascade' is an attractive cultivar with *L.* 'Pacific Beauty' as one of its parents. It is a cascading semiprostrate plant to 50 cm high with a spread of up to 1.5 m. The foliage is dark green with red new growth, and masses of two-toned pink blossoms appear in spring and again in autumn.

L. 'Pacific Beauty'

L. 'Pink Cascade'

Cultivation Grow in a sunny, well-watered position. All forms may be used in protected coastal gardens and are moderately frost-tolerant. Prune to shape after flowering.

Landscape Use The taller shrubs make beautiful screens and hedge plants, while the low-growing forms are suitable for rockeries or near ponds. 'Pink Cascade' makes an excellent weeping container plant and is a good cut flower.

Leptospermum rotundifolium

(syn. *L. scoparium* var. *rotundifolium*)

Origin NSW
Climate S, WT, M
Shade None to filtered
FAST-GROWING

Description A spreading dense shrub to around 2 m high with rounded green leaves. Well-displayed white, mauve or deep pink flowers are produced in spring and early summer. Various forms of this beautiful plant are available, including 'Julie Ann' an ornamental prostrate form with a spread of about 1 m and large pink flowers in profusion in spring.

Cultivation This species will grow in well-drained moist soils. It is frost-resistant and can be grown in protected coastal gardens. Lightly prune from early days to encourage good shape.

Landscape Use Grow as a decorative feature plant. 'Julie Ann' looks good edging a path or in a rockery.

Leptospermum rotundifolium

Leptospermum scoparium

MANUKA

Origin NSW, Vic., Tas.
Climate S, WT, M, CT
Shade None to filtered
FAST-GROWING
BIRD-ATTRACTING

Description A variable multistemmed shrub to around 3 m high. It has narrow, pointed foliage and bears white flowers massed along the stems during spring and early summer.

This species also occurs in New Zealand and has been the basis of many popular horticultural forms such as 'Red Damask', 'Ballerina' and 'Lambethii'.

Cultivation This hardy species will grow in most soils and conditions and is frost-resistant. Prune after flowering to shape.

Landscape Use Grow as a hardy hedge or windbreak.

Leptospermum scoparium

Leptospermum sericeum

Origin WA
Climate WT, M, SA
Shade None to light
BIRD-ATTRACTING

Description A silky spreading shrub to 2 m with grey-green leaves, bearing pale to deep pink flowers in spring.

Cultivation This species will grow in most soils, but requires perfect drainage and full sun. It will tolerate dry conditions and is moderately frost-resistant.

Leptospermum sericeum

Landscape Use A beautiful long-flowering shrub which can be used as a feature or planted to form a screen or hedge.

Leptospermum squarrosum

(syn. *L. persiciflorum*)

PEACH TEA-TREE

Origin NSW
Climate WT, M, CT
Shade None to light
BIRD-ATTRACTING
Description A bushy erect shrub to 2.5 m with sharply pointed foliage. The beautiful large pink flowers are produced on the old wood from late summer to autumn.

Leptospermum squarrosum

Cultivation A hardy species for most soils and conditions. It will tolerate periods of dryness and is frost-resistant. Prune if necessary, and then only lightly, as the flowers are produced on mature wood.

Landscape Use A pretty species for autumn flowers that is also suitable as a light screen.

LEUCOCHRYSUM

ASTERACEAE

This Australian genus of small herbaceous perennials was previously included in Helipterum *which was an illegitimate name and is not available for use. The most commonly cultivated species is* L. albicans *of which there is a number of varieties and forms. Protect from slugs and snail when young. Propagation is from seed. This species often self-sows in suitable conditions.*

Leucochrysum albicans

(syn. *Helipterum albicans*)

HOARY SUNRAY

Origin Qld, NSW, Vic.
Climate WT, M, CT, H
Shade None to light
CONTAINER PLANT
Description A variable perennial herb which has several forms. It grows to about 30 cm high and has narrow or broad, hairy grey leaves. It has shining yellow papery flowers in summer.

L. albicans ssp. *alpinum* is a particularly attractive alpine form with hoary grey foliage and papery white flowers with yellow centres.

Cultivation Although considered a perennial, this species is often short-lived and is best treated as an annual. It will grow in most well-drained, friable soils in an open sunny position and will tolerate very cold conditions.

Landscape Use An attractive plant for borders, rockeries or containers.

Leucochrysum albicans

L. albicans ssp. *alpinum*

LEUCOPHYTA

ASTERACEAE

This genus was previously included in Calocephalus *which has been taxonomically split.*

Leucophyta means 'white plant' and has only one species, the horticulturally well-known L. brownii *grown for its attractive silvery-white foliage. Propagation is from seed or from half-ripened tip cuttings.*

Leucophyta brownii
(syn. *Calcephalus brownii*)
CUSHION BUSH

Origin NSW, Vic., Tas., SA, WA
Climate S, WT, M, CT, SA
Shade None to filtered

SALT-TOLERANT
ORNAMENTAL FOLIAGE
CONTAINER PLANT

Description A very attractive compact shrub to around 1 m with silvery, slender branches with tiny grey leaves pressed tightly against them. The whole bush has a lovely silver sheen, and in spring and summer it is topped with pale yellow ball flowers at the ends of stems.

Cultivation A very hardy species which does best in an open sunny position with good drainage. It will tolerate dry conditions and is particularly good for seaside gardens as it is salt- and wind-resistant. It is frost-tolerant.

Landscape Use This is a charming shrub for the small or large garden. It makes a good foliage contrast against a background of dark green shrubs and brightly coloured flowers and is perfect for a rockery. It is also a good container plant for a courtyard or patio.

Leucophyta brownii

LINOSPADIX
ARECACEAE

A genus of about 10 species of small slender palms, which extends to New Guinea and has about six species in Australia. They bear long, showy strands of edible scarlet berries and make beautiful decorative plants for small shady gardens as well as excellent container plants. Propagation is from fresh seed, which is very slow to germinate.

Linospadix monostachya
WALKING STICK PALM

Origin Qld, NSW
Climate T, S, WT
Shade Filtered to full

CONTAINER PLANT
RAINFOREST PLANT

Description An elegant small palm to 3 m with dark green fronds arranged in a terminal cluster. The small flowers in long hanging spikes are followed by bright red edible berries.

Cultivation Grow in a soil rich in organic matter that is kept moist but well drained. It needs a protected position and will grow in quite heavy shade. If it is grown indoors apply small quantities of liquid fertiliser regularly.

Landscape Use An excellent palm for the small sheltered garden. It will live in a container indefinitely and is perfect for indoor use.

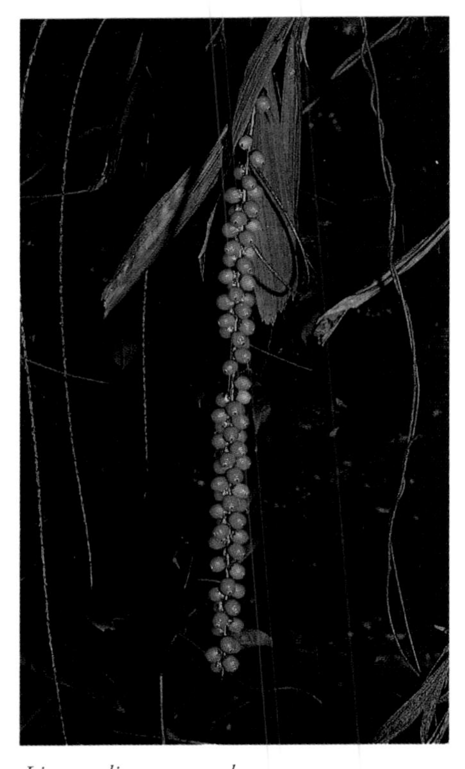

Linospadix monostachya

LIVISTONA
ARECACEA

Of the 30 species in this palm genus, about 20 occur in Australia. They are robust, tall palms with a single slender trunk and a crown of large shiny fan leaves. They make stately ornamental plants for the garden and for public places, or beautiful container specimens. Propagation is from fresh seed.

Livistona australis
CABBAGE PALM

Origin Qld, NSW, Vic.
Climate T, S, WT, M
Shade Light to filtered

ORNAMENTAL FOLIAGE
CONTAINER PLANT
RAINFOREST PLANT

Description A tall palm which may eventually reach a height of 25 m, but is usually much smaller in cultivation. It has a dense crown of deeply divided fan leaves and produces beautiful sprays of creamy yellow flowers in early spring followed by red fruit.

Cultivation This species prefers a moist position with some protection from strong sun and wind. It is frost-resistant.

Landscape Use A beautiful palm for the garden or park, either singly or in groves. It may be grown as a tub specimen for many years and used indoors when young.

Livistona australis

Livistona decipiens
WEEPING CABBAGE PALM

Origin Qld
Climate T, S, WT
Shade Light to filtered
ORNAMENTAL FOLIAGE
CONTAINER PLANT
RAINFOREST PLANT

Description A stately palm to around 10 m. It has circular fan-shaped fronds with long trailing ends that create a soft, weeping crown in mature specimens.

Cultivation Grow in a semishaded, protected position where there is plenty of moisture, but good drainage. It may be grown near the coast and is moderately frost-resistant.

Landscape Use This is an outstanding ornamental palm for the garden. Growth is slow and it may be grown in a container for many years for either indoors or on a patio.

Livistona decipiens

LOBELIA
LOBELIACEAE

There are more than 300 species of lobelias. The genus occurs naturally in many countries and has approximately 20 Australian species, found in all States. There are small annuals and herbaceous perennials, mostly with pale to deep blue flowers, and they look most effective in massed plantings or as rockery subjects. Propagation is from seed, half-ripened tip cuttings or root division.

Lobelia membranacea

Origin Qld
Climate T, S, WT, M
Shade None to filtered
FAST-GROWING
CONTAINER PLANT

Description A prostrate suckering plant with a spread to 1 m which bears masses of bright blue flowers in spring and summer.

Cultivation This species likes damp conditions with plenty of light. It is moderately frost-hardy.

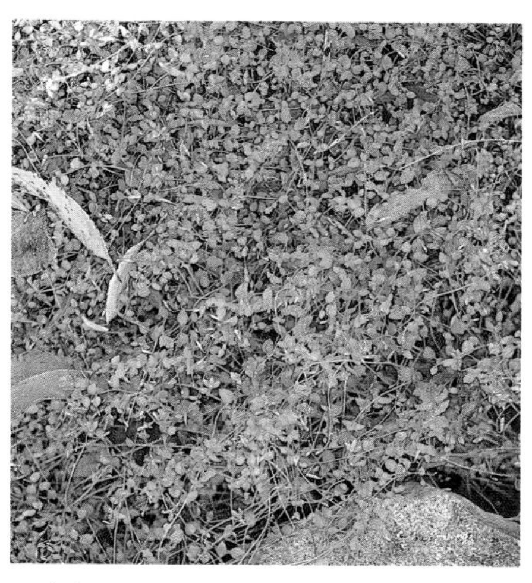

Lobelia membranacea

Landscape Use A charming carpeting species for moist positions in the rockery or near a water feature.

LOMANDRA
XANTHORRHOEACEAE

There are about 40 species of these decorative grassy plants, with approximately 25 native to Australia. Only a few species are in cultivation, but they are tough, easily grown plants. They have slender reed-like leaves and carry male and female flowers of separate flower spikes or separate plants. They are ideal feature plants for rockeries and near water features, as well as providing material for floral art, particularly dried arrangements. Propagation is from seed or by division of clumps.

Lomandra confertifolia
MATTING LOMANDRA

Origin Qld, NSW, Vic.
Climate T, S, WT, M, SA
Shade None to light
BIRD-ATTRACTING
CONTAINER PLANT

Description A small grass-like plant which grows to 30 cm high and 70 cm across. It has narrow light green leaves and produces short sprays of cream flowers amongst the foliage.

Cultivation This species needs a sunny position, where it will slowly spread over a large area. It is frost-resistant.

Landscape Use An attractive tufting species for the rockery, or as an edging or

Lomandra confertifolia

container plant. Its ability to spread makes it useful in soil binding.

Lomandra leucocephala
WOOLLY MAT-RUSH

Origin All Mainland States
Climate WT, M, SA
Shade None to light
FRAGRANT
CONTAINER PLANT
Description A tufted perennial plant with drooping grass-like leaves up to 50 cm long. The numerous dense, woolly spikes of fragrant cream flowers are produced mainly in spring and early summer, but may occur at other times.

Lomandra leucocephala

Flowers and foliage are long-lasting in indoor arrangements.

Cultivation Grow in a well-drained, sunny position. It will withstand dry periods and is frost-resistant.

Landscape Use An outstanding ornamental plant for the bush garden, rockery or container.

Lomandra longifolia
SPINY-HEADED MAT-RUSH

Origin Qld, NSW, Vic., Tas., SA
Climate T, S, WT, M, CT, SA
Shade None to filtered
FRAGRANT
BIRD-ATTRACTING
CONTAINER PLANT
Description A large tussock-grass-like plant to 70 cm high with narrow dark green arching leaves. Creamy spikes of fragrant flowers are produced in spring.

Cultivation A reliable plant that does well in most soils, including damp ones. It may be used in protected coastal gardens and is frost-hardy.

Landscape Use A graceful foliage plant for near pools, courtyards and rockeries. This is a foodplant of two attractive native skipper butterflies, *Trapeziles symmomns* and *T. eliena* which add beauty and interest to the garden.

Lomandra longifolia

LOPHOSTEMON

This genus of four species includes the well known Brush Box, L. confertus, *which was for many years known and sold as* Tristania conferta. *Galls can be a nuisance and when first noticed, affected stems should be removed and destroyed. Propagation is from fresh seed.*

Lophostemon confertus
(syn. *Tristania conferta*)
BRUSH BOX

Origin Qld, NSW
Climate T, S, WT, M
Shade None to light
FAST-GROWING
SPECIMEN PLANT
BIRD-ATTRACTING
RAINFOREST PLANT
Description An enormous tree in its rainforest habitat, but in cultivation reaching about 12 m. It has a dense, symmetrical crown of large, glossy leaves, and clusters of feathery white summer flowers which attract honeyeaters.

L. confertus 'Variegata' is a registered cultivar growing to 10 m, with yellow and green variegated foliage and attractive pinkish tan bark.

Cultivation A hardy and adaptable species for most deep, well-drained soils. It prefers an warm location with a plentiful supply of water and is frost-sensitive when young.

Landscape Use This is a very popular park and street tree in many towns and cities. It is an excellent shade tree and is suitable as a windbreak or screen. It will withstand trimming and may be used as a neat feature or lawn specimen.

Lophostemon confertus

MACADAMIA
PROTEACEAE

A small genus of about 11 species of nut-producing trees, of which about seven species are native to Queensland and northern New South Wales. Two species are cultivated commercially for their pleasant-tasting nuts encased in an extremely hard, bony shell. Macadamias have been proclaimed throughout the world as having the most delicious flavour of all nuts, but they also grow into very attractive, compact garden trees with long sprays of creamy blossoms. The nuts drop when dry and should be gathered, husked within a few days of harvesting, and then allowed to dry on racks in a dry place. They may be eaten raw or roasted in a slow oven. Pest problems such as macadamia cup moth, flower caterpillar, nutborer, twig-girdler and scale may attack macadamias, especially in subtropical areas. As there are many natural enemies, pests may be kept down to an acceptable level. If spraying is considered necessary consult your local nurseryman or agricultural department as to the most suitable control. Propagation is from seed, but trees will not bear fruit until at least six years old. Grafted trees come into bearing within four or five years of planting. They are available from nurseries in Queensland and New South Wales.

Macadamia integrifolia

MACADAMIA NUT; QUEENSLAND NUT; BAUPLE NUT

Origin Qld
Climate T, S, WT
Shade None to filtered
SPECIMEN PLANT
RAINFOREST PLANT
Description A handsome tall tree to around 20 m in the rainforest, but with a much lower branching growth in cultivation. It has a canopy of glossy, wavy-margined leaves that are usually in whorls of three. Pendulous creamy spikes of flowers in spring are followed by smooth, rounded nuts up to 3 cm in diameter.

Cultivation Grow in a moist, well-drained soil with plenty of compost added. The soil must not be allowed to dry out, especially during the spring and early summer. A layer of mulch will help keep the soil moist. Protect from wind and frost.

Landscape Use An ornamental shade tree that also provides nuts.

Macadamia integrifolia (tree)

M. integrifolia

Macadamia tetraphylla

MACADAMIA NUT; QUEENSLAND NUT

Origin Qld, NSW
Climate S, WT, M
Shade None to filtered
SPECIMEN PLANT
RAINFOREST PLANT
Description A tall tree to 20 cm in the rainforest, but much lower in cultivation, with a rounded canopy of glossy, rich green leaves, toothed at the edges and are mostly in whorls of four. It has long, pendulous sprays of white or pinkish blossoms in spring followed by hard nuts with a roughened surface.

Cultivation Grow in a warm, sheltered position with plenty of moisture, but good drainage. A deep, well-composted soil is preferred. Once established, this species is capable of withstanding frosts that are not too severe.

Landscape Use An ornamental fruit and shade tree for large gardens, parks and streets.

Macadamia tetraphylla (fruit)

M. tetraphylla

MACROPIDIA

HAEMODORACEAE

A genus of only one species, the striking black kangaroo paw, M. fuliginosa. *It is closely related to other kangaroo paws (*Anigozanthos *species), but differs in the colour of the flowers and in the seed capsule, which contains only three seeds. Propagation is from seed, which is often unreliable, or by division of older plants.*

Macropidia fuliginosa

BLACK KANGAROO PAW

Origin WA
Climate WT, M
Shade None to light
CONTAINER PLANT

Description A tufted plant with flax-like leaves to 50 cm. It bears unusual black and greenish yellow flowers on stems up to 1 m tall. The flowers and stems are densely clothed with black hairs.

Cultivation Grow in a sandy soil with excellent drainage. It requires plenty of sun and may be susceptible to fungal disease in hot humid weather. It is frost-tender.

Landscape Use A marvellous rockery subject. In humid areas it is best grown in a container where conditions may be controlled.

Macropidia fuliginosa

MACROZAMIA

ZAMIACEAE

An Australian genus of some 14 species belonging to an ancient group of plants known as cycads. These palm-like plants with graceful, arching, glossy green fronds radiating from the top or crown of the plant are very slow-growing. In time, some mature species will form a trunk up to 2 m high, while others are low-growing with large underground stems, tapering into a thick taproot. Male and female cones are borne on separate plants near the centre of the crown and vaguely resemble pineapples. The seeds contain large quantities of starch and were eaten by Aborigines after elaborate preparation to remove harmful substances that are known to cause severe vomiting. The leaves are poisonous to livestock. Propagation is from seed taken from the female cone and only half buried in the propagation mixture. The seeds germinate readily, but early seedling growth is very slow.

Macrozamia communis

Macrozamia communis

COMMON ZAMIA

Origin NSW
Climate S, WT, M
Shade None to full
ORNAMENTAL FOLIAGE
CONTAINER PLANT

Description Widely distributed in eastern New South Wales, this species is the one most commonly cultivated. The stem is usually mostly underground, although a short trunk may develop. Numerous glossy dark green fronds up to 2 m long arch outwards from the central stem.

Cultivation This species requires a deep, well-drained soil and needs some shade when young, although it will tolerate full sun when mature. It is moderately frost-resistant.

Landscape Use A beautiful feature plant for the rockery or for a prominent position in the garden. It makes a decorative container plant when young and may be used in an airy, well-lit position.

Macrozamia riedlei

Origin WA
Climate S, WT, M
Shade None to full
ORNAMENTAL FOLIAGE
CONTAINER PLANT

Description This variable species may be almost trunkless or grow into a palm-like plant up to 4 m tall, although the trunk is usually 2 m high. The numerous fronds grow up to 2 m long.

Cultivation Grow in a deep, light-textured, well-drained soil in either full sun or partial shade. It is moderately frost-resistant.

Landscape Use A good feature for the garden or, in a container, for a veranda, patio or courtyard. It is suitable as an indoor plant in an airy, well-lit position.

Macrozamia spiralis
BURRAWANG

Origin NSW
Climate S, WT, M
Shade None to full
ORNAMENTAL FOLIAGE
CONTAINER PLANT

Description A small plant with no visible trunk, and with fronds up to 1 m long arching from the crown at ground level. The leaflets are slightly twisted around the main leaf stalk.

Cultivation This species needs a light-textured soil with good drainage. It will grow in full sun when established and will withstand dry conditions. It is moderately frost-resistant.

Macrozamia spiralis

Macrozamia riedlei

Landscape Use A handsome plant as a feature or for bordering drives and wide pathways. It is an excellent container plant for many outdoor uses, or for indoors in an airy, well-lit position.

MARSILEA

MARSILIACEAE

A genus of 65 species of ferns, six of which occur in Australia. They are found in all States, usually in swamps or in inland areas subject to temporary flooding. In appearance, these mostly aquatic ferns have fronds resembling a four-leaf clover which float on the surface of the water. These interesting ferns produce their spores in a specialised protective capsule about the size of a small pea, known as a sporocarp. These spores are rich in carbohydrates, and Aborigines once collected the sporocarps in great numbers from nardoo M. drummondii, *and ground them into a flour from which they made cakes. These ferns grow well in moist parts of the garden, around or in water features or floating attractively in shallow ponds or aquariums. Propagation is from divisions of rhizomes.*

Marsilea drummondii

Marsilea drummondii
COMMON NARDOO

Origin All States except Tas.
Climate S, WT, M, SA
Shade None to filtered
CONTAINER PLANT
Description A small fern bearing a number of erect fronds with silky, clover-like leaflets on slender stalks up to 30 cm long.

Cultivation Grow in moist parts of the garden, or anchor in muddy bottoms of shallow pools with sufficient water to float the leaves. It will recover from frost.

Landscape Use A dainty plant around or in water features, shallow streams or ponds. It may be grown in an aquarium or in a wide shallow container.

Marsilea mutica

Marsilea mutica
RAINBOW NARDOO

Origin All States except Tas.
Climate S, WT, M, SA
Shade None to filtered
CONTAINER PLANT
Description This small fern has a branching, creeping rhizome that sends

up thin stalks terminating in a group of four with glossy, clover-like leaflets with an attractive brown or green band.

Cultivation Grow in moist parts of the garden, or anchor in shallow pools with sufficient water to float the leaves. It will recover from frost.

Landscape Use A dainty plant around or in water features, shallow streams or ponds. It may be grown in an aquarium or in a wide shallow container.

MAZUS

SCROPHULARIACEAE

A genus of about 20 species of prostrate herbaceous plants of which one species, the swamp mazus M. pumilio, *occurs in Australia. Propagation is by division of stems.*

Mazus pumilio

SWAMP MAZUS

Origin Qld, NSW, Vic., Tas., SA
Climate S, WT, M, CT
Shade None to filtered

FAST-GROWING
CONTAINER PLANT

Description A prostrate, suckering plant which forms a dense mat up to 1 m across. It has shiny light green leaves with lobed margins, and produces small mauve flowers throughout the summer months.

Cultivation This species is best suited to a moist situation, where it will quickly form a dense carpet. It will tolerate permanently boggy conditions and is frost-resistant.

Landscape Use An excellent ground cover for borders, for small areas or among shrubs, where it will act as a moisture-conserving mulch. It looks beautiful in a rockery and is ideal for softening the appearance of cement edges around pools. A good container plant if kept moist.

Mazus pumilio

MELALEUCA

MYRTACEAE

There are approximately 150 species in this genus mostly native to Australia, with a few species extending to Indonesia and Malaysia. They are often known as paperbarks as some species have papery, textured white or grey bark readily separated into layers. Others have hard or furrowed bark. Melaleucas often have bottlebrush type flowers, which are distinguished from those of the closely related genus Callistemon *by having the colourful stamens united in bundles instead of being free. The abundant flowers, which are a favourite nectar source for birds, come in many different colours — white, yellow, orange, pink, red and shades of purple. Some species are known as honey myrtles and several produce honey of an excellent quality.*

Most melaleucas are decorative fast-growing shrubs or small trees suitable for adverse conditions. They are generally frost-hardy, have the ability to withstand urban pollution and some degree of coastal exposure and, unlike many native plants, will tolerate moist sites which are poorly drained.

Melaleucas are very desirable ornamental shrubs suited to many landscaping requirements. Different species are variously suitable for hedges, screens, specimen plants, street planting, public parks, rockeries, ground cover and containers. They respond very well to pruning, and many are exceptionally good for cut flowers.

Melaleucas are relatively free of pests and diseases. Occasional white scale may be noticed on some species and this may be controlled by applications of white oil. Propagation is from seed, which usually germinates readily.

Melaleuca armillaris

BRACELET HONEY MYRTLE

Origin NSW
Climate T, S, WT, M, CT, SA
Shade None to full

FAST-GROWING
BIRD-ATTRACTING
SALT-TOLERANT
DROUGHT-RESISTANT

Description A fast-growing bushy shrub or small tree to around 5 m with fine,

Melaleuca armillaris

crowded dark green leaves. Numerous small white brush flowers appear in late spring and often again in late autumn, providing food for nectar-eating and insectivorous birds. A pinkish mauve flowering form is also available.

Cultivation This hardy, fast-growing shrub is adaptable to a wide range of conditions. It will tolerate coastal exposure and will grow in poorly drained soils. It is moderately frost-resistant. Prune after flowering to encourage branching if a dense shrub is desired. Alternatively, side branches may be removed to promote a tree-like habit.

Landscape Use An attractive plant suitable for use as a feature, background street tree, windbreak or clipped hedge, especially in exposed coastal areas.

Melaleuca bracteata

Origin Qld, NSW, NT, SA, WA
Climate T, S, WT, M
Shade None to filtered

FAST-GROWING
AROMATIC FOLIAGE
BIRD-ATTRACTING

Description A tall, bushy shrub or small tree to around 6 m with soft linear foliage. Numerous white brush flowers occur in summer.

Melaleuca bracteata

M. bracteata 'Revolution Gold'

M. bracteata 'Golden Gem' is a low, spreading cultivar to around 2 m high and 1.5 m across, with fine yellow foliage, and white flowers in spring and summer.

M. bracteata 'Revolution Gold' is an upright, tall cultivar to 5 m, with bright yellow foliage, and white flowers in summer.

M. bracteata 'Revolution Green' is an upright, bushy cultivar to 5 m, with fine, bright green foliage, and white flowers in summer.

Cultivation A very hardy shrub for wet, humid conditions. It may be grown in protected coastal gardens and is frost-resistant. Prune lightly to shape.

Landscape Use This species and its tall cultivars are excellent screen or windbreak plants. The golden foliage forms contrast well with other shrubs, and *M. bracteata* 'Golden Gem' makes an attractive low screen as well as a good container plant.

Melaleuca calothamnoides

Origin WA
Climate WT, M, CT, SA
Shade None to light

FAST-GROWING
BIRD-ATTRACTING

Description A multibranched small shrub to 2 m with fine grey-green foliage. The unusual green flowers ageing to pale red occur from spring to summer.

Cultivation This shrub is suitable for growing in sandy soils in a moist situation with good drainage. It will however, tolerate periods of dryness. It is frost-tender. Prune to shape.

Landscape Use This shrub with its unusual flowers may be planted singly, or will form a good fence screen.

Melaleuca capitata

Origin NSW
Climate WT, M, CT
Shade None to filtered

BIRD-ATTRACTING

Description A small rounded shrub to 2 m high with narrow dark green leaves

Melaleuca calothamnoides

that end in a soft point. Large rounded heads of pale yellow flowers are produced in late spring and early summer.

Cultivation This species likes good drainage, but a plentiful supply of moisture. It is frost-tolerant. Lightly prune when young to encourage compact habit.

Landscape Use As it will grow in part shade, this is a good plant for growing beneath trees. It makes an ornamental screen and flowers are suitable for picking.

Melaleuca capitata

Melaleuca elliptica
GRANITE HONEY MYRTLE

Origin WA
Climate WT, M, SA
Shade None to light
BIRD-ATTRACTING
DROUGHT-RESISTANT

Description A bushy shrub to around 3 m and 2.5 m across, with a slightly spreading, weeping habit. It has oval grey-green leaves and through spring and summer produces showy red flower spikes which attract honeyeaters.

Cultivation This adaptable species will grow in most soils with good drainage. It will tolerate extended dry periods and is moderately frost-resistant. Prune to encourage neat growth and, when mature, to maintain vigour.

Melaleuca elliptica

Landscape Use Of attractive appearance all year, this species will trim to a good hedge, fence screen or windbreak.

Melaleuca ericifolia
SWAMP PAPERBARK

Origin NSW, Vic., Tas.
Climate WT, M, CT, H
Shade None to heavy
FAST-GROWING
FRAGRANT
BIRD-ATTRACTING
SALT-TOLERANT

Description A tall, bushy shrub or small tree to around 4 m, with very dark green, linear foliage. It produces numerous creamy white flowers in late spring.

Melaleuca ericifolia

Cultivation This exceptionally hardy species will grow in permanently wet and salty soil. It will withstand severe coastal exposure and is frost-resistant. Prune to maintain compact growth.

Landscape Use An excellent plant for coastal gardens, where it can be used as a protective hedge or windbreak for plants less tolerant of salt spray.

Melaleuca filifolia
(syn. *Melaleuca nematophylla*)
WIRY HONEY MYRTLE

Origin WA
Climate WT, M
Shade None to light
FAST-GROWING
BIRD-ATTRACTING

Description This erect, open shrub growing to 2 m high has needle-like leaves to 10 cm long which are not prickly. During spring it bears large terminal pink or purple pompom flowers tipped with yellow.

Cultivation This species prefers a well-drained soil and an open sunny position. It will withstand dry periods and is moderately frost-resistant.

Landscape Use A beautiful melaleuca for use as a feature, or for colour in group planting.

Melaleuca filifolia

Melaleuca fulgens
SCARLET HONEY MYRTLE

Origin WA
Climate WT, M, CT, SA
Shade None to light
BIRD-ATTRACTING

Description A rather open, erect shrub to 2 m, with narrow grey-green leaves.

Melaleuca fulgens

M. fulgens (salmon-coloured form)

M. fulgens (red-coloured form)

It has showy gold-tipped scarlet bottlebrush flowers in spring and early summer.

Various colour forms are also in cultivation. The salmon-coloured form is particularly attractive and blooms during

M. fulgens (purple-coloured form)

late winter and spring. The purple-coloured form flowers mainly in summer. All attract honeyeaters and insectivorous birds to the garden.

Cultivation This species likes an open, sunny position with good drainage. It will withstand dry periods, but does best with plenty of water. It is frost-tender when young. Prune after flowering to maintain a compact shape.

Landscape Use An attractive shrub for the garden or for use as a hedge or windbreak.

Melaleuca gibbosa
SLENDER HONEY MYRTLE

Origin Vic., Tas., SA
Climate WT, M, CT
Shade None to light
BIRD-ATTRACTING
Description A densely spreading weeping shrub to around 2 m high and a similar width, with many slender

Melaleuca gibbosa

branches covered in small crowded leaves. It bears masses of dainty mauve brushes in spring and summer.

Cultivation This adaptable species will grow in most soils and conditions if adequate moisture is provided. It may be used in coastal gardens with some protection and it is frost-resistant. Prune back leafless twiggy branches to improve appearance.

Landscape Use A graceful, long-flowering shrub for an informal garden. It can be used as a light hedge or screen.

Melaleuca hypericifolia
HILLOCK BUSH

Origin NSW
Climate S, WT, M, SA
Shade None to light
FAST-GROWING
BIRD-ATTRACTING
SALT-TOLERANT
Description A dense shrub to 3m high and 2.5 m across, with attractive, oval foliage on slightly weeping branches. The leaves may turn reddish bronze during winter. The abundant orange-red brushes appear from late spring to midsummer and provide a good source of nectar for a variety of honeyeaters.

Cultivation This hardy and popular shrub is adaptable to a wide range of conditions. It will grow in permanently wet to very dry soil, and will withstand coastal exposure. It will tolerate light frosts. Flowers are produced on old wood and are often hidden among the foliage. Judicious pruning may display flowers to better advantage and pruning should be carried out immediately after flowering.

Landscape Use Of good appearance all year, this sturdy species is an excellent garden or park shrub. It will form an attractive informal hedge or fence shrub.

Melaleuca incana
GREY HONEY MYRTLE

Origin WA
Climate S, WT, M, CT, SA
Shade None to filtered
SPECIMEN PLANT
BIRD-ATTRACTING
ORNAMENTAL FOLIAGE
CONTAINER PLANT
Description A graceful, woolly shrub to 2.5 m high and a similar width, with weeping branches and feathery grey-

Melaleuca hypericifolia

Melaleuca incana

green leaves. Numerous small pastel yellow brushes are produced in spring. Flowers are attractive to a variety of birds and are ideal for picking.

Cultivation This hardy species prefers a sunny, moist position, but will tolerate periods of dryness. It may be grown in protected coastal gardens and is moderately frost-resistant when mature.

Landscape Use A beautiful weeping shrub that may be used as a feature. It may be used as a thick edge or fence screen or be grown in a large tub.

Melaleuca laterita
ROBIN RED BREAST

Origin WA
Climate S, WT, M, CT, SA
Shade None to light
SPECIMEN PLANT
AROMATIC FOLIAGE
BIRD-ATTRACTING
CONTAINER PLANT

Description An erect shrub to 2 m with fine, aromatic, light green foliage. It produces many large orange-red brushes during summer and still has some through autumn and early winter, providing a good source of food for honeyeaters.

Cultivation A hardy shrub that likes good drainage, but a plentiful supply of moisture. A good mulch will help to retain moisture. It is frost-tolerant when mature, but young plants should be protected. Prune to encourage compact habit and to stimulate new growth.

Landscape Use A beautiful shrub which may be used as a windbreak plant. It may be trimmed to make an attractive tub specimen.

Melaleuca laxiflora

Origin WA
Climate WT, M
Shade None to light
BIRD-ATTRACTING

Description A spreading, open shrub to 1.5 m high and similar width, with a number of stems. The narrow leaves are blue-green, and abundant purple-pink flowers in loose spikes are borne in late spring and summer.

Cultivation This hardy species does well in most well-drained soils, including limy ones. It likes a sunny, open position and is moderately frost-resistant when mature. Prune to shape.

Melaleuca laterita

Melaleuca laxiflora

Melaleuca linariifolia

Landscape Use A pretty plant either singly or in groups.

Melaleuca leucadendron
NORTHERN PAPERBARK; CAJEPUT

Origin Qld, NT, WA
Climate T, S, WT
Shade None to light

FAST-GROWING
SPECIMEN PLANT
FRAGRANT
AROMATIC FOLIAGE
BIRD-ATTRACTING

Description A tall, handsome tree to 12 m or more high with a weeping habit and beautiful whitish papery bark. It has long, lanceolate leaves and bears long, scented creamy white brushes in summer and autumn, attracting a variety of honeyeaters and insectivorous birds.

Melaleuca leucadendron

Cultivation A good hardy tree for warm climates in moist or boggy situations. It will grow in protected coastal gardens, but is tender to severe frost.

Landscape Use A graceful tree for specimen or street planting. It is particularly useful on large properties in positions where drainage is poor, such as around dams and along creek banks.

Melaleuca linariifolia
SNOW-IN-SUMMER

Origin Qld, NSW, SA
Climate T, S, WT, M, CT
Shade None to light

FAST-GROWING
SPECIMEN PLANT
FRAGRANT
BIRD-ATTRACTING

Description A beautiful bushy tree to 8 m with cream-coloured papery bark and attractive soft fine foliage. Masses of fragrant, fluffy white brushes cover the plant in summer, attracting a variety of honeyeaters and insectivorous birds. The flowers are beautiful in indoor arrangements.

M. linariifolia 'Snowstorm' is a bushy shrub to 2 m with light green foliage, and prolific white brush flowers in spring and summer.

Cultivation Grow in a sunny, moist position. It is suitable for protected seaside planting and is moderately frost-resistant.

M. linariifolia 'Snowstorm'

Landscape Use A beautiful specimen plant. It will form an excellent screen or windbreak and may be used as a park or street tree. 'Snowstorm' is ideal as a low shrub or in large tubs.

Melaleuca megacephala

Origin WA
Climate WT, M, CT, SA
Shade None to light

BIRD-ATTRACTING

Description A dense, upright shrub to 2.5 m high. It has greyish green ovate leaves, and bears pale yellow flowers in dense rounded heads at branch ends during the spring months. A second flowering may occur in autumn.

Cultivation Grow in a light-textured, well-drained soil. May be used in protected coastal gardens and is moderately frost-tolerant when once established.

Melaleuca megacephala

Landscape Use This is an attractive shrub in foliage and flower and may be used as a feature or as a screening plant.

Melaleuca nesophila
SHOWY HONEY MYRTLE

Origin WA
Climate S, WT, M, CT, SA
Shade None to light
FAST-GROWING
SPECIMEN PLANT
BIRD-ATTRACTING

Description A large, bushy shrub to 4 m high with elliptical, leathery leaves. The abundant pinkish mauve pompom flowers appear during the summer months. They are attractive to honeyeaters and are good for picking.

Cultivation This hardy species is adaptable to most soils and conditions. It likes plenty of moisture with good drainage, and is suitable for coastal planting with some protection. It is moderately frost-resistant. Prune lightly after flowering to shape bush. This melaleuca may be grown as a small tree by removing lower branches.

Melaleuca nesophila

Landscape Use This long-flowering species may be used as a feature, or as a fast-growing screen or windbreak.

Melaleuca nodosa

Origin Qld, NSW
Climate T, S, WT, M
Shade None to light
FAST-GROWING
BIRD-ATTRACTING

Description A dense shrub to 3 m tall with fine, dark green foliage on stems which may be upright or arching. Abundant pale yellow ball flowers cover the bush during the spring months.

Cultivation This adaptable species will grow in most well-drained soils. It needs adequate moisture during dry periods and may be grown in protected coastal gardens. It is moderately frost-resistant. Prune to maintain shape.

Landscape Use A beautiful feature or fast-growing screen plant.

Melaleuca nodosa

Melaleuca pulchella
CLAW FLOWER

Origin WA
Climate WT, M, CT, SA
Shade None to light
BIRD-ATTRACTING
CONTAINER PLANT

Description A small shrub to 1 m high with spreading, arching branches to 1.5 m across, crowded with spirally arranged leaves. The brightly coloured claw-shaped mauve-pink flowers appear in spring and early summer.

Cultivation This adaptable species will grow in most soils and conditions. It will tolerate dry periods and is moderately frost-resistant. Prune immediately after flowering to encourage good flower production and compact shape.

Landscape Use An easily grown species for the garden foreground, or in a large part of the rockery where it has room to spread. It makes an attractive container plant.

Melaleuca pulchella

Melaleuca quinquenervia
BROAD-LEAVED PAPERBARK

Origin Qld, NSW, NT
Climate T, S, WT, M
Shade None to filtered
FAST-GROWING
BIRD-ATTRACTING

Description A shapely tree to 12 m or more in cultivation, with beautiful, thick, papery bark, and dull green leaves forming a shapely crown. It bears numerous cream bottlebrush flowers in late summer and autumn, providing food for many species of birds.

Cultivation This species inhabits swampy coastal areas and will thrive better than most trees in wet and saline

Melaleuca quinquenervia (tree)

M. quinquenervia

conditions. It may be grown in protected coastal areas, but it is frost-sensitive.

Landscape Use This well-known avenue and park tree is particularly useful for poorly drained sites.

Melaleuca radula
GRACEFUL HONEY MYRTLE

Origin WA
Climate WT, M, CT, SA
Shade None to filtered
BIRD-ATTRACTING

Description An open shrub to 2 m high and a similar width, with slender, arching branches and narrow foliage. The small mauve brush flowers tipped with gold appear during spring and summer.

Cultivation This hardy species likes a sunny, well-drained position. Although it will withstand periods of dryness, it is suitable for moist conditions and is moderately frost-resistant. Prune regularly to encourage a compact shape.

Landscape Use A good ornamental shrub that is also useful as an attractive light screen.

Melaleuca radula

Melaleuca scabra
ROUGH HONEY MYRTLE

Origin WA
Climate WT, M
Shade None to light
BIRD-ATTRACTING
CONTAINER PLANT

Description A low-growing shrub which may be erect or spreading, growing to around 1 m tall with a similar spread. It

Melaleuca scabra

has very slender leaves and has masses of bright, deep pink terminal flowers with gold tips in spring.

Cultivation This species likes a well-drained soil and a sunny open position. It will tolerate periods of dryness and is frost-resistant. Prune to maintain a compact shape.

Landscape Use The spreading form of this species makes a wonderful rockery feature. It may be used as a ground cover, edging plant or container specimen.

Melaleuca spathulata

Origin WA
Climate WT, M, CT, SA
Shade None to light
SPECIMEN PLANT
BIRD-ATTRACTING
CONTAINER PLANT

Description A many-branched, spreading shrub to 1.5 m high and a similar width, with tapered foliage. Masses of bright pink pompom flowers are produced at the ends of branches during late spring. They make excellent cut flowers for indoors.

Cultivation This hardy species will grow in most soils with good drainage. It prefers full sun and is moderately frost-resistant. Prune immediately after flowering to eliminate bare branches and to encourage good flower production the following season.

Landscape Use An outstanding small shrub to use as a feature or grow as a pretty, low hedge.

Melaleuca spathulata

Melaleuca squamea

Origin NSW, Vic., Tas., SA
Climate WT, M, CT
Shade None to filtered
BIRD-ATTRACTING
Description An open, upright shrub to 2 m with soft, oval pointed foliage and slightly arching branches. It bears terminal mauve pompom flowers during spring.

Cultivation In nature this species mostly occurs in swampy conditions, and it will accept poorly drained soils. It is frost-resistant. Prune after flowering to promote bushy growth.

Landscape Use This pretty shrub is particularly useful for growing in moist areas around water features, ponds or dams.

Melaleuca squamea

Melaleuca squarrosa
SCENTED PAPERBARK

Origin NSW, Vic., Tas., SA
Climate S, WT, M, CT
Shade None to filtered
FAST-GROWING
FRAGRANT
BIRD-ATTRACTING
Description A bushy, rounded shrub to 3 m, densely covered with slender branches with heart-shaped leaves. Numerous showy cream flower spikes with a sweet perfume are produced in late spring and early summer. These are very attractive to honeyeaters and are ideal for picking.

Cultivation This species prefers moist conditions and is ideal for the poorly drained site in the garden. It will tolerate saline conditions and is frost-resistant. Prune to maintain good shape.

Melaleuca squarrosa

Landscape Use An attractive plant for growing as a screen or windbreak in very wet areas.

Melaleuca steedmanii

Origin WA
Climate WT, M, CT, SA
Shade None to light
BIRD-ATTRACTING
CONTAINER PLANT
Description A bushy or open shrub which may reach 1.5 m. It has narrow grey-green leaves and bears rich red, gold-tipped flowers in spring. This species attracts nectar-feeding and insectivorous birds. A purple-flowering form is also in cultivation.

A long flowering cultivar known as 'Paynes Hybrid' has *M. steedmanii* as one of its parents. It bears showy bright red flowers in spring, summer and autumn.

Cultivation Grow in an open sunny position with good drainage. It will tolerate periods of dryness and is tolerant of light frosts. Prune regularly to encourage good shape and vigour.

Landscape Use A good garden shrub and very attractive in flower. It may be trimmed to form a compact container plant.

Melaleuca steedmanii

M. steedmanii (purple-flowering form)

Melaleuca styphelioides
PRICKLY PAPERBARK

Origin Qld, NSW
Climate T, S, WT, M, CT, SA
Shade None to light
FAST-GROWING
SPECIMEN PLANT
BIRD-ATTRACTING
Description A very attractive large bushy shrub or medium-sized tree which may

reach a height of 10 m in favourable conditions. It has beautiful white to tan papery bark and an attractive dense crown of rather prickly deep green leaves. The delicate creamy white flowers are produced in great numbers during late spring and summer. This plant provides shelter and food for honeyeaters.

Cultivation This species is often found inhabiting swampy areas and is very hardy in poorly drained soils, although it will tolerate dry conditions. It is suitable for coastal planting with some protection and is frost-resistant. Although this melaleuca looks good with multiple stems, it may be trained as a tree by removing the lower branches.

Landscape Use This beautiful shade tree may be used as a specimen, street or park tree. It is ideal for windbreaks and screens in wet or harsh conditions.

Melaleuca styphelioides

Melaleuca thymifolia

Melaleuca thymifolia
THYME HONEY MYRTLE

Origin Qld, NSW
Climate S, WT, M, CT
Shade None to light

FAST-GROWING
AROMATIC FOLIAGE
BIRD-ATTRACTING
CONTAINER PLANT

Description A low, spreading, compact shrub to about 1 m high and 1 m across. The small branches are numerous and are densely crowded with blue-green foliage which is aromatic when crushed. The deep mauve, fringed flowers are produced along the stems over a long period in spring and summer.

Cultivation This hardy species will adapt to most soils and conditions. It prefers moist situations, but will also tolerate periods of dryness and frost. It is suitable for coastal gardens with some protection. Light trimming will maintain compact growth.

Landscape Use A beautiful plant for a small garden, rockery or container. It can be grouped near ponds or water features and can also be used in street landscapes and public parks.

Melaleuca viminea

Origin WA
Climate S, WT, M
Shade None to light

FRAGRANT
BIRD-ATTRACTING

Description A dense, rounded shrub to 3 m in diameter. The arching branches reach almost to the ground and are well covered with lush, bright green foliage.

Melaleuca viminea

Masses of perfumed white flowers in terminal heads are produced from late spring to early summer, attracting a variety of nectar-feeding and insectivorous birds.

Cultivation This hardy species likes a sunny, open position with plenty of moisture. It is frost-resistant. Prune lightly after flowering to encourage fresh new growth.

Landscape Use A very shapely weeping shrub for use as a feature or in group planting. It will form an excellent screen or windbreak.

Melaleuca violacea
VIOLET HONEY MYRTLE

Origin WA
Climate WT, M, CT
Shade None to filtered

BIRD-ATTRACTING
CONTAINER PLANT

Description A low, spreading, sometimes horizontal shrub to 1.5 m across, with a height up to 1 m. It has stem-clasping, heart-shaped leaves and bears clusters of small violet or purple flowers in spring.

Cultivation This adaptable shrub will grow in most soils and conditions. It is suitable for growing in moist situations, but will withstand dry periods. It is frost-resistant. Prune to promote fresh new growth.

Landscape Use A very attractive edging, small garden or rockery plant. It makes an ideal tub specimen for courtyards and patios.

Melaleuca violacea

Melaleuca wilsonii

Melaleuca wilsonii
WILSON'S HONEY MYRTLE

Origin Vic., SA
Climate WT, M, SA
Shade None to light

AROMATIC FOLIAGE
BIRD-ATTRACTING
CONTAINER PLANT

Description A dense shrub, with a variety of forms from prostrate, of up to 2 m across, to upright, which may reach a height of 1.5 m. It has narrow, pointed leaves that have a citrus scent when crushed, and beautiful magenta flowers clustered along the branches in the late spring months. These are excellent for attracting birds and are exceptionally good as cut flowers.

Cultivation This species is hardy in moist soils, provided they are well-drained. It will withstand periods of dryness and is frost-resistant. Light pruning in early stages will encourage bushy growth and mature plants should be pruned lightly immediately after flowering to promote fresh new growth.

Landscape Use A beautiful border or small garden shrub. The prostrate form may be used as a ground cover, rockery or container plant.

MELASTOMA
MELASTOMATACEAE

This tropical genus of approximately 70 species is closely related to the well-known exotic Tibouchina *(lasiandra). Australia has only one species and it makes a most attractive ornamental shrub providing good foliage contrast, showy flowers and edible fruit. The fruit stains the mouth black if eaten and this property gave rise to the name* Melastoma, *derived from the Greek words* melas, *black, and* stoma, *mouth. Propagation is from seed, which germinates readily, or from half-ripened tip cuttings.*

Melastoma affine
(syn. *M. polyanthum*)
NATIVE LASIANDRA

Origin Qld, NSW, NT, WA
Climate T, S, WT, M
Shade Light to full

FAST-GROWING
SPECIMEN PLANT
ORNAMENTAL FOLIAGE

Description A attractive rounded shrub to approximately 2 m with large, fleshy

Melastoma affine

dark green leaves with three prominent veins. The large flowers are deep pinkish purple and appear for a long period of time in summer and autumn. These are followed by edible dark berries.

Cultivation This species prefers light shade in a warm position in well-composted soil. It needs plenty of moisture and is frost-tender. Prune to shape after flowering.

Landscape Use A good-looking, off-season flowering shrub that will enhance a water feature and will blend well with palms and tree ferns.

MELIA

MELIACEAE

A small genus which occurs outside Australia, with a variety of one species extending to Australian rainforests. The white cedar Melia azedarach *var.* australasica *is one of the few deciduous native plants, and is a popular street tree grown for shade and ornament. The larvae of the white cedar moth may severely defoliate white cedars, but do not seem to attack other plants. They are dark brown caterpillars and are covered with hairs which can cause irritation. They feed on the foliage at night and during the day congregate and hide at the base of the tree. Tree banding with sacking or hessian is a simple and effective means of control. The caterpillars will gather and hide under the sacking during the day where they may be removed and destroyed. Propagation is from seed, which germinates readily.*

Melia azedarach *var.* australasica

WHITE CEDAR

Origin Qld, NSW
Climate T, S, WT, M, SA
Shade None to light

FAST-GROWING
SPECIMEN PLANT
FRAGRANT
BIRD-ATTRACTING
DROUGHT-RESISTANT
RAINFOREST PLANT

Description A handsome deciduous tree to 10 m with delicate bipinnate leaves which turn yellow before falling in winter. The beautiful fragrant sprays of lilac flowers appear in spring and are followed by prolific yellow berries which persist

Melia azedarach var. *australasica*

throughout winter, attracting many varieties of birds. The berries are reported to be poisonous to humans and livestock.

Cultivation A hardy tree for most warm, well-drained situation. It is drought- and frost-resistant.

Landscape Use A beautiful perfumed tree for specimen and street planting. It is suitable for dry inland areas, providing good summer shade and surviving severe drought.

MICROMYRTUS

MYRTACEAE

An Australian genus of 16 species of small heath-like shrubs with tiny crowded leaves and masses of very small white and pink flowers crowded towards the branch ends. The compact habit and the profuse display of flowers make these ornamental shrubs ideal for foregrounds, rockeries and containers. The cut flowers are long-lasting indoors. Propagation is from half-ripened tip cuttings.

Micromyrtus ciliata

FRINGED HEATH MYRTLE

Origin NSW, Vic., SA
Climate WT, M, CT, H, SA
Shade None to light

AROMATIC FOLIAGE
BIRD-ATTRACTING
CONTAINER PLANT

Description This popular garden shrub varies in habit from prostrate up to 1 m across to upright and may eventually reach a height of 1 m. The branches are usually arching and are crowded with tiny aromatic leaves, and masses of pinkish white flowers in late winter and spring. Flowers deepen to red with age and are retained for many weeks, making excellent cut flowers. Several forms are available from nurseries and it is best to check that you are getting the variety you prefer.

Cultivation This hardy plant will thrive in most well-drained, sunny positions. Once established it will withstand dry periods and is frost-resistant.

Landscape Use The low, spreading form is an ideal ground cover for sloping banks, between shrubs and as a border. All forms are good rockery and container plants.

MUEHLENBECKIA

POLYGONACEAE

A genus of some 15 species of twining or sprawling shrubs of which 10 occur in Australia. Although the flowers are inconspicuous, M. axillaris *with thin, wiry stems and dainty round leaves has become a popular ground cover. Propagation is by division.*

Muehlenbeckia axillaris

MATTED LIGNUM

Origin NSW, Vic., Tas.
Climate S, WT, M, CT, H, SA
Shade None to full

ORNAMENTAL FOLIAGE

Description A loosely matted creeping vine with thin, wiry stems and small, rounded dark green leaves. It has tiny green flowers in summer.

Cultivation This adaptable and hardy species will do well in most situations and thrives when plenty of moisture is available. It is frost-resistant.

Landscape Use A pretty, vigorous ground cover that will trail over rocks, sleepers and walls and will climb if given support.

MYOPORUM

MYOPORACEAE

There are approximately 15 species of this genus represented in Australia and found in all States. They are extremely hardy shrubs or small trees, and include two species commonly cultivated as ground covers. Propagation is from half-ripened tip cuttings, which strike easily.

Myoporum debile

AMULLA

Origin Qld, NSW
Climate S, WT, M, SA
Shade None to light

BIRD-ATTRACTING
DROUGHT-RESISTANT
CONTAINER PLANT

Description A prostrate, trailing plant to 1 m across with long, narrow, slightly blue star flowers in spring and summer. These are followed by ornamental cream or pinkish purple berries.

Cultivation This species is suited to most soils if grown in a well-drained dry position. It will tolerate light frosts.

Micromyrtus ciliata

Muehlenbeckia axillaris

Myoporum debile

Landscape Use An attractive, cascading ground cover for borders, rockeries or containers.

Myoporum floribundum
SLENDER BOOBIALLA

Origin NSW, Vic.
Climate WT, M, CT, H
Shade Light to filtered

FAST-GROWING
SPECIMEN PLANT
BIRD-ATTRACTING
ORNAMENTAL FOLIAGE

Description A slender, weeping shrub to 3 m high with long narrow leaves drooping from the long arching branches. Small white flowers are borne along the branches during the summer months.

Cultivation Suited to most soils, this species requires a well-drained position, with light shade. It is frost-resistant. Prune lightly to shape.

Myoporum floribundum

Landscape Use A beautiful weeping shrub suitable for specimen planting.

Myoporum insulare
BOOBIALLA

Origin NSW, Vic., Tas., SA, WA
Climate WT, M, SA
Shade None to light

FAST-GROWING
BIRD-ATTRACTING
SALT-TOLERANT
DROUGHT-RESISTANT

Description A dense, compact bush or small tree to 4 m high with fleshy, light green foliage to ground level. The small white flowers with purple dots that are produced in spring and summer are followed by purple, fleshy berries.

Cultivation A very hardy plant for most well-drained positions. It will withstand extreme coastal exposure and is drought-tolerant. It is frost-resistant. Prune to shape.

Landscape Use An excellent screen or windbreak plant for inland areas as well as for exposed coastal positions, where it will effectively form a barrier against salt spray, wind and spray.

Myoporum insulare

Myoporum montanum
WATER BUSH

Origin Qld, NSW, Vic., SA, NT
Climate WT, M, SA
Shade None to light

BIRD-ATTRACTING
DROUGHT-RESISTANT

Description This medium, rounded shrub is found along watercourses in inland areas. It grows to 3 m high and has narrow leaves and small, white flowers dotted with purple, followed by purplish berries. The latter were eaten by Aborigines.

Cultivation Grow in a light, well-drained soil. This species will tolerate drought and frost. It should not be planted close to drains.

Landscape Use A very suitable hedge or windbreak for inland areas.

Myoporum montanum

Myoporum parvifolium

(syn. *M. humile*)

CREEPING BOOBIALLA

Origin NSW, Vic., SA, WA
Climate S, WT, M, CT, SA
Shade None to filtered

FAST-GROWING
BIRD-ATTRACTING
SALT-TOLERANT
DROUGHT-RESISTANT
CONTAINER PLANT

Description A prostrate trailing plant up to 1 m across with a layering habit. It has fleshy bright green leaves and has dainty white star flowers in spring and summer. These are followed by round green or purple berries. A form with purplish foliage and a good carpeting form with clear pink flowers and broad leaves are also in cultivation.

Cultivation This hardy species is not fussy about soils, provided the drainage is good. It is drought- and frost-resistant and will tolerate extreme coastal exposure.

Landscape Use An excellent ground cover suitable for stabilising banks, binding sand or suppressing weeds. It is an attractive border, rockery or container plant and will creep beautifully over retaining walls. It is recommended for municipal or public landscaping where low cover is required.

Myoporum parvifolium

NEOSEPICAEA

BIGNONIACEAE

A genus of four species of rampant climbers of which two extend to rainforests of northern Queensland. Neosepicaea jucunda *is cultivated in tropical gardens for its lush foliage and attractive deep pink flowers and its ability to cover large areas. Propagation is from half-ripened tip cuttings.*

Neosepicaea jucunda

JUNGLE VINE

Origin Qld
Climate T, S, WT
Shade Light to filtered

FAST-GROWING
BIRD-ATTRACTING
ORNAMENTAL FOLIAGE
RAINFOREST PLANT

Description A strong creeper that has large glossy green leaves composed of three shiny leaflets and in spring produces large sprays of dark pink tubular flowers which are most attractive to honeyeaters.

Neosepicaea jucunda

Cultivation This rainforest species requires a moist, semishaded position. It will grow as far south as Sydney in a sheltered, warm, frost-free location. It is frost-tender. It will withstand hard pruning and may be trained as a large shrub.

Landscape Use A lush tropical climber for covering trellis, walls or fences. A good screen vine for shady places.

NEPHROLEPIS

DAVALLIACEAE

A widespread genus of about 30 species with about six species found in Australia. The widely distributed fishbone fern N. cordifolia *is commonly cultivated throughout Australia for its adaptability and hardiness as an indoor, container and garden fern. Propagation is by division of the rhizomes, which produce new plants on long runners.*

Nephrolepis cordifolia

FISHBONE FERN

Origin Qld, NSW, NT
Climate T, S, WT, M
Shade None to full

CONTAINER PLANT
RAINFOREST PLANT

Description The well-known fishbone fern has pale green fronds up to 1 m long. The creeping rhizome has many narrow runners which produce fleshy tubers that develop into new plants, quickly forming a dense clump.

Cultivation This very hardy fern will grow in full sun or total shade although it looks at its best in a filtered light position. It needs plenty of moisture and some protection from harsh winds. It is frost-tender.

Landscape Use A rapidly spreading fern that looks good near a water feature set among rocks. It is suitable for growing in containers and may be used indoors.

NOTHOFAGUS

FAGACEAE

A genus of about 35 species of evergreen and deciduous trees found only in the Southern Hemisphere. Australia has three species. These trees, although they could be regarded as too large for the average garden, are extremely slow-growing and make beautiful specimens for cool climates. Nothofagus *species can also be cultivated as pot plants and make interesting bonsai subjects. Propagation is from seed.*

Nothofagus cunninghamii

MYRTLE; MYRTLE BEECH

Origin Vic., Tas.
Climate M, CT, H
Shade Light to full

SPECIMEN PLANT
ORNAMENTAL FOLIAGE
RAINFOREST PLANT

Description A rather slow-growing tree to 35 m, but usually much less in cultivation. The fern-like leaves are shiny, toothed and oval and young spring foliage is in pink to deep bronzy tonings. Small light brown flowers are produced in summer.

Cultivation Grow in a cool, moist, shaded position with some protection from winds. It requires a rich, deep soil with good drainage., but should not be allowed to dry out. It is frost-and snow-tolerant.

Landscape Use An extremely attractive tree with lacy foliage suitable for specimen planting or for growing in a protected bush setting for contrasting foliage. It makes a superb container plant and may be used indoors.

OLEARIA

ASTERACEAE

A large genus of more than 100 species with approximately 75 species found throughout Australia. It consists of small herbaceous plants to fairly large shrubs noted for their attractive clusters of daisy-like flowers in shades of white, pink, blue or mauve. They are hardy in cultivation and many species make decorative garden plants. Small insectivorous birds feed on the insects that are attracted to the flowers. Propagation is from half-ripened tip cuttings.

Olearia erubescens

MOTH DAISY BUSH

Origin NSW, Vic., Tas., SA
Climate WT, M, CT, H
Shade None to light

BIRD-ATTRACTING
CONTAINER PLANT

Description A shrub to 1 m tall with narrow oblong leaves and a silky underside. Clusters of white daisy flowers appear in spring and early summer.

Nephrolepis cordifolia

Olearia erubescens

Nothofagus cunninghamii

Some forms have mauve flowers.

Cultivation Grow in a well-drained, sunny position. It is frost-resistant. Prune after flowering to remove old wood and to keep bush shapely.

Landscape Use A hardy floriferous shrub that looks exceptional when mass-planted.

Olearia microphylla
BRIDAL DAISY BUSH

Origin Qld, NSW
Climate WT, M, SA
Shade None to filtered
BIRD-ATTRACTING
CONTAINER PLANT
Description A small erect shrub to around 1 m with tiny dark green leaves. It produces masses of small white daisy flowers in late winter and spring.

Cultivation Grow in a sunny or partially shaded, well-drained position. It is frost-resistant. Tip prune regularly or immediately after flowering to encourage compact growth.

Landscape Use A pretty shrub for the garden foreground, rockery or container.

Olearia microphylla

Olearia phlogopappa
(syn. *O. gunniana*)
DUSTY DAISY BUSH; OTWAY DAISY BUSH

Origin NSW, Vic., Tas.
Climate WT, M, CT, H
Shade None to light
BIRD-ATTRACTING
Description An upright, slender bush to 1.5 m high with greyish woolly leaves.

It has small but very showy white flowers covering the bush in spring to summer. Pale pink and blue flowering forms are also available.

Cultivation Grow in a sunny, well-drained position with considerable moisture. It is frost-resistant. Prune lightly from early days and especially after flowering to maintain a compact bush.

Landscape Use A free-flowering species to grow among other shrubs or as a pretty trimmed hedge along a pathway.

Olearia phlogopappa

Olearia pimeleoides

Origin Qld, NSW, Vic., SA, WA
Climate WT, M, SA
Shade None to filtered

BIRD-ATTRACTING
DROUGHT-RESISTANT

Description This is a common and widespread shrub of drier inland areas. It is a rounded shrub to 1 m with grey felty foliage, and large white daisy flowers on single stems during the spring months.

Cultivation Grow in a dry, well-drained, sunny position. It is drought- and frost-tolerant. Prune lightly to shape if necessary.

Landscape Use A lovely shrub for the drier garden. A good feature plant for the rockery.

Olearia ramulosa

Origin Qld, NSW, Vic., Tas., SA, WA
Climate WT, M, CT, H, SA
Shade None to filtered

BIRD-ATTRACTING
CONTAINER PLANT

Description A variable and widespread shrub which may be low-growing and spreading to 1.5 m across or upright to around 1.5 m high. It has narrow leaves, and bears white or lilac daisy flowers from late spring through to autumn.

Cultivation This hardy and adaptable plant will grow in most positions, including poorly drained spots. It will withstand a considerable amount of shade and is frost-resistant.

Landscape Use An attractive summer-flowering plant for among other shrubs in the garden. It may also be grown in a container.

Olearia pimeleoides

Olearia ramulosa

OMALANTHUS

EUPHORBIACEAE

There are three Australian species in this genus of about 35 species of shrubs and small trees. They are grown for their colourful heart-shaped leaves, attractive both indoors and in the garden. Propagation is from fresh seed or from half-ripened tip cuttings taken in warm weather.

Omalanthus populifolius

(syn. *Homalanthus populifolius*)

NATIVE BLEEDING HEART

Origin Qld, NSW
Climate T, S, WT, M
Shade Light to full

BIRD-ATTRACTING
ORNAMENTAL FOLIAGE
CONTAINER PLANT
RAINFOREST PLANT

Description A tall bushy shrub or small tree up to 5 m tall, with deep green heart-shaped leaves which turn a brilliant red as they age. The small greenish flowers are insignificant.

O. stillingiifolius is similar in appearance but only grows from 1 to 3 m tall and has smaller leaves.

Cultivation Grow in a shady location with good drainage. It appreciates a

Omalanthus populifolius

humus-enriched soil in a warm, frost-free position. Prune to shape.

Landscape Use An attractive background foliage plant for the garden near, a water feature or at the edge of the garden 'rainforest', imitating its natural habitat.

OREOCALLIS

PROTEACEAE

A small genus of subtropical trees with three species extending to Australia. These are superb tall trees with decorative foliage, and spectacular red flowers in late spring and early summer. They need a warm climate but will flower well as far south as Sydney. Propagation is from fresh seed.

Oreocallis *sp.* nova

(sometimes sold as Oreocallis wickhamii*)*

TREE WARATAH; RED SILKY OAK

Origin Qld
Climate T, S, WT, M
Shade None to filtered
SPECIMEN PLANT
BIRD-ATTRACTING
RAINFOREST PLANT

Description A tall tree to 25 m in its rainforest habitat, but it can be expected to reach around 10 m in cultivation. It has a spreading canopy of dark green entire leaves and produces spectacular large red waratah-like flower clusters in spring. These are rich in nectar and attract parrots and honeyeaters to the garden. Flowers are long-lasting when cut for indoors.

Cultivation Grow in a warm, sheltered position. It needs a well-composted soil, and plenty of moisture but good drainage. Once established, it will tolerate light frost. Dense growth may be encouraged by pruning after flowering.

Landscape Use A magnificent specimen tree which needs plenty of room to display its full beauty.

Oreocallis sp. *nova*

ORTHROSANTHUS

IRIDACEAE

A small genus of tufted perennials of which five species are native to Australia. They are often called morning iris because their blue flowers open early in the morning and wither during the day. The flowers are produced in quantities and the plants therefore make good rockery or container subjects. Propagation is from seed or by careful division of older plants.

Orthrosanthus laxus

MORNING IRIS

Origin WA
Climate WT, M, CT
Shade Light to filtered
CONTAINER PLANT

Description A tufted perennial with long narrow leaves and loose panicles of pale or deep blue flowers which each last for one day. There are usually a number of buds and flowering continues for some time during spring.

Cultivation Grow in a lightly shaded position in most soils with good drainage but plenty of moisture. It is frost-resistant.

Landscape Use Provides an attractive springtime display of blue flowers for the border, rockery or container.

Orthrosanthus laxus

Orthrosanthus multiflorus

MORNING FLAG

Origin Vic., SA, WA
Climate WT, M, CT
Shade None to filtered
CONTAINER PLANT

Description A tufted perennial with erect, linear pale green leaves to 75 cm and

Orthrosanthus multiflorus

flower spikes with numerous blue flowers that last only for a day each but are produced for many weeks during spring.

Cultivation This hardy plant will grow in most soils and conditions, including wet spots. It is frost-resistant.

Landscape Use An excellent border, rockery or container plant.

OXYLOBIUM

FABACEAE

An Australian genus of approximately 40 species of shrubs or small trees which light up the bush with their golden pea flowers in spring. They add colour and interest to the native garden and are generally hardy in a well-drained, sunny position. Propagation is from seeds, which have a hard coat and require hot water treatment prior to sowing.

Oxylobium robustum

Origin Qld, NSW
Climate S, WT, M
Shade None to filtered
FAST-GROWING
BIRD-ATTRACTING
Description A rounded, spreading shrub to 2 m with long narrow leaves to 5 cm. Clusters of bright yellow pea flowers are produced on branch ends during spring and early summer.

Cultivation Grow in a humus-enriched soil with good drainage. It may be grown in protected coastal gardens and is fairly frost-resistant. Prune to shape.

Landscape Use A colourful plant to use for screening or as a background shrub.

Oxylobium robustum

Oxylobium scandens

NETTED SHAGGY PEA

Origin NSW
Climate S, WT, M
Shade None to light
CONTAINER PLANT
Description A trailing plant which will form a compact mat to around 1 m in diameter. It has leathery oval leaves and bears bright orange pea flowers in loose clusters during spring and early summer.

Cultivation This species requires a sunny, well-drained position. It may be grown in protected coastal gardens, but is slightly frost-tender.

Landscape Use An attractive ground cover for small areas between shrubs, in the rockery or cascading from containers.

Oxylobium scandens

OZOTHAMNUS

ASTERACEAE

A genus of about 55 species of shrubs occurring in southern and eastern Australia as well as New Zealand and New Caledonia. This genus was previously included under the revised Helichrysum. *They are aromatic shrubs with flower heads grouped in panicles. The tiny individual flower heads are surrounded by thin papery, white, cream or brown bracts. Propagation is from half-ripened tip cuttings or from seed.*

Ozothamnus diosmifolius

(syn. *Helichrysum diosmifolium*)

BALL EVERLASTING; SAGO FLOWER

Origin Qld, NSW
Climate S, WT, M
Shade None to filtered
FAST-GROWING
AROMATIC FOLIAGE
Description A tall, erect shrub to around 2 m with fine dark green or grey-green foliage that has a marvellous spicy fragrance in some plants. The many tiny ball flowers appear in great clusters during spring and summer. These are excellent for picking for fresh flowers, and if they are dried the brittle leaves may be stripped and the flowers used in all sorts of dried arrangements.

Cultivation Grow in most well-drained soils in either full sun or shaded situations. It will withstand some dryness and is frost-resistant. Take lots of cut flowers or prune to maintain shape.

Landscape Use This very beautiful plant may be grown under trees and is ideal for the bush garden.

Ozothamnus diosmifolius

PANDANUS

PANDANACEAE

A large and complex genus of some 600 species found throughout the world, with approximately 20 species extending to tropical and subtropical areas in Australia. They are mostly small, sparsely branched trees with a dense crown of sword-shaped leaves arranged in a spiral formation; because of this they are often given the common name of screw pine. Most species have prop-like roots which grow from the lower part of the main trunk into the ground, forming extra supports. Mature screw pines form interesting shapes and look superb in tropical landscaping. Propagation is from fresh seed.

Pandanus pedunculatus
SCREW PINE

Origin Qld, NSW
Climate T, S, WT
Shade None to light

SPECIMEN PLANT
BIRD-ATTRACTING
SALT-TOLERANT
ORNAMENTAL FOLIAGE

Description A branched, spreading small tree to around 5 m with well-developed prop roots. The long leaves with sharp spines are arranged in spiral fashion. The white flowers are produced in a dense cluster which eventually develops into a large, pineapple-like fruit.

Cultivation Grow in a sunny position with good drainage. This is an excellent species for exposed coastal gardens in warm areas. It is frost-tender.

Landscape Use A beautiful, sculptured feature plant for a tropical or seaside garden.

Pandanus pedunculatus (fruit)

P. pedunculatus

PANDOREA
BIGNONIACEAE

A small genus of climbing plants of which three species occur in Australia. Two species are popular in cultivation for their handsome foliage and spectacular, long-lasting displays of tubular bell flowers. They are excellent climbers for trellises, for pergolas or for covering fences and may be grown in large containers. A number of attractive cultivars are available. Propagation is from fresh seed or from half-ripened tip cuttings.

Pandorea jasminoides
(syn. *Tecoma jasminoides*)
BOWER CLIMBER

Origin Qld, NSW, Vic.
Climate T, S, WT, M, CT
Shade Light to filtered

FAST-GROWING
CONTAINER PLANT
RAINFOREST PLANT

Description An attractive climbing plant with a lush cover of deep green, glossy pinnate leaves and sprays of large, pale pink trumpet flowers with a dark red throat. This plant has a long flowering period from late spring to autumn.

A pure white flowering form is also in cultivation.

Cultivation This species likes a rich, moist soil and a lightly shaded position, although it will grow in full sun. It will tolerate some frost when established.

Landscape Use An excellent climber suitable for pergolas or trellises. It may be grown in a large tub in a courtyard or patio.

Pandorea jasminoides

Pandorea pandorana
WONGA WONGA VINE

Origin Qld, NSW, Vic., Tas., WA
Climate S, WT, M, CT
Shade Light to full

FAST-GROWING
CONTAINER PLANT
RAINFOREST PLANT

Description A vigorous, woody climber with shiny green foliage divided into leaflets. The clusters of tubular bell flowers are usually creamy white with reddish throats but can be variable. They are produced in profusion during the spring months.

P. pandorana 'Golden Showers' is a tall, woody climber with masses of gold and brown bell flowers during spring.

P. pandorana 'Snow Bells' has masses of pure white flowers in spring and summer.

Cultivation Grow in a sunny or shaded position in a well-composted soil with plenty of moisture. It is frost-resistant.

Landscape Use A beautiful climber that will grow on any support. It is ideal for covering sheds, trellises or old tree stumps and works very well on a wire swimming pool enclosure.

Pandorea pandorana 'Golden Showers'

P. pandorana 'Snow Bells'

P. pandorana

PARASERIANTHES

MIMOSACEAE

This genus of shrubs and small trees occurs chiefly in tropical parts of the world. There are three Australian species which were previously included in the genus Albizia. *There are attractive plants with decorative ferny foliage and showy fluffy flowers. They are grown for shade, for quick-growing shelter and as ornamental street trees. In summer the pea-shaped pods provide the hard coated seeds used for propagation. Although seeds germinate readily, they must be scarified by either sanding lightly or nicking with a sharp razor blade before sowing.*

Paraserianthes lophantha

(syn. *Albizia lophantha*)

CAPE WATTLE

Origin WA
Climate WT, M, SA
Shade None to filtered

FAST-GROWING
FRAGRANT
BIRD-ATTRACTING
SALT-TOLERANT

Description This very fast-growing tree to 8 m has soft, finely divided foliage, and scented greenish yellow flowers on dense cylindrical spikes occurring from autumn through to spring.

Paraserianthes lophantha

Cultivation This species is suited to most soils, including the light sandy soils of coastal areas, where it will tolerate salt-laden winds. It is somewhat frost-tender.

Landscape Use Being a rapid grower, this plant is useful for quick shade, screen or windbreak planting.

PASSIFLORA

PASSIFLORACEAE

There are over 500 species of this large genus of tendril climbers which includes the edible passionfruit P. edulis. *Only about four Australian species occur and they are grown for their attractive foliage and showy flowers. Propagation is from fresh seed and half-ripened tip cuttings.*

Passiflora aurantica
BLUNT-LEAVED PASSIONFRUIT

Origin Qld, NSW
Climate T, S, WT
Shade Light to filtered
FAST-GROWING
BIRD-ATTRACTING
RAINFOREST PLANT

Description A slender, wiry vine with glossy, lobed dark green leaves and attractive salmon pink flowers with deep red centres. The flowers only open for one day, but they continue to be produced throughout the year.

Cultivation Grow in a warm, sheltered, moist position with some shade. It is frost-tender.

Landscape Use A pretty, light climber that may be allowed to climb trees in a shady part of the garden. It may also be used on a trellis, fence or pergola.

Passiflora aurantica

Passiflora cinnabarina
RED PASSIONFLOWER

Origin NSW, Vic.
Climate S, WT, M
Shade None to light
FAST-GROWING
BIRD-ATTRACTING

Description A fairly strong climber with lobed leaves, and red passion flowers along the stems in late spring and summer. These are followed by small fruits which are enjoyed by many birds.

Cultivation Grow in a sheltered position in full sun or light shade with plenty of moisture, but good drainage. It is moderately frost tolerant.

Landscape Use A fast-growing and attractive fence, wall or pergola cover.

Passiflora cinnabarina

PATERSONIA
IRIDACEAE

There are about 20 species of these iris-like plants with about 18 occurring in Australia. They are perennial clump-forming plants, often with strap-like leaves, and produce attractive three-petalled flowers which are usually shades of blue or purple, but yellow and white flowers are also seen. The flowers usually each last less than a day, but flowering occurs over a long period because of the many buds produced. These beautiful wildflowers have adapted to cultivation and look most attractive when planted en masse as a border or in the rockery. Propagation is from seed, which is easily germinated.

Patersonia occidentalis
NATIVE IRIS

Origin Vic., Tas., SA, WA
Climate WT, M, CT
Shade None to filtered
CONTAINER PLANT
Description A tussock-forming species with narrow, grass-like leaves to 50 cm, and abundant purple flowers in spring through to early summer.

This species now includes the form sometimes sold as *P. longiscapa*.

Cultivation This adaptable species will thrive in most soils provided the drainage is very good. It can withstand moist conditions as well as periods of dryness. It is frost-resistant.

Landscape Use A good long-flowering species that makes an excellent rockery or container plant.

Patersonia sericea
SILKY PURPLE FLAG

Origin Qld, NSW, Vic.
Climate S, WT, M, CT
Shade None to light
CONTAINER PLANT
Description A low clump-forming plant with grass-like, silky leaves to around 30 cm. The deep violet flowers are produced on woolly stems and have silky flower bracts. Each flower lasts only a few hours, but a succession of buds ensure a good display during spring and summer.

Cultivation This species prefers good drainage in a light-textured soil. It is frost-resistant.

Landscape Use Plant in groups as a border, in the rockery or in a container.

Patersonia sericea

Patersonia occidentalis

PAVONIA
MALVACEAE

There are about 200 species in this genus, but only one occurs in Australia. It is P. hastata, *known as the Pink Pavonia, an open, spreading shrub with small, pink hibiscus-like flowers. It is very hardy and is suited to informal landscapes. Propagation is from seed, which germinates readily.*

Pavonia hastata
PINK PAVONIA

Origin Qld, NSW
Climate S, WT, M, SA
Shade None to light
FAST-GROWING
Description A small, open spreading shrub to 1 m with rough, arrow-shaped leaves. The small hibiscus-like flowers are pale pink with a red centre and are produced in abundance in summer and autumn. The plant will seed itself readily, but not all plants produce flowers that open fully, so ensure that the parent is a successful flowering form.

Cultivation A hardy plant that will adapt to most soils and conditions in full sun

Pavonia hastata

or part shade. It is frost-resistant. Prune regularly to encourage compact shape.

Landscape Use A good foreground plant for the bush garden.

PELARGONIUM

GERANIACEAE

A large genus of over 200 species of which many exotic species and cultivars have become familiar garden plants. There about seven Australian species and some of these are well worth a place in the garden. Propagation is from seed or from half-ripened tip cuttings, which strike readily.

Pelargonium australe

Pelargonium australe

AUSTRAL STORKSBILL

Origin All States

Climate S, WT, M, CT, H

Shade None to light

AROMATIC FOLIAGE
CONTAINER PLANT

Description A low, spreading or rounded shrub to 50 cm high and 50 cm across, with aromatic, heart-shaped, fleshy leaves. The clusters of flowers are usually white or pale pink with rose or purple veins and are produced in spring and summer.

Cultivation A hardy plant for most soils with good drainage. It likes full sun and is frost-resistant. Prune to shape.

Landscape Use A good spreading plant for border, rockery or container.

Pelargonium rodneyanum

MAGENTA STORKSBILL

Origin NSW, Vic., SA, WA

Climate WT, M, SA

Shade None to light

CONTAINER PLANT

Description A low-growing, stemless plant to 15 cm which forms a thick tap root and a rosette of leaves. Masses of magenta flowers are borne on long slender flowering stems in summer.

Cultivation Grow in a sunny, well-drained position. This species is not fussy about soil, but likes fairly dry conditions. It is frost-resistant.

Landscape Use A very showy rockery, border or container plant.

Pelargonium rodneyanum

PERSOONIA

PROTEACEAE

This attractive genus of shrubs and small trees is endemic to Australia, except for one species which occurs in New Zealand. They produce masses of tubular to bell-shaped yellow flowers at the ends of the branches, followed by edible yellow or green fruit called geebungs. This is an Aboriginal name for the fruit and it is now generally used as a common name for all species. They make decorative garden plants and, although difficult to propagate, are available from specialist nurseries. Propagation is from seed or from half-ripened tip cuttings, which are difficult to strike.

Persoonia chamaepitys

MOUNTAIN GEEBUNG

Origin NSW

Climate WT, M, CT, H

Shade None to filtered

CONTAINER PLANT

Description A prostrate, spreading plant to 1 m across, with soft, bright green

Persoonia chamaepitys

needle-like foliage. Clusters of bright yellow flowers are produced towards the ends of the branches in late spring and summer.

Cultivation Grow in a light-textured, well-drained soil in a sunny or lightly shaded position. It is frost-resistant.

Landscape Use This is a beautiful cascading ground cover for a border, rockery or container.

Persoonia levis
BROAD-LEAF GEEBUNG

Origin NSW, Vic.
Climate WT, M
Shade None to light
BIRD-ATTRACTING
ORNAMENTAL FOLIAGE
Description This erect shrub with leathery, bright green, broad-lanceolate leaves grows to around 4 m. It has dark red, flaky bark and bears small, bright yellow flowers along the stems in summer, followed by fleshy fruits.

Cultivation Grow in a warm, sunny position with good drainage. It is frost-resistant.

Landscape Use An attractive foliage plant for use as a background or in groups.

Persoonia levis

Persoonia oxycoccoides
(syn. *P. nutans*)

Origin NSW
Climate WT, M, CT, H
Shade None to light
CONTAINER PLANT
Description A prostrate to slightly upright shrub to 60 cm high and up to 2 m wide. It has small, oval, light green leaves and bears masses of yellow flowers from spring through summer.

Persoonia oxycoccoides

Cultivation Grow in a well-drained, sunny position with adequate moisture in dry months. It is frost-resistant.

Landscape Use An attractive plant for border, rockery or container.

Persoonia pinifolia
PINE-LEAF GEEBUNG

Origin NSW
Climate WT, M, CT
Shade Light to filtered
SPECIMEN PLANT
ORNAMENTAL FOLIAGE
Description A graceful large shrub to 4 m high with arching branches clothed in soft, pine-like foliage. Bright yellow flowers hang in terminal bunches in late summer and autumn, followed by pale green succulent fruit. Foliage and flowers

Persoonia pinifolia

are beautiful for indoor arrangements.

Cultivation Grow in a lightly shaded location with good drainage. This species does well in fairly dry conditions. It is frost-resistant.

Landscape Use An exceptionally attractive shrub for the bush garden. It may be used as a feature, as a light screen or in a small group planting.

PETROPHILE

PROTEACEAE

This genus of some 40 species is confined to Australia, with the greater number of species occurring in Western Australia. They are attractive small to medium-sized shrubs, mostly with stiff, prickly foliage, prominent flowers and grey seed cones resembling miniature pine cones. A number of species are in cultivation and some are most ornamental. Flowers, foliage and cones are excellent in floral arrangements. Propagation is from seed or half-ripened tip cuttings taken in autumn, which may be slow to strike.

Petrophile biloba

GRANITE PETROPHILE

Origin WA
Climate WT, M, CT, SA
Shade None to filtered

BIRD-ATTRACTING
ORNAMENTAL FOLIAGE
CONTAINER PLANT

Description An erect shrub to around 1.5 m high. It has lobed, prickly leaves and produces pale pinkish grey flowers clustered along the branch ends during spring. These are very long-lasting when picked for indoors.

Petrophile biloba

Cultivation Grow in a light-textured soil with very good drainage. It will withstand dry periods and is moderately frost-resistant. Prune to encourage compact growth.

Landscape Use A decorative and unusual shrub for garden or container.

Petrophile linearis

PIXIE MOPS

Origin WA
Climate M, SA
Shade None to light

CONTAINER PLANT

Description A small shrub to 50 cm with curved entire leaves. Woolly mauve flowers are produced at branch ends during spring.

Cultivation Grow in a very well drained sandy soil in full sun. It thrives in dry conditions and will not tolerate excessive humidity. It is hardy to light frosts.

Landscape Use A beautiful rockery or container subject.

Petrophile linearis

Petrophile serruriae

Origin WA
Climate M, SA
Shade None to light

CONTAINER PLANT

Description A fairly upright shrub to 2 m with finely divided, prickly leaves on

Petrophile serruriae

arching stems. Many small heads of slightly furry cream, or rarely pink, flowers are produced towards branch ends in late spring.

Cultivation This species demands excellent drainage and an open, airy sunny position. It is frost-resistant.

Landscape Use Grow in an elevated position to provide good drainage and to allow the flowers on drooping branches to be shown to advantage. It is well suited to a large container.

Petrophile sessilis
PRICKLY CONESTICKS

Origin NSW
Climate WT, M
Shade None to light
ORNAMENTAL FOLIAGE
CONTAINER PLANT

Description An erect, slender shrub to 2 m tall with divided, stiff, needle-like foliage. The stalkless white to pale yellow cone flowers appear in late spring and summer.

Cultivation Grow in a sunny, well-drained location in a light soil. It is frost-resistant.

Landscape Use An attractive foliage plant that looks good when not in flower. It is prickly and should not be grown too close to narrow paths.

Petrophile sessilis

PHEBALIUM
RUTACEAE

There are about 45 species in this genus, all Australian except for one which occurs in New Zealand. The genus is closely related to Boronia *and includes some very lovely shrubs with starry clusters of white, yellow or pink flowers with long, fluffy stamens. Propagation is from half-ripened tip cuttings taken in autumn.*

Phebalium nottii
PINK PHEBALIUM

Origin Qld, NSW
Climate WT, M
Shade Light to filtered
CONTAINER PLANT

Description A small, dense shrub to around 1 m in cultivation. It has oblong dark green leaves and bears loose clusters of bright pink flowers during spring. This is one of the prettiest phebaliums, but it is not always available and is often difficult to maintain in cultivation.

Cultivation This understorey shrub of open forests prefers light shade and a cool root run supplied by a good mulch. It needs perfect drainage and is frost-resistant.

Landscape Use A lovely plant for growing beneath taller shrubs and trees.

Phebalium nottii

Phebalium squamulosum
SCALY PHEBALIUM

Origin Qld, NSW, Vic., SA
Climate S, WT, M, CT
Shade Light to full
BIRD-ATTRACTING

Description A variable shrub ranging in size from 1 m to 3 m. It has narrow leaves with a silvery undersurface, and bears masses of bright yellow terminal flowers in spring.

Phebalium squamulosum

Cultivation Grow in a lightly shaded location with reasonable moisture, but good drainage. Apply a good mulch to keep roots cool in hot months. It is frost-resistant.

Landscape Use A very pretty shrub to brighten a shady corner. The lower growing varieties are suitable for the larger part of the rockery.

Phebalium stenophyllum
NARROW-LEAF PHEBALIUM

Origin NSW, Vic.
Climate WT, M
Shade Light to filtered
CONTAINER PLANT

Description A small, rounded shrub to a little over 1 m. It has narrow dark green

Phebalium stenophyllum

leaves with rolled-back edges and produces showy clusters of bright yellow flowers in late winter and spring.

Cultivation This species is quite hardy and prefers a light-textured soil with good drainage. It will withstand dry periods and is moderately frost-resistant.

Landscape Use The bright yellow display of flowers makes this an outstanding ornamental shrub for the garden foreground.

Phebalium whitei

Origin Qld
Climate S, WT, M
Shade Light to heavy
CONTAINER PLANT

Description A small erect shrub up to 1 m high but often less. It has oblong dark green leaves and conspicuous bright yellow flowers in spring.

Cultivation This species prefers a moist but well-drained soil and some shade. It is moderately frost tolerant. Lightly prune to shape.

Landscape Use An ornamental plant for growing in the shade of taller shrubs and trees.

Phebalium whitei

Phebalium woombye

Origin Qld
Climate S, WT
Shade None to filtered
CONTAINER PLANT

Description A rounded, open shrub to around 1.5 m. The narrow, elliptical leaves have a silvery undersurface, and clusters of starry white flowers occur in spring. A lovely pink-flowering form from around Bundaberg is available from specialist nurseries in Queensland.

Cultivation This species prefers a sandy, well-drained soil with a good mulch. It may be grown in a protected seaside garden and is frost-resistant. Tip prune regularly to encourage a compact habit.

Landscape Use An attractive shrub for the rockery or bush garden, where it will tolerate some shade.

Phebalium woombye

P. woombye (pink-flowering form)

PIMELEA

THYMELAEACEAE

Of the 90 species of pimeleas, approximately 80 occur in Australia, with representatives in all States. They are small to medium, soft-wooded shrubs with neat foliage and showy heads of terminal flowers in shades of white, yellow, pink and red. The flowers are very attractive to butterflies. Although many species have great horticultural potential, some are difficult to propagate and are short-lived in cultivation. The only readily available species in nurseries are P. ferruginea *and* P. rosea, *and these are regarded as reliable garden plants. Propagation is from seed or from half-ripened tip cuttings.*

Pimelea ferruginea

(syn. *P. decussata*)

PINK RICE FLOWER

Origin WA
Climate WT, M, CT, SA
Shade None to filtered
CONTAINER PLANT

Description A compact, rounded shrub to 1 m with glossy, oval stem-clasping leaves. Masses of bright pink pincushion heads of flowers are produced at branch ends from late winter through spring.

P. ferruginea 'Bonnie Petite' is a small shrub with very deep pink flowers for long periods from spring.

P. ferruginea 'Magenta Mist' grows to a rounded 1 m and bears masses of magenta heads of flowers.

Cultivation Grow in a well-drained soil in full sun or partial shade. It may be used in a protected seaside garden and is frost-resistant. Prune lightly after flowering to maintain a compact shape.

Pimelea ferruginea 'Magenta Mist'

P. ferruginea

Landscape Use A very floriferous species that may be used as a feature; as a pretty hedge along a path; in a rockery pocket; or as a pot plant.

Pimelea ligustrina
TALL RICE FLOWER

Origin Qld, NSW, Vic., Tas., SA
Climate S, WT, CT, H
Shade Light to heavy
FAST-GROWING
Description A tall, open shrub to 2 m with soft lanceolate leaves. Drooping white pincushion flowerheads on slender stems appear in summer. A low growing compact form to 1 m high with a similar spread is also in cultivation.

Pimelea ligustrina

Cultivation This hardy plant likes a well-composted soil with good drainage. It will grow well in quite heavy shade and is frost- and snow-resistant.

Landscape Use A lovely understorey plant for the bush garden.

Pimelea linifolia
SLENDER RICE FLOWER

Origin Qld, NSW, Vic., Tas., SA
Climate S, WT, M, CT, H, SA
Shade None to filtered
FAST-GROWING
CONTAINER PLANT
Description A widespread species which varies from very low-growing to a slender, erect shrub of 1 m. It has narrow foliage and bears showy heads of flowers on the ends of branches for most of the year. The flowers are usually white, but a pretty pink-flowering form with fine foliage is also in cultivation.

Pimelea linifolia

P. linifolia (pink-flowering form)

Cultivation Grow in a well-drained soil in either full sun or partial shade. It may be used in a protected seaside garden and is frost-resistant. Tip prune after flowering to encourage bushiness.

Landscape Use A dainty border, rockery or container plant.

Pimelea rosea
PINK RICE FLOWER

Origin WA
Climate WT, M, CT, SA
Shade None to filtered
CONTAINER PLANT
Description A small, branched shrub to 1 m high, with sparse, narrow, lanceolate foliage. Deep pink terminal flowerheads occur during spring. A pure white form is also in cultivation and flowers prolifically.

Cultivation Grow in a sandy, well-drained soil in either full sun or dappled sunlight. It is frost-resistant. Prune lightly straight after flowering to encourage compact growth.

Landscape Use A pretty plant for growing among other shrubs and under trees. It is suitable for a rockery or for containers.

Pimelea rosea

Pimelea spectabilis

Origin WA
Climate WT, M, SA
Shade Light to filtered
CONTAINER PLANT
Description A small, erect shrub to around 1 m with narrow grey-green foliage. The large, nodding white flowerheads, sometimes flushed with

pink, are produced on long slender stems during spring.

Cultivation This very beautiful species is difficult to grow and is often short-lived. It requires dappled sunlight and good drainage in a light to medium soil. It is frost-resistant. Prune after flowering.

Landscape Use A very showy plant for the rockery or container.

Pimelea spectabilis

PIPER

PIPERACEAE

There are about nine Australian species of this large tropical genus comprising approximately 2,000 species of bushy shrubs and rampant vines. Piper nigrum *of South-east Asia provides the commercial condiment pepper. Valued for their handsome glossy heart-shaped leaves and ability to thrive in shady areas a few pepper vines are cultivated in Australia. Propagation is from cuttings.*

Piper novae-hollandiae

GIANT PEPPER VINE

Origin Qld, NSW
Climate T, S, WT
Shade Filtered to heavy

ORNAMENTAL FOLIAGE
AROMATIC FOLIAGE
CONTAINER PLANT
RAINFOREST PLANT

Description A moderately vigorous climber that clings to supports by numerous adventitious roots. The large glossy heart-shaped leaves on young plants become ovate on mature branches. Crushed leaves are aromatic. Tiny flowers are followed by clusters of small red fruits. When dried, the peppercorns may be ground and used as pepper.

Cultivation Grow in a moist, humus-enriched soil with reasonable drainage. The plant requires a fibrous support on which to cling. It will grow well in heavy shade, but is frost tender.

Landscape Use A beautiful vine for a warm shady garden. If given suitable support it can be grown in a container and used on a veranda or indoors.

Piper novae-hollandiae

PITTOSPORUM

PITTOSPORACEAE

A genus of trees and shrubs comprising about 150 species with about 10 occurring in Australia, including representatives in all States. They are hardy in cultivation and most species make very decorative garden subjects with handsome glossy foliage, fragrant flowers and long-

lasting, colourful fruits. They are used for hedges, screens and windbreaks, as ornamental lawn specimens and for street planting. The pittosporum leaf miner Phytobia pittosporophyllii *may cause damage to the leaves of some species. Leaf miners are difficult to control and although damaged leaves are unattractive, the plant will not be seriously affected. Pittosporums may become infested with scale pests such as pink wax scale and white wax scale. As mature scales are difficult to kill it is best to spray the young scales with white oil during early summer before too much scale covers the insect. Propagation is from fresh seed.*

Pittosporum revolutum
YELLOW PITTOSPORUM

Origin Qld, NSW, Vic.
Climate S, WT, M
Shade Filtered to full

FAST-GROWING
FRAGRANT
BIRD-ATTRACTING
RAINFOREST PLANT

Description A tall, open shrub to around 3 m with large, glossy green leaves with a felty underside. Clusters of fragrant yellow flowers in spring are followed by showy orange fruit which open to reveal bright scarlet sticky seeds. A variety of birds feed on the fruit.

Cultivation Grow in a partially shaded location in a moist, well-composted soil. It is moderately frost-resistant.

Landscape Use As this species tolerates shady conditions, it is best for planting under existing trees or in the bush garden.

Pittosporum revolutum

Pittosporum rhombifolium

Origin Qld, NSW
Climate T, S, WT, M
Shade None to filtered

SPECIMEN PLANT
FRAGRANT
BIRD-ATTRACTING
RAINFOREST PLANT

Description An attractive, upright tree which grows to around 8 m in cultivation. It has glossy green oval foliage forming a neat dense cover. The clusters of small white perfumed flowers are followed by showy bunches of bright orange berries in autumn and winter.

Cultivation This hardy and adaptable species will grow in any well-drained soil, but needs plenty of moisture. It may be used in protected seaside gardens and it is frost-resistant.

Landscape Use Although slow-growing at first, this trouble-free tree will soon develop into a neat specimen for garden, lawn, park or street.

Pittosporum rhombifolium

P. rhombifolium (fruit)

Pittosporum undulatum
SWEET PITTOSPORUM

Origin Qld, NSW, Vic.
Climate S, WT, CT, H
Shade Light to filtered

FAST-GROWING
FRAGRANT
BIRD-ATTRACTING
RAINFOREST PLANT

Description A small bushy tree to around 8 m in cultivation. It has wavy dark green leaves and produces sweetly perfumed creamy white flowers in spring. These are followed by small bright orange berries which attract a variety of birds to the garden.

Cultivation This hardy and adaptable tree will thrive in almost any conditions where ample moisture is available. It may be grown in protected coastal gardens. Young plants are slightly frost-tender.

Landscape Use This species will quickly form a good screen or windbreak. As it will tolerate considerable shade it is ideal for growing under taller trees or in the 'rainforest' part of the garden.

Pittosporum undulatum

PLATYCERIUM
POLYPODIACEAE

This genus of ferns contains about 15 species with four present in Australia. They grow either on trees (epiphytes) or on rocks (lithophytes), and two magnificent species are common in cultivation. These are the Elkhorn P. bifurcatum *and the Staghorn* P. superbum. *They attain large clumps with age and have two types of fronds, fertile and infertile. The infertile fronds are the nest leaves which wrap around and anchor the fern to its host. As new backing leaves develop each year, the old ones wither and form a peaty mass providing protection for the roots and a catchment area for moisture and nourishment. The fertile fronds extend outwards and are usually pendent and lobed at the ends. These produce brown patches of spore material and are shed before being replaced by new fronds.*

These long-lived ferns make beautiful specimen plants for mounting on a tree or a large wooden slab. Small brown spots at the tips of the fronds indicate the presence of the staghorn fern beetle. It is a tiny dark purple beetle, with four reddish spots, which lays its eggs under the surface of the fronds. Remove and destroy affected parts of the frond as soon as damage is noticed. Beetles can be removed by hand. Elkhorns are also attacked by this beetle. Propagation is by division of clumps of the Elkhorn or from spores of the Staghorn.

Platycerium bifurcatum
ELKHORN

Origin Qld, NSW
Climate T, S, WT, M
Shade Light to filtered
ORNAMENTAL FOLIAGE
RAINFOREST PLANT

Description This widespread fern has deeply lobed green nest leaves which turn brown with age. The pendulous fertile fronds, up to 1 m long, are forked two or three times. Small new plants develop on the margins of the nest leaves, continually adding to the size of the clump. These can be carefully removed, making sure an ample layer of peat is left as a backing.

Cultivation This species may be mounted on a large hardwood slab with plenty of room for development. It requires a semishaded position with good sunlight and must be kept moist, especially in summer. In cooler climates, it must be given protection from frosts and winds.

Landscape Use A beautiful plant for verandas, patios, courtyards and on trees

Platycerium bifurcatum

in the garden. It is well suited to the 'rainforest' part of the garden.

Platycerium superbum

(syn. *P. grande*)

STAGHORN

Origin Qld, NSW
Climate T, S, WT, M
Shade Light to full

ORNAMENTAL FOLIAGE
RAINFOREST PLANT

Description This spectacular fern from rainforests has large green backing leaves which eventually form an extensive collecting area. The pendulous fertile fronds, up to 2 m long, are lobed several times. A large spore-bearing patch is formed on the undersurface around the first division. As this species does not produce plantlets, propagation must be from spores.

Cultivation This species may be mounted on a piece of tree or tied to a large hardwood slab. Care should be taken not to wire across the central crown or growing points. Place in a semishaded position protected from harsh sun and frost and kept moist. In cooler climates, it is best kept fairly dry during the dormant winter months.

Landscape Use Place on fences, walls or trees to create a tropical atmosphere around the home or grow in the 'rainforest' part of the garden.

Platycerium superbum

POA

POACEAE

A worldwide genus of grasses of which some 30 species are found in Australia. Some are ornamental and look good in a bush garden or used in association with rocks or water. Propagation is from seed or by division of clumps.

Poa australis

BLUE TUSSOCK GRASS

Origin NSW, Vic., Tas., SA, WA
Climate WT, M, CT, H
Shade None to filtered

CONTAINER PLANT

Description A grassy clump with soft, narrow grey-green leaves to 30 cm high. Decorative flower heads are produced in spring and summer.

Cultivation A very hardy grass that will grow in most well-drained soils and in

Poa australis

most positions. It likes plenty of moisture and is frost-resistant.

Landscape Use A rockery pocket is the perfect home for this silvery grass. It also looks good edging a path in the bush garden.

POLYSTICHUM
ASPIDIACEAE

Of the 175 species of this widespread genus, only four are known to occur in Australia. They have an erect rhizome covered with many brown scales, and numerous erect fronds spreading in a crown. They are extremely hardy ferns in the garden and make excellent container plants. Some species produce reproductive bulbils on the tips of the mature fronds; these grow into young plants as the fronds wither and die. Propagation is from these small plants or from spores.

Polystichum formosum
BROAD SHIELD FERN

Origin Qld, NSW, Vic.
Climate S, WT, M
Shade Light to filtered
CONTAINER PLANT
Description This species has attractive, feathery, arching fronds to about 60 cm tall. They are light green and harsh to the touch and do not produce young plants at the tips.

Cultivation This hardy fern will grow in full sun, but is at its best in a shady location. It needs plenty of moisture and protection from severe frosts.

Landscape Use A very pretty fern for a shady garden or near a water feature. It looks good in a large container if given reasonable room.

Polystichum proliferum
MOTHER SHIELD FERN

Origin NSW, Vic., Tas.
Climate S, WT, M, CT, H
Shade None to heavy
CONTAINER PLANT
RAINFOREST PLANT
Description This widespread fern is common in gullies, forests and alpine areas. It has dark green, arching to spreading fronds to over 1 m high and these produce bulbils near the tips.

Polystichum formosum

Polystichum proliferum

Cultivation A very hardy fern in the garden, suited to a well-drained, sunny or shaded position. It needs plenty of moisture, especially if grown in the sun, and is snow- and frost-resistant.

Landscape Use A good cold climate fern. It looks good in a sizeable rockery pocket or in a large container.

PRATIA

LOBELIACEAE

A group of some 35 species of small herbaceous plants of which 13 species occur in Australia. Some are prostrate creepers and make useful ground cover and rockery plants in moist and shady places in the garden.

Pratia pedunculata *is widely available in nurseries and even supermarket chains. Propagation is easy, by division or from seed.*

Pratia pedunculata

TRAILING PRATIA

Origin NSW, Vic., Tas., SA
Climate S, WT, M, CT, H
Shade None to full
CONTAINER PLANT
Description A small, prostrate, mat-forming plant to 1 m across with small soft green oval leaves. It bears masses of dainty star-like white or pale blue flowers in spring and summer.

Pratia pedunculata

Cultivation This species prefers a moist shaded position and will form a good cover in poorly drained areas. It will withstand cold conditions, including frost and some snow.

Landscape Use This very attractive ground cover is ideal for rockery, border, water feature, between paving and as a miniature lawn alternative.

PROSTANTHERA

LAMIACEAE

A large endemic genus with around 65 species ranging in size from small foliage shrubs. Most have aromatic foliage and produce masses of spring and summer flowers in shades of blue to purple, red, yellow and white. Along with members of the family Myrtaceae, it is the mint bushes that impart that wonderful Australian bush fragrance of hot, sunny days, making them a favourite native plant among bushwalkers and gardeners alike. In garden situations they are extremely fast-growing and flower well even when quite small. As many species prefer some shade they may be planted in the bush garden or beneath the overhead cover of eucalypts. Some of the small species make charming subjects for the small garden, rockery or container. Plant a mint bush next to a path, window or gateway where the scent may be enjoyed after a shower of rain or on a hot day. Mint bushes are usually free from pests and diseases, but are somewhat short-lived under cultivation. In extended periods of rain, particularly in heavy soils, the roots may become affected by root rot, thus perfect drainage is essential for healthy growth. Tip pruning should be carried out throughout the life of the plant to ensure dense and compact growth. Propagation is easiest from half-ripened tip cuttings, which strike readily.

Prostanthera aspalathoides

SCARLET MINT BUSH

Origin NSW, Vic., SA
Climate WT, M, CT, SA
Shade None to filtered
AROMATIC FOLIAGE
DROUGHT-RESISTANT
CONTAINER PLANT
Description A dense, rounded shrub to less than 1 m tall with small linear leaves.

Prostanthera aspalathoides

P. aspalathoides (yellow-flowered form)

The tubular scarlet flowers are produced for most of the year, with a main flush in late spring. A yellow-flowered form is sometimes available.

Cultivation This species likes a light, well-drained soil and a sheltered position. It will withstand dry conditions and is frost-resistant. Prune after flowering to promote vigour and compact growth.

Landscape Use A good rockery or container plant.

Prostanthera cruciflora

GREY MINT BUSH

Origin NSW
Climate WT, M
Shade Light to filtered
CONTAINER PLANT
Description A rounded soft shrub to 1 m with pale grey-green wavy foliage. The small white to pale mauve flowers open to form a cross shape during spring.

Prostanthera cruciflora

Cultivation This species prefers some shade and a well-drained position. It is frost-resistant. Prune back after flowering to encourage compact shape.

Landscape Use A lovely grey-foliaged plant for contrast in the garden. It may be grown in a container.

Prostanthera cryptandroides

Origin NSW
Climate WT, M, CT
Shade Light to filtered

AROMATIC FOLIAGE
CONTAINER PLANT

Description A small, dainty shrub to 75 cm with narrow sticky leaves which are highly aromatic. Many small mauve flowers are produced along the stems for most of the year, with a new flush in spring.

Cultivation This hardy species will grow in most soils, provided the drainage is good. It needs plenty of water, especially during the summer, and is frost-resistant. Prune lightly to maintain a neat shape.

Landscape Use This pretty little plant blooms through autumn and into early winter when very little else flowers. It is an asset to any native garden and looks good as a foreground, rockery or container plant.

Prostanthera cuneata
ALPINE MINT BUSH

Origin NSW, Vic., Tas.
Climate WT, M CT, H
Shade Light to filtered

AROMATIC FOLIAGE
CONTAINER PLANT

Description A variable compact shrub which may be low and spreading to 1.5 m across or upright to 1 m high. The attractive, strongly aromatic leaves are dark green and glossy and are crowded along the branches. The large white or pale mauve flowers with purple blotches in the throat almost cover the plant in summer.

Prostanthera cuneata

Prostanthera cryptandroides

Cultivation This species occurs naturally in alpine areas and does best in a cool situation with adequate moisture in summer. It likes good drainage and will tolerate frost and snow. Prune after flowering to prevent legginess.

Landscape Use An ornamental plant for among other shrubs or under trees. The spreading form makes an excellent ground cover, rockery plant or container plant.

Prostanthera denticulata

Origin NSW, Vic.
Climate WT, M, CT
Shade Light to filtered

AROMATIC FOLIAGE
CONTAINER PLANT

Description A variable spreading shrub which may be prostrate to 1 m across or upright to 60 cm. The slightly rough foliage is aromatic, and masses of mauve to purple flowers occur in spring and summer.

Cultivation This species needs a light, well-drained soil in a warm, partially shaded position. It will tolerate dry periods, but benefits from summer watering. It is frost-resistant. Prune to shape.

Landscape Use A good rockery or foreground species.

Prostanthera denticulata

Prostanthera incana
HOARY MINT BUSH

Origin NSW
Climate WT, M, CT
Shade Light to filtered

CONTAINER PLANT

Description A dense, rounded shrub to 1.5 m with soft, hairy, crinkled leaves. Small clusters are produced near the ends

Prostanthera incana

of the branches during spring. A white-flowered form is also available.

Cultivation This hardy species likes partial shade in a well-drained position. It will withstand periods of dryness and may be used in protected coastal gardens. It is moderately frost-resistant.

Landscape Use An attractive compact shrub for the garden, rockery or large tub.

Prostanthera incisa
CUT-LEAF MINT BUSH

Origin NSW
Climate WT, M, CT
Shade Light to filtered
AROMATIC FOLIAGE
CONTAINER PLANT
Description A spreading but compact shrub to 2 m with very aromatic oval toothed leaves. The small mauve flowers are produced in showy clusters during the spring months.

Cultivation Grow in a moist position in a well-mulched soil with good drainage. It does best in dappled shade and is frost-hardy. Prune after flowering.

Landscape Use A showy species that blends well with tree ferns near a water feature or sheltered part of the garden. It is also suited to a large tub.

Prostanthera lasianthos
VICTORIAN CHRISTMAS BUSH

Origin Qld, NSW, Vic., Tas.
Climate WT, M, CT, H
Shade Light to full
FAST-GROWING
AROMATIC FOLIAGE
Description A variable tall shrub or small tree from 2 to 5 m. It has dark green lanceolate toothed leaves and produces an abundance of large white flowers, spotted purple in the throat, around Christmas time. Pale mauve and pink flowered forms are also available.

P. lasianthos var. *subcoriacea* from the Grampians in Victoria is a smaller form to 2 m with white flowers in late spring and early summer.

Cultivation This species occurs naturally in cool, moist forests and prefers some shade and a well-composted soil with good drainage. It is tolerant of cold, frost and some snow. Prune after flowering to shape.

Landscape Use As this species will thrive under overhead cover, it is ideal for the bush garden or under trees. It will also form a good screen.

Prostanthera magnifica
MAGNIFICENT MINT BUSH

Origin WA
Climate M, SA
Shade None to light
FAST-GROWING
CONTAINER PLANT
Description An upright shrub to 1.5 m high with thick lanceolate leaves. The large mauve flowers have an enlarged calyx which deepens to a rich reddish colour with age. Flowering time is from late winter through to early summer.

Cultivation This very decorative Western Australian is rather tricky in cultivation. It prefers fairly dry conditions in sandy soil with very good drainage. It resents humidity and is slightly frost-tender.

Landscape Use A beautiful shrub for the garden or for the container, where conditions may be controlled.

Prostanthera incisa

Prostanthera lasianthos

Prostanthera magnifica

Prostanthera melissifolia
BALM MINT BUSH

Origin Vic.
Climate WT, M, CT, H
Shade Light to heavy
FAST-GROWING
AROMATIC FOLIAGE
CONTAINER PLANT

Description A rounded, dense shrub to 3 m with strongly aromatic toothed oval leaves. Loose clusters of purple flowers are borne towards branch ends in late spring and summer.

A prolific pink-flowering form is also in cultivation.

Cultivation A hardy species that enjoys a moist well-composted position with good drainage. It will tolerate frost and light snow. Prune to shape after flowering.

Landscape Use A very colourful shrub that may be grown beneath the overhead cover of larger trees. It is also useful as a screening plant.

Prostanthera melissifolia

P. melissifolia (pink-flowering form)

Prostanthera nivea
SNOWY MINT BUSH

Origin Qld, NSW, Vic.
Climate WT, M, CT
Shade None to filtered
FAST-GROWING

Description An open, slender shrub to 3 m with narrow light green leaves. Sprays of snowy white flowers are produced in late spring.

P. nivea var. *induta* is a more compact form to 2 m with silvery foliage and with large pale blue flowers covering the bush for a long period in spring.

Cultivation An adaptable species that will grow in most well-drained soils and most conditions. It will tolerate periods of dryness and is frost-resistant. Prune immediately after flowering to encourage compact growth.

Landscape Use A very attractive species in a ferny area or near a pond.

Prostanthera nivea

P. nivea var. *induta*

Prostanthera ovalifolia
PURPLE MINT BUSH

Origin Qld, NSW
Climate WT, M, CT
Shade Light to filtered
FAST-GROWING
AROMATIC FOLIAGE

Description An upright bushy shrub, usually to around 2 m tall. The oval leaves are strongly but pleasantly aromatic, and masses of purple flowers are produced in spring.

There are several forms of this species, including a dwarf bushy type and one with variegated foliage. A most attractive variety with foliage tinged with purple is also in cultivation.

Cultivation This is one of the most reliable mint bushes and the most popular in cultivation. It will grow in most well-drained soils in full sun or semishade and may be planted in protected coastal gardens. It is frost-resistant. Prune after flowering to maintain compact shape and encourage vigour.

Prostanthera ovalifolia

Landscape Use Grow near a path for its striking display of flowers and for the scent of the foliage when it is brushed against. It may be grown in a large container in the courtyard and it also makes an attractive fence screen.

Prostanthera phylicifolia

Origin Qld, NSW, Vic.
Climate WT, M, CT, H
Shade Light to filtered
FAST-GROWING
CONTAINER PLANT
Description An erect shrub to 1.5 m with thick, narrow, stem-clasping leaves. The pale mauve flowers, which are borne in the leaf axils, are blotched yellow or purple in the throat. These occur during spring.

Cultivation A hardy plant for a cool, moist position with dappled shade. It will withstand frost and snow. Prune after flowering to encourage compact growth.

Landscape Use A robust cold climate species for the garden, rockery or container.

Prostanthera phylicifolia

Prostanthera *'Poorinda Ballerina'*

Origin Cultivar (*P. phylicifolia* x *P. lasianthos*)
Climate WT, M, CT, H
Shade Light to filtered
FAST-GROWING
CONTAINER PLANT
Description An attractive rounded shrub to 2 m with narrow foliage, and with

Prostanthera 'Poorinda Ballerina'

masses of white flowers tinged purple during the spring months.

Cultivation A hardy shrub which likes a well-mulched soil in a moist, partially shady location. It is frost-resistant. Prune immediately after flowering and lightly at other times to maintain bushiness and vigour.

Landscape Use Grow among other shrubs in the garden, as a hedge, or neatly trimmed in a large container.

Prostanthera rhombea

Origin NSW
Climate WT, M, CT
Shade None to filtered
AROMATIC FOLIAGE
CONTAINER PLANT
Description A spreading small shrub to 1 m high and a similar width, with tiny,

Prostanthera rhombea

rounded aromatic leaves. Pale mauve flowers are produced along the wiry branches during spring.

A pink-flowering form is also available.

Cultivation A hardy and adaptable plant that will grow in full sun or shade in dry or moist conditions. It is frost-resistant. Prune to maintain a lovely domed shape.

Landscape Use An attractive shrub with interesting foliage for along a pathway, in a large pocket or in a container.

Prostanthera rotundifolia
ROUND-LEAF MINT BUSH

Origin NSW, Vic., Tas.
Climate WT, M, CT
Shade None to filtered
FAST-GROWING
AROMATIC FOLIAGE
CONTAINER PLANT
Description A bushy, rounded shrub to 1.5 m with aromatic rounded leaves. The abundant lilac flowers almost cover the bush in spring.

P. rotundifolia var. *rosea* is a compact form with masses of rose pink spring flowers.

Cultivation A fairly hardy and adaptable shrub for most well-drained soils with adequate summer moisture. It will grow in full sun or dappled shade and is frost-

Prostanthera rotundifolia

resistant. Prune immediately after flowering to maintain an attractive shape.

Landscape Use A pretty, aromatic shrub for near a pathway as a single plant, or trimmed to form an attractive hedge. Both forms look good in a container.

Prostanthera scutellarioides

Origin NSW
Climate WT, M, CT, H
Shade Light to filtered
CONTAINER PLANT

Description An erect, open shrub to around 1 m high. It has linear, pointed leaves with curled-back margins, and produces small but numerous purple flowers during spring.

Cultivation This species likes good drainage and a light-textured soil. It will withstand dry periods but benefits from adequate water during summer. It is frost-resistant. Prune to keep compact.

Landscape Use A colourful small shrub for the garden foreground or in a container.

Prostanthera sieberi

Origin NSW
Climate WT, M
Shade Light to filtered
FAST-GROWING
AROMATIC FOLIAGE

Description A wispy open shrub to 2 m with toothed oval leaves which are strongly aromatic. The mauve or purple flowers are borne in profusion in spring.

Cultivation This species will tolerate considerable shade in a well-mulched soil with good drainage. It is frost-resistant. Prune to encourage compact growth.

Prostanthera sieberi

Prostanthera scutellarioides

Landscape Use A good shrub for background or under trees in the bush garden, where the scent from the leaves will fill the air on hot days or after rain.

Prostanthera striatiflora
STREAKED MINT BUSH

Origin Qld, NSW, SA, NT, WA
Climate WT, M, SA
Shade None to light
AROMATIC FOLIAGE
CONTAINER PLANT

Description An erect, round shrub to 1.5 m with sweetly aromatic oblong

Prostanthera striatiflora

leaves. The large creamy white flowers with purple striations occur in late spring and summer.

Cultivation This species, which occurs in dry inland areas, likes lots of sun and excellent drainage in a light soil. It will withstand dry conditions and is frost-resistant.

Landscape Use A very showy shrub for a dry position in the garden. It may be grown in a large container, where conditions may be controlled.

Prostanthera teretifolia

Origin NSW
Climate WT, M
Shade Light to filtered
AROMATIC FOLIAGE
ORNAMENTAL FOLIAGE

Description An upright, open shrub to 2 m with a silvery green appearance. The grey-green leaves are narrow, sticky and very aromatic. Showy sprays of violet flowers are produced during spring.

Cultivation This species will grow in most soils, provided the drainage is good and adequate water is supplied during hot dry weather. It is frost-resistant. Tip prune regularly and especially immediately after flowering to encourage a more compact shape.

Landscape Use The grey-green foliage combined with pretty violet flowers makes a lovely contrast plant for growing among other shrubs in the garden.

Prostanthera teretifolia

PULTENAEA

FABACEAE

A large Australian genus of about 130 species known as bush peas. They vary in height from prostrate ground covers to large woody shrubs and they provide a bright display of spring flowers in shades of mostly yellow, orange and red. There are a number of species in cultivation. Most are fast-growing and are hardy under a wide range of conditions provided the drainage is good. Propagate from half-ripened tip cuttings or from seed, which should first be soaked in hot water and left overnight.

Pultenaea cunninghamii

GREY BUSH PEA

Origin Qld, NSW, Vic.
Climate S, WT, M
Shade None to light
ORNAMENTAL FOLIAGE
CONTAINER PLANT

Description This variable species may be an erect plant up to 1 m or a low, spreading, prostrate plant to 2 m across. The prostrate form is the one most often sold at nurseries. It has attractive light green diamond-shaped leaves on slender spreading stems, and bears masses of small orange and red pea flowers during spring and summer.

Cultivation Grow in an open, well-drained position with a good supply of mulch. It is frost-resistant.

Landscape Use A most attractive, well-behaved ground cover for between shrubs, as a border, scrambling over rocks or in a large container.

Pultenaea cunninghamii

Pultenaea daphnoides

LARGE-LEAF BUSH PEA

Origin NSW, Vic., Tas., SA
Climate WT, M, CT
Shade Light to full
FAST-GROWING

Description An erect, slender shrub up to 2 m tall. It has dark green wedge-shaped leaves with a small point and produces terminal clusters of yellow and red pea flowers during spring.

Cultivation This species, which inhabits forests and woodlands, will tolerate fairly shady conditions. It likes plenty of moisture but needs good drainage and a well-mulched soil. It is moderately frost-resistant.

Landscape Use A common and widespread bushland species that will provide a bright display of colour among other shrubs or beneath tall trees.

Pultenaea daphnoides

Pultenaea villosa

BRONZE BUSH PEA

Origin Qld, NSW
Climate S, WT, M
Shade None to light
FAST-GROWING

Description A slightly weeping round shrub to 1.5 m with small soft green leaves that turn bronze during winter.

Pultenaea villosa

P. villosa 'Wallum Gold'

The bright yellow and red pea flowers are produced during spring.

P. villosa 'Wallum Gold' is a prostrate, spreading form to 1 m across with an almost year-round display of golden pea flowers.

Cultivation A hardy species for a well-drained, sunny position. It may be grown in a protected seaside garden and is frost-resistant.

Landscape Use The tall-growing form is a most attractive species for the garden or for a large part of the rockery. 'Wallum Gold' is an excellent ground cover for foliage, flowers and form.

RANUNCULUS

RANUNCULACEAE

Of this large and widespread genus of some 400 species, Australia has about 35 representatives, found in all States. Many occur in damp locations and make very pretty plants for a moist rockery pocket, around a pond or in a ferny part of the garden. Propagate from seed or by division.

Ranunculus graniticola

GRANITE BUTTERCUP

Origin NSW, Vic.
Climate WT, M, CT, H
Shade None to light
CONTAINER PLANT

Description A small perennial species which forms a rosette of divided leaves and bears yellow flowers during summer.

Cultivation This species occurs naturally in alpine regions and will tolerate very cold conditions, including frost and snow. It needs plenty of moisture and a sunny position.

Landscape Use Grow in a moist rockery pocket or in a container.

Ranunculus graniticola

Ranunculus lappaceus

AUSTRAL BUTTERCUP

Origin All States except WA
Climate S, WT, M, CT, H
Shade None to light
CONTAINER PLANT

Description A small perennial plant with deeply lobed leaves and with enamelled yellow flowers on long, slender stems.

Cultivation Grow in a moist, sunny position. It is frost-resistant. If conditions are right, it will self-sow readily.

Landscape Use A pretty, robust species for around ponds or in moist parts of the garden.

Ranunculus lappaceus

RESTIO

RESTIONACEAE

A genus of rush-like plants. The Tassel Cord-rush, R. tetraphyllus, *with decorative, soft, feathery stems, is commonly seen in florist shops and is used as a foliage contrast in arrangements. It makes an outstanding feature plant for damp sites near a water feature. Propagation is by division of clumps.*

Restio tetraphyllus

TASSEL CORD-RUSH

Origin All States except WA
Climate S, WT, M, CT
Shade None to full
ORNAMENTAL FOLIAGE
CONTAINER PLANT

Description This creeping plant to over 1 m high will form a bright green tussock to 50 cm across of soft, feathery, weeping foliage. It produces rusty brown flowers along the tips during spring.

Cultivation A hardy plant for most situations, including quite heavy shade. It will tolerate poorly drained soils and is frost-resistant.

Restio tetraphyllus

Landscape Use A most decorative plant for use beside a pond or in a moist rockery pocket. It may be grown in a container if ample water is supplied.

RHODANTHE

ASTERACEAE

This Australian genus of annual or short-lived perennial plants was previously included in Helipterum *which is an illegitimate name and is not available for use.* Rhodanthe *means 'pink flower' and refers to the often conspicuous white or pink soft papery bracts that surround the flowerheads. They are valued as cut flowers, both fresh and for use in dried arrangements. Flowers with delicate stems can be wired. This is easily done by pushing a length of florist's wire into the cut stem at the back of the flowerhead. The wire should not protrude at the front. As the flower dries its centre will grip the wire which will remain firmly in place. Propagation of annuals is by seed, which may be sown directly into the soil in late autumn in frost-free areas for an early spring display or up to spring in cooler areas.* R. anthemoides *can also be propagated by half-ripened tip cuttings.*

Rhodanthe anthemoides

(syn. *Helipterum anthemoides*)

CHAMOMILE SUNRAY

Origin Qld, NSW, Vic., Tas.
Climate WT, M, CT, H
Shade Light to filtered
CONTAINER PLANT
Description A small, rounded perennial to 30 cm high with a spread to 60 cm across. It has aromatic, narrow, grey-green leaves and bears masses of white papery flowerheads from late winter to spring. A number of attractive cultivars are available including the compact, long-flowering 'Paper Star' and 'Paper Cascade' with purplish pointed buds and a spectacular floral display in spring and summer.

Cultivation This species does best in a humus-rich well-drained soil, preferring morning sun and protection from strong afternoon sun in hot climates. It is frost-tolerant. Tip prune young plants to encourage branching. When flowering has finished, moderately cut back to promote fresh new growth.

Rhodanthe anthemoides

Landscape Use An attractive edging and rockery, pot and basket plant.

Rhodanthe chlorocephala *ssp.* rosea

(syn. *Helipterum roseum*)

Origin WA
Climate WT, M, SA
Shade None to light
CONTAINER PLANT
Description An annual that grows to 40 cm, with smooth, narrow leaves and erect stems of white, pink or deep pink papery flowers with yellow or black centres in spring.
Cultivation In frost-free areas sow seed directly into the soil from May to July. It appreciates a well-prepared soil and plenty of sunlight.
Landscape Use A very showy annual which provides plenty of flowers for display and indoors. It looks best when mass-planted, either as a bedding annual, as a border or in the bush garden where it may be left to set seed and produce further displays.

Rhodanthe chlorocephala

Rhodanthe manglesii

(syn. *Helipterum manglesii*)
MANGLES' EVERLASTING; PINK SUNRAY

Origin WA
Climate WT, M, SA
Shade None to light
CONTAINER PLANT
Description An annual to 40 cm high with small round leaves and slender branching stems. Pendulous silvery buds open to pink or white papery flowerheads often with a darker inner ring of colour. Flowers appear from late winter to late spring.
Cultivation Sow seed direct in a well-drained position in full sun or part shade. Water moderately and feed lightly when the buds first appear. When young protect from slugs and snails.
Landscape Use This reliable and showy annual is an ideal choice for mass planting and looks good in rockery, cottage and meadow gardens. The flowers dry well if picked when the buds are just beginning to open and hung upside down to dry in small bunches.

Rhodanthe manglesii

RHODODENDRON

ERICACEAE

A large genus of over 500 species of which only one occurs in Australia. Rhododendron lochae *with its beautiful bright red flowers is found only at altitudes above 1,000 m in far northern Queensland. It is available from a few specialist nurseries and is easily cultivated in mild climates if protected from wind and direct sunlight. Propagation is from half-ripened tip cuttings or seed.*

Rhododendron lochae

AUSTRALIAN RHODODENDRON

Origin Qld
Climate S, WT, M
Shade Filtered to full
CONTAINER PLANT
RAINFOREST PLANT
Description A small, spreading shrub to around 1 m high and a similar width with glossy leaves. The waxy, bright red tubular flowers hang in terminal clusters. These appear mainly in spring and summer.
Cultivation Grow in a cool, shaded part of the garden in a well-mulched soil during summer. It is moderately frost tolerant. The species has been successfully grown as a container plant in an orchid mixture with good drainage.
Landscape Use For a shady part of the garden or in a container which may be brought indoors to show off its superb flowers.

Rhododendron lochae

RICINOCARPOS

EUPHORBIACEAE

A small genus of about 15 species native to Australia. They are attractive shrubs with showy, waxy white or pink star flowers. Only one species, R. pinifolius, *has proved reliable in cultivation and it is available from some native plant nurseries. Propagation is from half-ripened tip cuttings.*

Ricinocarpos bowmanii

PINK WEDDING BUSH

Origin Qld, NSW
Climate WT, M, SA
Shade None to light
CONTAINER PLANT

Description An erect, bushy shrub to around 1 m high. It has linear, stem-clasping leaves and produces abundant star-like flowers during spring.

Cultivation This very pretty species is not often seen in cultivation, and is available only sometimes from a few specialist nurseries. It likes a light-textured soil with very good drainage and moderately frost-resistant.

Landscape Use A lovely plant for garden foreground, rockery pocket or container.

Ricinocarpos bowmanii

Ricinocarpos pinifolius

WEDDING BUSH

Origin Qld, NSW, Vic., Tas.
Climate S, WT, M, CT, SA
Shade None to filtered
FAST-GROWING
FRAGRANT

Description A well-branched, erect shrub up to 2 m with linear dark green leaves. The dainty white star flowers are lightly perfumed and are produced in profusion during spring.

Cultivation Grow in a light, sandy soil with good drainage. It may be used in seaside gardens with a little protection and is frost-resistant.

Landscape Use A very pretty plant when in flower, for use among other shrubs.

Ricinocarpos pinifolius

RULINGIA

STERCULIACEAE

A small genus which extends beyond Australia, with approximately 20 endemic species. They range in size from low-growing prostrate shrubs to quite tall bushes and bear attractive, but small, star-shaped flowers. Rulingia hermanniifolia *has become a popular ground cover and rockery plant. Propagation is from half-ripened tip cuttings.*

Rulingia dasyphylla

(syn. *R. pannosa*)

KERRAWANG

Origin Qld, NSW, Vic.
Climate S, WT, M
Shade None to light
FAST-GROWING
CONTAINER PLANT

Description A spreading, woody shrub up to 3 m high and 3 m across, with dull green, narrow leaves. The pinkish white flowers in spreading clusters are produced during spring.

Cultivation An adaptable species for most well-drained soils and most locations. It is frost-resistant. Prune to shape.

Landscape Use With pruning, this species may be shaped to form an attractive hedge or screen. It may also be grown in a large container.

Rulingia dasyphylla

Rulingia hermanniifolia

WRINKLED KERRAWANG

Origin NSW
Climate WT, M, SA
Shade None to light
CONTAINER PLANT

Description A sprawling prostrate shrub up to 2 m across with attractive, dark green, wrinkled leaves. It bears masses of small pink and white star flowers in spring, followed by deep red, bristly fruits.

Cultivation An adaptable species for most well-drained soils. Although it will grow in partial shade, growth is more compact in full sun. It may be used in protected coastal gardens and is frost-resistant.

Rulingia hermanniifolia

Landscape Use An attractive shrub for use as a ground cover or edging plant, in a rockery or in a container.

SARCOCHILUS

ORCHIDACEAE

A genus of some 12 endemic species of mostly epiphytic orchids which are confined to rainforests and moist gullies of eastern Australia. The small flowers which grow in racemes are either spreading or bell-shaped; some are very beautiful and some have a delightful perfume. Some species will grow in pots and others may be mounted on tree fern slabs, cork or tree limbs with persistent bark. Plants will grow in areas where the summer is hot, provided they are given cool, shaded conditions. In areas with a temperate climate, they are easily grown in bush houses or shadehouses. They will not tolerate excessive heat or frost and prefer to be kept well shaded and moist at all times. Propagation is from seed or by division.

Sarcochilus falcatus

ORANGE BLOSSOM ORCHID

Origin Qld, NSW, Vic.
Climate T, S, WT, M
Shade Filtered to full
FRAGRANT
RAINFOREST PLANT

Description This is the species with the widest distribution in Australia and it is quite variable, ranging in size from small, compact plants to large clumps. It has fleshy pale green leaves and sprays of two to ten flowers in shades of white or cream, with a striped labellum. These appear in spring and in some forms have a beautiful perfume resembling that of orange blossoms.

Cultivation This species is best mounted on a host and may be grown outside in the garden if mild, shaded conditions are provided. It requires a moist, humid atmosphere and resents extreme heat and cold.

Landscape Use An epiphytic orchid for a moist, shady part of the garden or in a bush house or shadehouse.

Sarcochilus falcatus

SCAEVOLA

GOODENIACEAE

A genus of approximately 100 species of which about 80 are found in Australia. They are mostly spreading herbs or small shrubs. A number are in cultivation and their pretty, fan-shaped flowers in white and shades of mauve or blue make them ideal edging and rockery plants. Propagation is from half-ripened tip cuttings.

Scaevola aemula

FAIRY FAN FLOWER

Origin NSW, Vic., Tas., SA, WA
Climate S, WT, M, CT, SA
Shade None to light
CONTAINER PLANT

Description This widespread and variable species may be spreading to 1 m across or upright to 50 cm. It has bright green leaves with toothed margins and produces prolific mauve-blue, fan-shaped flowers over long periods in spring and summer.

'Purple Fanfare' is a very good selected form of *S. aemula*. It spreads to 2 m across and bears large purple flowers for most of the year.

Cultivation Grow in a well-drained soil with plenty of moisture during hot, dry weather. It is frost-resistant and may be used in coastal gardens with some protection. Take cut flowers for the house or prune back after flowering to maintain vigour and shape.

Landscape Use A very attractive border plant that will cascade over edging. It is

Scaevola aemula

an excellent rockery, basket and container plant.

Scaevola albida

Origin Qld, NSW, Vic., SA
Climate S, WT, M, CT
Shade None to filtered
CONTAINER PLANT
Description A dense, suckering plant with a spread up to 1 m. It has bright green, fleshy leaves and bears white or pale lilac fan-shaped flowers during spring and summer.

'Mauve Clusters' to 1 m across is a compact ground covering form of *S. albida*. It bears masses of mauve flowers for most of the year.

Cultivation This species does best in a well-drained position with adequate moisture. It may be grown in protected coastal gardens and is frost-resistant. Prune untidy branches.

Landscape Use A profusely flowering plant which will happily trail and spread over steps, sleepers, rocks, pots and baskets.

Scaevola albida

Scaevola calendulacea
DUNE FAN FLOWER

Origin All States except WA
Climate T, S, WT, M
Shade None to filtered
BIRD-ATTRACTING
SALT-TOLERANT
Description This soft, trailing cover plant spreads to 2 m across. It has bright green, fleshy leaves and produces blue-mauve fan flowers in small, erect heads during spring and summer. These are followed by attractive purple berries which are relished by parrots.

Scaevola calendulacea

Cultivation This plant is found on dunes close to the sea and is an excellent sand binder. It will withstand salt spray and exposure and prefers a light soil. It is frost-tender.

Landscape Use An ideal plant for covering banks in seaside gardens.

Scaevola hookeri
CREEPING FAN FLOWER

Origin NSW, Vic., Tas.
Climate WT, M, CT, H
Shade None to filtered
CONTAINER PLANT
Description A prostrate, creeping plant with a spread to 1 m. It has succulent, irregularly toothed leaves and bears masses of dainty white to pale mauve fan flowers from late spring through summer.

Scaevola hookeri

Cultivation Occurring naturally in subalpine areas, it is hardy to extreme cold and snow. It prefers a moist situation in full sun or partial shade.

Landscape Use An attractive creeping plant for a cool, moist rockery or garden foreground.

Scaevola ramosissima
HAIRY FAN FLOWER

Origin Qld, NSW, Vic.
Climate S, WT, M, CT
Shade None to filtered
CONTAINER PLANT
Description A low-growing perennial with wiry branches to 60 cm high and 1 m across. The linear leaves are small, and large purple fan flowers are produced in spring and summer.

Cultivation Grow in a well-drained, sandy soil in full sun or part shade. It is frost-resistant. Lightly trim to shape into compact bush.

Landscape Use A small, showy plant for a rockery or container. As it will tolerate dappled shade it may be used as a foreground understorey plant.

Scaevola ramosissima

Scaevola striata
ROYAL ROBE

Origin WA
Climate WT, M
Shade None to light
CONTAINER PLANT
Description A hirsute, prostrate plant which spreads by suckering to 1 m across. The coarsely toothed leaves are hairy. Very bright blue-purple flowers are produced at branch ends during spring and summer.

Scaevola striata

Cultivation Grow in a light to medium soil with good drainage. Once established, it will withstand periods of dryness, but it is slightly frost-tender.

Landscape Use A pretty, trailing plant for a rockery, border or container.

SCHEFFLERA

ARALIACEAE

This large genus of over 200 species has two or three Australian species found mainly in tropical rainforests, including the well-known Umbrella Tree, S. actinophylla. *This common street and garden tree in Queensland and New South Wales is known throughout the world as a hardy indoor pot specimen, as it can survive quite harsh conditions for a long time. Plants are usually pest-free, but may sometimes be attacked by scale, which can be controlled by white oil spray. Propagation is from fresh seed or from cuttings of side shoots.*

Schefflera actinophylla

(syn. *Brassaia actinophylla*)

UMBRELLA TREE

Origin Qld
Climate T, S, WT, M
Shade None to full

FAST-GROWING
BIRD-ATTRACTING
ORNAMENTAL FOLIAGE
CONTAINER PLANT
RAINFOREST PLANT

Description This well-known tree will reach up to 15 m in its rainforest habitat,

Schefflera actinophylla

but is usually no more than 10 m high in cultivation. It has large compound leaves which resemble an umbrella, and honey-rich red flower spikes which radiate from the top of the tree. These attract a variety of nectar-feeding birds.

Cultivation In warmer areas, this species will grow well in most well-drained soils if given plenty of water during its early growth. In cool areas it needs protection from frost. As a container plant, it is suitable for indoors. It will withstand hard pruning.

Landscape Use A handsome foliage tree for gardens, streets or parks to provide shade and a tropical touch. Grow as a container plant for verandas, patios, around pools, foyers and indoors.

SCLERANTHUS

CARYOPHYLLACEAE

A small genus of mostly cushion plants of which five species are found in Australia. Scleranthus biflorus *is widely distributed in eastern Australia and has been cultivated for a number of years as a mossy, carpeting plant in rockery landscaping. Propagation is by division.*

Scleranthus biflorus

CANBERRA GRASS; KNAWEL

Origin Qld, NSW, Vic., Tas.
Climate S, WT, M, CT, H
Shade None to light

CONTAINER PLANT

Description A bright green cushion-like plant with a spread of up to 40 cm diameter. It has tiny, narrow leaves

Scleranthus biflorus

crowded on spreading stems, and minute green flowers appearing in late spring.

S. uniflorus is very similar, but produces pretty white flowers in summer.

Cultivation Grow in a sunny but moist position. It is best to plant it in a weed-free area, as weeds will grow through the carpet and spoil the appearance. It is frost-resistant and forms from alpine regions are snow-tolerant.

Landscape Use A decorative, moss-like plant for use as a container, border, ground cover or rockery subject where it will spread over and around rocks in a most attractive way.

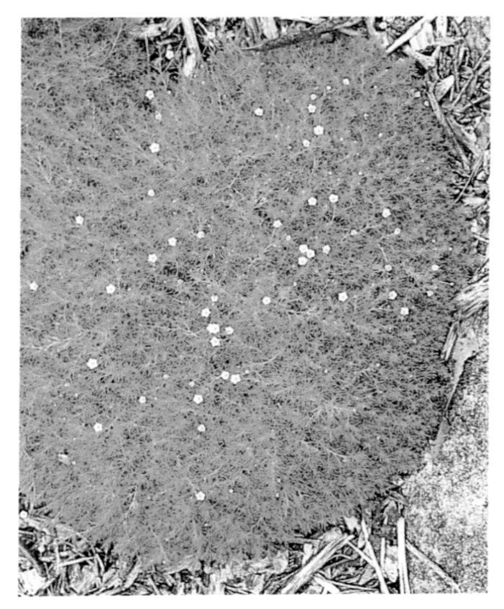

S. uniflorus

SOLLYA

PITTOSPORACEAE

This is a small genus of three species of shrubs or climbers endemic to Western Australia. The Bluebell Creeper, S. heterophylla, *is popular in cultivation and may be used as a twining climber or be allowed to form a bushy shrub. Propagation is either from seed or from half-ripened tip cuttings taken in the warmer months.*

Sollya heterophylla

(syn. *S. fusiformis*)

BLUEBELL CREEPER

Origin WA
Climate WT, M, CT, SA
Shade None to filtered
FAST-GROWING
CONTAINER PLANT

Description A rather vigorous climber or shrub with oval, pointed leaves, and dainty, hanging bluebell flowers in spring and summer. There are also white and pink flowered forms. All are followed by sprays of berries which turn blue as they ripen.

Cultivation An adaptable and hardy plant which will tolerate a wide range of garden conditions in most well-drained soils. It is frost-resistant.

Landscape Use This species may be trained to climb fences and trellises or be allowed to cascade down slopes or cascade from hanging baskets or large containers. It can be pruned to a compact bush and used as a hedge or screen.

Sollya heterophylla

SOWERBAEA

ANTHERICACEAE

An Australian genus of five species of small, grass-like herbs. They occur in moist situations and their clusters of dainty flowers make them attractive plants for a damp rockery pocket or near a pond. Propagation is from seed or by division of clumps.

Sowerbaea juncea

VANILLA LILY

Origin Qld, NSW, Vic., Tas.
Climate S, WT, M, CT
Shade None to light
FRAGRANT
CONTAINER PLANT

Description A small tufted plant with grey-green cylindrical leaves to 40 cm high. The pink or lilac, sweetly scented flowers are produced in clustered heads at the ends of long, slender stalks during spring.

Cultivation Grow in a sunny position in a moist but well-drained soil. It is frost-resistant.

Landscape Use Grow in groups in the rockery, close to a water feature or grow as a container plant with a plentiful supply of water.

Sowerbaea juncea

SPRENGELIA

EPACRIDACEAE

A small genus of four species of heath-like shrubs which occur mostly in moist, swampy places in the eastern States. Sprengelia incarnata *is a particularly attractive species and its flowers last well when cut for indoors. Propagation is from ripe seed or from half-ripened tip cuttings taken in autumn which may be slow to strike.*

Sprengelia incarnata

PINK SWAMP HEATH

Origin NSW, Vic., Tas., SA
Climate WT, M, CT
Shade None to filtered
CONTAINER PLANT

Description A widespread and variable species to 1 m or more. It has rigid, pointed, stem-clasping leaves and produces attractive star-shaped pink

Sprengelia incarnata

flowers grouped towards branch ends in spring and summer.

Cultivation Grow in a moist but well-drained situation with plenty of compost added to the soil. It is frost-resistant. Tip prune regularly to promote compact growth.

Landscape Use An ornamental plant for poolsides or near ponds. It may be grown in a container if adequate moisture is supplied.

SPYRIDIUM

RHAMNACEAE

This Australian genus of about 30 species consists of prostrate to medium-sized shrubs with downy grey leaves and silvery bracts surrounding the small flowers. A few species are in cultivation for the ornamental colour contrast of the foliage and flowers. Propagation is from half-ripened tip cuttings.

Spyridium parvifolium

AUSTRALIAN DUSTY MILLER

Origin NSW, Vic., Tas., SA
Climate WT, M, CT
Shade None to filtered
ORNAMENTAL FOLIAGE
CONTAINER PLANT
Description An upright, rounded shrub which reaches up to 3 m, but usually less. The grey-green, rounded leaves have a silky undersurface and the white flowers produced in spring and early summer are surrounded by whitish floral leaves.

S. parvifolium 'Australflora Nimbus' is a prostrate form with a spread to 1 m.

Cultivation An adaptable shrub for most well-drained soils and positions. It will tolerate fairly dry conditions and the prostrate form is suited to seaside gardens. It is frost-resistant. Trim to shape.

Landscape Use A beautiful shrub for its grey foliage effect among other shrubs or as a feature. The prostrate form is a pretty trailer for the rockery or container.

Spyridium parvifolium

STENOCARPUS

PROTEACEAE

This genus of some 25 species extends beyond Australia to Malaysia, Indonesia and New Caledonia. There are about eight native species, of which the Firewheel Tree, S. sinuatus, *is the most ornamental and most widely cultivated species. Any signs of scale insect may be removed by an application of white oil. Propagation is from fresh seeds which are released when ripe. Seeds germinate quite well but growth in the young stages is generally slow.*

Stenocarpus sinuatus

FIREWHEEL TREE

Origin Qld, NSW
Climate T, S, WT, M
Shade None to filtered
SPECIMEN PLANT
BIRD-ATTRACTING
ORNAMENTAL FOLIAGE
CONTAINER PLANT
RAINFOREST PLANT
Description A slow-growing tree which may reach 10 m or more in cultivation. It has a dense crown of variable, wavy dark green foliage which may be deeply lobed or entire. The very showy, wheel-shaped orange or red flowers are borne in clusters

Stenocarpus sinuatus

during summer and into autumn, attracting a variety of honeyeaters.

Cultivation This species prefers a deep, rich, moist soil and a warm, protected position. In southern areas it is frost-tender when young.

Landscape Use A very attractive ornamental tree as a specimen for a small or large garden. It is a successful street tree and in its early years may be grown in a container as an indoor or courtyard plant.

STICHERUS

GLEICHENIACEAE

A genus of 100 species of ferns with three representatives in Australia. They are beautiful terrestrial ferns with a creeping underground rhizome and numerous fronds branched in an umbrella-like manner. They are ideal for a moist spot in the garden or for growing in a large container with room to spread. Propagation is from spores or by taking a division of rhizome containing a few small fronds.

Sticherus flabellatus

UMBRELLA FERN

Origin Qld, NSW, Vic.
Climate T, S, WT, M
Shade Light to filtered

ORNAMENTAL FOLIAGE
CONTAINER PLANT

Description A tall, erect fern with fronds that grow up to 1.5 m. The fronds grow from an underground rhizome and are branched at the top like the frame of an umbrella.

Cultivation This slow-growing fern prefers a semishaded garden situation where ample moisture is present. When grown in a container it must have good drainage, but never be allowed to dry out.

Landscape Use A beautiful plant for the understorey or beside a pond. If space is left around this fern it will slowly form a colony.

STYPANDRA

PHORMIACEAE

A small endemic genus of six species of perennial herbs represented in all States. They are attractive clump-forming plants with mostly blue flowers on slender

Sticherus flabellatus

stems in loose terminal clusters. Propagation is from seed or by division.

Stypandra glauca
NODDING BLUE LILY

Origin Qld, NSW, Vic., SA, WA
Climate S, WT, M, SA
Shade Light to filtered
CONTAINER PLANT
Description A tall-growing, robust perennial plant up to 1 m. It has grass-like foliage and produces bunches of stamens near branch ends during spring.

Cultivation Grow in a well-drained, lightly shaded position. Once established, it will tolerate dry periods and is frost-resistant.

Landscape Use An ornamental plant for the garden, rockery or container.

Stypandra glauca

SWAINSONA
FABACEAE

A genus of 85 species of mostly perennial plants confined to Australia except for one endemic New Zealand species. The genus has recently been revised (1993) and now includes the celebrated Sturt's Desert Pea, which was previously known as Clianthus formosus. *It is South Australia's official floral emblem. A small number of species are available at specialist nurseries and make desirable garden plants, as they are quick growing, provide a long flowering season and are able to withstand periods of dryness. Several species of* Swainsona *have a reputation for being poisonous to cattle and sheep. Propagation is from seed, which require soaking in warm water until they swell, and are then planted in the position in which they are to grow. Sowing of seed is best done in the spring months.*

Swainsona formosa

Swainsona formosa
(syn. *Clianthus formosus*)
STURT'S DESERT PEA

Origin Qld, NSW, SA, WA, NT
Climate WT, M, SA
Shade None to light
CONTAINER PLANT

Description A prostrate creeping annual or perennial with woolly greyish pinnate leaves and spectacular heads of large, shiny, red pea-shaped flowers with prominent bosses, or bumps, in the middle, usually black but sometimes red and rarely white.

Cultivation Because this plant resents root disturbance, it is best to buy seeds and sow in spring in the position in which it is to grow. It has an exceptionally long tap root and if it is to be grown in a container, deep pots should be used. It demands excellent drainage and does best in sandy soil in full sun. Once the plant is established, watering should be kept to a minimum. In areas with high rainfall, it is best under eaves or in a position where water can be controlled. It is frost-tender.

Landscape Use A magnificent cascading plant for a deep rockery pocket, raised garden bed or container.

S. formosa

Swainsona galegifolia
SMOOTH DARLING PEA

Origin Qld, NSW, SA
Climate WT, M, SA
Shade None to light
DROUGHT-RESISTANT
CONTAINER PLANT

Description A soft perennial plant to 1 m with light green, pinnate leaves, and numerous spikes of white, pink, mauve or dark red pea flowers during spring and summer.

Swainsona galegifolia

Cultivation Grow in a well-drained, dry position. It will tolerate dry conditions and frost. Prune back each winter.

Landscape Use A most attractive plant for among other shrubs, in the rockery or in a large tub.

Swainsona greyana
HAIRY DARLING PEA

Origin Qld, NSW, Vic., SA
Climate WT, M, SA
Shade None to light
DROUGHT-RESISTANT
CONTAINER PLANT

Description A soft perennial to 1 m with hairy, grey-green pinnate leaves. The pea flowers, which may be white, mauve or vivid pink, appear in long sprays during spring. These large flowers are suitable for cutting.

Cultivation A hardy plant for a well-drained dry position. It will tolerate drought and frost. Prune back each winter.

Landscape Use A free-flowering and attractive-foliaged plant for the foreground in the garden, or a larger part of the rockery.

SYNCARPIA
MYRTACEAE

A small genus of trees closely related to Eucalyptus *with a few very attractive species found in Australia. The strong,*

Swainsona greyana

durable timber is widely used in wharf construction and is highly resistant to decay, marine borers and fire. Species have been planted for timber as well as specimen, shade and shelter trees in streets and parks. They have very few pests and diseases, but the hairy lumps often found under the leaves of the Turpentine are caused by wasp galls. The tree is not usually seriously affected and control is not really necessary. Propagation is from ripened seed, which germinates readily.

Syncarpia glomulifera

TURPENTINE

Origin Qld, NSW
Climate T, S, WT, M
Shade None to filtered

FAST-GROWING
SPECIMEN PLANT
BIRD-ATTRACTING

Description A handsome, dense-foliaged, straight tree to around 15 m in cultivation. It has a thick fibrous bark and has dark green leaves grouped in fours, covered with fine hairs beneath and hairy all over when young. The lovely white fluffy blossoms in spring and summer are followed by fused, woody capsules.

Cultivation Grow in a rich, well-drained soil with a plentiful supply of water. It may be used in protected coastal gardens and is moderately frost-tolerant. It will withstand lopping and trimming and may be shaped to form a short, dense tree.

Landscape Use An attractive specimen and shade tree for large gardens, streets or parks. It makes an excellent wind and shelter break.

Syncarpia glomulifera

SYZYGIUM

MYRTACEAE

A cosmopolitan genus of shrubs and trees containing many species which were formerly included in the larger genus Eugenia. *About 50 species occur in Australia and most are found in eastern rainforests, thriving in rich conditions with plenty of moisture. They are beautiful, mostly medium-sized trees with neat glossy foliage, having colourful new growth and pretty fluffy flowers followed by ornamental fruits which attract a variety of birds. Many nurseries sell their plants under the old generic name of* Eugenia. *Plants are subject to scale attack, on leaves and stems, which can be controlled with white oil. Propagation is from fresh seed which may be slow to germinate.*

Syzygium australe

(syn. *Eugenia australis*)

SCRUB CHERRY

Origin Qld, NSW
Climate T, S, WT
Shade None to light

SPECIMEN PLANT
BIRD-ATTRACTING
ORNAMENTAL FOLIAGE
CONTAINER PLANT
RAINFOREST PLANT

Description A small to medium-sized tree to around 10 m in cultivation. It has a dense crown of bright green, glossy leaves with attractive bronze new growth. It bears clusters of small white flowers in spring followed by pink to dark red, edible oval fruit.

Cultivation Grow in a well-drained position with a good supply of moisture and with humus added to the soil. It is moderately frost-resistant.

Landscape Use An attractive specimen tree for use as a feature, for shade or as a screen. When young, it may be grown in a container.

Syzygium australe

Syzygium leuhmannii

(syn. *Eugenia leuhmannii*)

RIBERRY; CHERRY SATINASH

Origin Qld, NSW
Climate T, S, WT, M
Shade None to filtered

SPECIMEN PLANT
BIRD-ATTRACTING
ORNAMENTAL FOLIAGE
CONTAINER PLANT
RAINFOREST PLANT

Description A bushy medium-sized tree to no more than 10 m in cultivation. It has glossy pointed ovate leaves. Flushes of new leaves are bright pink and appear several times a year. Clusters of small white flowers in late spring and summer

Syzygium leuhmannii

S. leuhmannii (foliage)

are followed by masses of small pinkish-red fruit.

Cultivation This popular and adaptable species does well in humus-enriched, well-drained soils with a good supply of moisture. It is moderately frost tolerant.

Landscape Use Plants are bushy when quite young and may be pruned to a hedge or screen. It makes a fine specimen tree in the garden or may be contained in a tub for several years. This species also makes a beautiful indoor plant for a well-lit situation.

Syzygium paniculatum

(syn. *Eugenia paniculatum*)

MAGENTA CHERRY

Origin NSW
Climate S, WT
Shade None to filtered

SPECIMEN PLANT
BIRD-ATTRACTING
ORNAMENTAL FOLIAGE
CONTAINER PLANT
RAINFOREST PLANT

Description A small tree to 8 m with a dense crown of aromatic glossy leaves, and dark red new growth. The clusters of fluffy white flowers in summer are followed by rounded magenta fruits, which are a showy feature in autumn. A small compact form to 3 m is also in cultivation.

Cultivation Grow in a moist, well-drained position in a humus-enriched soil. It may be grown in protected coastal areas, but will tolerate only light to moderate frosts.

Landscape Use A beautiful flowering and fruiting tree to use as a feature or a screen. As it is slow-growing, it may be grown in a container for a courtyard or brought indoors.

Syzygium paniculatum

Syzygium wilsonii

(syn. *Eugenia wilsonii*)

POWDER PUFF LILLY PILLY

Origin Qld
Climate T, S, WT
Shade Filtered to full

SPECIMEN PLANT
BIRD-ATTRACTING
ORNAMENTAL FOLIAGE
CONTAINER PLANT
RAINFOREST PLANT

Description A very beautiful shrub which grows to around 3 m, with weeping branches of shiny foliage and attractive crimson young growth. Large, pendent red pompom flowers appear in spring and early summer. These are followed by bunches of white fruit.

Syzygium wilsonii

Cultivation Grow in a rich soil with ample moisture. It prefers semishade in a protected position and is frost-tender.

Landscape Use This outstanding shrub is ideal for planting under trees. It is also suitable for a large container and may be brought indoors.

TECOMANTHE

BIGNONIACEAE

A genus of climbers found beyond Australia with one species extending to Queensland. Tecomanthe hillii, *a beautiful twining plant, is uncommon in the field and well worth a place in the garden. Propagation is from seed or half-ripened tip cuttings.*

Tecomanthe hillii

(syn. *Tecoma hillii*)

PINK TRUMPET VINE; FRASER ISLAND CREEPER

Origin Qld
Climate T, S, WT
Shade Filtered to full

FAST-GROWING
ORNAMENTAL FOLIAGE
RAINFOREST PLANT

Description A vigorous twining plant with attractive glossy, dark green leaves. The large deep pink bell flowers with a

Tecomanthe hillii

paler throat are produced in clusters during spring.

Cultivation This species prefers semishade and rich, moist soil. It needs good drainage and shelter from hot winds and frost.

Landscape Use An outstanding climber for fences, pergolas or trellises. It is spectacular when in flower and the lush foliage looks attractive at all times.

TELOPEA

PROTEACEAE

There are four endemic species of Telopea *confined to south-eastern Australia. The name* Telopea *is derived from the Greek* telopos, *meaning 'seen from afar', because the crimson heads of flowers stand out in the distance. The Aboriginal name 'waratah' referred to the spectacular New South Wales Waratah,* Telopea speciosissima, *but is now the accepted vernacular name of all species.* T. speciosissima *is the floral emblem of New South Wales and is one of the most familiar of native plants. It has been used widely in applied art, particularly as a motif in woodcarving, textile, ceramic and glassware design. It has attracted artists from the earliest days of settlement to current times and is grown commercially for high quality cut flowers. All species are highly ornamental and make beautiful garden plants. Propagation is from seed in early spring.*

Telopea mongaensis

BRAIDWOOD WARATAH

Origin NSW
Climate WT, M, CT, H
Shade None to full

SPECIMEN PLANT
BIRD-ATTRACTING
CONTAINER PLANT

Description An open, upright shrub which grows from 1.5 m to 3 m high. The thick, leathery leaves are up to 15 cm long and fresh growth is an attractive yellow-green. The large, open crimson flowerheads are produced in terminal clusters from late October to summer.

Cultivation A hardy shrub for a well-mulched soil with good drainage. It will grow in quite heavy shade or in full sun if a cool root area and adequate water are provided. It is frost-hardy and is suitable for cultivation in cool climates. Although pruning is not usually necessary, the cutting of flowers will keep the shrub bushy.

Landscape Use A beautiful shrub for the garden or in a large container.

Telopea mongaensis

Telopea speciosissima

NEW SOUTH WALES WARATAH

Origin NSW
Climate WT, M, CT, H
Shade None to light

SPECIMEN PLANT
BIRD-ATTRACTING

Description A slender, erect shrub to 3 m tall, with toothed or lobed leathery leaves. The large crimson flowerheads consist of many small flowers densely

Telopea speciosissima

Telopea 'Wirrimbirra White'

packed in a globular arrangement and surrounded by a collar of large red bracts. They are produced during spring and provide large quantities of nectar for a variety of honeyeaters. This waratah is a magnificent cut flower and is cultivated for the florist trade.

'Wirrimbirra White' is the cultivar name given to the rare white-flowered form of *Telopea speciosissima*. It is occasionally available from specialist growers.

Cultivation Grow in a deep, extremely well drained soil with adequate water provided until the plant is established. A mulch of leaf mould or compost will keep the roots cool in summer. This species is moderately frost-resistant. The beautiful flowers can be cut with long stems or left on the plant and pruned back as soon as they are finished. This is essential for maintaining vigour and ensuring good flowering in the following season.

Landscape Use A magnificent feature plant.

TEMPLETONIA

FABACEAE

A small endemic genus comprising eight species of attractive pea-flowered shrubs, of which the ornamental T. retusa *has been in cultivation for a number of years. Propagation is from seed, which needs to be covered with boiling water and left to stand 24 hours.*

Templetonia retusa

COCKIES TONGUES

Origin SA, WA
Climate WT, M, CT, SA
Shade None to filtered
BIRD-ATTRACTING
SALT-TOLERANT

Description A rounded, spreading shrub which grows from 1.5 to 2.5 m high, with grey-green, leathery foliage. The abundant, large scarlet pea flowers are produced during winter and early spring. There is also a yellow flower form.

Cultivation This species prefers a sunny, well-drained position in the garden. It will grow in sandy soil and is very lime-tolerant. It may be grown in exposed seaside gardens and will withstand periods of dryness and frost.

Landscape Use A showy winter-flowering shrub for the garden or to use as a screen or low windbreak in dry or coastal areas.

Templetonia retusa

TETRATHECA

TREMANDRACEAE

A genus of around 40 species of tiny shrubs with abundant white, pink or purple pendent flowers. Several are cultivated and are popular as edging, rockery or container subjects. They are very pretty wildflowers of the bush and as they are mostly undershrubs, they enjoy dappled shade and a cool root run in the garden. Propagation is from fresh seed which germinates easily in moist, sharp sand. Propagation is also from half-ripened tip cuttings.

Tetratheca ciliata

Tetratheca ciliata

PINK BELLS

Origin Vic., Tas., SA
Climate WT, M, CT
Shade Light to filtered
CONTAINER PLANT
Description A small, erect shrub to 30 cm with soft hairy leaves in whorls. The bright pink, pendent bell flowers are produced in late winter and during spring. A white-flowered form is also available.

Cultivation Grow in a well-drained soil in a partially shaded position. It is frost-resistant.

Landscape Use A very pretty rockery or border plant that looks most effective when grouped. It is also a good container plant.

Tetratheca thymifolia

Origin Qld, NSW, Vic.
Climate S, WT, M
Shade Light to filtered
CONTAINER PLANT
Description A compact, rounded shrub to around 60 cm with erect, hairy stems and rounded, hairy leaves in whorls around the stem. Masses of dainty bell flowers are produced from late winter to early summer. A white-flowered form is also available.

Cultivation This species enjoys a partially shaded position with good drainage. It is frost-resistant.

Landscape Use Grow in groups in a rockery or border. It is also a good container plant.

T. ciliata (white-flowered form)

Tetratheca thymifolia

T. thymifolia (white-flowered form)

THOMASIA

STERCULIACEAE

This genus of 31 species is endemic to Australia and all but one are restricted to Western Australia. They are beautiful small shrubs with rough or felty leaves and with showy, pendent white, pink or purple papery flowers, often produced in profusion for long periods. They are hardy and long-lived in cultivation. Propagation is from half-ripened tip cuttings.

Thomasia macrocarpa

LARGE-FRUITED THOMASIA

Origin WA
Climate WT, M, CT, SA
Shade None to filtered
CONTAINER PLANT

Description A small, spreading shrub to around 1 m high with a similar width. It has heart-shaped, furry leaves with lobed or toothed margins and produces abundant mauve pendulous flowers during spring. Cut sprays of foliage and flowers are very pretty for indoor arrangements.

Cultivation Grow in a light-textured, well-drained soil. It will tolerate light frost. Prune or take flowers for indoors to keep the bush compact.

Landscape Use A very attractive small shrub for the garden foreground, rockery or container.

Thomasia macrocarpa

Thomasia petalocalyx

PAPER FLOWER

Origin Vic., SA, WA
Climate WT, M, SA
Shade None to filtered
SALT-TOLERANT
CONTAINER PLANT

Description A small, spreading shrub to 1 m with hairy, oblong leaves with wavy edges. The pinkish mauve flowers hang in loose clusters from late winter through spring.

Cultivation A hardy species for most well-drained soils and position. It is extremely salt-tolerant and may be used in exposed coastal gardens. It is frost-resistant. Prune lightly after flowering to shape.

Landscape Use Not a spectacular species, but excellent for seaside gardens. It may also be grown in a container.

Thomasia pygmaea

Origin WA
Climate WT, M
Shade None to filtered
CONTAINER PLANT

Description A small, rounded shrub to 60 cm high. It has small, rounded leaves and masses of papery, nodding flowers which are pinkish mauve with small red dots. These are produced in spring and early summer and when cut they make pretty, long-lasting posies.

Cultivation Grow in a light-textured soil with good drainage. It will accept some shade and is moderately frost-tolerant.

Landscape Use A very attractive small shrub for the garden edge, rockery or container.

Thomasia pygmaea

Thomasia petalocalyx

THRYPTOMENE
MYRTACEAE

An Australian genus of approximately 35 species of shrubs with representatives in all States. They are most ornamental shrubs with arched branches and minute aromatic leaves; they are covered with masses of small white or pink flowers in winter and spring. They make perfect long-lasting cut flowers. Propagation is from half-ripened tip cuttings taken in autumn.

Thryptomene calycina
GRAMPIANS HEATH MYRTLE

Origin Vic.
Climate WT, M, H, CT
Shade None to filtered

FAST-GROWING
SPECIMEN PLANT
AROMATIC FOLIAGE
CONTAINER PLANT

Description A rounded, bushy shrub to 2 m high with small aromatic leaves. Small white flowers with a dark centre are packed along the stems during the winter and early spring months. They are beautiful as a cut flower and last well indoors.

Cultivation Grow in a light-textured soil with good drainage and a good mulch. In very cold areas, it may need the shelter of tall trees. It is frost-resistant when established. Prune after flowering or take long sprays of flowers for the house. This will help maintain a shapely and vigorous plant.

Landscape Use A beautiful feature plant to plant under trees or along a path, or to train as a hedge. It is ideal for the bush garden and looks splendid in a large container.

Thryptomene calycina

Thryptomene saxicola
ROCK THRYPTOMENE

Origin WA
Climate S, WT, M, CT
Shade None to filtered

FAST-GROWING
AROMATIC FOLIAGE
CONTAINER PLANT

Description A spreading or weeping shrub to 1 m high. The arching branches are crowded with flat leaves that are aromatic when crushed. Masses of tiny pale to deep pink flowers are produced mainly in winter and spring, but some are present for most of the year. They are excellent long-lasting cut flowers.

Cultivation This is the most often cultivated species. It is adaptable and hardy and will thrive in most well-drained positions. It will tolerate moderate frost. Prune back after flowering or take cut flowers to encourage abundant flowering and compact growth.

Landscape Use A dainty, pendulous shrub for the foreground, in the rockery, at the top of steps, in a raised garden bed or in a large container.

Thryptomene saxicola

TODEA
OSMUNDACEAE

This small fern genus consists of two species with only one, T. barbara, *occurring in eastern Australia from Queensland to Tasmania and South Australia; it is also found in New Zealand and South Africa. It grows beside creeks and in moist rock crevices and will attain a large size in a favourable situation. It is a most attractive garden specimen and will thrive in a protected, moist location. Propagation is from fresh spores.*

Todea barbara
KING FERN

Origin Qld, NSW, Vic., Tas., SA
Climate T, S, WT, M, CT
Shade Light to filtered

ORNAMENTAL FOLIAGE
CONTAINER PLANT

Description A slow-growing species with several crowns of glossy green fronds up to 3 m long arising from a fibrous broad trunk which may reach up to 1.5 m tall in elderly, healthy specimens.

Cultivation This adaptable fern prefers a rich, moist situation with reasonable drainage. It likes dappled shade and is frost-tolerant.

Landscape Use A beautiful fern for under trees or as a feature plant near a pond or water garden.

Todea barbara

TOONA

MELIACEAE

A genus of only one species endemic to Australia. Famous for its beautiful furniture timber, the Red Cedar Toona australis *also makes a large, handsome specimen tree when given room for plenty of development. It is one of the few deciduous native trees and usually loses its leaves late in winter or early in spring. The Red Cedar has been eagerly sought for its very valuable timber since the earliest days of settlement, and has now become rare in its natural rainforest habitat. It is a magnificent tree and one worthy of preservation by cultivation. Propagation is from fresh seed.*

Toona australis

(syn. *Cedrela toona* var. *australis*)

RED CEDAR

Origin Qld, NSW
Climate T, S, WT, M
Shade None to light

FAST-GROWING
SPECIMEN PLANT
FRAGRANT
RAINFOREST PLANT

Description A tall deciduous tree which may reach up to 20 m or more in cultivation. New spring foliage is bright red, turning bronze and then light green with age, forming a dense spreading crown. The fragrant white flowers are produced on long branching sprays during spring.

Cultivation Grow in a rich, deep soil with good drainage but adequate moisture. Young plants may need protection from harsh conditions until established. It is frost-tender.

Landscape Use A beautiful specimen and shade tree for large parks, gardens and properties.

Toona australis

TRISTANIOPSIS

MYRTACEAE

A genus of around 30 species of tall shrubs and trees of which three occur in eastern Australia. Some species were previously know as Tristania. Tristaniopsis laurina *is the most commonly planted species and because of its small compact growth is valued as a street tree. Propagation is from seed.*

Tristaniopsis laurina

(syn. *Tristania laurina*)

WATER GUM

Origin Qld, NSW, Vic.
Climate T, S, WT, M
Shade None to full

SPECIMEN PLANT
BIRD-ATTRACTING
RAINFOREST PLANT

Description A small, compact tree which usually reaches no more than 6 m in cultivation. It has dark green, glossy leaves with dark red new growth and produces a good display of small yellow flowers in clusters during summer.

Cultivation This tree often grows near streams and thrives in most situations with ample water. It will grow in full sun or heavy shade and is suitable for growing in poorly drained soils. Once established, it is moderately frost-tolerant.

Landscape Use A decorative small tree for use as a shade or lawn specimen. It is suitable for small gardens where space is available, and is an ideal street tree, as its growth may be attractively controlled to avoid power lines.

Tristaniopsis laurina

VERTICORDIA

MYRTACEAE

There are some 50 species of these beautiful small shrubs that are found almost entirely in Western Australia, and are collectively known as feather flowers owing to their deeply divided fringed calyces. They are particularly ornamental plants but have a reputation for being difficult garden subjects, especially in the eastern States where they are grown mostly by enthusiasts. For best results in summer rainfall areas, grow in a raised, fast draining bed of light soil mixed with gravel. Plants are available from specialists in Western Australia, although occasionally some species are sold in Sydney and Melbourne nurseries, V. plumosa *being the most common. Most species make excellent cut flowers, and dried flowers will retain their colour for a year or longer. Propagation is from half-ripened tip cuttings.*

Verticordia chrysantha

GOLDEN FEATHER FLOWER

Origin WA
Climate WT, M
Shade None to light

CONTAINER PLANT

Description A small, rounded shrub to around 80 cm with crowded linear leaves. It bears masses of bright golden yellow flowers during spring.

Cultivation Grow in a sunny, open position with excellent drainage. Once established, it will withstand a dry summer and is frost-resistant.

Landscape Use Ideal for a raised garden bed, rockery or container.

Verticordia grandiflora

CLAW FEATHER FLOWER

Origin WA
Climate M, SA
Shade None to light

CONTAINER PLANT

Description A small, open shrub up to 80 cm with bright green, crowded leaves. The large bright yellow flowers produced in spring turn an attractive red-brown with age.

Cultivation Grow in an open, sunny position in a light, well-drained soil. It is moderately frost-resistant.

Landscape Use A beautiful small ornamental plant for the raised garden bed, rockery or container.

Verticordia chrysantha

Verticordia grandiflora

Verticordia grandis

Verticordia grandis

SCARLET FEATHER FLOWER

Origin WA
Climate M, SA
Shade None to light
CONTAINER PLANT
Description An open, spreading shrub to 1 m high with attractive greyish rounded leaves. The large scarlet flowers are produced along the upper branches during spring.

Cultivation Grow in a light, sandy soil with excellent drainage. It resents humidity and enjoys a dry summer. It is moderately frost-resistant.

Landscape Use A very showy species ideally suited to a rockery, where excellent drainage is assured.

Verticordia picta

PAINTED FEATHER FLOWER

Origin WA
Climate M, SA
Shade None to light
CONTAINER PLANT
Description A small, upright, spreading shrub to 50 cm tall, with very narrow leaves. The deep pink flowers are cup-shaped and are more prominent than the fringed calyx lobes. They appear during the spring months.

Cultivation This species requires excellent drainage in a light-textured soil. It will withstand a dry, hot summer and is moderately frost-resistant.

Verticordia picta

Landscape Use A very ornamental species when in flower, suited to a raised garden bed or rockery.

Verticordia plumosa

PLUMED FEATHER FLOWER

Origin WA
Climate WT, M, CT
Shade None to light
FAST-GROWING
CONTAINER PLANT
Description An open, rounded shrub to 60 cm with crowded linear blue-green

Verticordia plumosa

foliage. It has masses of small mauve-pink cup-shaped flowers arranged in dense heads during the spring months.

Cultivation This is the most commonly cultivated verticordia and one of the most successful in eastern gardens. It likes a sandy soil with very good drainage and prefers fairly dry conditions during summer. It is frost-resistant.

Landscape Use A most ornamental plant for a container or rockery.

VIMINARIA

FABACEAE

A genus of one species found only in Australia. Viminaria juncea *is known as Native Broom or Golden Spray and is a most delightful tall, weeping shrub found in moist temperate areas in all States except Northern Territory. It is an ornamental species with many landscape uses and is hardy in most garden situations. Propagation is from seed, which needs to be covered with boiling water and left to stand overnight before sowing.*

Viminaria juncea

(syn. *V. denudata*)

NATIVE BROOM; GOLDEN SPRAY

Origin All States except NT
Climate S, WT, M, CT
Shade Light to filtered

FAST-GROWING
SPECIMEN PLANT

Description An upright small tree or tall shrub up to 6 m with bright green, slender almost leafless branches and a graceful, weeping habit. In late spring and early summer, small bright yellow pea flowers are produced along the branches.

Viminaria juncea

Cultivation This species is suited to most soils and conditions. It needs plenty of water and does not mind poorly drained areas. It is frost-resistant.

Landscape Use An attractive, fine-textured background shrub or specimen. In nature it is often found near streams and it is ideally suited to growing at the edges of a pond or pool.

VIOLA

VIOLACEAE

A large genus of some 500 species of annual or perennial herbs found in many parts of the world. Australia has about five species of Native Violets which make attractive bedding, rockery or ground cover plants. Propagation is from seed or by division.

Viola betonicifolia

PURPLE VIOLET

Origin Qld, NSW, Vic., Tas., SA
Climate S, WT, M, CT, H
Shade Light to full

CONTAINER PLANT

Description An erect, tufted plant to 20 cm with elongated leaves produced in a basal rosette. Large mauve or purple flowers on stalks to 10 cm long appear during spring and summer.

Cultivation This adaptable species will grow in a variety of soils and situations, but does best in a moist sheltered position. It is frost- and snow-tolerant.

Viola betonicifolia

Landscape Use A dainty plant for a border, rockery pocket or container.

Viola hederacea

IVY-LEAF VIOLET

Origin Qld, NSW, Vic., Tas., SA
Climate S, WT, M, CT, H
Shade None to full

FAST-GROWING
CONTAINER PLANT
RAINFOREST PLANT

Description A spreading ground cover which will form extensive mats up to 2 m across of small, round, ivy-shaped leaves arising from long thin runners. The white and purple flowers are produced on upright stems for a long period from spring to winter.

V. hederacea 'Baby Blue' has smaller leaves and pale blue flowers.

Cultivation This species will grow in most soils and will thrive in moist areas with some shade. It is frost-tolerant and moderately snow-tolerant.

Landscape Use An excellent ground cover for the rockery, between paving, around steps, cascading down walls, as a border, or in a flower pot or hanging basket.

Viola hederacea

WAHLENBERGIA

CAMPANULACEAE

A large, widely distributed genus with approximately 15 species occurring in Australia in all States. They are annual or perennial herbs with showy, blue, bell-shaped flowers and they usually flower over a long period. Propagation is from seed, or by division of underground stems in some species.

Wahlenbergia gloriosa
ROYAL BLUEBELL

Origin NSW, Vic.
Climate WT, M, CT, H
Shade None to filtered
CONTAINER PLANT
Description This pretty prostrate plant is the official floral emblem of the Australian Capital Territory. It spreads by suckering to 50 cm across and has crinkled oblong leaves to 3 cm long. The large vivid, bluish-purple flowers are borne on long stems from mid-spring to late summer.

Cultivation Royal Bluebell occurs naturally in alpine grasslands and is ideal for the cold climate garden. It does best in full or partial sun and needs a cool root-run and good drainage. Provide ample water during dry periods.

Landscape Use An extremely attractive border, rockery or container plant.

Wahlenbergia gloriosa

Wahlenbergia stricta
TALL BLUEBELL

Origin All States except NT
Climate WT, M, SA
Shade None to light
CONTAINER PLANT
Description An erect herbaceous plant to 60 cm high. It has grassy foliage and produces masses of pale blue flowers on slender stems in spring and summer.

Cultivation This species is easily grown from seed. It prefers a light-textured soil with good drainage, and a sunny position. It is frost-resistant.

Wahlenbergia stricta

Landscape Use This colourful plant looks best in massed displays as an edging, in the rockery or cottage garden.

WESTRINGIA
LAMIACEAE

This endemic genus of around 30 species of small to medium shrubs is found in all States. A few are in cultivation, but it is the widely grown Coastal Rosemary that is a favourite amongst public landscape designers because of its low maintenance needs and fresh appearance, even under the harshest conditions. Propagation is from seed or from half-ripened tip cuttings.

Westringia fruticosa
(syn. *W. rosmariniformis*)
COASTAL ROSEMARY

Origin NSW
Climate S, WT, M, CT, H, SA
Shade None to filtered
FAST-GROWING
SALT-TOLERANT
DROUGHT-RESISTANT
CONTAINER PLANT
Description A rounded, bushy shrub to 2 m with narrow dark green leaves with a silky grey undersurface. The dainty white flowers clustered around the stems are produced throughout the year, with a main flush in late spring.

Cultivation An extremely hardy species that will grow in all soils and situations. It grows wild along the coast, often down to beach level, and is tolerant of the harshest salt-laden winds. It will also withstand drought and frost.

Westringia fruticosa

Landscape Use This is an excellent screen or hedge plant for seaside gardens, especially for the holiday house, requiring minimal maintenance. It may be cut for indoor arrangements or be grown in a container and used as a temporary indoor plant.

Westringia glabra
VIOLET WESTRINGIA

Origin NSW, Vic.
Climate S, WT, M, CT, SA
Shade Light to filtered
FAST-GROWING
CONTAINER PLANT
Description A bushy shrub to 1.5 m with smooth, oval leaves in whorls of four. The numerous lilac flowers are produced over a long period from late winter to summer.

Cultivation This species prefers dappled shade and a well-drained position. It will

Westringia glabra

withstand fairly dry conditions and is frost-resistant. Prune after flowering to shape.

Landscape Use An attractive bushy shrub that may be used as a screen, or be pruned to form a dense hedge.

Westringia longifolia
(syn. *W. linifolia*)

WINGED WESTRINGIA

Origin NSW
Climate S, WT, M, CT, SA
Shade None to full

FAST-GROWING
DROUGHT-RESISTANT
CONTAINER PLANT

Description An open shrub to 2 m with fine foliage in whorls of three. The white to pale mauve flowers are produced freely several times a year.

Cultivation A hardy and adaptable plant for a sunny or shaded position. It will grow in heavy soil and will withstand drought and frost. Prune regularly if a dense shrub is required.

Landscape Use A very pretty wispy shrub for under trees or in the bush garden. It may be used as a fence screen or be grown in a container.

Westringia *'Wynyabbie Gem'*

Origin Hybrid (*W. fruticosa* x *W. eremicola*)
Climate S, WT, M, SA
Shade None to light

FAST-GROWING
SPECIMEN PLANT
SALT-TOLERANT
DROUGHT-RESISTANT

Description A compact, bushy shrub to 1.5 m with slender grey-green leaves. Clusters of mauve flowers are produced throughout the year.

Cultivation A hardy species for most well-drained soils in full sun. It may be grown in exposed coastal gardens and is frost-resistant. Prune regularly to shape.

Landscape Use A most attractive shrub for use as a feature or screening plant in seaside gardens.

Westringia longifolia

Westringia 'Wynyabbie Gem'

XANTHORRHOEA

XANTHORRHOEACEAE

A genus of around 20 endemic species of very long-lived plants known as grass trees or blackboys. They look superb in the Australian landscape and are a marvellous addition to any native garden, adding texture and interest and attracting a variety of birds. They are plants with trunk above or below the ground, depending on species and age. The very long, narrow leaves are crowded at the top of the stem, from which also arises the long cylindrical flower spike. Mature specimens are often available from nurseries specialising in native plants. Propagation is from seed which may take up to a year to germinate.

Xanthorrhoea australis

AUSTRAL GRASS TREE

Origin NSW, Vic., Tas., SA
Climate S, WT, M, CT, SA
Shade None to light

SPECIMEN PLANT
BIRD-ATTRACTING
ORNAMENTAL FOLIAGE
CONTAINER PLANT

Description This species may have a short or tall trunk, depending on its age. An elderly specimen may reach 2 m or more with a single or forked trunk. It has a crown of long, narrow, grass-like leaves and may have a skirt of older dead leaves. The small creamy white flowers are crowded along a long, thick flower spike.

Cultivation Once established, this species is very hardy. It needs a well-drained, open sunny position in a light-textured soil. It will withstand dry conditions and is frost-resistant.

Xanthorrhoea australis

Landscape Use A mature plant with a well developed trunk makes a spectacular feature plant. Younger plants with a fine crown of foliage look splendid in a rockery or in a container.

ZIERIA

RUTACEAE

An Australian genus of over 20 species of shrubs with aromatic foliage and starry flowers. They are closely related to boronias and, although not as showy in flower, some species are cultivated for their compact growth and ornamental foliage. Propagation is from half-ripened tip cuttings taken in autumn.

Zieria cytisoides

DOWNY ZIERIA

Origin Qld, NSW, Vic., Tas.
Climate S, WT, M, CT, H
Shade None to filtered
AROMATIC FOLIAGE
ORNAMENTAL FOLIAGE
CONTAINER PLANT
Description A neat, rounded shrub to around 1 m high and across with aromatic, grey, felty leaflets in threes. Small clusters of pink or white flowers occur in spring.

Cultivation A hardy and adaptable species that will grow in either sandy or clay soil with good drainage. It is frost-resistant.

Landscape Use An attractive grey foliage shrub for colour contrast or as a feature.

Zieria cytisoides

Its compact habit makes it a good tub subject.

Zieria laevigata

ANGULAR ZIERIA

Origin Qld, NSW
Climate WT, M
Shade Light to filtered
AROMATIC FOLIAGE
CONTAINER PLANT
Description This small, erect shrub grows to just under 1 m tall. It has angular branches and fine, bright green foliage with small clusters of white or pale pink star flowers in winter and spring. These make pretty cut flowers.

Cultivation A hardy species for a well-drained, partly shaded position. It is frost-resistant. Prune lightly after flowering.

Zieria laevigata

Landscape Use An attractive species for under trees, in the rockery or in a container.

Zieria smithii

Origin Qld, NSW, Vic.
Climate WT, M
Shade Light to filtered
AROMATIC FOLIAGE
Description A rounded shrub to 1.5 m high. It has divided, strongly aromatic foliage and bears masses of white or pale pink star flowers in clusters during spring.

Cultivation A hardy species for most well-drained soils and position. It is frost-resistant. Prune lightly after flowering to maintain compact growth.

Landscape Use A shapely, freely flowering shrub for the garden. Its attractive foliage has rather a strong odour that is not considered pleasant by all.

Zieria smithii

Glossary

Acute Ending in a sharp point.
Alternate Of leaves on a stem, arranged at different levels, not opposite each other.
Annual A plant that completes its life cycle in one year.
Axil The angle between a stem and leaf.

Bipinnate Of leaves or fronds, twice divided in a pinnate manner.
Bract A modified leaf which surrounds or encloses a flower or group of small individual flowers.
Bulbil A small bulb produced on a frond which develops into a plantlet.

Calyx Outer series of floral leaves, each one a sepal.
Capsule A dry fruit that opens when mature to release the seeds.
Compound leaf A leaf divided into two or more leaflets.
Cultivar A variety of a plant produced in cultivation.
Cuneate Wedge-shaped.

Decumbent Lying along the ground, but with the tip growing upwards.
Dormant Temporary inactive growth.
Drupe A succulent fruit with a stone enclosing the seed or seeds.

Elliptic Narrow, oval and tapering at both ends.
Endemic Confined to a particular region or country.
Entire Of leaf, having a smooth margin, not divided or toothed.
Epiphyte A plant which grows on another plant, but is not parasitic.
Exotic A plant introduced from a foreign country.

Floriferous Bearing numerous flowers.
Frond The leaf of a fern or palm.

Glabrous Smooth, without hairs.
Gland A liquid-secreting organ, usually on leaves.
Glaucous Covered with bloom, giving a greyish appearance.

Habitat The environment in which a plant grows.
Head A compact cluster of flowers.
Herbaceous A perennial plant which dies down each year after flowering.
Hirsute Covered with rather long coarse hairs.
Hoary Densely covered with minute white hairs, giving a white or greyish appearance.

Inflorescence Arrangement of flowers on plant.

Labellum Front petal of an orchid appearing as a lip or tongue.
Lanceolate Shaped like a lance, broadest in the lowest half and tapering to both ends.
Larva The immature stage of insects which is usually the one which causes the most damage to plants, e.g. caterpillars and grubs.
Leaflet A segment of a compound leaf.
Lichen A plant organism composed of fungus and algae forming a crust on rocks, tree-trunks and soil.
Linear Long and narrow with parallel sides.
Lobe A rounded division of leaf, petal or other plant organ.

Mallee A shrubby eucalypt with several stems arising from the base or below ground level.
Mealy Covered with dry flour-like powder.

Node A joint on a stem where leaves or bracts arise.

Obovate Egg-shaped with the broadest part above the middle.
Opposite Of leaves, at the same level but on opposite sides of the stem.
Ovate Egg-shaped with the broadest part at the base.

Panicle An irregular much-branched spray of flowers.
Pendent Hanging downwards.
Pendulous Hanging downwards.
Perennial A plant living for more than two years.
Phyllode A flattened leaf stalk which functions as a leaf.
Pinnate Of leaves, divided once with leaflets arranged on each side of a central stalk.
Procumbent Trailing or spreading along the ground without rooting.
Prostrate Lying closely on the ground.
Pseudobulb Bulb-like thickened stem of some orchids.
Pubescent Covered with short soft downy hairs.
Pungent Ending in a stiff sharp point.

Raceme An unbranced spray of stalked flowers along a common stem.
Recurved Of leaves, curved or curled downwards or backwards.
Resinous Covered with sticky secretion.
Revolute Of leaves, margins rolled backwards.
Rhizome An underground stem.
Rhomboid(al) Roughly quadrangular (i.e. having four sides).
Rosette An arrangement of leaves radiating from a centre, usually near the ground.

Scarify Of seed, removal of dormancy of hard-coated seeds such as *Acacia* and the family Fabaceae by rubbing with emery paper or nicking with a razor blade.
Sepal A leaf-like segment of the calyx.
Serration Of a margin, with sharp forward-pointing teeth.
Simple Of a leaf, not divided into leaflets.
Spathe A large leafy bract enclosing a flower cluster.
Spike An arrangement of stalkless flowers along an individual stem.
Spore A reproductive body which does not contain an embryo.
Stamen Male part of a flower which comprises a pollen-bearing anther and supporting filament.
Stigma The part of the flower than receives the pollen.
Striation A marking with parallel lines or ridges.
Style The main descending root of a plant.

Terete Slender and circular in cross-section.
Terminal At the end or apex.
Terrestrial Growing in the ground.
Trifoliate A compound leaf having three leaflets.

Umbel A cluster of individual flower stalks all arising from the same point.

Valve Segment of a capsule which lifts to release the seeds.

Wallum An area of coastal sandplain from south-east Queensland into northern New South Wales.
Whorl A ring of flower petals or leaves encircling a stem.

Guide to Native Plant Nurseries

There are many nurseries throughout Australia which stock or specialise in native plants. The following list of nurseries is by no means complete, but is a collection of those that have been the most helpful or interesting during the preparation of this book. It is best to make enquiries first before writing for a catalogue.

Queensland

ANDERSON ROAD NATIVE PLANT NURSERY

Anderson Road
Cairns Qld 4870
Tel (070) 36 2655

FAIRHILL NATIVE PLANTS

Alex Hansa
Fairhill Road
Yandina Qld 4561
Tel (074) 46 7088
Open 7 days
A large range of native plants suitable for sub-tropical and tropical east coast areas. Also a good range of ferns, palms and orchids.

Beautiful botanic garden which includes a water garden, rainforest section and a planting of species from the Wallum.

Interesting gallery with works of local artists and craftspeople. The book section has a range of native gardening books.

A comprehensive catalogue is available which includes an alphabetical list and descriptions and planting guide.

New South Wales

BUNDARA NATIVE NURSERY

Tom Gibian
37 Carters Road
Dural NSW 2158
Tel (02) 651 1962
Specialist in grevilleas and rainforest plants. Mainly a wholesale nursery, but will supply retail. Ring first.

CRANEBROOK NATIVE NURSERY

Betty and Anton Peeters
R23 Cranebrook Road
Cranebrook NSW 2750
Tel (047) 77 4256
Open 7 days
Also at:
238 Great Western Highway
Warrimoo NSW 2774
Tel (047) 53 6376
Open 7 days
A wide variety of native plants including those suitable for growing in the Blue Mountains, NSW.

At Cranebrook there are attractive display gardens set in peaceful surrounds with abundant birdlife.

A tip from Mrs Peeters for those whose gardens are prone to frost damage: if you know a frost is coming, protect plants facing east with plastic or hessian sheets. Alternatively, after a frost, hose the plants down so that the water (not the early morning sun) will thaw the frost.

FLORALANDS

Brian and Nola Parry
Woy Woy Road
Kariong NSW 2257
Tel (043) 40 1142
Open 7 days
Large selection of native plants including Hawkesbury sandstone flora and rainforest plants.

Extensive display gardens with a large variety of native plants suitable for cultivation in the Sydney–Gosford area.

HASTINGS WILDFLOWER NURSERY

Allan and Margaret Nixon
76–78 Hastings River Drive
Port Macquarie NSW 2444
Tel (065) 83 6473
Open 7 days
A large range of native plants suitable for growing in sub-tropical and warm temperate areas, many of which are growing in display gardens.

Plants arranged alphabetically.

LIMPINWOOD GARDENS

Russell and Sharon Costin
Limpinwood Valley
Via Chillingham
Limpinwood NSW 2484
Tel (066) 79 3353
Open weekdays; weekends by appointment
Large range of native plants including many outstanding grevilleas suitable for growing in sub-tropical areas. Also a good selection of fruit trees.

Extensive display gardens set in the magnificent scenery of the Macpherson

Ranges, a short drive from Murwillumbah, northern NSW. Apart from the large variety of native plants established and flowering in the gardens, there are also established fruit orchards which include many rare tropical and sub-tropical fruits. An interesting and beautiful garden for birds, flowers and views.

Catalogue is available.

SYDNEY WILDFLOWER NURSERY (SOUTH)
Michele Stewart, John and Penny Rose
9 Veno Street
Heathcote NSW 2233
Tel (02) 548 2818
Open 7 days
Delightful cottage nursery in glorious garden setting. Plants arranged alphabetically with heaps of information which can be supplemented by the dedicated and knowledgeable staff of native plant enthusiasts.

SYDNEY WILDFLOWER NURSERY (WEST)
Mark Ferrington
241 South Street
Marsden Park NSW 2765
Tel (02) 628 4448
Open 7 days
Plants arranged alphabetically. Display gardens around the nursery contain a large variety of native plants suitable for cultivation in hot dry areas west of Sydney. Garden planning advice.

SYDNEY WILDFLOWER NURSERY (NORTH)
Peter and Noreen Byrne
327 Mona Vale Road
Terry Hills NSW 2084
Tel (02) 450 1785
Open 7 days
Plants arranged alphabetically specialising in native plants for the Sydney region. Over 100 grevilleas. Fact and information sheets. Garden planning advice. Display garden developing.

TERANIA RAINFOREST NURSERY
Hugh and Nan Nicholson
Terania Creek Road
The Channon
Via Lismore NSW 2480
Tel (066) 886 204
Rainforest plant specialists. Mainly a wholesale nursery, but will supply large retail orders.

Descriptive plant list available.

Mail orders.

WIRREANDA NURSERY
End of Wirreanda Road
Ingleside NSW 2101
Tel (02) 450 1400
Open 7 days

A comprehensive range of well-known and popular varieties of native plants as well as many unusual and rarer species. Also a good range of tree ferns, ground ferns and rainforest species.

Attractive display gardens in a pleasant bushland setting.

WIRRIMBIRRA SANCTUARY
David G. Stead Memorial Wildlife Research Foundation of Australia
Hume Highway
Bargo NSW 2574
Tel (046) 84 1112
Open 7 days
A wide range of native plants available at the nursery including unusual species.

A large area of around 100 hectares of bushland sanctuary includes a section which has been established as a wildflower garden. Wirrimbirra is essentially designed as an educational project for nature conservation. The indigenous and planted flora is name-plated and catalogued for reference.

The foundation publishes a quarterly news sheet and a series of informative booklets in the *Your Australian Garden* series. Information regarding membership and other enquiries may be obtained from: The Secretary, Box 4840, G.P.O. Sydney 2001.

Victoria

AUSTRAFLORA NURSERY AUSTRALIA PTY LTD
Belfast Road
Montrose Vic 3765
Tel (03) 728 1222
Open 7 days
Situated in the Gumnut Village. Extensive range of native trees, shrubs, ground covers, climbers and ferns. An excellent display of plants seasonally in flower is situated near the shop.

Large tree-studded display gardens featuring rockery, rock pools, waterfalls and an interesting area with plants grown in a variety of containers. An entertaining children's playground is provided. Also tea room, gift shop and wheelchair independent access.

The *Austraflora Book of Australian Plants* is an excellent descriptive cultivation guide and catalogue.

KURANGA NATIVE NURSERY
393 Maroondah Highway
Ringwood Vic 3134
Tel (03) 879 4076
Open 7 days
A large selection of Australian plants including rainforest species, native grasses, aquatic plants, ferns, orchids and grafted plants. Also a good range of indigenous plants of the Greater Melbourne area; rare, unusual and hard-to-obtain plants.

Extensive display gardens include attractive container specimens.

Descriptive plant list and informative fact sheets available.

WHITE GUMS NURSERY
Neil Marriott
Along Warracknabal Road
At Deep Lead intersection
Postal address: Box 107, Stawell Vic 3380
Tel (053) 58 2885
Open Friday, Saturday and Sunday or by appointment
A small nursery specialising in rarer small native plants and a large selection of grevilleas.

Extensive display garden area featuring many grevilleas. Situated near the Grampians, Victoria.

Tasmania

WOODBANK NURSERY

Ken and Lesley Gillanders
Huon Highway
Longley Tas 7103
Postal address: RMB 303, Kingston Tas 7150
Tel (002) 39 6452
Closed Wednesdays and Thursdays or by appointment
General cold-climate plants that will tolerate very cold strong winds, snow and frosts; including native and species endemic to Tasmania.

Plant list available.

Mail orders April to end of September.

South Australia

NELLIE NURSERY

Tony Clark
46 Randell Street
Mannum SA 5238
Tel (085) 691 762
Open 7 days
Branch nursery:
129 Adelaide Road
Murray Bridge SA 5253
Tel (085) 325 188
Open 7 days
Large selection of native plants including those suitable for areas with low rainfall. Over 120 species of Eremophila in stock as well as many rare and unusual plants.

Mail orders.

Western Australia

BUSHLAND FLORA

Brian Hargett
Seed Supplier
17 Trotman Crescent
Yanchep WA 6035
Tel (09) 561 1636
Selected Western Australian and other wildflower seeds. Catalogue available, SSE. Mail orders.

LULLFITZ NURSERY

George Lullfitz
Caporn Street
Wanneroo WA 6065
Tel (09) 405 1607
Open 7 days
Specialises only in Western Australian species including a large range of waxflowers, verticordias, grevilleas, banksias, hakeas and ground covers.

George Lullfitz has written a small book called *Grow Native*. It is available in Western Australian news agencies and is a very useful guide to the plants and their cultivation available at his nursery.

NINDETHANA SEED SERVICE

Chester Pass Road
Baker's Junction
Albany WA 6330
Postal address: P.O. Box 2121, Albany WA 6330
Tel (098) 44 3533
Large selection of native plant seeds. Catalogue available. Mail orders.

WILDFLOWER NURSERY

274 Wanneroo Road
Kingsley WA 6065
Tel (09) 409 9811
Open 7 days
Branch nursery:
Shop 16
Homebase Shopping Centre
55 Salvado Road
Wembley WA 6014
Tel (09) 381 8644
Open 7 days
A large selection of native shrubs, trees, ferns and palms as well as hardy plants from other countries.

ZANTHORREA NURSERY

Alex and Jackie Hooper
155 Watsonia Road
Maida Vale WA 6057
Tel (09) 454 6260
Open 7 days
A good range of Australian plants including a large selection of Western Australian species.

Display gardens of a variety of plants available at nursery.

Descriptive catalogue, informative fact sheets and Bush Telegraph newsletter available.

Northern Territory

ALICE SPRINGS GARDEN NURSERY

Cliff Sturgess
Ross Highway
Alice Springs NT 5750
Tel (089) 52 5055
Open every day except Wednesdays

A good range of native plants including a large selection of local species.

Display gardens feature an interesting collection of eucalypts from the WA Goldfields that grow well in the Alice Springs area.

THE SOCIETY FOR GROWING AUSTRALIAN PLANTS

The Society is for people interested in Australian flora, its preservation and cultivation. Membership is on a subscription basis and members receive copies of the quarterly journal *Australian Plants* and a regional newsletter.
Enquiries for membership to:
Australian Plants
P.O. Box 410
Padstow NSW 2211

Further Reading

Adams, G. M. (1980), **Birdscaping Your Garden**, Rigby, Adelaide.

Anderson, R. H. (1967), **The Trees of New South Wales**, NSW Government Printer, Sydney.

Armitage, I. (1978), **Acacias of New South Wales**, New South Wales Region, Society for Growing Australian Plants, Sydney.

Australian Plant Study Group (1980), **Grow What Where**, Thomas Nelson (Australia) Ltd, Melbourne.

Australian Plant Study Group (1982), **Grow What Wet**, Thomas Nelson (Australia) Ltd, Melbourne.

Australian Plant Study Group (1983), **Grow What Basic**, Thomas Nelson (Australia) Ltd, Melbourne.

Baines, J. A. (1981), **Australian Plant Genera**, Society for Growing Australian Plants, Sydney.

Beadle, N. C. W., Evans, O. D. and Carolin, R. C. (1972), **Flora of the Sydney Region**, A. H. & A. W. Reed, Sydney.

Black, J. M. (1943–57), **Flora of South Australia**, parts 1–4, SA Government Printer, Adelaide.

Black, J. M. (1978), **Flora of South Australia**, part 1 (3rd edn), SA Government Printer, Adelaide.

Blackall, W. E. (1954), **How to Know Western Australian Wildflowers**, part 1, University of Western Australia Press, Perth.

Blackall, W. E. and Grieve, B. J. (1956–80), **How to Know Western Australian Wildflowers**, parts 2–4, University of Western Australia Press, Perth.

Blombery, A. M. (1967), **A Guide to Native Australian Plants**, Angus & Robertson, Sydney.

Blombery, A. M. (1972), **What Wildflower is That?**, Paul Hamlyn, Sydney.

Blombery, A. and Rodd, A. N. (1982), **Palms**, Angus & Robertson, Sydney.

Brooker, M. I. H. and Kleinig, D. A. (1983), **Field Guide to Eucalypts of South-Eastern Australia**, Inkata Press, Melbourne.

Brooks, A. E. (1973), **Australian Native Plants for Home Gardens**, 6th edn, Lothian Publishing Co., Melbourne.

Burbridge, N. T. (1963), **Dictionary of Australian Plant Genera**, Angus & Robertson, Sydney.

Burbridge, N. T. and Gray, M. (1970), **Flora of the Australian Capital Territory**, Australian National University Press, Canberra.

Canberra Botanic Gardens (1971–), **Growing Native Plants** (series), Australian Government Publishing Service, Canberra.

Chippendale, G. M. (ed.) (1968), **Eucalyptus Buds and Fruits**, Forestry & Timber Bureau, Canberra.

Chippendale, G. M. (1973), **Eucalypts of the Western Australian Goldfields**, Australian Government Publishing Service, Canberra.

Cochrane, R. G., Fuhrer, B. A., Rotherham, E. R. and Willis, J. H. (1968), **Flowers and Plants of Victoria**, A. H. & A. W. Reed, Sydney.

Costermans, L. (1981), **Native Trees and Shrubs of South-Eastern Australia**, Rigby, Adelaide.

Costin, A. B., Gray, M., Totterdell, C. J. and Wimbush, D. J. (1979), **Kosciusko Alpine Flora**, CSIRO, Melbourne and William Collins, Sydney.

Cribb, A. B. and Cribb, J. W. (1974), **Wild Food in Australia**, William Collins, Sydney.

Cribb, A. B. and Cribb, J. W. (1981), **Useful Wild Plants in Australia**, William Collins, Sydney.

Cribb, A. B. and Cribb, J. W. (1981), **Wild Medicine in Australia**, William Collins, Sydney.

Cunningham, G. M., Mulham, W. E., Milthorpe, P. L. and Leigh, J. H. (1981), **Plants of Western New South Wales**, NSW Government Printer, Sydney, in association with Soil Conservation Service of New South Wales.

Elliot, G. M. (1979), **Australian Plants for Small Gardens and Containers**, Hyland House, Melbourne.

Elliot, R. (1975), **An Introduction to the Grampians Flora**, Algona Guides, Melbourne.

Elliot, W. R. and Jones, D. L., **Encyclopaedia of Australian Plants Suitable for Cultivation**, Lothian Publishing Co., Melbourne, vol. 1 (1980), vol. 2 (1982), vol. 3 (1984), vol. 4 (1986), vol. 5 (1990).

Erickson, R., George, A. S., Marchant, N. G. and Morcombe, M. K. (1973), **Flowers and Plants of Western Australia**, A. H. & A. W. Reed, Sydney.

Everist, S. K. (1974), **Poisonous Plants of Australia**, Angus & Robertson, Sydney.

Galbraith, J. (1977), **Collins Field Guide to Wild Flowers of South-East Australia**, William Collins, Sydney.

Gardner, C. A. (1975), **Wildflowers of Western Australia**, West Australian Newspapers Ltd, Perth.

George, A. S. (1984), **The Banksia Book**, Kangaroo Press, Kenthurst, NSW.

Hall, N., Johnston, R. D. and Chippendale, G. M. (1970), **Forest Trees of Australia**, Australian Government Publishing Service, Canberra.

Holliday, I. and Watton, G. (1975), **A Field Guide to Banksias**, Rigby, Adelaide.

Jones, D. L. (1986), **Ornamental Rainforest Plants in Australia**, Reed Books Pty Ltd, Frenchs Forest, NSW.

Jones, D. L. and Clemesha, S. C. (1976), **Australian Ferns and Fern Allies**, A. H. & A. W. Reed, Sydney.

Jones, D. L. and Gray, B. (1977), **Australian Climbing Plants**, A. H. & A. W. Reed, Sydney.

Kelly, S. (1983), **Eucalypts**, vol. 1, rev. edn, Thomas Nelson (Australia) Ltd, Melbourne.

Kelly, S. (1983), **Eucalypts**, vol. 2, rev. edn, Thomas Nelson (Australia) Ltd, Melbourne.

Launceston Field Naturalists Club (1981), **Guide to Flowers and Plants of Tasmania**, M. Camerson (ed.), A. H. & A. W. Reed, Sydney.

Leigh, J., Boden, R. and Briggs, J. (1984), **Extinct and Endangered Plants of Australia**, Macmillan Co. Aust. Pty Ltd, Melbourne.

Leigh, J. Briggs, J. and Hartley, W. (1981), **Rare or Threatened Australian Plants**, Australian National Parks & Wildlife Service, Canberra.

Maiden, J. H. (1889), **The Useful Native Plants of Australia**, facsimile edn, Alexander Bros Pty Ltd, Melbourne.

Maloney, B., Walker, J. and Mullins, B. (1973), **All About Australian Bush Gardens**, Mulavon, Sydney.

Molyneux, B. (1980), **Grow Native**, Anne O'Donovan, Melbourne.

Molyneux, B. and Macdonald, R. (1983), **Native Gardens: How to Create an Australian Landscape**, Thomas Nelson (Australia) Ltd, Melbourne.

Newbey, K. (1968–72), **West Australian Plants for Horticulture**, parts 1–2, Society for Growing Australian Plants, Sydney.

Nuytsia (1970–), Bulletin of the Western Australian Herbarium, Department of Agriculture, Western Australia, WA Government Printer, Perth.

Rotherham, E. R., Briggs, B. C., Blaxell, D. F. and Carolin, R. C. (1975), **Flowers and Plants of New South Wales and Southern Queensland**, A. H. & A. W. Reed, Sydney.

Salter, B. (1977), **Australian Native Gardens and Birds**, Ure Smith, Sydney.

Simmons, M. (1981), **Acacias of Australia**, Thomas Nelson (Australia) Ltd, Melbourne.

Simpfendorfer, K. J. (1975), **An Introduction to Trees for South-Eastern Australia**, Inkata Press, Victoria.

Society for Growing Australian Plants, **Australian Plants**, quarterly, Society for Growing Australian Plants, Sydney.

Stead Memorial Wildlife Research Foundation, Miscellaneous publications, Stead Memorial Wildlife Research Foundation, Sydney.

Telopea (1975–), Contributions from the National Herbarium of New South Wales, NSW Government Printer, Sydney.

Whibley, D. J. E. (1980), **Acacias of South Australia**, SA Government Printer, Adelaide.

Williams, K. A. W. (1979), **Native Plants Queensland**, vol. 1, K. A. W. Williams, North Ipswich, Qld.

Williams, K. A. W. (1984), **Native Plants Queensland**, vol. 2, K. A. W. Williams, North Ipswich, Qld.

Willis, J. H. (1962–72), **A Handbook to Plants in Victoria**, vols 1 and 2, Melbourne University Press.

Wrigley, J. W. and Fagg, M. (1988), **Australian Native Plants**, 3rd edn, William Collins, Sydney.

Wrigley, J. W. and Fagg, M. (1989), **Banksias, Waratahs and Grevilleas**, Collins, Sydney.

Zacharin, R. F. (1978), **Emigrant Eucalypts: Gum Trees as Exotics**, Melbourne University Press, Melbourne.

Indexes

COMMON NAME INDEX

BIRD-ATTRACTING PLANTS

Acacia
acinacea
adunca
amblygona
aneura
baileyana
beckleri
binervata
binervia
boormanii
brachybotrya
buxifolia
calamifolia
cardiophylla
conferta
cultriformis
dealbata
deanei
decurrens

'Australflora Canterbury Gold'
australis
banksii
barklyana
baueri
beadleana
'Boongala Spinebill'
buxifolia
caleyi
'Canberra Gem'
'Clearview Robin'
'Coastal Glow'
crithmifolia
curvilobar
dielsiana
diffusa
diminuta
'Evelyn's Coronet'
floribunda
x *gaudichaudii*
glabrata
hilliana
'Honey Gem'
hookerana
insignis
intricata
'Ivanhoe'
johnsonii
juncifolia
juniperina
lanigera
laurifolia
lavandulacea
longifolia
longistyla
'Misty Pink'
muelleri
Mason's Hybrid ('Ned Kelly')
'Moonlight'
mucronulata
nudiflora
'Pink Parfait'
petrophiloides
'Poorinda Beauty'
'Poorinda Blondie'
'Poorinda Diadem'
'Poorinda Royal Mantle'
'Poorinda Tranquility'
pteridifolia
quercifolia
robusta
'Robyn Gordon'
rosmarinifolia
saccata
'Sandra Gordon'
sericea
'Shirley Howie'
speciosa
stenomera
'Superb'
synapheae
thelemanniana
triloba
tripartita
venusta
vestita
victoriae
whiteana
wilsonii
Hakea
bucculenta
cinerea
corymbosa
cucullata
eriantha
francisiana
gibbosa
laurina
lissocarpha
multilineata
petiolaris
propinqua
purpurea
sericea
suaveolens
teretifolia
trineura
verrucosa
victoriae
Homoranthus
darwinioides
flavescens
Isopogon
anemonifolius
anethifolius
cuneatus
dawsonii
dubius
formosus
trilobus
Kennedia
glabrata
macrophylla
microphilla
nigricans
prostrata
retrorsa
rubicunda
stirlingii
Kunzea
affinis
ambigua
sp. 'Badja Carpet'
baxteri
capitata
pulchella
recurva
Lagunaria patersonii
Lambertia
formosa
inermis
multiflora
Leptospermum
juniperinum
laevigatum
lanigerum
petersonii
polygalifolium
scoparium
sericeum
squarrosum
Lomandra
confertifolia
longifolia
Lophostemon confertus
Melaleuca
armillaris
bracteata
calothamnoides
capitata
elliptica
ericifolia
filifolia
fulgens
gibbosa
hypericifolia
incana
laterita
laxiflora
leucadendron
linariifolia
megacephala
nesophila
nodosa
pulchella
quinquenervia
radula
scabra
spathulata
squamea
squarrosa
steedmanii
styphelioides
thymifolia
viminea
violacea
wilsonii
Melia azedarach var. *australasica*
Micromyrtus ciliata
Myoporum
debile
floribundum
insulare
montanum
parvifolium
Neosepicaea jucunda
Olearia
erubescens
microphylla
phlogopappa
pimeleoides
ramulosa
Omalanthus populifolius
Oreocallis wickhamii
Oxylobium robustum
Pandanus pendunculatus
Paraserianthes lopantha
Passiflora
aurantica
cinnabarina
Persoonia levis
Petrophile biloba
Phebalium squamulosum
Pittosporum
revolutum
rhombifolium
undulatum
Scaevola calendulacea
Schefflera actinophylla
Stenocarpus sinuatus
Syncarpia glomulifera
Syzygium
australe
leuhmannii
paniculatum
wilsonii
Telopea
mongaensis
speciossima
Templetonia retusa
Tristania laurina
Xanthorrhoea australia

CONTAINER PLANTS

Plants that are happy in pots or tubs.

Acacia
acinacea
amblygona
drummondii
flexifolia
Actinodium cunninghamii
Actinotus helianthi
Adiantum
aethiopicum
formosum
hispidulum
Agathis robusta
Agonis flexuosa
Ajuga australis
Alocasia macrorrhiza
Alyxia ruscifolia
Angiopteris evecta
Anigozanthos
'Bush Gem' hybrids
flavidus
humilis
manglesii
pulcherrimus
rufus
viridis
Araucaria
bidwillii
cunninghamii
Archontophoenix
alexandrae
cunninghamiana
Asplenium
australasicum
bulbiferum
flabellifolium
Astartea heteranthera
Astroloma
conostephioides
pinifolium
Austromyrtus tenuifolia
Baeckea
astarteoides
camphorata
crenatifolia

'Poorinda Tranquility'
quercifolia
robusta
'Robyn Gordon'
rosmarinifolia
saccata
sericea
'Shirley Howie'
stenomera
'Superb'
synapheae
thelemanniana
thyrsoides
Guichenotia
ledifolia
macrantha
Hakea
myrtoides
verrucosa
Halgania cyanea
Hardenbergia
comptoniana
violacea
Hemiandra pungens
Hibbertia
dentata
empetrifolia
miniata
obtusifolia
pedunculata
procumbens
scandens
sericea
serpyllifolia
stellaris
stricta
Hicksbeachia pinnatifolia
Homoranthus
darwinioides
flavescens
Hovea
acutifolia
chorizemifolia
elliptica
linearis
pungens
trisperma
Hypocalymma
augustifolium
cordifolium
robustum
xanthopetalum
Isotoma axillaris
Ixodia achilleoides
Jasminum suavissimum
Kennedia
glabrata
microphylla
prostrata
Kunzea
affinis
capitata
Lechenaultia
biloba
formosa
laricina
Leea indica
Lepidozamia peroffskyana
Leptospermum
epacridoideum
polygalifolium
Leucochrysum albicans
Leucophyta brownii
Linospadix monostachyus
Livistona
australis
decipiens
Lobelia membranacea
Lomandra
confertifolia
leucocephala
longifolia
Macropidia fuliginosa
Macrozamia
communis
riedlei
spiralis
Marsilea
drummondii
mutica
Mazus pumilio
Melaleuca
incana
laterita
pulchella
scabra
spathulata
steedmanii
thymifolia
violacea
wilsonii
Micromyrtus ciliata
Myoporum
debile
parvifolium
Nephrolepis cordifolia
Olearia
erubescens
microphylla
ramulosa
Omalanthus populifolius
Orthrosanthus
laxus
multiflorus
Oxylobium scandens
Pandorea
jasminoides
pandorana
Patersonia
occidentalis
sericea
Pelargonium
australe
rodneyanum
Persoonia
chamaepitys
oxycoccoides
Petrophile
biloba
linearis
serruriae
sessilis
Phebalium
nottii
stenophyllum
whitei
woombye
Pimelea
ferruginea
linifolia
rosea
spectabilis
Piper novae-hollandiae
Poa australis
Polystichum
formosum
proliferum
Pratia pedunculata
Prostanthera
aspalathoides
cruciflora
cryptandroides
cuneata
denticulata
incana
incisa
magnifica
melissifolia
phylicifolia
'Poorinda Ballerina'
rhombea
rotundifolia
scutellarioides
striatiflora
Pultenaea cunninghamii
Ranunculus
graniticola
lappaceus
Restio tetraphyllus
Rhodanthe
anthemoides
chlorocephala spp. *rosea*
manglesii
Rhododendron lochae
Ricinocarpos bowmanii
Rulingia
dasyphylla
hermanniifolia
Scaevola
aemula
albida
hookeri
ramosissima
striata
Schefflera actinophylla
Scleranthus biflorus
Sollya heterophylla
Sowerbaea juncea
Sprengelia incarnata
Spyridium parvifolium
Stenocarpus sinuatus
Sticherus flabellatus
Stypandra glauca
Swainsona
formosa
galegifolia
greyana
Syzygium
australe
leuhmannii
paniculatum
wilsonii
Telopea mongaensis
Tetratheca
ciliata
thymifolia
Thomasia
macrocarpa
petalocalyx
pygmaea
Thryptomene
calycina
saxicola
Todea barbara
Verticordia
chrysantha
grandiflora
grandis
picta
plumosa
Viola
bentonicifolia
hederacea
Wahlenbergia
gloriosa
stricta
Westringia
fruticosa
glabra
longifolia
Xanthorrhoea australis
Zieria
cytisoides
laevigata

FAST-GROWING PLANTS

Plants that have a growth rate of 1 m or more in one growing season.

Acacia
adunca
baileyana
binervata
binervia
boormanii
calamifolia
cardiophylla
dealbata
decurrens
drummondii
elata
floribunda
frimbiata
gracilifolia
howittii
iteaphylla
longifolia
myrtifolia
perangusta
podalyriifolia

pravissima
prominens
pycnantha
saligna
sophorae
spectabilis
suaveolens
terminalis
verniciflua
vestita
Adenanthos sericea
Agathis robusta
Agonis juniperina
Alphitonia petriei
Alyogyne huegelii
Angophora
costata
floribunda
hispida
Aotus lanigera
Araucaria cunninghamii
Baeckea
camphorata
virgata
Banksia
ericifolia
integrifolia
Bauera rubioides
Boronia
clavata
denticulata
Brachysema
celsianum
praemorsum
Buckinghamia celsissima
Callicoma serratifolia
Callistemon
citrinus
comboynensis
'Harkness'
'King's Park Special'
pachyphyllus
'Perth Pink'
salignus
subulatus
viminalis
Callitris rhomboidea
Calothamnus quadrifidus
Calytrix tetragona
Carpobrotus glaucescens
Casuarina
cristata
cunninghamiana
decaisneana
equisetifolia
glauca
littoralis
stricta
Chamelaucium uncinatum
Chorizema
cordatum
ilicifolium
Cissus antarctica
Clematis
aristata
microphylla
Commersonia bantramia
Cyathea cooperi
Dodonaea viscosa
Elaeagnus triflora
Eriostemon myoporoides
Eucalyptus
botryoides
caesia
camaldulensis
citriodora
eximia
globulus
gunnii
lehmannii
leucoxylon
maculata
mannifera ssp. maculosa
melliodora
microcorys
nicholii
pilularis robusta
saligna
scoparia
torquata
Eutaxia
cuneata
obovata
Faradaya splendida
Ficus
benjamina
macrophylla
rubiginosa
Geitonoplesium cymosum
Goodenia ovata
Grevillea
aquifolium
asplenifolia
banksii
barklyana
baueri
beadleana
'Clearview Robin'
curviloba
'Evelyn's Coronet'
x gaudichaudii
glabrata
'Honey Gem'
hookerana
'Ivanhoe'
longifolia
longistyla
'Misty Pink'
petrophiloides
'Poorinda Beauty'
'Poorinda Blondie'
'Poorinda Diadem'
'Poorinda Royal Mantle'
'Poorinda Tranquility'
pteridifolia
robusta
'Robyn Gordon'
rosmarinifolia
saccata
'Sandra Gordon'
speciosa
stenomera
'Superb'
venusta
vestita
victoriae
whiteana
'White Wings'
Hakea
cucullata
gibbosa
laurina
lissocarpha
multilineata
petiolaris
sericea
Hardenbergia
comptoniana
violacea
Hibbertia
cuneiformis
dentata
empetrifolia
scandens
Hibiscus
heterophyllus
splendens
Hovea acutifolia
Hymenosporum flavum
Indigofera australis
Ixodea achilleoides
Jasminum suavissimum
Kennedia
glabrata
macrophylla
nigricans
prostrata
retrorsa
rubicunda
stirlingii
Kunaea
ambigua
sp. 'Badja Carpet'
baxteri
recurva
Lagunaria patersonii
Lambertia inermis
Leea indica
Leptospermum
epacridoideum
juniperinum
petersonii
polygalifolium
rotundifolium
scoparium
Lobelia membranacea
Lophostemon confertus
Mazus pumilio
Melaleuca
armillaris
bracteata
calothamnoides
ericifolia
filifolia
hypericifolia
leucadendron
linariifolia
nesophila
nodosa
quinquenervia
squarrosa
styphelioides
thymifolia
Melastoma affine
Melia azedarach var. australasica
Myoporum
floribundum
insulare
parvifolium
Neosepicaea jucunda
Oxylobium robustum
Ozothamnus diosmifolius
Pandorea
jasminoides
pandorana
Paraserianthes lopantha
Passiflora
aurantica
cinnabarina
Pavonia hastata
Pimelia
ligustrina
linifolia
Pittosporum
revolutum
undulatum
Prostanthera
lasianthos
magnifica
melissifolia
nivea
ovalifolia
phylicifolia
'Poorinda Ballerina'
rotundifolia
sieberi
Pultenaea
daphnoides
villosa
Ricinocarpos pinifolius
Rulingia dasyphylla
Schefflera actinophylla
Sollya heterophylla
Syncarpia glomulifera
Tecomanthe hillii
Thryptomene
calycina
saxicola
Toona australis
Verticordia plumosa
Viminaria juncea
Viola hederacea
Westringia
fruticosa
glabra
longifolia
'Wyngabbie Gem'

FRAGRANT PLANTS

Acacia
adunca
baileyana
beckleri
binervia
boormanii
cardiophylla
cultriformis
dealbata
deanei
decurrens
flexifolia
floribunda
frimbiata
howittii
iteaphylla
longifolia
myrtifolia
podalyriifolia
pravissima
prominens
pubescens
pycnantha
suaveolens
Alocasia macrorrhiza
Alphitonia petriei
Alyxia ruscifolia
Boronia
clavata
floribunda
heterophylla
megastigma
pinnata
purdieana
serrulata
Buckinghamia celsissima
Callistemon pallidus
Cassia
artemisioides
odorata
Clematis aristata
Crinum pendunculatum
Crowea angustifolia
Dendrobium
canaliculatum
x *delicatum*
falcorostrum
gracilicaule
kingianum
linguiforme
ruppianum
speciosum
Elaeagnus triflora
Elaeocarpus reticulatus
Eucalyptus
eximia
melliodora
Faradaya splendida
Flindersia schottiana
Grevillea
australis
curviloba
'Moonlight'
triloba
whiteana
Hakea
lissocarpha
sericea
suaveolens
Hicksbeachia pinnatifolia
Homoranthus flavescens
Hymenosporum flavum
Indigofera australis
Jacksonia scoparia
Jasminum suavissimum
Kennedia glabrata
Kunzea ambigua
Lomandra
leucocephala
longifolia
Melaleuca
ericifolia
leucadendron
linariifolia
squarrosa
viminea
Melia azedarach var. *australasica*
Paraserianthes lopantha
Pittosporum
revolutum
rhombifolium
undulatum
Ricinocarpos pinifolius
Sarcochilus falcatus
Sowerbaea juncea
Toona australis

DROUGHT-RESISTANT PLANTS

Once established, these plants should survive in areas which receive less than 375 mm annual rainfall.

Acacia
aneura
beckleri
brachybotrya
calamifolia
cardiophylla
conferta
cultriformis
iteaphylla
lanuginoisa
myrtifolia
pendula
pycnantha
spectabilis
uncinata
Atriplex nummularia
Callistemon macropunctatus
Callitris glaucophylla
Carpobrotus modestus
Cassia
artemisioides
nemophilia
Casuarina
cristata
decaisneana
Dodonaea
microzyga
viscosa
Einadia nutans
Eremophila
bignoniiflora
bowmanii
calorhabdos
christopheri
decipiens
densifolia
drummondii
gilesii
glabra
laanii
latrobei
macdonnellii
maculata
merrallii
pachyphylla
Eucalyptus
caesia
calycogona
camaldulensis
campaspe
forrestiana
grossa
kruseana
lehmannii
leucoxylon
macrocarpa
pyriformis
torquata
woodwardii
Geijera parviflora
Gossypium sturtianum
Grevillea
alpina
anethifolia
juncifolia
petrophiloides
robusta
Melaleuca
armillaris
elliptica
Melia azedarach var. *australasica*
Myoporum
debile
insulare
montanum
parvifolium
Olearia pimeleoides
Prostanthera aspalathoides
Swainsona
galegifolia
greyana
Westringia
fruticosa
longifolia
'Wynyabbie Gem'

SPECIMEN PLANTS

These plants have some outstanding attribute that makes them attractive when seen individually.

Acacia
baileyana
beckleri
binervia
boormanii
cardiophylla
cultriformis
decurrens
floribunda
iteaphylla
melanoxylon
pravissima
prominens
pubescens
saligna
spectabilis
verniciflua
vestita
Acmena smithii
Agonis flexuosa
Angiopteris evecta
Angophora
costata
floribunda
hispida
Anigozanthos
flavidus
manglesii
pulcherrimus
rufus
viridis
Araucaria
bidwillii
cunninghamii
Archontophoenix
alexandrae
cunninghamiana
Backhousia citriodora
Baeckea linifolia
Banksia
aemula
ashybi
baueri
baxteri
coccinea
ericifolia
hookerana
integrifolia
media
menziesii
occidentalis
prionotes
repens
robur
serrata
speciosa
spinulosa
Boronia
denticulata
heterophylla

mollis
molloyae
muelleri
pinnata
rosmarinifolia
thujona
Brachychiton
acerifolius
bidwillii
discolor
rupestris
Buckinghamia celsissima
Callicoma serratifolia
Callistemon
citrinus
comboynensis
'Harkness'
'King's Park Special'
macropunctatus
pachyphyllus
pallidus
'Perth Pink'
pinifolius
rigidus
salignus
sieberi
speciosus
subulatus
viminalis
Callitris
columellaris
glaucophylla
macleayana
oblonga
rhomboidea
Calothamnus
quadrifidus
rupestris
sanguineus
villosus
Cassia artemisioides
Castanospermum australe
Casuarina
cunninghamiana
equisetifolia
littoralis
stricta
torulosa
Ceratopetalum gummiferum
Crowea 'Festival'
Cyathea
australis
cooperi
Davidsonia pruriens
Dendrobium
speciosum
striolatum
Dicksonia antarctica
Doryanthes
excelsa
palmeri
Dryandra
formosa
praemorsa
quercifolia
Elaeocarpus reticulatus
Eucalyptus
blakelyi
caesia
calophylla
campaspe
cinerea
citriodora
curtisii
elata
eximia
ficifolia
forrestiana
haemastoma
kruseana
lehmannii
leucoxylon
macrocarpa
mannifera ssp. maculosa
nicholii
preissiana
risdonii
rossii
scoparia
sideroxylon
torquata
woodwardii
Ficus
macrophylla
rubiginosa
Flindersia
australis
schottiana
Graptophyllum exelsum
Grevillea
acanthifolia
banksii
hilliana
'Honey Gem'
hookerana
'Ivanhoe'
johnsonii
longifolia
longistyla
'Misty Pink'
'Moonlight'
petrophiloides
'Poorinda Diadem'
robusta
'Robyn Gordon'
'Superb'
wilsonii
Hakea
bucculenta
cinerea
corymbosa
francisiana
laurina
multilineata
petiolaris
victoriae
Harpullia pendula
Hicksbeachia pinnatifolia
Hymenosporum flavum
Isopogon
anethifolius
formosus
Kunzea
baxteri
pulchella
Lagunaria patersonii
Lophostemon confertus
Macadamia
integrifolia
tetraphylla
Melaleuca
incana
laterita
leucadendron
linariifolia
nesophila
spathulata
styphelioides
Melastoma affine
Melia azedarach var. australasica
Myoporum floribundum
Nothofagus cunninghamii
Oreocallis wickhamii
Pandanus pendunculatus
Persoonia pinifolia
Pittosporum rhombifolium
Stenocarpus sinuatus
Syncarpia glomulifera
Syzygium
australe
leuhmannii
wilsonii
Telopea
mongaensis
speciosissima
Thryptomene calycina
Toona australis
Tristania laurina
Viminaria juncea
Westringia 'Wynyabbie Gem'
Xanthorrhoea australis

PLANTS WITH ORNAMENTAL FOLIAGE

Plants with unusual or beautiful foliage.

Acacia
baileyana
binervia
cardiophylla
cultriformis
glaucoptera
gracilifolia
iteaphylla
podalyriifolia
pravissima
pubescens
spectabilis
triptera
vestita
Actinotus helianthi
Adenanthos sericea
Adiantum
aethiopicum
formosum
hispidulum
Alocasia macrorrhiza
Angiopteris evecta
Asplenium
australasicum
bulbiferum
Atriplex nummularia
Banksia
baxteri
blechnifolia
speciosa
Blechnum
cartilagineum
nudum
patersonii
Callistemon salignus
Cassia artemisioides
Castanospermum australe
Casuarina
cristata
cunninghamiana
decaisneana
distyla
equisetifolia
glauca
littoralis
paludosa
stricta
torulosa
Cissus antarctica
Cordyline
petiolaris
stricta
Cyathea
australis
cooperi
Davallia pyxidata
Davidsonia pruriens
Dicksonia antarctica
Dodonaea boroniifolia
Dryandra
formosa
nivea
praemorsa
quercifolia
sessilis
Einadia nutans
Elaeagnus triflora
Eremophila
bowmanii
nivea
Eucalyptus
cinerea
cordata
gunnii
kruseana
risdonii
tetragona
woodwardii
Geitonoplesium cymosum
Gleichenia dicarpa
Graptophyllum exelsum
Grevillea
aquifolium
banksii

beadleana
caleyi
dielsiana
glabrata
hilliana
hookerana
insignis
longifolia
'Moonlight'
robusta
thyrsoides
whiteana
Hakea
cucullata
trineura
victoriae
Hicksbeachia pinnatifolia
Isopogon
anemonifolius
anethifolius
Jacksonia scoparia
Leea indica
Lepidozamia peroffskyana
Leucophyta brownii
Livistona
australis
decipiens
Macrozamia
communis
riedlei
spiralis
Melaleuca incana
Melastoma affine
Muehlenbeckia axillaris
Myoporum floribundum
Neosepicaea jucunda
Nothofagus cunninghamii
Omalanthus populifolius
Pandanus pendunculatus
Persoonia levis
Petrophile
biloba
sessilis
Piper novae-hollandiae
Platycerium
bifurcatum
superbum
Prostanthera teretifolia
Pultenaea cunninghamii
Restio tetraphyllus
Schefflera actinophylla
Spyridium parvifolium
Stenocarpus sinuatus
Sticherus flabellatus
Syzygium
australe
leuhmannii
paniculatum
wilsonii
Tecomanthe hillii
Todea barbara
Xanthorrhoea australis
Zieria
cytisoide

SALT-TOLERANT PLANTS

Plants that can withstand exposed coastal conditions of blustery sea winds and salty spray.

Acacia
longifolia
sophorae
Atriplex nummularia
Banksia
aemula
ericifolia
integrifolia
marginata
praemorsa
serrata
speciosa
Canavalia maritima
Carpobrotus
glaucescens
rossii
Casuarina
distyla
equisetifolia
stricta
Correa
alba
backhousiana
Einadia nutans
Eucalyptus
lehmannii
robusta
Frankenia pauciflora
Grevillea
'Coastal Glow'
nudiflora
pteridifolia (prostrate form)
Hakea suaveolens
Hibbertia scandens
Lagunaria petersonii
Melaleuca
armillaris
ericifolia
hypericifolia
Myoporum
insulare
parvifolium
Pandanus pendunculatus
Scaevola calendulacea
Templetonia retusa
Thomasia petalocalyx
Westringia
fruticosa
'Wynyabbie Gem'

PLANTS WITH AROMATIC FOLIAGE

Agonis
flexuosa
juniperina
Astartea
fascicularis
heteranthera
Backhousia citriodora
Baeckea
camphorata
linifolia
Boronia
anemonifolia
clavata
crenulata
deanei
denticulata
floribunda
fraseri
heterophylla
ledifolia
'Lipstick'
megastigma
microphylla
mollis
molloyae
muelleri
pilosa
pinnata
safrolifera
serrulata
thujona
Callistemon
citrinus
pallidus
Calytrix
alpestris
tetragona
Crowea
angustifolia
exalata
'Festival'
saligna
Darwinia
citriodora
grandiflora
oxylepis
Eriostemon
myoporoides
verrucosus
Eucalyptus
citriodora
nicholii
polybractea
Geijera parviflora
Homoranthus darwinioides
Hypocalymma augustifolium
Kunzea
affinis
ambigua
sp. 'Badja Carpet'
baxteri
capitata
recurva
Leptospermum
laevigatum
petersonii
Leucophyta brownii
Melaleuca
bracteata
laterita
leucadendron
thymifolia
wilsonii
Micromyrtus ciliata
Ozothamnus diosmifolius
Paraserianthes lopantha
Pelargonium australe
Piper novae-hollandiae
Prostanthera
aspalathoides
cryptandroides
cuneata
denticulata
incisa
lasianthos
melissifolia
ovalifolia
rhombea
rotundifolia
sieberi
striatiflora
teretifolia
Thryptomene
calycina
saxicola
Zieria
cytisoides
laevigata
smithii

RAINFOREST PLANTS

Acmena smithii
Adiantum
formosum
hispidulum
Agathis robusta
Alocasia macrorrhiza
Alphitonia petriei
Alysia ruscifolia
Angiopteris evecta
Araucaria
bidwillii
cunninghamii
Archontphoenix
alexandrae
cunninghamiana
Asplenium
australasicum
bulbiferum
Backhousia citriodora
Blechnum
cartilagineum
patersonii

Brachychiton
acerifolius
discolor
Buckinghamia celsissima
Calamus muelleri
Calanthe triplicata
Callicoma serratifolia
Callitris macleayana
Castanospermum australe
Ceratopetalum gummiferum
Cissus antarctica
Commersonia bantramia
Cordyline
petiolaris
stricta
Crinum pedunculatum
Cyathea cooperi
Davidsonia pruriens
Dendrobium
beckleri
falcorostrum
gracilicaule
kingianum
ruppianum
speciosum
Dicksonia antarctica
Doodia
aspera
caudata
Elaeagnus triflora
Elaeocarpus reticulatus
Faradaya splendida
Ficus
benjamina
coronata
macrophylla
rubiginosa
Flindersia
australis
schottiana
Geitonoplesium cymosum
Grevillea
hilliana
robusta
Harpullia pendula
Hicksbeachia pinnatifolia
Hymenosporum flavum
Leea indica
Lepidozamia peroffskyana
Linospadix monostachya
Livistona
australis
decipiens
Lophostemon confertus
Macadamia integrifolia
Macadamia tetraphylla
Melia azedarach var. *australasica*
Neosepicaea jucunda
Nephrolepis cordifolia
Nothofagus cunninghamii
Omalanthus populifolius
Oreocallis sp. *nova*
Pandorea
jasminoides
pandorana
Passiflora aurantica
Piper novae-hollandiae
Pittosporum
revolutum
rhombifolium
undulatum
Platycerium
bifurcatum
superbum
Polystichum proliferum
Rhododendron lochae
Sarcochilus falcatus
Schefflera actinophylla
Stenocarpus sinuatus
Syzygium
australe
leuhmannii
paniculatum
wilsonii
Tecomanthe hillii
Toona australis
Tristaniopsis laurina
Viola hederacea

SPECIES WITH COLOURFUL FRUIT

Acmena smithii	autumn to spring	pink or purple berry
Alyxia ruscifolia	spring and summer	orange to red drupe
Astroloma pinifolium	summer	pale green globular fruit
Billardiera cymosa	summer and autumn	reddish berry
B. scandens	summer and autumn	yellowish green oblong berry
Carpobrotus glaucescens	summer	purple to red oblong fruit
C. modestus	summer	purple oblong fruit
C. rossii	summer	purple to red rounded fruit
Cissus antarctica	autumn	black rounded berry
Cordyline petiolaris	summer and autumn	pendulous clusters of shiny red fruit
C. stricta	autumn and winter	reddish purple rounded berry
Dianella caerulea	summer	blue to purple rounded berry
D. revoluta	summer	dark blue, shiny oblong berry
Dodonaea cuneata	spring	reddish capsules
D. microzyga	spring	red or purple capsules
D. triquetra	spring and summer	green to purple capsules
D. viscosa	spring	pink to purple capsules
Einadia nutans	mostly autumn	bright red or yellow berry
Elaeocarpus reticulatus	winter	rounded shiny dark blue berry
Ficus macrophylla	autumn	rounded purple fruit
F. rubiginosa	autumn and winter	yellow to red rounded fruit
Harpullia pendula	spring	yellow-orange fruit
Leea indica	autumn	clusters of globular black fruit
Linospadix monostachya	autumn	pendulous string of waxy red fruit
Melia azedarach var. ***australasica***	autumn	globular yellow fruit
Myoporum debile	summer	green, purple or red rounded fruit
M. insulare	summer	bluish fruit
M. montanum	summer	reddish-purple fruit
Pittosporum revolutum	autumn	orange fruit
P. rhombifolium	autumn	clusters of orange globular fruit
P. undulatum	autumn and winter	orange to brown rounded fruit
Scaevola calendulacea	summer	purple succulent fruit
Sollya heterophylla	autumn	cylindrical blue fruit
Syzygium australe	summer and autumn	pink, purple or red fruit
S. paniculatum	autumn	magenta fruit
S. wilsonii	summer	cream oval fruit